Have You Considered My Servant Job?

STUDIES ON PERSONALITIES OF THE OLD TESTAMENT
James L. Crenshaw, Series Editor

Have You Considered My Servant Job?

Understanding the Biblical Archetype of Patience

SAMUEL E. BALENTINE

The University of South Carolina Press

© 2015 University of South Carolina

Published by the University of South Carolina Press
Columbia, South Carolina 29208

www.sc.edu/uscpress

Manufactured in the United States of America

24 23 22 21 20 19 18 17 16 15   10 9 8 7 6 5 4 3 2 1

Library of Congress Cataloging-in-Publication Data

Balentine, Samuel E. (Samuel Eugene), 1950–
  Have you considered my servant Job? : understanding the biblical archetype of
patience / Samuel E. Balentine.
    pages cm. — (Studies on personalities of the Old Testament)
    Includes bibliographical references and index.
    ISBN 978-1-61117-451-9 (hardcover : alk. paper) — ISBN 978-1-61117-452-6 (ebook)
  1. Bible. Job—Criticism, interpretation, etc. 2. Job (Biblical figure) 3. Patience—
Biblical teaching. I. Title.
    BS1415.52.B35 2015
    223'.106—dc23

                                                                            2014044828

This book was printed on recycled paper with 30 percent postconsumer waste content.

To Betty, Graham, and Lauren, thank you for the support and understanding that makes it possible for me to do what I do

CONTENTS

SERIES EDITOR'S PREFACE

Critical study of the Bible in its ancient Near Eastern setting has stimulated interest in the individuals who shaped the course of history and whom events singled out as tragic or heroic figures. Rolf Rendtorff's *Men of the Old Testament* (1968) focuses on the lives of important biblical figures as a means of illuminating history, particularly the sacred dimension that permeates Israel's convictions about its God. Fleming James's *Personalities of the Old Testament* (1939) addresses another issue, that of individuals who function as inspiration for their religious successors in the twentieth century. Studies restricting themselves to a single individual—for example, Moses, Abraham, Samson, Elijah, David, Saul, Ruth, Jonah, Job, Jeremiah—enable scholars to deal with a host of questions: psychological, literary, theological, sociological, and historical. Some, like Gerhard von Rad's *Moses* (1960), introduce a specific approach to interpreting the Bible, hence providing valuable pedagogic tools.

As a rule these treatments of isolated figures have not reached the general public. Some were written by outsiders who lacked a knowledge of biblical criticism (Freud on Moses, Jung on Job) and whose conclusions, however provocative, remain problematic. Others were targeted for the guild of professional biblical critics (David Gunn on David and Saul, Phyllis Trible on Ruth, Terence Fretheim and Jonathan Magonet on Jonah). None has succeeded in capturing the imagination of the reading public in the way fictional works like Archibald MacLeish's *J.B.* and Joseph Heller's *God Knows* have done.

It could be argued that the general public would derive little benefit from learning more about the personalities of the Bible. Their conduct, often less then exemplary, reveals a flawed character, and their everyday concerns have nothing to do with our preoccupations from dawn to dusk. To be sure some individuals transcend their own age, entering the gallery of classical literary figures from time immemorial. But only these rare achievers can justify specific treatments of them. Then why publish additional studies on biblical personalities?

The answer cannot be that we read about biblical figures to learn ancient history, even of the sacred kind, or to discover models for ethical action. But what remains? Perhaps the primary significance of biblical personages is the light they throw on the imaging of deity in biblical times. At the very least, the Bible constitutes human perceptions of deity's relationship with the world and its creatures. Close readings of biblical personalities therefore clarify ancient understandings of God. That is the important data that we seek—not because we endorse that specific view of deity, but because all such efforts to make sense of reality contribute something worthwhile to the endless quest for knowledge.

James L. Crenshaw
Robert L. Flowers Professor
Emeritus of Old Testament,
Duke University

PREFACE

In one way or another, I have been immersed in the story of Job for most of my professional life. For me, and perhaps also for the many others who instinctively resonate with Job's plight, his story is like a "tar baby"; once you enter into it fully, you never escape. The scars of engagement may fade over time, but they always leave a footprint. Tracing some of these footprints in the reception history of Job is the objective of this book.

My journey with Job and his interpreters will no doubt continue, for life itself seems to demand it. Even so I confess that after a lifetime's work, Job's story still unsettles me. I continue to pause before answering God's opening question, "Have you considered my servant Job?" (Job 1:8), because I know that any answer I may offer can be countered by a whirlwind voice. "Who is this that darkens counsel by words without knowledge?" (38:2). Like Job my first instinct is to retreat in silence (40:5). But also like Job, I am compelled to move beyond silence to explore what I can see and understand, limited as it may be, about the God who afflicts the righteous "for no reason" (2:3). I read and reread this ancient story because I must.

I am grateful to my friend Jim Crenshaw for inviting to me to contribute this volume to this distinguished series, and to Jim Denton and his colleagues at the press for their help in moving the manuscript to publication. Special thanks go to Grant Holbrook and Joe Perdue, who helped me in untold ways to prepare the manuscript for final submission.

INTRODUCTION

Oh, there's always Someone playing Job.

Archibald MacLeish, *J.B.*

Job is no longer man; he is humanity! A race which can feel, think, and speak in such a voice is truly worthy of a dialogue with the divine; it is worthy of conversing with its creator.

Alphonse de Lamartine, *Cours familier de littérature*

House, M.D. is an Emmy Award–winning American television drama series that began airing in 2004. The lead character, Dr. Gregory House, is an infectious disease specialist at the fictitious Princeton-Plainsboro Teaching Hospital (PPTH). A modern-day Sherlock Holmes, House is a brilliant, Vicodin-addicted diagnostician who thrives on solving medical puzzles, even as he alienates patients and colleagues with his antisocial behavior and unconventional thinking. In an episode broadcast in February 2009, House takes on the case of a young priest, Daniel Bresson, who claims to have seen a crucified, bleeding Jesus hovering on his doorstep.[1] In conversation with Bresson, House learns that he has been moved from one diocese to another, dogged at each stop along the way by the accusation that he had inappropriate contact with a boy in his first parish. Bresson insists he is innocent of the charge, and he continues to serve the church by working at a homeless shelter, but he survives day-to-day more by the scotch that numbs his despair than by faith in God's justice.

Bresson's symptoms suggest at first little more than an alcohol-induced hallucination. Additional symptoms quickly complicate his medical situation, however, so House begins to search for other causes. He runs an EEG to check for epilepsy, a CT scan to check for brain tumors; the results are negative. He tests Bresson's home for toxins, suspecting carbon monoxide poisoning but finds no corroborating evidence. When Bresson loses sight in his right eye, House runs a nerve conduction study, and when this also proves inconclusive, he suspects the spleen is the problem. Finally when Bresson breaks out in inflamed red welts all over his body, House zeroes in on the diagnosis: "Job's disease." It is the term used since the 1960s to describe persons suffering from chronic granulomas, manifest as severe abscesses of the skin, tissue, and organs. Based on his lingering suspicion that the molestation charges against the priest are true, House orders a blood test. "Father Nietzsche has AIDS," House announces. Ultimately this diagnosis also proves to be inaccurate, and with additional tests House finally determines that Bresson has Wiskott-Aldrich Syndrome, a genetic but treatable immune deficiency that is not connected to the HIV-AIDS virus.

As with all the episodes in this television series, this one is laced with subplots that connect to various philosophical and psychological issues. The episode begins not with the priest in the ER but with the invitation to House from Dr. Cuddy, the hospital administrator and dean of medicine at PPTH, to attend her daughter's Simchat Bat celebration. House has no desire to attend this ceremony—he believes "in medicine, not metaphysics"—and so he spends much of the rest of the episode thinking up ways to get out of going. With this lead-in, the television audience is invited to suspect that House has taken Bresson's case because a priest who has lost faith presents him with more than just another medical challenge. Consider the following exchange with Bresson:

HOUSE: So if I happen to cure you, what happens then? You start thinking that God was working through me some sort of miracle?

BRESSON: Do you think I'm an idiot?

HOUSE: That's what I'm testing.

BRESSON: Losing my faith wasn't a choice I made. It happened. It's gone.

HOUSE: But if it can magically disappear, it can magically reappear. And that's what you're hoping. Your job—

BRESSON: Sucks.

HOUSE: That's my point. You could make more money frapping decafs and yet you're still ministering to the meek. Why do the Lord's work if the Lord has left the building?

BRESSON: I've been with the church my entire adult life. It's my only marketable skill.

HOUSE: I detect the stink of leftover faith.

BRESSON: You want to talk about hypocrisy. What about you? You act like you don't care about anyone, but here you are saving lives.

HOUSE: Solving puzzles. Saving lives is just collateral damage.

BRESSON: Nice try, but I don't think you're looking to someone to prove you're right, I think you're looking for someone to prove you're wrong; to give you hope. You want to believe, don't you?

HOUSE: Yeah, I want to walk out and find myself in a forest of whore trees. But I don't think it's a good idea to tell people to go fornicate with fruit.

When the episode ends, the Simchat Bat ceremony at Dr. Cuddy's house has begun. Family and friends are gathered in celebration, both ritual and real. House sits alone in his apartment, his only company the repeating refrain from a Rolling Stones song he plays on his piano and sings to himself: "You can't always get what you want." The episode, titled "Unfaithful," takes its place in the show's archives, a rerun anticipating another viewing, continued consideration of answers to questions it invites but does not clearly provide. When a priest loses faith in God because he has been falsely accused, who is unfaithful to whom? When persons want to believe but cannot, who or what gives them hope sufficient to continue the search? To pull the string on the question that is perhaps most germane for what follows, when a person is afflicted with "Job's disease," what remains beyond the "stink of leftover faith"? As House poses the question to the priest, "Why do the Lord's work if the Lord has left the building?"

That a twenty-first-century television drama can script the ancient story of Job into an hour of prime-time entertainment speaks to our continuing identification with its abiding truths. As Elie Wiesel has said, "through the problems [Job] embodied and the trials he endured, he seems familiar—even contemporary."[2] The epigraphs that preface this chapter extend Wiesel's observation with two brief overviews of Job's modern readers.

Alphonse de Lamartine (1790–1869) was one of the notable poets of the French romantic school, along with Victor Hugo (1772–1821), and an outspoken advocate for a republican form of government when King Louis Philippe abdicated the throne in 1847. He served briefly in the provisional government and was nominated for the presidency, but having received little support from the voters, he quickly fell out of favor and was forced to the sidelines. By the time Napoleon seized power in 1848, Lamartine, along with many of his fellow poets who were calling for reform, was largely a voice crying in the wilderness. Echoes of his fortunes can be discerned in his literary work, especially in his essay on Job in *Cours familier de littérature,* a periodical published from 1856 to 1869. With the heart of a romantic, Lamartine found in Job the "epic poem of the soul" that gives voice to the "melancholy of declining age." "If there is any book which has portrayed the special poetry of old age—first its discouragement, bitterness, irony, reproach, complaint, impiety, silence, prostration, and then its resignation; that impatience which, of necessity, is transformed into virtue; and, finally, the consolation which by divine reverence raises up the crestfallen spirit;—then that book is most certainly the book of Job, that dialogue with the self, with one's friends, and with God."[3] Departing from the conventional focus on the prose account of

Job's exemplary patience and submission to sovereign power (Job 1–2, 42:7–17), Lamartine, the failed democrat, saw in Job's poetry (Job 3–42:6) a model that continued to inspire courageous defiance, long after Job's particular wars had shifted to other battlefields. "Job is the Prometheus of the word, raised to the heavens still shrieking, still bleeding, in the very claws of the vulture gnawing at his heart. He is the victim become judge, by the sublime impersonality of reason, celebrating his own torture and, like the Roman Brutus, casting up to heaven the drops of his blood, not as an insult, but as a libation to a just God!"[4]

If romantic poets of the nineteenth century found in Job a Promethean model for humanity's quest for justice, American playwrights of the twentieth century, chastened by the horrors of two world wars, writ large in the Holocaust and the bombings of Hiroshima and Nagasaki, found something different. In his 1956 Pulitzer Prize–winning play, *J.B.*, Archibald MacLeish stages the biblical story as a circus sideshow. God (Mr. Zuss) and Satan (Mr. Nickles) are cast as elderly, broken-down actors, who now earn their keep as circus vendors. Zuss has balloons tied to his belt; Nickles has a popcorn tray strapped across his shoulders. The halcyon days of their fame and stature are a fading memory. With an unvarnished assessment of their contemporary irrelevance, Nickles and Zuss join fragment to fragment to complete a single, telling, sentence.

NICKLES: The two best actors in America
    Selling breath in bags . . .
MR. ZUSS: and bags
    To butter breath with . . .
NICKLES: when they sell.[5]

Zuss wonders if the two of them should stage their own play. "Why not?" Zuss says, "Who cares?" Zuss will play the role of God in *Job*; Nickles agrees, reluctantly, to play the role of Satan. But who, Nickles asks, will play the role of Job, the one who "saw God / . . . By that cold disclosing eye / That stares the color out and strews / Our lives . . . with light . . . for nothing" (12)? The conversation that produces the answer unfolds as follows:

MR. ZUSS: Oh, there's always
    Someone playing Job.
NICKLES: There must be
    Thousands . . .
    Millions and millions of mankind
    Burned, crushed, broken, mutilated,
    Slaughtered, and for what? For thinking!
    For walking around in the world in the wrong

Skin, the wrong-shaped noses, eyelids:
Sleeping the wrong night in the wrong city
London, Dresden, Hiroshima.
There never could have been so many
Suffered more for less. . . .

MR. ZUSS: All we have to do is start.
Job will join us. Job will be there.

NICKLES: I know. I know. I know. I've seen him.
Job is everywhere we go,
His children dead, his work for nothing,
Counting his losses, scraping his boils,
Discussing himself with his friends and physicians,
Questioning everything—the times, the stars,
His own soul, God's providence. . . . (12–13)

MacLeish's "someone playing Job" is J.B. He is cast not as a falsely accused priest, as in *House, M.D.,* nor as Lamartine's Promethean rebel, but as a twentieth-century New England banker whose fortunes have been erased by circumstances he could not predict and cannot understand. His response to misfortune is essentially consonant with his biblical counterpart. He assumes that he, not God, is somehow responsible for his losses. "We have no choice but to be guilty," J.B. says. "God is unthinkable if we are innocent" (111). But Zuss's description of J.B. as he takes the stage provides a clue to MacLeish's reading of those who would play Job in the modern world: "Well," Zuss says to Nickles, "that's our pigeon" (44).

MacLeish's characterization of J.B. as a "pigeon" hints at his understanding of the role innocent sufferers must play in the modern world, if they are to remain faithful to the biblical script. We might take a first clue from the range of colloquial uses of the word. A pigeon is something used for target practice, like a "clay pigeon"; someone "gulled," that is, easily deceived or duped; or someone paid under the table, usually by the police, as an informer or a spy, like a "stool pigeon" or "stoolie." MacLeish himself glosses J.B.'s pigeonlike role in the play in several ways. Both Nickles and Zuss repeatedly acknowledge that J.B. is a "lousy actor," a "ham."[6] Nickles notes that J.B. seems always to need a "prompter" to tell him what to say, then adds, speaking to Zuss, "*Your* lines he was reading, weren't they?" (97). Even when he knows what he is to say, J.B. "muffs" his lines as badly as his life (92). He is "like a canary" (48); he sings praises to God on cue. He plays his part like a "mouth-organ"; "any idiot on earth," Nickles says, "given breath enough can breathe it" (75). By play's end even Zuss is fed up with the plasticity of J.B.'s performance. After all the trouble he took to show him "the wonder and mystery of the universe—the unimaginable might of things," Zuss says, "Job . . . just . . . sat!

Sat there! Dumb! Until it ended!" (137–38). Having seen enough, a deflated Zuss declares, "I'm sick of it. . . . Sick to death. I'd rather sell balloons to children . . . Lights!" (140).

MacLeish primes the play's last scene with a conversation between J.B. and Nickles. As if hoping that J.B. may yet grow into the performance that he (Nickles) has been waiting for from the beginning, Nickles puts his vendor's cap back on, squats down behind J.B., and says to him, "I wondered how you'd play the end." Again, J.B. seems clueless or disinterested. Nickles spells it out for him.

I'll tell you how to play it. Listen!
Think of all the mucked-up millions
Since this buggered world began
Said, No!, said Thank you!, took a rope's end,
Took a window for a door,
Swallowed something, gagged on something . . .

Job won't take it! Job won't touch it!
Job will fling it in God's face
With half his guts to make it spatter!
He'd rather suffocate in dung—
Choke in ordure— (147)

Nickles's last bit of directing is interrupted when J.B. hears someone approaching: "Listen! Do you hear? There's someone. . . . There is someone—Someone waiting at the door" (147–48). Unlike the biblical story, MacLeish scripts the final scene of his play for Job and his wife, not Job and God. It is Sarah who has come to him; God (or Zuss) is nowhere to be seen. A broken-down actor at the beginning of the play, Zuss now appears to be completely irrelevant to its ending. Sarah holds a twig from a forsythia bush that she has found growing, against all odds, in the ashes. It is symbolic of her undying love for her husband. "Why did you leave me alone?" J.B. asks. "I loved you," she responds. "I couldn't help you any more. You wanted justice and there was none—Only love." J.B. still needs directing to understand what Sarah is saying. "He [God] does not love," J.B. says, "He Is." "But we do," Sarah replies. "That's the wonder" (151–52). J.B. complains that it is too dark for him to see. Sarah puts her hands around his face and kisses him, then speaks these last words:

Then blow on the coal of the heart, my darling. . . .

It's all the light now.

Blow on the coal of the heart.
The candles in churches are out.

The lights have gone out in the sky.
Blow on the coal of the heart
And we'll see by and by . . .
We'll see where we are.
The wit won't burn and the wet soul smolders.
Blow on the coal of the heart and we'll know . . .

We'll know . . . (153)

As the curtain comes down, MacLeish adds a final piece of stage directing: "The light increases, plain white daylight from the door, as they work" (ibid.).

Sarah's last words are generally regarded as the signature for MacLeish's contemporary reading of Job. In the world of the 1950s, where millions of persons had suffered barbaric deaths "without cause," as a "Distant Voice" says in scene 7 of the play (96), conventional notions about the biblical God of justice and redemption are obsolete. Religion may be preoccupied with ultimate questions about the meaning of life and its intrinsic connection to belief in God, but as MacLeish suggests, the candles in the church, and the lights in the sky, have long since gone out. If there is any consolation at all for the sufferer, it will not be found in broken-down biblical scripts or the broken-down "actors" who try to bring them to life. The only meaningful consolation is what persons can offer each other, the wonder—and the work—of love that will not let go, no matter what. All else, like the staged setting for this play, is little more than a sideshow.

Commentators often note that MacLeish has taken a good deal of poetic license in his adaptation of the biblical story. In the midst of the near universal praise for his creative genius, one frequently finds the criticism that MacLeish has either ignored or distorted major aspects of his source text in order to write another version of the story that thinly masks his own denial of traditional notions about God's justice and benevolence.[7] Such criticisms are not without merit. In a seminal study of the different images of the biblical Job one finds in the Middle Ages, Lawrence L. Besserman notes that all who would retell the Joban story must face the hazards that come with interpreting or reinterpreting any classic text. He cites the warning of Samuel Johnson: "We have been too early acquainted with the poetical heroes to expect any pleasure from their revival; to show them as they already have been shown, is to disgust by repetition; to give them new qualities or new adventures, is to offend by violating received notions."[8] As Besserman says, "How could the story of Job be retold so as not to 'disgust by repetition' or 'offend by violating received notions'?"[9]

I cite Besserman's question at the outset of this study not to answer it but to agree that it is important to linger over it, especially if the objective is to write a book on the "personality" of Job. Which "biblical" Job should we focus on? The patient, submissive, and ever-faithful Job of the prologue/epilogue (Job 1–2, 42:7–17), which essentially provides the script for *J.B.* and the "Unfaithful" episode of *House*? Or the heroically defiant Job we encounter in the poetic middle of the book (Job 3–42:6), which is the script for Lamartine's nineteenth-century Promethean Job? Depending on the script we choose, Job plays his role in the modern world as someone who models either the integrity of righteous suffering or the integrity of noble rebellion. Similar questions press on our search for the personalities of other characters in this ancient story. As we shall see in the chapters that follow, the characterizations of Job's wife, his friends, the satan, and God shift from version to version, from Hebrew to Greek to Latin to English, from first to second, third, fourth, and more retellings and rereadings of the story.

On the one hand, this is hardly surprising. Truth conveyed as scripture is seldom, if ever, simple, assured, or uncontested. Instead, as Robert Alter has noted, from antiquity the Bible has served not to finalize the search for meaning but to open it up and keep it alive with the promise of new possibilities. It offers a "lexicon for imagining" how to live with or against its semantic sweep, sometimes embracing, sometimes resisting its script about God, the world, and the human condition. In this way the Bible gives birth to a "culture of exegesis" that survives to this day.[10] If we place the long and shifting history of the way the book of Job has been interpreted within Alter's conceptual framework, then we have ample reason to agree that this book and these characters have invited "imaginative allegiance" to insights that we recognize as both "ungraspable" and "continually mesmerizing."[11]

On the other hand, how should we adjudicate the different interpretations this classic text has evoked? Has MacLeish distorted the foundational text by "humanizing the biblical notion of redemption"?[12] Did Lamartine misunderstand or misrepresent Job by romanticizing his poetic eloquence as the cries of humankind? We can and we should scrutinize the differences between the Job(s) of the Bible and the Jobs of our interpretations. But before equating these differences with errors that do violence to the text, we should pause to consider that the text itself is the generative source for multiple, sometimes conflicting, readings. Why does the poet in the eighteenth century read Job differently than the playwright in the twentieth century or the television producer in 2009? Why do different religious traditions commend particular aspects of Job's character—the one that has by far the most traction is his proverbial patience—at the expense of some other part of his profile, even when it is firmly anchored in the scriptural deposit that informs a faith perspective? Such questions invite exegesis of the "culture of exegesis" that the book of Job has produced. What historical, social, cultural, and religious contingencies frame the way we read Job? The pursuit of these questions will be a part of the following exploration of the various personalities who have a role in the book of Job. Definitive answers will no doubt be elusive, and error—to the extent that such an evaluation applies to the exegetical task—will always be a possibility. But as Lewis Thomas, a medical doctor and essayist, has observed, we learn by "trial and *error*," not "trial and *rightness*."[13]

A final introductory comment. The story that unfolds in the book of Job begins with a question from God: "Have you considered my servant Job?" (Job 1:8). By any assessment of the history of Job's claim on the way successive generations have been compelled to return to this book, the answer to this question must surely be "Yes, we have." What follows is my effort to remain faithful to the originating question and to its abiding imperative to sustain the quest. Whether compelled by God or invited by those who, irrespective of notions about God, have lent their insights to the journey, I believe MacLeish is fundamentally correct. "There's always Someone playing Job."

PROLOGUE

"There was once a man in the land of Uz whose name was Job"

Turn it and turn it again, for everything is in it.

Mishnah ʾAbot 5:22

Re-reading is a minor key of everlastingness.

George Steiner, *Grammars of Creation*

First Reading

Like all good stories, the biblical story of Job consists of a beginning, middle, and end. A prose prologue (Job 1–2), offered from the perspective of a guiding narrator, introduces the major characters in the order of their appearance in the story.

Job, the "blameless and upright" man who "feared God and turned away from evil" (1:1), the narrator tells us, is "the greatest of all the people of the east" (1:5).

God, who has been caucusing with "heavenly beings" in the divine council, sets the story in motion by addressing the one named the satan with a presenting question: "Have you considered my servant Job? There is no one like him on the earth, a blameless and upright man who fears God and turns away from evil" (1:8; cf. 2:3).

The satan responds to God with counterquestions that invite scrutiny both of Job's piety—"Does Job fear God for nothing?" (1:9)—and of God's nature and character: "Have you not put a fence around him and all that he has?" (1:10). In response to these questions, God grants the satan permission to launch a series of tests, which result in Job's loss of his wealth and possessions, the deaths of his children, and his affliction with physical suffering (1:13–19, 2:7–8). Confronted by all these adversities, Job persists in his fidelity to God, a conclusion underscored by his own actions and words (1:21, 2:10), by God's confirming assessment (2:3), and by the narrator, who twice reminds readers that "in all this Job did not sin" (1:22, 2:10b).

Job's wife enters and speaks one line. Her words to her husband echo parts of
   what both God and the satan have said thus far: "you still persist in your
   integrity" (2:9a; cf. God's words in 2:3) and "curse God and die" (2:9b; cf. the
   satan's words in 1:11, 2:5).
Three friends, Eliphaz, Bildad, and Zophar, come to "comfort and console" Job
   (2:11–13). When they see him from a distance, they weep, tear their robes,
   throw dust in the air, and sit with him on the ground for seven days and
   seven nights.

   Through the words and actions of these characters, the prologue introduces
the outline of what was surely a conventional story in the ancient world about a
righteous person who maintains his faith in the face of great affliction. Telltale
signs that will soon complicate the story, especially the satan's questions about
God's governance of Job's world and God's admission that all that has turned it
upside down, including the deaths of his children, has happened "for no reason"
(2:3), are temporarily muted by the narrator's last words in chapter 2: "no one
spoke a word . . . for they saw that his suffering was very great" (2:13).
   The middle of the story (Job 3–42:6) is conveyed through poetry instead of
prose. The narrator, the satan, and Job's wife disappear, leaving the stage to Job,
his three friends (Eliphaz, Bildad, and Zophar), God, and a fourth friend, Elihu,
who appears for the first time in chapters 32–37. The plotline advances through
the speeches of each of these characters. If initially "suffering [that] was very
great" silenced all speech (2:13), now Job's suffering requires the consideration of
a torrent of words before any decisive action can be contemplated. It is Job's
words, not God's (cf.1:7–8), that set the pace the others in this drama must follow.
When Job curses the day of his birth (3:1–10), then repeatedly questions why he
was born into such a life of misery (3:11–26), he insists that innocent suffering is
an issue that neither his friends nor his God can ignore if they are to remain a
part of his story. The three friends who had come to comfort him are the first to
accept the challenge. Through three cycles of dialogues (Job 4–14, 15–22, 23–27),
they try to nudge or coerce Job toward their answers to his questions. Their tac-
tics vary from cycle to cycle, but their objective remains the same throughout.
The principle of divine justice that defines their world—and their place within it
as spokespersons for God—simply put, is this: God can be trusted to reward the
righteous and punish the wicked. From this they deduce, with invincible conviction, that if Job suffers, then he must be guilty of sin, in which case God promises
forgiveness and restoration in exchange for his confession and repentance (e.g.,
8:5–7, 11:13–20, 22:21–27). Job's only recourse, as Eliphaz concludes in the last
cycle, is to "agree with God, and be at peace" (22:21). Job counters that he is innocent; he cannot repent of sins he has not committed (e.g., 6:28–30, 9:21, 10:7, 16:17,

19:6–7). In his final response to the friends, he declares his innocence and, by implication, God's guilt in afflicting him "for no reason," and he insists that in doing so his conscience is completely clear (27:1–6). As his debate with the three friends limps to an unresolved end, Job takes an oath, swearing his innocence and demanding that his accuser—God—appear in court (31:35–37). If Job is to be condemned as guilty, then God must produce the evidence; if God cannot do this, then it is God, not Job, who risks indictment in the court of justice.

When Elihu appears, he claims for himself the role of the "answerer" this story needs (cf. 32:1, 3, 5, 6, 12, 17, 20). He speaks for 159 uninterrupted verses, but his contribution receives no response from Job. Elihu does however anticipate the final dialogue in the middle section, when at long last God "answers Job out of the whirlwind" (38:1, 40:6). God's two speeches (38:1–39:30, 40:1–34 [Heb: 41:26]) and Job's two responses (40:3–5, 42:1–6) bring this middle section to a close. The conventional rendering of Job's last words in 42:6—"therefore I despise myself and repent in dust and ashes" (NRSV)—appears to leave him just where his friends had urged him to be: in abject penitence before God. But as we shall see, a number of intractable ambiguities deny the certainty many have claimed for this reading.

The prose epilogue in 42:7–17 provides the story's ending. As in the prologue, a narrator appears, now to offer two final judgments. The first (42:7–9) is God's judgment *against* the friends, "who have not spoken about me what is right"; the second (42:10–17) is God's judgment *for* Job, which results in the restoration of his wealth, family, and place in society. "After this," the narrator says in conclusion, "Job lived one hundred and forty years, and saw his children, and his children's children, four generations. And Job died, old and full of days" (42:16–17).

Most commentators agree that the final form of the biblical book that conveys the story as sketched above (excluding the Elihu speeches) dates between the sixth and fifth centuries B.C.E., that is, to the exilic or early postexilic period, when the Babylonian destruction of Jerusalem (586 B.C.E.) raised acute questions about the justice of God and innocent suffering. Antecedent texts from Mesopotamia, Egypt, and Syria-Palestine, some of which date to the second millennium B.C.E., confirm that stories about a righteous, Job-type sufferer circulated widely in the ancient Near East. When Job makes his biblical appearance in the land of Uz, therefore, we can be sure that he was following in the footsteps of a host of others who had long been traveling similar paths. To return once more to the observation by Zuss in MacLeish's *J.B.*, "there's always Someone playing Job."

If there is always someone playing Job, then there is also always someone reading, interpreting, and adapting Job's story for the world in which they live. The journey from second-millennium ancient Near Eastern texts about a Joblike sufferer to the Bible's version of the book of Job is case in point. The only reference to Job in the Old Testament outside the book of Job occurs in Ezekiel (early sixth century), where Job is ranked, along with Noah and Dan'el, a legendary Canaanite king, as one of the righteous heroes from whom ancient Israelites drew inspiration in times of crisis (Ez 14:14, 20). From this brief mention, there is no way to know for certain whether the story Ezekiel knows is the same one we read in Job 1–2 or a different one, perhaps, as has been argued, an ancient Job epic that predates both.[1] We can see, however, that within the Old Testament itself, the received story about Job expands from a single, allusive reference to his exemplary righteousness to a forty-two-chapter account of his life in the land of Uz. This observation sets the table for a closer examination of the basic plotline as sketched above. As we shall see, the final form of the book itself reflects the ways ancient authors and readers adapted what they received to construct a much more complicated story than any simple plotline can adequately convey.

Second Readings

The prose prologue (1–2) and epilogue (42:7–17) likely constitute the oldest form of the Joban story. Taken together, they constitute a coherent account of a righteous individual who is tested by misfortune and rewarded by God for his perseverance. The story invites consideration of whether affliction causes a "blameless and upright" person to curse God, then dismisses any such notion, apparently without objection, as transparently "foolish" (2:10). There are no specific indicators for locating this version of the story in any one particular period of Israel's history, but we can plausibly speculate that it would have had resonance with an audience in either the eighth century, before the devastations wrought by Assyrian, Egyptian, and Babylonian conquests, or perhaps in the sixth century, when assurances in the early aftermath of these conquests remained persuasive. In either setting this account of Job's story would have recruited readers who can hear Job's last words in the prologue, "Shall we receive the good at the hand of God, and not receive the bad?" (2:10), and remain confident that the answer is not ambiguous.

The dialogues between Job and his three friends (Job 3–31) and between Job and God (38:1–42:6) that stand at the center of the book are written in poetry, not prose, and are dominated by the speeches of the characters, not their actions. Drawn primarily from the genres of lament and disputation, these speeches provide characterizations of the friends, Job, and God that stand in marked contrast with what we find in the prologue and epilogue. The friends, who are silent and sympathetic in the prologue, become increasingly strident interlocutors. Job, whose piety in the prologue is undisturbed by either doubts or complaints, fills the center of the book with curses, laments, and direct challenges to God's moral governance of the world. God, who is content to speak approvingly *about* Job's fidelity in the prologue and epilogue, now speaks *directly* to Job, though whether to commend or rebuke him requires further analysis.

It is possible that the author of the dialogues is the same person who crafted the prologue/epilogue, in which case we should suppose that he chose to recast the traditional story about Job's unflinching fidelity to God by inserting these dialogues in the middle, thus strategically transforming the simple "all's-well-that-ends-well" conclusion into a much more complicated story. It is also possible that the dialogues should be attributed to a different and later author, who found the existent story about Job overly simplistic and woefully inadequate for the world in which he lived. A strong case can be made for locating this author in the time of the Babylonian exile (586–38 B.C.E.), when the massive destruction and losses suffered by the Israelites traumatized all explanation. From this general period come texts such as Lamentations, Deutero-Isaiah, portions of Jeremiah and Ezekiel, and a number of Jerusalem lament psalms (e.g., Pss 44, 69, 74, 79, 102, 137), all of which give expression in various ways to doubt and despair that could not be silenced by simple appeals to patience. By splicing the prologue and the epilogue with the dispute between Job and his friends, this Joban poet offers a template for exploring the rift between God's promises and the on-the-ground misery that threatens to nullify them. The friends urge Job to stay inside old certainties about God's justice and mercy; Job refuses, insisting that they are whitewashing the truth with lies (13:4) and speaking falsely for God (13:7). Whether attributed to the same author or a later one, the dialogues constitute a rereading that requires a retelling of the Joban story.

The speeches of Elihu (32–37) clearly constitute a further addition to the traditional story of Job. A number of historical-critical arguments, both stylistic and substantive, support this assessment. Elihu is not mentioned in either the prologue or epilogue; neither the friends (Eliphaz, Bildad, Zophar) nor Job speak of or to him; his speeches begin with a prose introduction (32:1–5) that differs in tone and style from the introductions to the other characters; he is the only character in the book who has an Israelite name and a genealogy that suggests Israelite origins; he explicitly cites the words of Job and the three friends; he not only anticipates God's speeches but also speaks as if he has a script of these speeches in hand (cf. 37:14–24). All these reasons in fact only provide critical confirmation of what the narrator (and author?)[2] announces when Elihu makes his first appearance in the story. When the three friends "ceased to answer Job," Elihu "became angry."[3] He was angry at Job "because he justified himself rather than God." And he was angry at the friends "because they had found no answer, though they had declared Job to be in the wrong" (32:1–5). We are invited to read Elihu reading Job. His speeches provide "the first commentary" on what had become, in effect, the book of Job he had received.[4]

As with all the component parts of this book, the Elihu speeches are impossible to date with precision. The evidence, especially the significant number of Aramaisms in the speeches, suggests a late Persian or early Hellenistic dating that is consonant with the intellectual milieu of late wisdom texts such as Ecclesiastes and Sirach and protoapocalyptic texts such as Daniel 1–6.[5] Such a date places the author as reader within the general context of an Israelite living in a world of foreign hegemony, where long-held convictions about God's power, justice, and compassion are strained by current realities. Unlike the author of the dialogues, however, who crafted Job's dispute with the friends to challenge, or subvert, orthodoxy, the author of the Elihu speeches seeks to review, buttress, and transport the old certainties into the new realities of his world. He supplies the answers to Job's questions that have thus far been lacking in this story. For example he accents former certainties about God's indisputable sovereignty, now clouded by the reality of foreign kings who exercise political control over Israel, with new affirmations of God's irresistible power (36:5, 22; 37:22–24). He buttresses former certainties about God's moral governance of the world, now called into question by the injustices the righteous suffer without redress, with new assertions promising that the wicked cannot hide from God's judgment (34:10–30). He reclaims former beliefs about God's readiness to respond to the sufferer's cry, now thinned by experiences of prolonged divine silence, by inscribing both God's silence (35:5–13) and human suffering (33:14–20) into a purposive divine revelatory process. He invokes praise of God's creation as an antidote to suffering (36:26–37:13) not to argue that humans must bow to the mysterious power of the Almighty, as Job's friends have pressed him to do, but to invoke a sense of wonder and awe that invites humans into an encounter with something larger than their own personal need.

Third Readings

Thus far I have provided an overview of the major characters and participants in this story and briefly sketched the outlines of the compositional history of the "book." My objective in doing so has been to demonstrate that from its first appearance in scripture, Job's story has been read and reread, interpreted and reinterpreted, appropriated and reappropriated by different authors for different times, places, and purposes. This process of translating the received story from its originating context(s) into new settings and for different readers continues long after the story in its Hebrew version attains some form of stability. In subsequent chapters I will continue to track this ongoing process in the Greek translation of Job in the Septuagint (LXX) (third century B.C.E.), which both omits from and adds to what we have in the Masoretic text; in the pseudepigraphal *Testament of Job* (*T. Job*) (first century B.C.E.–first century C.E.), which in both style and substance significantly recasts the biblical story; in the Church Fathers, medieval Jewish commentators, and the vast number of nonclerical readers—artists, novelists, playwrights, poets, and others—who come belatedly to this text. As preface to this discussion, however, it is instructive to pause at this point in order to consider one of the primary issues that generate such different readings and interpretations of the biblical Job.

The book of Job begins in prose, shifts to poetry in the middle, and then ends by returning to prose. This shifting from one form of presentation to another and back again invites attention to the question of genre.[6] The Job we meet in the prose prologue and epilogue is different than the Job we encounter in the poetic dialogues that stand at the center of the book. The Job of the prose continues to bless God in the midst of undeserved suffering and is rewarded by God for his unfailing fidelity. The Job of the poetry curses undeserved suffering and challenges God's fidelity to him. In response to God's "answer," Job moves first to silence (40:4–5) and then, apparently, to contrition (42:6). These starkly contrasting descriptions have typically been explained by assigning them to different authors, and while this mitigates the jarring impact readers feel when moving from one part of the book to another, it does little to help us understand why prose should be the vehicle for one characterization of Job's story and poetry for another and different characterization.

The didactic tale (Job 1–2 + 42:7–17) features a *narrator*, who conveys its beginning and ending from the perspective of an omniscient spectator who knows what truth the reader should discern.[7] This truth is conveyed as both simple—it is essentially beyond disagreement and dispute—and normative, that is, readers can agree to its authoritative claim on the way they live. Job *is* "blameless and upright" (1:1), the narrator states categorically. He *is* "the greatest of all the people in the east" (1:3); when afflicted, he *does* fall on the ground, worship, and bless God (1:20–21); he "*did not* sin" (1:22); the Lord does "restore the fortunes of Job" (42:10) and *does* "bless the latter days of Job more than his beginning" (42:12); and Job *does* die "old and full of days" (42:17).

The narrator reinforces these assertions by repeating them at strategic points in the narrative (cf. 1:1, 6-8, 22; 2:1-3, 10), which increases the likelihood that readers will agree to their importance, and he adds supporting details that constructively explicate the basic challenges Job overcomes en route to securing his reward (the satan's proposed testing of Job [1:9–12; 2:4–7]; the messengers who report the execution of Job's plotted misfortunes [1:13–19]; and the wife's encouragement to curse God [2:9]). In unfolding the story, the narrator omits superfluous details that might distract the reader's attention; for example there is no attention to Job's genealogy, his origins in the land of Uz, or the relevance of his non-Israelite/Gentile status, all issues that, as we shall see, later commentators take up with great interest. Other details that might trigger questions or provoke interpretations opposite to the narrator's intention are minimized; they are present in the story line but not really pertinent to understanding its primary message. For example the narrator does not linger over the possibility that God, by first inviting and then agreeing to the satan's proposal to test Job (1:12, 2:6), is complicit in Job's misfortune; he cites God's admission to having been "incited" by the satan to destroy Job "for no reason" (2:3) but does not encourage readers to pursue what this means.

Finally the narrator privileges the principle of the story over the particulars. What is most important is the overarching truth that may be extracted and applied to any person in any time and place, not the individual circumstances that may raise questions about its specific application. As the narrator says after introducing Job to the reader, "This is what Job always did" (1:5). An implicit universalizing also applies to the narrator's advocacy for a larger truth: this is who God always is; this is the way the world always works; this is the way everyone who is "blameless and upright" should always respond to unexpected misfortune.

The wisdom dialogue in the center of the book (Job 3–42:6) represents a different way of conceptualizing reality and its claims on readers. Beginning with chapter 3 and continuing through 42:6, the narrator disappears. The story now advances through the speeches of one character to another, their entry onto the stage signaled by only a conventional recognition of the change of speaker: "Job said" (3:2), "Then Eliphaz the Temanite answered" (4:1), "Then Job answered" (6:1), "Then Bildad the Shuhite answered" (8:1), "Then Job answered" (9:1), "Then the Lord answered Job" (38:1), "Then Job answered the Lord" (40:3), and so on. No third party steps into the middle of these conversations to comment on or critique them for the reader; dialogic, not monologic, perspectives sustain the story line. The only exception occurs in 32:1–5, where a narrator tells us that Elihu speaks because he is "angry." When Elihu the character speaks, however, he presents himself not as angry but as divinely inspired (32:18). Thus here too readers must decide how to assess what he says.

Instead of simple, authoritative assertions about the way the world works, the dialogues prize competing perspectives. Different characters may align themselves with a shared viewpoint; they may press their conversation partner to yield to its truth; but try as they will, they cannot control the response they receive. The dialogues continue by debating the issues. Points of contradiction rather than agreement move the conversation from cycle to cycle, with roughly equal time allotted for each set of speakers to express themselves without interruption, until the conversation stalls, with no party being able to claim the upper hand. Job's three friends assert in alternating speeches what they believe is a normative view of human suffering in relation to God's justice and mercy. While essentially agreeing with this norm, Job resolutely disagrees that it functions as it should for him, and he matches their assertions with questions and counterassertions of his own. When he last speaks directly to his friends, his words indicate just how far apart they remain: "Far be it from me to say that you are right; until I die I will not put away my integrity from me" (27:5). The dialogues between God and Job reflect a different dynamic. God clearly has the upper hand, in a sense, commanding center stage for 159 verses, compared to just 9 verses allotted to Job's response. But even with a conventional rendering of Job's response, there is no agreement between God and Job on a fundamental question that underlies the whole of their "conversation": "Why have you made me your target?" (7:20).

Finally, whereas the didactic tale privileges principle and minimizes contingencies, the dialogues place Job's mitigating circumstances opposite the friends' norming assertions. The friends urge Job toward truths they believe transcend his particular circumstances. Job insists that if their assertions about God's justice cannot adequately address his experiences of brokenness and loss—seven sons and three daughters dead "for no reason"—then all claims for transcendent justice are nothing more than a lie masquerading as the truth. "Look at me and be appalled," Job says to his friends, "and lay your hand on your mouth" (21:5; cf. 6:28, 13:17, 21:2).

Both the didactic tale and the wisdom dialogue are constructive genres. Both draw upon a range of social values that are deeply engrained and widely appreciated. If we read the beginning and ending of the didactic tale as a set piece, bracketing for the moment the wisdom dialogue, then the narrator maps a world of "ready-made truth"[8] that cannot be subverted by passing problems. All gaps between the way the world "ought" to work and the way it "is" in any particular time and place are either denied or minimized as inconsequential. Normative truths are sufficient to account for specific experiences. The narrator, like a wise and knowing parent, seeks to instill in his readers the childlike discipline of trusting in time-tested virtues they may not understand. When trust is lacking, obedience bridges between resistance and compliance, between doubt and affirmation molded by more experience.

The wisdom dialogue also calls upon established ways of thinking about God, the world, and the human condition, and it too, when read on its own, apart from the didactic tale, makes a constructive contribution to the reader's understanding. The pursuit of truth, as modeled by the dialogues between Job and his friends and Job and God, makes room for multiple perspectives. Each "I" who speaks contributes something that has the potential to change and be changed by the legitimate response of another. No one voice can claim a monopoly on truth, which is inevitably larger and more complex than any one person or any one system of thought can contain. The dialogues invite exploration of the gaps between what ought to be and what is, not to explain them or to minimize their impact but to acknowledge that truth most often lies at the intersection of incommensurate ideas. Consequently the dialogues find and shape readers who, for whatever reason, are not content with ready-made answers that stifle curiosity or imagination. What can be asserted can be questioned; what can be affirmed can be pressed by wonderment, suspicion, or denial. This intellectual process may of course be tiresome and frustrating—hence the abiding appeal of the authoritative voice that ends debate—but it is also generative. In its restlessness with bordered answers, the dialogue probes uncharted territory in search of new discoveries. If the didactic tale "infantilizes readers" by offering "paternal assurances" that require obedience, even when comprehension is lacking, then the dialogues acknowledge that readers do not always remain infants.[9] When they grow up and begin to think for themselves, they should not be expected to exchange their independence for the tyranny of imposed assertions they can no longer accept.[10]

The wisdom dialogue that provides the template for the Joban poet is, of course, anchored not to modern or postmodern constructs of the psyche but to regnant social and cultural values in the ancient Near East. Nonetheless with good reason we might suspect that the Joban poet would endorse the following sentiment: "There lives more faith in honest doubt, / Believe me, than in half the creeds."[11] If we did not know the author of these words was Alfred Lord Tennyson (1809–92), we might read them as the signature of the poet who long ago insisted that Job's "Why?" questions be factored into every assertion about truth and justice, especially when the presenting issue is how to respond to someone whose "suffering was [read *is*] very great" (Job 2:13).

It is relatively easy to read and interpret these two genres, the prose and the poetry, separately, as if they were two discrete accounts of the Joban story. Much of the history of Joban interpretation accents either the patient Job of the prose or the rebellious Job of the poetry. It is a far greater challenge to hold both genres together, to begin with the prose, read through the poetry, then end by returning to the prose, which invites a final assessment of the whole story. What is the interpretive impact of having to shift our reading strategies back and forth between these different ways of telling and retelling the story? Does the prose effectively frame our reading of the poetry at the center? Should we conclude that despite a temporary lapse into defiance, Job begins and ends as a moral exemplar of resolute faith in the midst of adversity? Does the poetry that dominates the center of the book effectively determine our reading of the beginning and ending prose? Should we conclude that despite a temporary resolve to trust in God's justice and mercy, Job is primarily a moral exemplar of loyal opposition to God? Such either-or reading strategies are not without merit; they have had and no doubt will continue to have wide appeal for interpreters of this book. Even so, we must wonder if in making our choice for one or the other of these strategies we are in fact settling for a finalized reading that the final form of the book (intentionally?) resists.

Rereading Is a Minor Key of Everlastingness

The language I have used above—first, second, third "readings"—connects with the methodology of "reception history," which, since the 1970s, has become increasingly prominent in biblical studies. I am not especially concerned to conform to what is still a developing set of criteria for this approach, but I do agree with one of its fundamental principles: "Readings give meanings to texts."[12] I agree with the premise that it is important and necessary to discern, as clearly as possible, what the (original) author of a text meant to say, thus I begin subsequent chapters with a conventional historical-critical overview of the Job texts I address, which situates the texts in a particular historical-cultural context that I assume was important for its first reading. The question remains, however: once an author or editor has completed work on a text that is "finalized," how do later readers, whose historical and cultural contexts may be very different, read and appropriate the text they have received? Original readings (however determined) may get us to the bedrock of the excavation process, but they provide only a foundation, a touchstone, for the subsequent readings that are constructed on top of them. My assumption throughout is that the meanings subsequent interpreters build on the foundations of the Job text are important. Each successive reading adds a layer of interpretation. Each layer is a witness to historical and cultural contingencies that shape both academic and ordinary apprehensions of the text; each layer is a reminder that critical analysis of what the text means to contemporary readers is at least as important as what it meant to its presumptive first readers and hearers. The question is not whether the first or the third reading is correct. It is whether and to what extent rereadings enlarge our understanding and our appropriation of ancient texts in new, perhaps surprising ways.

Biblical texts have a life after their composition and final editing. Subsequent readers may or may not know the history of a text's composition. They may or may not know or value how a text has been altered or embellished in translation, from Hebrew to Greek to Latin to English. The text they read and interpret is the text they receive. For readers of Job, particularly, the biblical account remains "a value-laden, imaginatively energizing" text, as Alter suggests, "a timeless inscription of fixed meanings" that remains "continually mesmerizing"—in sum a canonicity of God, the righteous, and good and evil that still nourishes readers.[13]

George Steiner ultimately affirms this observation, but he puzzles over whether the travails of history may have slammed the door on scripture's relevance for contemporary readers. Given the "core-tiredness" of life at the beginning of the twenty-first century, rooted in the hideous barbarity of war, disease, deportation, ethnic cleansing, and political murder, why read scripture at all? "*Stricto sensu,*" he says, scripture seems to have "nothing left to say" that makes a difference.[14] Nevertheless Steiner insists that a core hunger for apprehending the grammars of creation compels a rereading of scripture. Scripture in general, and the book of Job in particular, Steiner suggests, enables readers to experience "something of God's choice of the poetic in counterblast to the challenges of the ontological, the ethical, and the religious."[15] We are possessed by a "shared nativity," manifest in art, literature, and religious beliefs, that is "older than reason and incised . . . in the collective soul."[16] "Are the great stories going to continue to be told," Steiner asks, and "will the characters which enact them continue to be born?"[17]

Steiner's answer is a beleaguered, knowing yes, even if this answer commits him to a "baffled engagement with transcendence."[18] If, as he says, "only certitude ages," then reading and rereading Job may be the key to "the fraught miracle of [our] survival."[19] When third parties to a dialogue become not only listeners but also active readers, then "rereading is a minor key to everlastingness."[20]

PART I

Introduction to the Characters in the Didactic Tale (Job 1–2 + Job 42:7–17)

1

THE JOB(S) OF THE DIDACTIC TALE

A Saint in the Making

[The] outstanding and much esteemed history of the saintly Job.

Theodore, bishop of Mopsuestia

You are the Emancipator of your God,

And as such I promote you to a saint.

Robert Frost, *A Masque of Reason*

The Job we meet in the didactic tale that frames the book (Job 1–2 + Job 42:7–17) needs little introduction. In forty-five verses, less than 1 percent of the total book, the Job we perhaps know best emerges. He is a righteous man who endures undeserved affliction without complaint and is in the end restored and rewarded by God. For many readers this one-sentence characterization can be condensed still further—and finalized—with a single phrase: "the patience of Job." Whether we know this phrase from reading the New Testament (Jas 5:11) or from listening to the proverbial wisdom passed along by our elders, many of us have archived "Job" in our memories under the general rubric "patience."

"Patience" is, however, an *inferred* virtue of the Job in the didactic tale. The narrator tells us that both he and God know Job to be "blameless and upright" (1:1, 8; 2:3); that despite undeserved affliction "Job did not sin or charge God with wrongdoing" (1:22; cf. 2:10); that when his wife urged him to curse God, he dismissed her as foolish (2:9–10); and that in the end God restored Job's fortunes and blessed him (42:10,12). In conveying this information, neither the narrator nor God ever use the word *patience* to describe Job's character,[1] although both assume to know things about Job that he does not know about himself. The same is true for the satan, who recognizes that Job may be a more complex character than either God or the narrator allow—"Does Job really fear God for nothing?" (1:9)— but in this case the satan claims to know that Job will indeed curse God when his circumstances change. The satan expects Job to be *impatient* with God, although this is never explicitly stated. Neither does Job describe himself as patient. He speaks the two lines he is given (1:21, 2:10), but in both cases the narrator immediately provides an addendum that effectively removes any consideration of his interior motives. Job *did not sin,* the narrator assures us (1:22, 2:10), even though "his suffering was very great" (2:13).

The narrator, God, and the satan "narrate Job"; he is for them more an example of the "blameless and upright" man than a person with subjective emotions and motivations. In sum the Job of the didactic tale is a "spectacle," an object in a "scientific" experiment that will be conducted according to a predetermined set of circumstances. As soon as God poses the opening question, "Have you considered my servant Job?" everyone becomes a voyeur. God watches Job to see what he will do and say; the satan watches Job; and we readers watch the both of them watching Job. We all know more about Job than he knows about himself, and while there may be some uncertainty about specific twists and turns the story might take, we cannot imagine, given the careful structuring of the narrative, anything but a positive ending.[2]

How then does "the patience of Job" come to be, effectively, the sum truth not only of the didactic tale, but also in many respects of the entire book? Three primary interpretive moves are required. First, interpreters must focus on the framing didactic tale and its account of Job's piety and fortitude in the face of suffering and loss. Coupled with his ultimate reward and restoration, Job emerges in this reading as a moral exemplar of heroic dimensions; as suggested by the title for this chapter, he is a saint in the making. Second, interpreters must essentially ignore, minimize, or rationalize the "impatient" Job who dominates the poetic dialogues that stand at the center of the book (Job 3–42:6).[3] His complaints about God's justice, his doubts about God's presence, and his determination to establish his own innocence by prosecuting God's guilt must be viewed as a regrettable but understandable character flaw. It is a sin of temporary despair, which is overcome by Job's repentance and redeemed by God's forgiveness. In this reading even a rebellious Job remains a paragon of patience, a reminder that fortitude trumps human frailty in the divine economy. Third, for interpreters to identify patience as the most important and imitable Joban virtue, they must successfully argue that Job's patience sets a principled precedent that transcends the particular circumstances of any one time or place. Such patience must have a generic suasion that reaches across historical and cultural contingencies, beyond ethnic and religious identities. The point may be sharpened by referring once more to James 5:11, the single mention of Job in the New Testament. When the author of this epistle says to his first-century audience, "You have heard of the patience of Job," he must be able to assume that they know the word *patience* is a sufficient summation of the entire story.

In different ways and for various reasons, early Jewish and Christian exegetes made each of these interpretive moves. Beginning with the LXX and still more decisively with the *T. Job,* patience emerges as the dominant trope for reading Job. Rabbinic interpretation both informed early Christian exegesis and reacted to it. By the time of the Latin fathers of the church (Jerome, Augustine, Gregory the Great), the accent on Job's patience and fortitude was so deeply rooted in the interpretive tradition that it would not be dislodged until the nineteenth century, when historical-critical approaches placed the unity of the book and thus its presumed unitary focus under close scrutiny. Contemporary biblical scholarship has tended to dismiss the "patient Job" as a relic of the very orthodoxy the "rebellious Job" of the dialogues refuses to embrace. We will assess this alternative characterization of Job in subsequent chapters, but first it is instructive to recognize that the "patience of Job" has long been, and likely will remain, an enormously generative summons to heroic, saintly virtues that no society, ancient or modern, can afford to erase from its collective memory.[4]

"Patience Is Better than Anything" (*T. Job* 27:7)

Early rabbinic commentators were well aware of the contradictions between the pious and God-fearing Job of the prose tale and the rebellious Job of the rest of the book. While Christian interpreters from the second to the nineteenth centuries largely resolved this issue by minimizing or ignoring the poetic dialogues, the rabbis, "as conscientious exegetes . . . had perforce to read the Hebrew book of Job as it stood."[5]

At the center of what proved to be an unresolved debate among the rabbis was the question about Job's origins. The Hebrew book describes Job as a non-Israelite from the "land of Uz," a Gentile who was a worshipper of Israel's God YHWH (1:1, 21). Some rabbinic commentators regarded Job, along with Abraham and Joseph, as one of three persons who were "God-fearing" (*Gen. Rabbah* 21). Others viewed Job as the most pious Gentile who ever lived (*Deut. Rabbah* 2:4). As a righteous Gentile, Job demonstrates that it is possible to be a faithful worshipper of the one true God even outside the boundaries of Israel. He is regarded, for example, as one of the seven Gentile prophets who prophesied to the nations before the Torah was given to Israel. The seven are identified as "Balaam and his father; Job from the land of Uz; and Eliphaz the Temanite; and Bildad the Shuhite; and Zophar the Naamathite; and Elihu the son of Barachel the Buzite" (*Seder ʿOlam Rabbah* 21). Other rabbis, convinced that a man with Job's virtues must have been an Israelite, argued that he was one of the Israelite prophets, along with Elijah, who preached to the Gentiles (*Baba Batra* 15b). Still others insisted that because Job is described as a "whole-hearted" or "perfect" man (*tām* [Job 1:1]), he must have been born circumcised (*ʾAbot de Rabbi Nathan* 2).

The rabbis could not ignore, however, Job's suffering, which in rabbinic thinking could not be gratuitous. Job must have sinned, thus meriting his affliction as part of God's inviolable justice. Raba interpreted Job 2:10—"In all this Job did not sin with his lips"—to mean that he did sin within his heart; because God knew that Job would soon open his mouth to speak curses (cf. Job 3), God was justified in punishing him (*Baba Batra* 16a). Some rabbinic accounts trace Job's origins to the time of Moses, when he was said to have served as one of Pharaoh's counselors, along with two other Gentiles, Jethro and Balaam, during the time of the Israelite's enslavement (*B. Soṭah* 11a; *B. Sanhedrin* 106a; *Exod. Rabbah* 1:9). Balaam is said to have persuaded Pharaoh to issue the decree that all male children be drowned. For this he is remembered as the model of the wicked Gentiles who seek the destruction of the people of Israel. When the decree was issued, Jethro is said to have fled Pharaoh's court, renounced his former life, and joined the Jewish community. He thus becomes the model of the Gentile proselyte to Judaism. Job, by contrast, is reported to have been silent in the face of Pharaoh's decree. He is punished by God because he did nothing to prevent Israel's affliction.

In a similar line of argumentation, the rabbis recognize Job's reputation for righteousness but qualify it as less than that exemplified by Israel's revered ancestors. Baskin cites a comment from *Pesiqta Rabbati* 47 as typical:

> The Holy One, blessed be He, said to Job: Why raisest thou a cry? Because suffering befell thee? Dost thou then perhaps consider thyself greater than Adam, the creation of my own hands? Because of a single command that he made nothing of, I decreed death for him and his progeny. Yet he did not raise a cry. Or consider thyself greater than Abraham? Because he ventured to say "Whereby shall I know that I shall inherit it?" (Gen 15:8), I put him to trial after trial. . . . Yet he did not raise a cry. Or consider thyself greater than Isaac? Because he persisted in loving Esau I made his eyes dim. . . . Or consider thyself greater than Moses? Because he spoke in anger to Israel, saying, "Hear now, ye rebels" (Num 20:10), I decreed as punishment for him that he could not enter into the land. Yet he did not raise a cry.[6]

If Job had not complained, as this discussion goes on to make clear, then he would have been listed along with the ancestors of Israel in the daily prayers of the faithful. People would have prayed "God of Abraham, God of Isaac, God of Jacob and God of Job." Job's complaints, especially his remonstrations against God, were an indication to some that he served God out of fear, not love, that his righteousness was a careful and calculated hedge against losing his possessions. Devotion motivated by fear crumbles under the weight of adversity; it reveals a man who claims to be righteous not only as a fraud but also a rebel. Rabbi Akiba compares Job's love for God to that of Abraham and others and finds him wanting. When God ordered Abraham to offer his only son Isaac as a burnt offering, he was silent

(Gn 22); when God afflicted Hezekiah, he begged God for mercy (2 Kgs 20); but when God sent suffering to Job, he "remonstrated when punished, as it is said, 'I will say unto God; Do not condemn me; make me to know wherefore Thou contendest with me' (Job 10:2)" (*Semahot* 8; *Midrash Teharot* 26:2). Because of such rebellion, Akiba identified Job with the wicked, such as Gog and Magog, who were punished in Gehenna (*M. 'Edduyot* 2:10). *Baba Batra* 15b makes a similar case against Job by arguing that even if he was the most righteous of Gentiles, he forfeited life in the world to come because he questioned God's justice.[7]

This overview of rabbinic interpretation may be sufficient to confirm Baskin's assertion that "there are almost as many Jobs as Rabbis who speak about him."[8] The rabbis' inability, or refusal, to resolve the differences between the pious and patient Job of the prose narrative and the defiant and impatient Job of the poetic dialogues was likely influenced by, even as it contributed to, the more pietistic and more unitary focus on the "saintly" Job that began to take root in early Jewish and Christian communities with the appearance of the LXX and the *T. Job*. We turn to these rereadings of Job in the following paragraphs, but before doing so it is instructive to consider Baskin's caveat:

> Such texts as the *Testament of Job* [and the LXX] . . . glorified the pious sufferer of Job 1 and 42 as an innocent and paradigmatic model of patience under duress. The outraged and outspoken Job of the rest of the book is totally ignored in these works, which had an immense impact on Christian views of Job. The rabbinic respect for Scripture could not sanction so cavalier an approach to holy writ, and instead demanded descriptions of Job's obvious wrongdoings, justifications of his undoubtedly deserved punishment, and condemnations of his intemperate and occasionally blasphemous complaining. The flawed figure who thus emerged explains the hesitation some Rabbis felt to grant Job full forgiveness and access to the world to the come. At the same time the rather one-dimensional Job, championed by the authors of those pietistic texts, and their adherents, was also disavowed.[9]

The LXX is the oldest surviving translation of Job, and as such it represents an early move toward elevating the patient Job over the impatient Job. The Greek translators produced not only a shorter version of the Hebrew text,[10] they also changed its characterization of Job by supplying information not found in rabbinic sources and by subtly softening or eliminating many of Job's impious statements. Two significant additions are made to the prose tale, the most important of which for our purposes here is the addendum in Job 42:17a–e.[11] Where the Hebrew text ends with the words "and Job died, old and full of days," the LXX adds "And it is written that he will rise again with those the Lord raises up" (42:17a).[12] The affirmation that Job's suffering finds its ultimate reward in his resurrection effectively removes a major tension in the book. If all present wrongs are righted when Job rises again, then, as Baskin notes, "the central issue of the Book of Job, the existence of unjustified suffering in the universe of a just God, is neatly vitiated."[13]

The addendum continues by supplying a genealogy for Job that identifies him with Jobab of Genesis 36:33–34 (LXX 42:17b–c).[14] We have seen above that the rabbis debated Job's origins, some arguing that he was a righteous Gentile (though not as righteous as Abraham), others that his very righteousness indicated he must be an Israelite. The LXX translators move beyond this question by linking Job's righteousness, as a Gentile descended from Esau, the eponymous ancestor of the Edomites, to Abraham. With Job's being fifth in descent from Abraham, virtually all arguments negatively comparing Job to Abraham are muted.

The *T. Job* (first century B.C.E.–first century C.E.) clearly draws upon the LXX. Like the LXX the *Testament* identifies Job with Jobab of Genesis 36 (e.g., *T. Job* 2:1; LXX Job 42:17d); it reproduces and embellishes the LXX's version of the speech of Job's wife (*T. Job* 21–25, 39–40; LXX Job 2:9a–e); and it relies on and amplifies numerous concepts and phrases in the LXX's description of Job's wealth, piety, and generosity (*T. Job* 9–15; LXX Job 29–31). For all these and other indications of its reliance on the LXX, the *Testament* is however essentially a fundamentally different account of Job's story.

The *Testament*'s Job knows from the outset that he will suffer for his beliefs but will be rewarded by God in the end if he perseveres; thus unlike the biblical Job, he neither complains about his afflictions nor accuses God of wrongdoing. He learns from an angel that an idolatrous temple belongs to Satan. When Job resolves to destroy the temple, the angel warns him in advance that if he does so, he will have to endure Satan's wrath as the price for his ultimate victory (*T. Job* 4:3–11).[15]

Roughly 40 percent (twenty-one of fifty-three chapters) of the *Testament* is devoted to describing Satan's attacks on Job. The losses of Job's cattle, his children, and his health (*T. Job* 16–25) basically follow but embellish the biblical sequence of events. The description of these losses is, however, prefaced by a lengthy account detailing Job's generosity and charity toward others (*T. Job* 9–15). Numerous examples are cited of Job using his wealth to provide hospitality and care for strangers in need (e.g., 9:2–6, 10:1–4). Job's generosity inspired charitable acts by others; even those who had insufficient resources of their own wished to follow his example (12:1–3). There is also a description of Job as a musician that adds a further dimension to his characterization as a healer of the afflicted (14:1–5). Later representations of Job, as we will see, especially in medieval art and iconography, develop this motif by depicting Job as the patron saint of music.

Job endures his losses without complaint. When Satan strikes him physically with a severe plague from head to toe, Job extends his mercies even to the worms that eat his flesh (20:7–9). The enormity of Job's wealth, exceeded only by his resolve to expend it in service to others, underscores the losses to both Job and his community when Satan takes everything away and leaves him in abject poverty. Ultimately, however, Satan fails to break Job's will, as the angel had promised, and he concedes defeat (27:2–5).

The *Testament*'s description of Job's restoration, followed by an epilogue, also departs from the biblical version. Even before reporting that God rewarded Job by doubling his possessions, the *Testament* says that Job resumed doing good works for the poor (44:3–5). Further, as he prepares to divide his estate among his children, he exhorts them to remember his lifelong concern: "And now, my children. . . . Above all, do not forget the Lord. Do good to the poor. Do not overlook the helpless. Do not take to yourselves wives from strangers" (45:1–3). The biblical version reports that Job gave his daughters "an inheritance along with their brothers" (42:15). The *Testament* expands upon this brief comment by saying that Job gave each of his daughters three multicolored cords (*chordas*) "whose appearance was such that no man could describe, since they were not from earth but from heaven, shimmering with fiery sparks like the rays of the sun" (46:7–8). These cords, Job explains, are the ones he received from God. When God said to him, "Gird up your loins" (Job 38:2, 40:7), Job put on these cords, and immediately the worms and the plagues disappeared from his body. He gives them now to his daughters as "a protective amulet (*phulaktērion*) of the Father" (47:5–11). Place these cords across your breasts, Job instructs them, "so that it may go well with you all the days of your life" (46:7–9). When the daughters put on the cords, their hearts are changed; they lose interest in earthly concerns and begin to speak and sing in the language of the angels (chaps. 48–50). The *Testament*'s epilogue reports that as Job was dying, he gave his daughter Hemera a lyre, his daughter Kasia a censer, and his daughter Amaltheia's Horn a kettle drum. As Job's soul ascended toward the east in a gleaming chariot sent from heaven, his daughters, girded with their cords, "blessed and glorified God each one in her own distinctive dialect" (52:4–7). Nereus, Job's brother, accompanied by "the poor and the orphans and all the helpless," leads in singing a final lament for the one whose name would be "renowned in all generations forever":

> Woe to us today! A double woe!
> Gone today is the strength of the helpless!
> Gone is the light of the blind!
> Gone is the father of orphans!
> Gone is the host of strangers!
> Gone is the clothing of widows!
> Who then will not weep over the man of God? (53:1–8)

The primary virtue that characterizes the *Testament*'s Job as a "man of God" is perseverance, or patience, in the face of innocent suffering. The biblical Job, the LXX Job, and the rabbinic Job, as noted above, are also portrayed, in different ways, as patient, but the *Testament*'s Job surpasses them. By using more than half of its retelling of Job's story (twenty-seven of fifty-three chapters) to accent Job's patience, the Job of the *Testament* emerges as the prototype of faithful endurance. Job begins his farewell address to his children in *T. Job* 1:5 by describing himself as one who has been "fully engaged in endurance." After reviewing his life of suffering and his triumph over Satan, Job exhorts his children to follow his example: "Now then, my children, you also must be patient in everything that happens to you. For patience is better than anything" (27:7). Between chapters 1 and 27, a word for endurance or patience occurs an additional nine times (4:6, 10; 5:1; 11:10; 21:4; 26:4, 5; 27:4, 7). In short Job's patience is a critical aspect of almost everything he wants to tell his children about his life. Cees Haas has shown that a cluster of three different words—*hypomonē, karteria,* and *makrothymia* (and their related verbs)—are used in these passages, often side by side, to convey related but not identical dimensions of Job's perseverance.[16]

Hypomonē occurs in *T. Job* 1:5, 4:6, 5:1, and 26:4. The basic meaning of the verb (*hypomenō*) is "to hold out," "to stand firm," or "to endure." The noun form thus conveys the idea of steadfastness or, as more typically rendered in English translations, "perseverance" or "fortitude." In the *Testament hypomonē* is the general term that covers the specific ideas associated with the two other words, *karteria* and *makrothymia*.[17] In *T. Job* 4:6 and 5:1, the context for "standing firm" is Job's battle with Satan. The backdrop for this battle in chapters 2–4 makes it clear that Job *chooses* to engage Satan; the battle is not imposed on him, nor he is coerced into fighting. Instead Job sees the sacrifices being offered to an idol in a nearby temple and wonders whether the god worshipped there is "the God who made heaven and earth, the sea too, and our very selves" (2:4). When an angel reveals to him that this idol is not the true God but the "devil by whom human nature is deceived," Job "begs" the angel for permission to destroy to destroy the temple (3:3, 6). The angel assures Job that he can successfully destroy the temple, but before Job embarks on his mission, the angel conveys to him "all the things which the Lord has charged me to tell you" (4:1). God's message to Job, in advance of the action Job has already decided to take, is that Satan will rise up against him by inflicting him with plagues, destroying his possessions, and carrying off his children, but if Job remains patient (*ean hypomeinēs* [4:6]), if he "stands firm," then he will survive the battle and God will reward him with a name "renowned in all generations of the earth" and will repay him for his losses by doubling his estate (4:7; cf. 44:5). In *T. Job* 5:1 Job says to his children, who have been listening to his account of these events, that he responded to the angel's warning by saying, "Till

death, I will endure (*hypomeinō*): I will not step back at all." Having made his decision with full knowledge of the consequences, Job takes fifty youths and destroys the temple, then returns to his house, secures the door, and waits for
Satan's counterattack (5:2–3).

The *Testament*'s description of Satan's attack (chaps. 6–8, 16–20) essentially
follows the biblical version of the story, but it accents Job's perseverance by reporting that after Satan destroys his possessions, Job stands firm by glorifying God
(16:7). After Satan kills his children, Job is initially confused and speechless, but
once he remembers the angel's promise of his ultimate victory (18:5), he takes
courage. He likens his journey to that of a sailor who sets off to a distant city
(likely the heavenly Jerusalem) to gain a portion of its wealth and splendor. In
mid-ocean winds and waves threaten to sink his ship. He immediately throws his
cargo overboard, saying, "'I am willing to lose everything in order to enter the city
so that I might gain . . . things better than the payload.' Thus, I also considered my
goods as nothing compared to the city about which the angel spoke to me" (18:8).

In the context of the battle against Satan, and the sea waves that symbolize
Satan's attacks, the *Testament* uses *hypomonē* to describe Job's determination to
stand firm against powerful, life-threatening enemies. Satan is stronger than any
human enemy Job might confront (cf. 27:2); if Job does not hold his ground, if he
retreats one step, Satan will surely overcome him. Such steadfastness is not a passive response to adversity, as the word *patience* usually connotes. It is an active
refusal to back down in the face of danger, a resolve that requires Job to summon
all his strength to stay the course. Job's resolve is not based on his own capacity
to withstand the forces arrayed against him; it is not based on any self-generated
confidence that he can escape the suffering Satan will inevitably cause him. It is
instead driven by his decision to believe in and commit himself to the angel's
promise. If he holds his ground when Satan rises up against him, then he will
suffer grievous losses, but he will not die (4:4–5). As Job himself seems to realize
in *T. Job* 18:8, he must be willing to lose everything, even his life, to actualize the
angel's assurance.

The *Testament*'s use of *hypomonē* to describe standing firm in the battle is consistent with the use of this word in the Hellenistic Jewish literature of the period.
A particularly good example is 4 Maccabees (second century B.C.E.–second century
C.E.), which retells the story from 2 Maccabees of the martyrdom of Eleazar and
seven Jewish brothers, along with their mother, during the reign of Antiochus Epi-
phanes.[18] In describing the martyrs' resolve to stand fast in their dedication to the
Law, even when faced with extreme torture, the author uses the word *hypomonē*
twenty-three times. Eleazar is described as the "best" of those who, by "courage
and endurance" (*hypomonē*), resisted the tyrant's decrees (4 Macc 1:7, 11). When
Antiochus threatened him with torture if he did not eat the food forbidden by

Jewish law, Eleazar responded that the Law "trains us in courage, so that we endure (*hypomenein*) any suffering willingly" (5:23). Having paid for his convictions with his life, Eleazar, like the *Testament*'s Job, is praised by comparing him to a "skillful pilot" who "steered the ship of religion . . . and though buffeted by the stormings of the tyrant and overwhelmed by the mighty waves of torture, in no way did he turn the rudder of religion until he sailed into the haven of immortal victory" (7:1–2; cf. *T. Job* 18:6–8). By these acts his ancestors declared, Eleazar "strengthened our loyalty to the law through your glorious endurance (*hypomonōn*)" (7:9). The determination to stand fast against the torture Antiochus inflicted is described with graphic detail in the accounts of the martyrdom of the seven brothers, who followed Eleazar's example by declaring that "if the aged men of the Hebrews . . . lived piously while enduring (*hypomeinantes*) torture, it would be even more fitting that we young men should die despising your coercive tortures" (9:6).[19]

Hellenistic Jewish literature clearly exerted influence on the New Testament and other early Christian literature that praised similar notions of the believer's perseverance in the face of suffering. Although the Epistle of James is the only New Testament book that cites Job as an exemplar, the general commendation of perseverance of faith in God in times of extreme duress is a staple of New Testament texts (e.g., Matt 10:22, 24:13; Mark 13:13; Rom 5:3–4; 2 Tim 2:12; Jas 1:2–4, 5:7–11). Clearly for New Testament writers Jesus is the most important example of the one who is steadfast in times of trial: "Let us run with perseverance (*hypomonēs*) the race that is set before us, looking to Jesus the pioneer and perfecter of our faith, who for the sake of the joy that was set before him endured (*hypemeinen*) the cross, disregarding its shame, and has taken his seat at the right hand of the throne of God. Consider him who endured (*hypomemenēkota*) such hostility against himself from sinners" (Heb 12:1–3).[20]

In addition to this generalized New Testament summons to perseverance, the notion of standing firm in the battle against Satan, so prominent in the *Testament,* is also widely attested in early Judaism and Christianity. In the "Apocalypse of Sedrach" (second to fifth century C.E.), Sedrach wonders why God created the world, since life is filled with so much undeserved suffering. If Satan is the cause of the suffering bequeathed from Adam to every mortal, then why did God himself not vanquish Satan, rather than leave the fight to those who seemed destined to lose it ("Apocalypse of Sedrach" 5:3–6)?[21] In *Joseph and Aseneth,* the devil pursues Aseneth because she, like the *Testament*'s Job, has broken her Egyptian idols into pieces and stopped offering sacrifices and libations to "deaf and dumb gods." She prays to God to deliver her from the "primaeval Lion" (cf. *T. Job* 27:1) who seeks to devour her (*Joseph and Aseneth* 12:7–10).[22]

The battle Satan wages against believers, and the exhortation to stand their ground against his assaults, is adopted by New Testament writers. For example in

Ephesians 6:10–20, believers are summoned to "put on the whole armor of God" (cf. 4 Macc 13:16: "Let us put on the full armor of self-control") in order to be able to "stand against" (*stēnai pros*) the devil and "withstand" (*antistēnai*) his assaults on that evil day. The Revelation of John is in many ways preoccupied with the believers' battle against Satan, who uses superhuman powers to wage war against the church. Revelation 13:5–10 (cf.14:12), for example, exhorts believers to have the "endurance (*hypomonē*) and faith (*pistis*) of the saints."

Karteria occurs in *T. Job* 4:10 and 27:4. Like *hypomonē, karteria* is also used in the context of Job's battle against Satan, but it conveys a different image. Whereas *hypomonē* describes standing firm against an opponent, *karteria* signifies the physical toughness that enables one not only to withstand but also to defeat an opponent. More specifically both *T. Job* 4:10 and 27:4 describe the contest between Job and Satan as a wrestling match, a man-to-man, no-holds-barred fight in the arena in which one of the combatants is eventually forced to surrender. The *Testament* uses the imagery of an "athlete" (*athlētēs* [4:10, 27:3]) to describe Job and Satan exchanging blows in a contest that will decide who has the *karteria,* the stamina, to hold out the longest. In *T. Job* 4:10 the angel describes Job as a "sparring athlete" who will endure Satan's assault and win "the crown." Job's "crown," as the angel announces in advance, will be not only the earthly prize for having bested Satan but also the heavenly reward of "being raised up in the resurrection" (4:9; cf. 40:3). In *T. Job* 27:3–4 Satan describes himself as a wrestler whose stamina fails; as his war with Job goes on, he grows weary (*diaphōnēsantos*) and loses strength. In the end Satan "cries out in defeat" and concedes that his supposedly weaker opponent has overthrown him and pinned him. As a result the vanquished Satan limps away in shame and disgrace (27:2–6).

Hellenistic Jewish literature also uses *karteria* to describe the stubbornness or toughness that enables a person to outlast a stronger opponent. In *Quod omnis probus liber sit*, Philo describes a wise man who "willingly and patiently endures (*egkapterōn*) the blows of fortune" (v. 24) and "will not obey just anyone who gives him orders, even though he menaces him with outrage and tortures and threats however dreadful" (v. 25). Philo compares such "stubborn endurance" to that which a combatant ("pancratiast") must display if he is to wear down his adversary and claim the victory (v. 26).[23]

Fourth Maccabees uses *karteria* in a similar way, often alongside *hypomonē*, as in the passage just cited from Philo. The mother who remained unwavering (*karteria*) in her piety as she watched her seven sons tortured and burned by Antiochus is a prime example (4 Macc 15:14; cf. 9:28, 11:12, 13:11, 14:9). Even more than the noble Eleazar and the seven Jewish brothers, she models the toughness in the face of adversity that characterizes an entire nation committed to observance of God's law (4 Macc 15:29–32). As in the *Testament,* 4 Maccabees describes

the crown of victory these noble "athletes" (*athlētēs* [6:10, 17:15]) win for their perseverance in heavenly, not earthly, terms. The ultimate reward is life everlasting
(4 Macc 17:11–16; cf. 7:3; 9:8, 22; 14:5–6; 16:13; 18:23).[24]

The New Testament also speaks of receiving the "crown of God's glory" (1 Pt
5:4) or the "crown of righteousness" for having "fought the good fight . . . finished
the race . . . and kept the faith" (2 Tm 4:7–8). Similarly Paul encourages believers
who are vulnerable to despair not to "lose heart," for present afflictions will not
prevail against "an eternal weight of glory beyond all measure" (2 Cor 4:16–17).
For Paul, as for other New Testament writers, the model for stubborn faith—or to
use the New Testament's preferred term, "obedience" (*hypakoē*)—is Jesus, who
"humbled himself and became obedient to death, even death on the cross" (Phil
2:8). In his obedience Jesus likens himself "to those who share the faith of Abraham" (Rom 4:16, 19–20).

From Abraham to the *Testament*'s Job to the Hellenistic Jewish literature that
provides the template for the New Testament, we can plot the trajectory of a generally consistent exhortation to believers to exhibit the stubbornness of faith that
merits God's reward of the "crown of life" (*stephanon tēs zōēs)*, which, according
to the author of the Epistle of James, awaits those who "endure" (*hypomenei*) and
overcome the temptation to give up (Jas 1:12; cf. Rv 2:10; 3:11; 4:4, 10).

The third word the *Testament* uses to describe Job's perseverance is *makrothymia* (21:4, 26:5, 27:7, 28:5, 35:4). It is a near synonym for *hypomonē* and *karteria*,
but unlike these two *makrothymia* does not occur in the context of a battle
against Satan. Instead it conveys the idea of being long-suffering, waiting patiently, or persevering over an extended period of time of temptation and trial.
The *Testament*'s Job suffers on the dung heap outside the city for forty-eight years
(21:1). During this time he not only experiences his own losses and afflictions, but
also sees with his own eyes the suffering inflicted upon his wife. Job initially
expresses contempt for those who abuse his wife—"The gall (*alazoneias;* "arrogance") of these city fathers! How can they treat my wife like a female slave?"—
but then he says that he regained his "patient capacity to reason" (*anelambanon
logismon makrothymon*) (21:3–4). Implicit in this use of *makrothymia* is the idea
that perseverance as patience requires one to restrain feelings of anger and wrath;
instead of yielding to such passions by expressing them, one waits patiently and
expectantly for God's saving intervention. Job has modeled such patience by refusing to speak a word against God throughout his ordeal. When he lost his
possessions, he glorified God and "did not blaspheme" (T. *Job* 16:7). When he
learns that his children have been killed, he blesses the God who gives life and
takes it away (19:4). Once Satan concludes that he cannot provoke Job to speak
contemptuously (*oligōrian* [20:1; cf. 13:4–5, 14:4–5]) against God, he resorts to
using Job's wife against him. Tricked by Satan's ruse, Job's wife loses patience

and becomes despondent (24:10). In her weakness (25:10a) she urges Job "to speak some word against God" (25:10b). Here again Job insists on waiting patiently for God's intervention, and he urges his wife to join him in "enduring (*hypomeno-men*) all things" (26:4): "Rather, let us be patient (*makrothymēsōmen*) till the Lord, in pity, shows us mercy" (26:5; cf. 24:1).

The *Testament*'s account of Job's sufferings in chapters 19–27 is in general agreement with LXX Job 1–2. Job's response in *T. Job* 26:4, for example, is almost a verbatim quotation of LXX Job 2:10 (cf. *T. Job* 19:4 and LXX Job 1:21). But the *Testament*'s description of Job's perseverance is very different than the LXX.[25] The LXX's Job uses *makrothymēsō* in 7:16 to declare that he does *not* have the patience to endure his suffering and wishes to die: "For I will not live forever, or I would be patient. Let me alone, for my life is empty" (cf. LXX Job 6:11: "For what is my strength, that I endure [*hypomenō*]"). In general the Job portrayed in LXX Job 1–2 can be described as patient (though only LXX Job 2:10 uses a word [*hypoisomen*] for patience), and the Job of the dialogues is less rebellious in the LXX than in the biblical version, but the patience of the *Testament*'s Job exceeds anything found in its source documents. Indeed in the *Testament* even Job's friends demonstrate "patience" (*makrothymēsōmen*; 28:4; 35:4) in the ways they try to comfort him in his suffering.[26]

The *Testament*'s account of Job's successful perseverance in the face of Satan's attack ends with chapter 27. The latter half of the *Testament* shifts the attention to Job and his three friends (28–45), the inheritance Job bequeaths to his three daughters (46–50), and a concluding epilogue (51–53). In important ways chapter 27 provides an apt segue to the rest of the book, for here, as Haas has noted, the three major aspects of Job's perseverance—"standing firm" in battle (*hypomonē*), "stamina" or "toughness" in winning the contest (*karteria*), and "patience" in the face of trial and temptation (*makrothymia*)—come together. Because Job has stood firm (4:6, 5:1), Satan withdraws from the battle, conceding that he no longer has the strength to fight on (27:1–2). Satan then acknowledges that Job has won the wrestling match, because he has proven himself to be the tougher, more determined combatant (27:3–5 [esp. verse 4]; cf. 4:10). Finally, having failed to get Job to speak out against God, Satan leaves in disgrace, because, as *T. Job* 27:7 makes clear, Job has demonstrated patience in the face of suffering: "Now then, my children, you also must be patient (*makrothymēsate*) in everything that happens to you. For patience (*makrothymia*) is better than anything." From the first words of Job's address to his children (1:5) to this, his summation of all that he has endured at the hands of Satan, the *Testament*'s Job demonstrates that by every meaning of the word, he can justly claim to be a model of perseverance.[27]

The use and context of *makrothymia* in the *Testament* corresponds closely with other Greek and Hellenistic texts. In Sir 2:1–18 a teacher reminds his students that those who "fear God" must prepare themselves to be tested, but if they persevere, then their "reward will not be lost" (v. 8; cf. vv. 9–10). To convey the idea of perseverance, the teacher uses all three words found in the *Testament:* "Set your heart right and be steadfast" (*karterēson* [v. 2]); "in times of humiliation be patient" (*makrothymēson* [v. 4]; cf. Prv 25:15 with reference to mastering one's tongue in the face of adversity); "Woe to you who have lost your nerve" (*hypomonēn* [v.14]). In Bar 4:25 Mother Zion assumes the teacher's role, reminding her exiles that they, like she, have suffered great sorrows (cf. Bar 4:9–16), but if they "endure with patience (*makrothymēsate*) the wrath that has come upon [them] from God," then God will deliver them from the hand of the enemy (cf. *Pss. Sol.* 16:15, with *hypomeinai*). Similarly in the *Testament of Joseph,* Joseph describes for his children his perseverance in the face of the temptation by the shameless Egyptian woman who tried to seduce him away from his commitments to God (*T. Jos.* 2:7).

The New Testament uses *makrothymia* primarily to describe God's "patience" in delaying deserved judgment in order to give time for believers to realize their sins and repent (e.g., Rom 2:4, 9:22; 1 Tm 1:16). When it uses the same word with reference to human beings, the New Testament typically describes the patience required to wait for the fulfillment of God's promises (e.g., Heb 6:12, 15). In this context the Epistle of James equates the "endurance (*hypomonēn*) of Job" (Jas 5:11) with the patience (*makrothymōn*) of the farmer who plants his crop and waits for the rain to bring it to fruition (Jas 5:7); with the patience (*makrothymias*) of prophets "who spoke in the name of the Lord" and had to wait for the word to be fulfilled (Jas 5:10); and by extension with believers, who must be patient (*makrothymēsate*) in suffering, "strengthen (their) hearts" (Jas 5:8), and not "grumble" against one another (Jas 5:9; cf. vv.12–18).

The testamentary genre that provides the template for the *Testament of Job* typically contains moral exhortations (e.g., *T. Isaac* 4:11–54). The *T. Job* is considerably less hortatory than other Jewish testaments, but it does offer two examples that are particularly instructive, because both provide an important context for assessing the legacy of Job's perseverance, in all of the aspects we have identified above. In *T. Job* 27:7 Job concludes his account of the patience he has exemplified in defeating Satan by exhorting his children to be patient in everything that happens to them, "for patience is better than anything." In *T. Job* 45:1–3, as Job lies on his deathbed, just before he divides his inheritance, he gives his children his final instructions: "Do not forget the Lord. Do good to the poor. Do not overlook the helpless. Do not take to yourselves wives from strangers." These two exhortations indicate that from Job's perspective there is an ethical component to the virtue of patience. Patience is not solely or even primarily about Job's securing a personal victory by standing firm, being tough, and persevering against suffering; it is rather a virtue he exercises in the service of others, particularly those whose resources do not afford them the luxury of deciding how they will live.

An important aspect of Satan's attack on Job is the loss of his great wealth. Job suffers these losses willingly, with the full knowledge that if he perseveres, then he will be rewarded not only in this world, with a double repayment of his goods, but also in the heavenly world, when he is raised up in the resurrection (4:7–8). The *Testament* underscores Job's eschatological focus repeatedly (e.g., 18:6–8, 36:3, 38:1–5, 39:11–12, 41:5, 46:7–8) and gives it sustained attention in chapters 32–33.[28] In response to Eliphas's lament about the loss of Job's wealth, especially his repeating question, "Now where is the splendor of your throne?" (32:2, 3, 4, 5, 6, 7, 9, 10, 11, 12), Job explains that his "throne is in the upper world, and its splendor and majesty come from the right hand of the Father" (33:3). Eliphas assumes that because Job has lost his wealth, he has also lost the honor and status that comes with riches. Job counters that his real throne awaits him in the "holy land," where splendor and majesty derive from "the changeless one," where true fortunes do not "disappear" but instead exist in a kingdom that lasts "forever and ever" (33:5, 7, 9). Job's focus on heavenly rewards, however, does not compromise his clear conviction that in this life he must use his wealth for persistent care of the poor and needy. Toward this end, after Job has successfully persevered against Satan but before his possessions are restored, he resumes his commitment to doing "good works for the poor" (44:3–5).

In sum the *Testament* connects Job's personal perseverance with his persistent ethical obligation to care for the poor. The promise of a heavenly reward for such perseverance is clearly a sustaining motivation for the way Job chooses to live and die. But if the legacy he leaves to his children is a life "fully engaged in endurance" (1:5), and if it is true that "patience is better than anything" (27:7), then his children, and we his readers, must be able to discern the ethical imperative that connects his two exhortations: "You . . . must be patient in everything that happens to you. . . . Do good to the poor. Do not overlook the hapless" (27:7, 45:2–3). For his perseverance, with all its this-worldly imperatives and its otherworldly rewards, the angel promises Job that his name will be "renowned in all generations of the earth" (4:6). As Patrick Gray has noted, "The Letter of James appears to be the first place where the angel's promise is kept."[29]

The Letter of James is roughly contemporaneous with the *Testament of Job*. Although this does not necessarily indicate literary dependence, it does provide a relative chronology that suggests the author of James, and his audience, was familiar with the *Testament*'s portrait of the patience of Job.[30] Gray has demonstrated, however, that a narrow focus on James's singular reference to Job's "endurance" (*hypomonēn* [Jas 5:11]) overlooks the way he uses and adapts the *Testament*'s broader moral-theological framework for understanding Job as an exemplar of patience. Gray identifies three congruent concerns in the *Testament* and James.[31]

James commends the virtue of Joblike patience (*hypomonē*) not only in James 5:11 but also in his opening exhortation to be joyful when faith is tested, because this produces "endurance," which in turn leads to "mature and complete" believers (Jas 1:2–4). Anyone who "endures" (*hypomenei*) temptation "will receive the crown of life that the Lord has promised to those who love him" (Jas 1:12; cf. *T. Job* 4:10). Further James connects endurance *(hypomonē)* with the imperative to be patient during extended times of waiting for God's intervention. As the *Testament*'s Job urges his wife to be "patient" (*makrothymia*) in suffering and to resist the temptation to speak negatively about God (26:5–6), so James urges his readers to have the "patience" (*makrothymia*) of farmers and prophets (5:7–8, 10), who know they must wait expectantly for God to bring their work to fruition; in the meantime they should not "grumble against one another" (5:9; cf. 3:13–18, 4:11–12, 5:12–16).

A major aspect of Job's piety in the *Testament* is the use of his wealth to care for the poor. This *ethical* component is also a primary feature of the "endurance" James commends to his readers. Believers must be "doers of the word and not merely hearers," which James insists will be evident in their "care for the orphans and widows" (1:22, 27). Because God has "chosen the poor in the world to be rich in faith and to be heirs of the kingdom," those who profess faith in God are morally obligated to use their resources to care for the needy. James condemns those who lack the compassion and generosity Job exemplified. If those with "gold rings" and "fine clothes" discriminate against "the poor in dirty clothes," then they become "judges with evil thoughts" (2:1–4). If they see a brother or sister who is naked and hungry and do not give them clothing and food, then their faith is dead (2:14–17). If those blessed with great wealth "weep" and "wail" over their own miseries but do not hear and respond to the cries of the oppressed, then they will experience God's judgment. Moths will eat their clothes; rust will destroy their silver and gold; and fire will consume their flesh (5:1–6). At his death Job was mourned by the poor, the orphans, and the helpless, who had been sustained by his hospitality and charity (*T. Job* 53:1–8). James warns those who "know the right thing to do and fail to do it" (4:17) that their ending will be very different: "judgment will be without mercy to anyone who has shown no mercy" (2:13).

Both the *Testament* and James place the imperative to faithful endurance within an *eschatological context.* Job understands the difference between the wealth he accumulates and distributes in this world and the true reward that awaits him in heaven. Similarly James contrasts the "wisdom from below," which tempts believers toward earthly interests that are destructive (3:14–16, 4:1–33, esp. verse 3), with the "wisdom from above" that God gives, which is "peaceable, gentle, willing to yield, full of mercy and good fruits, without a trace of partiality or hypocrisy" (3:17; cf. 1:5, 17; 3:15). "Friendship with the world," James warns, is "enmity with God" (4:4). In other words if believers choose to see reality the way the world defines it, if they choose to be friends with the world by sharing its perspective, then they will live by the logic of selfishness, greed, violence, and murder.[32] On the other hand, when believers choose to be friends with the God who "gives to all generously and ungrudgingly" (1:5), they remain "unstained by the world." The way they demonstrate that their friendship with God is pure and undefiled is to care for the poor in the same way God cares for them (1:27, 2:5).

The way James weaves together these three aspects—endurance, care for the poor, and the promise of eschatological reward—indicates his familiarity with, if not his dependence upon, the *Testament*'s description of the patience of Job. Moreover James uses these motifs to construct a moral discourse directed to first-century Christians that functions in a manner very similar to Job's testamentary instructions to his children. When James urges his readers not to grumble but instead to pray and sing when facing trials (1:3; 5:9, 13), we can hear the echo of Job's exhortation to his maidservants and his wife (*T. Job* 14:4–5; cf. 26:1–6). When James says that if believers resist the devil then he will flee (Jas 4:7), we know that this is consonant with the angel's advice to Job and with Job's own experience (*T. Job* 4:4, 27:2–6). When James tells his readers that before they act they should say, "If the Lord wishes, we will live and do this or that" (4:15), they remember that the *Testament*'s Job received, and then lived in conformity with, a similar instruction (4:2, 19:4).[33] These and other thematic parallels between the *Testament* and James are a strong indicator that these two texts, one Jewish, the other Christian, are the major sources for the tradition about the patience of Job.

As this tradition begins to take shape, however, it is instructive to note how James adapts it for his own world. Although he seems to be familiar with the testamentary genre, he utilizes it not to offer instructions from parents to children but to address a community, an *ekklēsia,* that is defined not by genealogy but by a shared faith in Jesus Christ (2:1). This community is not facing the death of its patriarch but the death of the world as they know it. There is little information in the letter about the specific circumstances of the composition, but it seems likely that James is addressing readers who understand themselves to be among "the poor" who are called into God's kingdom and are subject to the legal and economic pressures imposed on them by the rich (cf. 2:1–6, 5:1–6). These pressures threaten the solidarity of the community with eruptions of anger (1:19–20), jealousy (4:1–2), arrogance (4:6, 10, 16; cf. 3:14–15), and slander (4:11–12). To a community who knows the right way to live but needs to be aroused from inactivity to do it (4:17), James says that the judgment of the "last days" is imminent. In 5:7–11 he uses judicial language to remind them that "the coming of the Lord" (*parousia*) is near (vv. 7, 8). His words convey urgency, because the "Judge" who comes to vindicate the righteous and punish the wicked is "standing at the doors" (v. 9). In the interim between the present and the almost-but-not-yet-future, James exhorts his readers to live with patience (*makrothymia:* vv. 7–8). The eschatological context for this exhortation is quite different from that which frames the *Testament*'s profile of Job's endurance, even though James uses Job as an example for this community. As Gray notes, "James thus employs the example of Job in the maintenance of an emergent Christian identity and accompanying social ethic foreign in many ways to its original setting."[34]

The analogues for the patience James commends are laborers who cry out to God for a just dispensation of their wages (5:4), farmers who have planted their crops but must wait for the rain (5:7), and the prophets, exemplified by Jeremiah and Habakkuk, who have suffered in delivering their words from God and must wait for God to validate their messages. To persevere in such fraught interim times, believers must "strengthen their hearts" (5:8) and stay focused on what God has promised, despite present realities that tempt them to yield to despair. Until stingy employers pay workers what they are owed, until the weather changes from death-dealing dryness to life-giving rain, until prophetic words become present reality, believers must have the "endurance of Job" (*hypomonēn:* v. 11).

As they have *heard* (ēkousate) of Job's endurance, so believers have "*seen* (*eidete*) the purpose of the Lord (*to telos kuriou*), how the Lord is compassionate and merciful." James is likely referring to the end of the Joban story, probably to the *Testament*'s version of this story, and not to the *parousia* of the Lord.[35] Nevertheless by connecting what readers have "heard" about Job with what they have "seen," James effectively blurs the distinction between God's past blessings of Job and God's abiding compassion and mercy for those James addresses (cf. 1:5, 17; 2:13; 4:6). With the words "we call blessed those who showed endurance (*hypomeinantas*)" (5:11), James returns his readers to the opening exhortation that guides the entire epistle. The summons is for believers to consider it a joy when they face trials and temptations (1:2). The promise is that those who persevere because of their love for God are "blessed" and will receive the crown of life (1:12).

Saintly Patience: The Construction of the Heroic Job

The *Testament of Job* and the Letter of James accent Job's exemplary patience as his primary virtue. Although James is the only New Testament writer to cite Job, subsequent Christian interpreters appropriate his commendation of Job as a model for Christian behavior and extend it by identifying patience as both heroic and saintly. In his second-century treatise *Of Patience,* Tertullian describes Job's patience as a heroic "example and testimony to us" of the faithfulness God expects and requires.[36] In the late fourth century, the apocryphal *Apocalypse of Paul* extends this heroic imagery by identifying Job as one of the saints Paul meets in heaven.[37]

An important aspect of Job's characterization as a saintly hero is his depiction as an "athlete" who wages a courageous battle *for* God *against* Satan. The image of Job as a noble warrior is nascent in both the *T. Job* (e.g., 4:10, 27:3–4) and other Hellenistic Jewish texts (cf. Wis 5:17; 4 Macc 6:10, 13:16, 17:15), as noted above. The Greek fathers often invoke the imagery of Job as a wrestler in an athletic contest. In the third century, Origen describes him as a "most strong athlete" and paraphrases Job's complaint, "I call aloud but there is no justice" (Job 19:7), as the words of a wrestler: "As an athlete in the stadium I cried, yet judgment by no means came; still I keep wrestling."[38] In the fourth century, Chrysostom uses the same imagery to describe the conversation between Satan and God in the heavenly assembly that led to Job's testing (cf. Job 1:6–12).[39] Early Christian writers extend this imagery by identifying Job as the archetypical soldier of Christ (1 Cor 9:25; 2 Cor 10:3–6; 2 Tm 2:3–4; Eph 6:11–17; 1 Thes 5:8) who prefigures both the strife and the victory of all the Lord's warriors.[40] Jerome, for example, gives a classic Christian interpretation of the very difficult passage in Job 19:25, "I know that my Redeemer lives, and that at the last he will stand upon the earth,"[41] in which he exalts Job as "the athlete of the Church." "No one since the days of Christ speaks so openly concerning the resurrection as [Job] did before Christ. . . . He hopes for a resurrection; nay, rather he knew and saw that Christ his redeemer, was alive, and at that last day would rise again from the earth. The Lord had not yet died, and the athlete of the Church saw his redeemer rising from the grave."[42]

The earliest, most extensive use of martial imagery to depict Job's primary virtue is Prudentius's fifth-century poem *Psychomachia,* which allegorizes the battle between virtues and vices (e.g., chastity vs. lust, humility vs. pride, good works vs. avarice). Each virtue and vice is personified differently; various biblical figures who exemplify the virtues are used to illustrate their defeat of the opponent. In the battle between patience and anger, patience, feminized as long-suffering Patientia, is assaulted by her rival, Ira (wrath, anger), who is unable to defeat her tactical strategy of remaining bravely undisturbed (lines 128–31).[43] Patientia wins the battle with the help of Job, the battle-scarred escort who has stood by her side throughout the fight. As Patientia and Job march off to lend their support to other virtues, Job, "panting from the slaughter of many a foe," smiles as he remembers "his thousands of hard-won fights, his own glory and his foes' dishonour." From the spoils of victory, he gains restitution for all his losses and "carries home things that shall no more be lost" (lines 163–71).[44] Two ninth-century manuscript illuminations reinforce the imagery. In one Job takes Patientia by the hand and leads her through the battle lines. She is depicted as an elderly, slump-shouldered woman; she wears an ankle-length robe and carries a cane in her right hand, hardly the attire of one engaged in battle. Job, on the other hand, is depicted as a young soldier in full battle gear (helmet, armor, shield, and sword).[45] The second illumination, located on the following page of the same manuscript, depicts Patientia and Job much the same way, although now they are seated outside a fortified castle, overseeing the soldiers fighting in the foreground.[46]

The development and survival throughout the Middle Ages of Job's characterization as a saintly, heroic warrior rests heavily on Gregory the Great's influential *Moralia in Job* (sixth century). As Ann W. Astell has noted, Gregory "extends the image of the mighty wrestler and gladiator and uses it repeatedly both to unify his encyclopedic exposition of the text and to qualify the Book of Job as a heroic biblical poem."[47] At the outset Gregory compares his exposition of Job's virtues to storytellers who narrate a wrestling match by first describing the physical characteristics of the contestants.

> But it is the custom of narrators, when a wrestling match is woven into the story, first to describe the limbs of the combatants, how broad and strong the chest, how sound, how full their muscles swelled, how the belly below neither clogged by its weight, nor weakened by its shrunken size, that when they have first shewn the limbs to be fit for the combat, they may then at length describe their bold and mighty strokes. Thus because our athlete was about to combat the devil, the writer of the sacred story, recounting as it were before the exhibition in the arena the spiritual merits in this athlete, describes the members of the soul, saying, *And that man was perfect and upright, and one that feared God, and eschewed evil;* that when the powerful setting of the limbs is known, from this very strength we may already prognosticate also the victory to follow. (1.3.4)[48]

As he describes how Job was attacked by Satan, by his wife, who acted on Satan's behalf, and by his friends, especially Elihu, who served Satan's purposes, Gregory explains that Job fought back like a true soldier of God.

> It is the aim of enemies, when they come up face to face, to send off some in secret, who may be so much the more free to strike a blow in the flank of the hostile force, in proportion as he that is fighting is more eagerly intent upon the enemy advancing in front. Job, therefore, being caught in the warfare of this conflict, received the losses which befel him like foes in his front; he took the words of his comforters like enemies on his flank, and in all turning round the shield of his stedfastness, he stood defended at all points, and ever on the watch, parried on all sides the swords directed against him. By his silence he marks his unconcern for the loss of his substance; the flesh, dead in his children, he bewails with composure; the flesh in his own person stricken, he endures with fortitude; the flesh in his wife suggesting mischievous persuasions, he instructeth with wisdom. (1.5.11)

Such heroic fortitude, Gregory says, exemplifies what it means to be a champion who uses the "shield of patience" to stand "strong and erect" against the enemy (3.10.17).

Gregory builds this portrait of Job as a heroic warrior by explaining Job's outbursts in the middle of the biblical story (Job 3–31) not as rash and rebellious but instead as the true measure of passion in the face of suffering. As Gregory argues, "The weightiness of true virtue consists not in dulness of heart" (2.16.28). Humble obedience to trial and suffering, the willingness to say yes to what God wills, requires passion, not apathy. Indeed, according to Gregory, Job's passionate response to felt sorrow prefigures Christ's own passion; it is the embodiment of the true wisdom Christ lived and died to impart (1.6.13–14; cf. 1.24.33). Gregory's characterization of Job as a soldier of Christ, a *miles Christi,* results in a double-sided portrait of Job. "On the historical and moral levels it is the portrait of a patient Christian saint, and on the allegorical level, the portrait of a type or pre-figuration of Christ."[49]

Gregory's Christological approach to Job's suffering provides the basis for a redefinition of heroic virtues in the Middle Ages. Homeric heroes publicly displayed their courage on the battlefield; in a contest of physical strength, they excelled in the kind of power that "changes men into gods" (*Iliad* 24.258). Gregory retains the use of martial imagery to describe Job's behavior, but by allegorizing his battle as a lifelong contest between the church and Satan, Gregory effectively shifts the definition of a hero to accent spiritual, rather than physical, virtues. As a spiritual warrior, Job's fortitude exceeds that of his Homeric counterparts, because it is equated with humble obedience to God's will, not with his fighting skills. In this way Job becomes the archetype for Christ and hence "for all the saints, male and female, whose steadfast virtue, subjected to satanic testing through serial misfortunes, merits the reward of restored happiness."[50] As Astell has demonstrated, the archeology of heroism in the Middle Ages can be traced from its foundation in Gregory's exegesis of Job as a soldier of Christ to its subsequent development as the template for medieval knighthood.

Astell identifies four periods in the development of medieval knighthood, each connected with a different representation of Job.[51] It is instructive to follow her discussion of these four faces of the knightly Job and adapt them for our objectives: heroic self-divestment; spiritual discipline and physical combat; saintly crusader; and penitent knight.

In the early Christian period, Job's willingness to sacrifice everything in order to serve God more fully becomes a model for heroic self-divestment.[52] As Christ stripped himself of heavenly glory (Phil 2:6–11), so Gregory's Job, when confronted with the loss of his goods and the death of his children, boasts that it is better to be "humbly denuded of virtues" and lie prostrate dressed in humility than to stand in strength and claim "no need of divine aid" (*Moralia,* 2.53.85). Astell cites Saint Martin of Tours (fourth century) as an early exemplar of one who modeled Job's sacrifice of wealth and honor in order to clothe the poor by becoming himself poor and naked. Stripping himself of glory, Martin offered to march at the head of the emperor's troops, armed only with the sign of the cross.[53]

Still more instructive as an example of Job's naked vulnerability to suffering is Saint Sebastian (third century). A successful commander of the Praetorian Guard in Rome, according to the legend, Sebastian used his position to help Christians through the time of persecution orchestrated by emperors Maximilian and Diocletian.[54] When Diocletian discovered Sebastian's subversive acts, he ordered him to be stripped of his rank, tied to the stake, shot with arrows, and left for dead. Miraculously Sebastian did not die, and a few days later he appeared on the steps of the palace and publicly rebuked the emperors for their cruelty to Christians. At this point the emperors ordered the soldiers to beat Sebastian to death with clubs and, as a final indignity, to throw his body in the sewer. Again their plans were thwarted, this time by a woman who came to be known as Saint Irene, who recovered his body and had it buried, we are told, at the feet of the apostles in a crypt in Sebastiano alla Polveriera, one of the seven churches of Rome on the Via Appia.

At least by the ninth century, artists began associating Sebastian's martyrdom with Job's suffering and heavenly reward.[55] Although the legends of Saint Sebastian make no mention of Job, artists discerned a connection between Job's assault by "archers" and their "arrows" (Job 6:4, 16:13) and Sebastian's nude body, filled with the arrows of the Roman soldiers. In medieval altarpieces Sebastian is often positioned opposite Job, with both saints facing either the Madonna or a depiction of Christ's resurrection.[56] At the center of Giovanni Bellini's fifteenth-century *San Giobbe Altar,* for example, the Madonna, holding the infant Jesus in her lap, sits on a throne, flanked by saints Job and Francis on the left and saints Sebastian and Dominic on the right.[57] By placing Job and Sebastian in the foreground, Bellini draws the viewer's attention to their similar features. Both are naked, except for the loincloth that covers their midsection. Job's hands are raised in prayer; Sebastian's are tied behind his back, a gesture that depicts his surrender to the soldiers' arrows, two of which, as Bellini shows, have hit their mark. Both have been "denuded" by their suffering; both are calm and serene as they gaze upon the promised blessing of the Madonna and child.[58]

Following the eleventh-century Investiture Controversy, the Crusades introduced a new era in which Job became the model for the soldier of Christ who combines both spiritual discipline and physical combat to confront the enemies of the church. With the founding of the Knights Templar (1119) and the religious order of knighthood, both Templar and crusader "[were] placed under the explicit patronage of Job."⁵⁹ Writing to Hugh of Payns, the founder of the Knights Templar, Bernard of Clairvaux "reliteralize[d]" the Joban allegory of spiritual warfare in support of "a new sort of chivalry [that] has appeared on earth."⁶⁰ As Christ once appeared in the flesh to "cast out the princes of darkness," he accomplished the "redemption of His people" through "the arm of His valiant men"—the Templars.⁶¹ The Knights of the Temple, Bernard said, waged a double war with two swords. With a spiritual sword—a life of prayer and devotion to the church—they waged war against the temptations of flesh and blood; with a physical sword, they be-came defenders of Christians and protectors of peace. Both swords, Bernard ar-gued, were sacred; both exemplified Christ's passion for the church; and both must be used as necessary when the soldier-crusader takes up the cross against the forces of evil in the world. In sum, as Astell puts it, "The Templar should pos-sess both the strength of the knight (*militis fortitude*) and the gentleness of the monk (*monachi mansuetudo*) and discipline soul and body accordingly."⁶²

In identifying the roles of the clergy and the laity during the Crusades, Bernard distinguished three respective social orders—prelates, consecrated celibates, and married people. The three orders were based on Ezekiel 14:14, which lists the righ-teous as Noah, Daniel, and Job. In this biblical hierarchy, Job, according to Bernard, is the model for the laity.⁶³ Normally engaged in secular pursuits, the laity become knights of the church. Like Job they brave great dangers to respond to the church's call to defend the true faith. They arm themselves for the conflict like a warrior, with helmet, a coat of armor, and a shield, but their most important weapon, the sword, is made in the form of a cross, an outward sign that even as Christ defeated death through crucifixion, the true knight will defeat the enemies of the cross with his sword.⁶⁴ Bernard thus placed the Knights Templar and the crusaders under both the patronage of Job and the sign of the cross. As Beverly Kennedy notes, Bernard advanced the belief "that God himself ordained knighthood to undertake the task of temporal governance."⁶⁵ As God selected Job to be his champion in the conflict with Satan, so the church summons the true knight to suffer the pains of hell if need be in order to secure and defend God's reign on earth.

In the late Middle Ages, the Bernardine ideal of the saintly warrior on a cru-sade for Christ was no longer persuasive, owing largely to the undeniable gap between the ideal and the reality. The scandalous conduct of so many crusaders made it imperative to draw a finer distinction between true knights, who killed and died only for the sake of securing the heavenly kingdom on earth, and false knights, whose ulterior motives sabotaged any claim to be Christlike. To sustain the "myth" of the Bernardine ideal, it proved necessary to create purely fictional characters such as the completely "unblemished Galahad" of the quest for the Holy Grail.⁶⁶ Sir Galahad emerges, however, as Raymond Bolgar notes, as little more than a "cardboard figure" whose virtues are so extraordinarily heavenly that he no longer seems fully human: "Galahad gave such a display of strength and skill and slew so large a number that he seemed to them no normal man, but a fiend burst in among them to destroy them all"; Galahad, wielding the sword of the strange belt, smote to the right and left, dealing death at every stroke, and performed such feats that all who saw him thought him no mere mortal but a monster of some sort."[67] Galahad's counterpart, as depicted in *Sir Gawain and the Green Knight* (fourteenth century) and in Thomas Malory's *Tale of the Sankgreall* (1469), is Lancelot, the humbled and penitential knight who exemplifies Job's humility.

Lancelot is constructed as a more human figure, a warrior whose success derives not from his extraordinary military exploits but from an ordinary humility that enables him to recognize and confess his shortcomings. Shortly after leaving Camelot, Lancelot finds himself alone in the forest at night. He takes off his armor and lies down near an abandoned chapel to sleep. A strange knight appears to him, denounces him as a sinner, seizes his horse and his arms, and takes them away. Lancelot is convicted and spends the rest of the night lamenting his sins and praying for forgiveness. He begins by quoting Job's words as his own, "cursing the day he was born" (cf. Job 3:1).[68] A few days later, having confessed and renounced his adulterous affair with Guinevere, Lancelot encounters a hermit who reminds him of the virtues he possessed when he first became a knight: virginity, humility, long-suffering, rectitude, and charity.[69] The list of virtues recalls those attributed to Job in Job 1:1, virtues Lancelot compromised by yielding to Guinevere's seductive charms. The hermit explains that when the "Old Enemy" saw that Lancelot possessed Joblike perfection, he determined to use Guinevere, as Satan used Eve, to tempt Lancelot to forsake his virtues. The strategy parallels Gregory the Great's description of the way Satan used Job's wife to break down Job's defenses (*Moralia,* 3.8.12–14). As Satan, according Gregory, used the words of Job's wife like a javelin thrown in ambush (*Moralia* 3.8.14), so the hermit says that through Guinevere's glance, Satan "let fly a dart which caught [Lancelot] undefended."[70]

In one respect Lancelot's sin makes him the antitype of the Joban saint who exemplified the ideal crusader. Once this ideal model for the hero yielded to reality, however, it is the Job who sits on a dung heap in humility, meditating upon and embracing his miserable human condition, who becomes Lancelot's moral exemplar. When Lancelot sees himself as "naked of all the virtues that should clothe a Christian,"[71] he prays for forgiveness. Christ rewards him by removing his sins and clothing him with patience and humility. It is Lancelot, the Joblike "penitent self-conqueror,"[72] who now redefines the heroic ideal of the soldier for Christ in the later Middle Ages.

Edmund Spenser's depiction of the Redcrosse Knight in *The Faerie Queene* (1596) marks a pivotal turning point in the concept of the heroic Christian warrior.[73] Unlike Lancelot, who does penance for his sins and so ultimately over-comes his faults, Redcrosse must learn to endure his mortal fallibilities, especially the despair that accompanies his constant failures. Such suffering, which may lead one to prefer death to life, Spenser suggests, is the only route to true knowl-edge of God's grace and mercy. Redcrosse's journey toward this knowledge leaves him, at the end of the age of chivalry, with "old dints of deepe wounds" in his armor.[74] He is the embodiment of "a new Job whose patience must endure his own mutability," by God's grace.[75]

Spenser introduces Redcrosse as a Christian knight who bears on his shield and upon his heart the sacramental signs of "a bloudie Crosse" in "deare remem-brance of his dying Lord." He is, however, also joyless and subject to despair: "Right faithful true he was in deede and word, / But of his cheere did seeme too solemne sad" (1.1.2). His joylessness is explicated in his battle against Sans Joy, who struck him so hard "that twise he reeled, readie twise to fall" (1.2.6). Through successive, nearly fatal, encounters with personifications of his own character, Redcrosse limps toward a climatic encounter with a "man of hell" who calls him-self Despair. Despair sits "low . . . on the ground," like Job on his dung heap,[76] "musing full sadly in his sullein mind" (1.9.35). Spenser characterizes Despair as a ragged old hermit who lives in caves haunted by shrieking owls, wailing ghosts, and the noiseless carcasses of suicide victims, the "rustie knife" they used to end their lives still "fast fixed" in their corpses. With allusions to Elihu's counsel to Job, Despair confronts Redcrosse with his past sins and the inexorable justice of God: "Is not his law, Let euery sinner die: / Die shall all flesh?" (1.9.47; cf. Job 34:15). Despair concludes his speech by offering a conscience-stricken Redcrosse a rusty knife of his own. Like the corpses that inhabit his world, Redcrosse is encouraged to use it as they did and "enioy eternall rest," for "ease after warre" and "death after life does greatly please" (1.9.40).

Una, the woman who has been traveling with Redcrosse throughout his jour-ney, rescues him from the cave of Despair. Seeing that "her knight was feeble, and too faint; / And all his sinews woxen weake and raw" (1.10.2), Una brings him to the House of Holiness, where the matron of the house, Dame Celia, "the Heavenly Lady," and her three daughters, Fidelia (Faith), Speranza (Hope), and Charissa (Love), devote themselves to comforting those in trouble. The porter, an aged man named Humility, leads Una and Redcrosse to a spacious hall, where other atten-dants, Zeal and Reverence, bring them to Celia. After a night of rest, Una asks Faith if she will allow Redcrosse to enter her school and learn from the instruc-tions she and her sisters can offer. Faith teaches him from her "sacred Booke" of the marvelous wonders of God's heavenly grace, but Redcrosse feels so wretched and grieved over his wrongdoings that once again he despairs "to end his wretched dayes: / So much the dart of sinfull guilt the soule dismayes" (1.10.19, 21). Then comes Hope, who offers "comfort sweet, / And taught him how to take assured hold / Vpon her siluer anchor," but Redcrosse remains unhappy, "disdeining life, desiring leaue to die" (1.10.22). Seeing that Redcrosse needs more attention, Celia brings to him a doctor who has wonderful powers to cure the "disease of grieued conscience." His name, an echo of the biblical story about the man from Uz, is "*Patience*" (1.10.23). With the help of his attendant, Repentance, Patience "asswag'd the passion of his plight"; "his paine endur'd, as seeming now more light," Redcrosse grows well and strong again (1.10, 24, 30). Finally Una brings Redcrosse to the third daughter, Love, who teaches him about love and righteousness and how to shed all wrath and hatred, like "many soules in dolours had fordonne" (1.10.34). To guide him along the path to heaven, Love delivers Redcrosse into the hands of Mercy. Should he stumble on his continuing journey, Mercy is there to bring him safely to the end (1.10.36).

Spenser's depiction of the hero as a penitent knight who, like all flawed mortals, must win the battle against despair, draws upon the literary and intellectual contexts of Protestantism in Tudor England. The sources available to him were no doubt many, for as Andrea Hopkins has shown, the narrative of the sinful knight who repents and is finally forgiven is the central pattern of the Middle English romance tradition from the mid-fourteenth century onward.[77] Lawrence Besserman has noted that aspects of this encounter with despair are already present in Middle English morality plays such as *The Castle of Perseverance* (c.1400) and *Mankind* (c.1465), both of which use explicit references to Job to tell the story of an Everyman, a Humanum Genus, who is assaulted by and temporally succumbs to doubts but is finally saved through penitence and God's mercy.[78] In *The Castle of Perseverance,* Mankynde comes into the world paraphrasing Job's words in Job 1:21 ("Naked I came from my mother's womb, and naked shall I return there"): "ful bare/ And bare schal beryed be at hys last ends."[79] In *Mankind* Mercy reminds Mankynde that Job "was of yowr nature and of yowr fragylyte" and that if he is to achieve the final victory as "Chrystys own knyght" in the battle between the soul and the body, he must have the "grett pacyence of Job in tribulacyon" and a Joblike "remors and memory of hymsylff."[80] Mankynde's response to Mercy is to inscribe himself with a memento mori adapted from Elihu's rebuke to Job in Job 34:15, the same scripture Spencer's Despair quotes to Redcrosse: "Remember, man, that you are dust and will return to dust."[81]

As Astell has noted, this association of Job, and the hero, with despair reopened the question of whether Job was in fact guilty of sin and thus deserving of punishment. Protestant theologians (e.g., Martin Luther, John Calvin, Theodore Beza) typically answered this question by following Gregory's exegetical approach (e.g., *Moralia*, 2.16.28). They reasoned that the despairing Job who speaks in the dialogues of the biblical book exemplifies the frailty and imperfections that afflict all saints.[82] Job's doubts about God's mercy, justice, and grace pushed him to the brink of suicide, but they were part of God's providential testing, a test that in the end the saint successfully passed.

Donald Beecher connects Redcrosse's vulnerability to despair, and indirectly Job's temporary lapse into weakness, with the kind of religious depression that came to be described by physicians and theologians alike in the sixteenth and seventeenth centuries as melancholy.[83]

The most encyclopedic account of this malady is Robert Burton's *The Anatomy of Melancholy* (1621), which draws a distinction between the despair of the "reprobate" that is final and incurable and the "temporal despair" that befalls "the best of God's children."[84] As biblical examples of this latter type, Burton cites David, who, "when he was oppressed . . . cried out, 'O Lord thou hast forsaken me,'" and Job, whose heart was so grieved and his conscience so wounded that he wished "to be strangled and die [rather] than to be in his bonds."[85] Christians frequently fall victim to this "temporary passion," as David did in Psalms 88 and 102. Job, Burton says, "doth often complain in this kind."[86] Indeed Job's anguished cries "are no new thing," for even "God's best servants and dearest children have been so visited and tried," including "Christ in the Garden [who] cried, 'My God, my God, why hast thou forsaken me?'"[87] Yet "neither David nor Job did finally yield to despair." David humbled himself, confessed his sin, and received God's mercy. "Job would not leave his hold, but still trusted in him, acknowledging him to be good God."[88] Job's victory over despair, Burton says, citing Saint Gregory, is a victory over the "melancholy humor itself," which is the "ordinary engine" the devil uses to tempt the merry righteous "to some dissolute act."[89]

Spencer's Redcrosse Knight "stands at the apogee of a continuous tradition of heroic poetry" mediated in large measure from classical times to the Middle Ages through Job.[90] As a biblical hero who divests himself of everything to oppose Satan, as a soldier whose virtuous intentions sanctify combat against the enemies of God, as a penitent warrior whose humility is the key to victory, and as an ordinary mortal who, by God's grace, triumphs over despair, Job provides a template for heroism that significantly shaped the culture and values of religious and secular thinkers from the third to the seventeenth centuries. In the end the "cruell marks" and "old dints" in Redcrosse's armor may be an apt metaphor for the promise and the peril awaiting those who would model themselves after the Joban hero.[91]

Saint Job

Crusader knights are not the only ones during the Middle Ages placed under Job's patronage. In the fourteenth and fifteenth centuries, Job was also venerated as the patron saint of musicians.[92] How his saintly virtues come to be associated with both crusaders who kill in the service of the church and musicians who comfort and heal in the service of the church is part of the complex trajectory of Joban interpretation. There are but two oblique references to Job and music in the Hebrew text. In the first (21:12) Job laments that the wicked "sing to the tambourine and the lyre and rejoice to the sound of the pipe" while oppressing the righteous; in the second (30:31) Job concedes that his own lyre and pipe have been co-opted for mourning. Neither of these references fully explains the *Testament*'s embellishment of Job as a musician: in *T. Job* 14:1–5 he plays the lyre to cheer up his maidservants; in *T. Job* 52:2 he gives two of his daughters musical instruments, a harp and a drum, as presents. From such relatively meager accounts, the legend of Job as musician develops, incrementally adding details that likely derive from the hagiography that grows up around the belief that music has a therapeutic effect on the afflicted.[93] The late fifteenth-century English poem "The Life of Holy Job" weaves together biblical and apocryphal details, including the first literary account of Job paying minstrels to comfort him on the dunghill with scabs from his body that turn into gold:

> This sore syk man syttyng on this foule Dongehill,
> There came mynstrelles before him, playing meryly,
> Money had he none to reward aftyr his will,
> But gave theym the brode Scabbes of his sore body,
> Whiche turned vnto pure golde, as sayth the story.[94]

The Middle French mystery play *La Pacience de Job* (1475) contains two scenes that connect with the English poem. In one scene Satan, disguised as a beggar, approaches Job at his lowest moment and asks for alms. Job gives him some of the worms from his body, and when Satan shows them to Job's wife, they appear to her as pieces of gold. In another scene later in the play, Job's friends, Robin, Gason, Le Pasteur, and Le Messaiger, come to comfort him; because they have nothing they can give as gifts, they cheer him with a concert played on their musical instruments. In the final scene of the play, once Job has recovered, he praises God for all his blessings and asks those who are with him to join in singing the words "Te deum laudamus."[95] Besserman notes that *La Pacience de Job* "represents the first clear literary evidence to account for the very popular medieval iconographic motif of Job serenaded on his dunghill by musicians."[96] His observation is reinforced by the illustration used on the cover of the 1570 edition of the play published in Paris by Simon Calvarin, which shows a haloed Job sitting on a mound, listening with pleasure to two musicians, a drummer and a flute player.[97]

Pictorial representations of Job in the company of musicians date to the fourteenth century. The earliest may be the picture of a haloed and sore-covered Job seated before three musicians in a fourteenth-century illumination of a Greek manuscript. One musician plays a psaltery, a second plays on a stringed instrument with a bow, and the third plays a drum. Job extends his right hand to them, a gesture that could indicate either his pleasure upon hearing their music or his caution. The latter could be suggested by the Greek text from Job 21:12—"They take up the harp and lyre and make merry to the sound of melody"—that accompanies the illumination, which is part of Job's complaint that the wicked celebrate life with a full symphony of musical sounds without a thought to the righteous who mourn.[98]

The transformation of Job's friends into musicians and of Job himself into the patron saint of musicians emerges over time in artistic representations. In a mid-fifteenth-century illumination, for example, Jean Fouquet locates Job and his three friends, dressed in colors representative of the monarchy, the church, and parliament, respectively, in the foreground. In the middle distance, Fouquet shows Job's wife, accompanied by three musicians carrying instruments, walking on the road that leads to Job.[99] By the late fifteenth century, the transformation appears to be complete, as for example in the illumination that accompanies Pierre de Nesson's *Paraphrase des neufs lecons de Job,* which shows Job giving a coin to friends who are depicted as three musicians holding a harp, a portable organ, and a lyre.[100]

Job was venerated as a saint, particularly as the patron saint of musicians, in many places north and south of the Alps, especially in the northern half of Belgium, in Karlo, Brussels, Antwerp, and Wezemaal. The "Cult of Saint Job" centered in Wezemaal, a small village in the former duchy of Brabant, is of particular importance. From the mid-fifteenth to the mid-sixteenth centuries, pilgrims made the journey to the Church of Saint-Martin in Wezemaal, where the main object of devotion was a wooden statue of Saint Job, depicted as a priest, holding a placard in his right hand that says in Flemish "The Lord gives, and the Lord takes away," and in his left hand what appears to be a fiery chalice or the Host of the Eucharist.[101] From 1450–1550 pilgrim badges were struck for the use of those making the journey to Wezemaal. Twenty-five of these badges are extant; without exception they show Job sitting on the dung heap rewarding the three musicians playing before him. These badges are especially interesting because the oldest of them, dating to around 1450, depict Job not only as the patron saint of musicians but also, in a clear connection with the church's statue of Saint Job, as a priest who offers the sacrament of communion by which all those who are afflicted may be healed and reunited in the fellowship of the saints.

The pilgrimages to the Cult of Saint Job in Wezemaal reached their apex in 1515, with more than twenty thousand recorded visitors to the village. In the first half of the sixteenth century, Saint Cecilia gradually took over Job's role as the patron saint of music, and the veneration of Saint Job shifted to accent his legendary powers as an intercessor for those afflicted with skin diseases such as leprosy.

In the aftermath of the great syphilis epidemic that swept through Italy and then France, Belgium, and England in 1495–1525, which killed an estimated one million people, this dreaded disease was called "le mal Monseigneur saint Job."[102] Numerous hospitals emerged during this period throughout Western Europe bearing the name Saint Job,[103] perhaps none more important for our purposes here than the San Giobbe hospital founded in Venice in the late fourteenth century.[104] The name Giobbe identified both the hospital and the Franciscan church associated with the hospital not only with the biblical Job but also with the section of the city that was home to the poor and afflicted underclass of Venice. These persons, known as *giopen,* apparently made up the majority of the population in this area, although it is unclear whether this was by official decree or by personal choice. Presumably if someone in Venice during the fourteenth century asked where Giobbe was, they would be directed to this part of the city, where people with "Job's disease," and those committed to their care, were located.

Giovanni Bellini's *Pala di San Giobbe,* as noted above, was painted for a side altar in the chapel of the San Giobbe hospital. At the center of the composition, the Madonna and child sit on a throne underneath a golden dome; the inscription in the apse above reads AVE VIRGINEI FLOS INTERMERATE PVDORIS, "Hail undefiled flower of virgin modesty." Mary's left hand is raised, evoking the intercessory gesture of the worshipper/viewer.[105] The saints surrounding the throne, from left to right, are Frances, John the Baptist, Job, Dominic, Sebastian, and Louis of Toulouse. Bellini places Job closest to the virgin, on her right or favored side. Job, aged and with a long white beard, raises his hands in prayer. Sebastian, his counterpart on the opposite side of the throne, is youthful; his hands are bound behind his back, the conventional posture of one tied to the stake. Although both Job and Sebastian are venerated intercessors for the sick, here Job is shown as praying not only for the viewer but also for Sebastian, who looks directly across at him.[106]

Some twenty years later, Bellini's younger contemporary Vittore Carpaccio painted *The Presentation of Jesus in the Temple* (1510) for the same chapel. Bellini's influence on Carpaccio's style is clear, especially in the similar grouping of the three young minstrels who sit below the Madonna and child. Another Carpaccio painting, *Meditation on the Passion* (c.1495), also shows Bellini's influence but extends the depiction of Saint Job's intercession in a suggestively new direction. At the center of this painting, Carpaccio locates not the Madonna and child, who remind viewers of the Annunciation and the Incarnation, but a dead Christ, the iconographic type for the Man of Sorrows who awaits resurrection. Christ sits not on an ornate throne in a vaulted church apse but on a cracked and deteriorating throne that is placed in the middle of a countryside landscape. Christ slumps wearily toward the right, his eyes closed, as if in contemplation of the wounds he has suffered, which are visible in his hands and his side and in the crown of thorns that has fallen to the ground beside his feet. In the ruined upper left corner of the throne, weeds and flowers have begun to grow over and obscure a Hebrew inscription. The words *Israel* and *voice* can be definitively identified,[107] which suggests to some interpreters that Carpaccio depicted Christ sitting on the shattered throne of Israel, inviting his faithful servants to contemplate the meaning of his sacrificial death.[108]

Christ's throne divides the landscape into halves, each detailed with symbolism. To the left is a dead tree, bending toward a deserted mountain trail, where a leopard is about to devour a doe; a wolf looks on from a cave just above, waiting to scavenge any remains left behind. The imagery suggests a world of death, unrestrained force, and hapless victims. To the right the landscape is filled with images of life and possibilities: trees and plants are full with foliage; walled villages are safe and secure; and animals (leopard, doe, and red bird) inhabit the same world without fear or intimidation. This left-right, death-life backdrop provides the context for Carpaccio's depiction of two saints who sit with the dead Christ. On the left is Saint Jerome, identified by his books, his rosary, and his lion,[109] each of which recalls Jerome's symbolic interpretation of Job 19:25–26:

> Job, example of patience, what mysteries are not embraced in his teachings? In them each single word is full to the senses. And (though I pass over other things) he prophesies the resurrection of the body as no other has written of it, either openly or implicitly. "I know," he said, "that my Redeemer liveth, and that on the last day I shall rise again from the earth, and I shall gather my skin once more about me, and in my flesh I shall see God. Whom I myself shall look upon, I and none other, and whom my eyes shall behold. This my hope reposes in my breast. (Job 19:25–26)[110]

Jerome's interpretation of Job sets the tone for Christian interpreters throughout the Middle Ages, especially Gregory the Great, who quotes in full the passage above in the Citreaux manuscript of *Moralia in Job*.[111] With regard to the conceptions of Job current in Carpaccio's time, Frederick Hartt notes that the *Moralia* was reprinted in Venice in 1480 and 1494. This work would have been part of the Venetian theological discussion about Job in the late fifteenth century that was available to Carpaccio.[112]

To the right, opposite Jerome, Carpaccio places Saint Job, depicted, in close imitation of Bellini's Job at San Giobbe, as elderly and bearded. Job is seated on the side of the painting where symbols of life and peace define the landscape, yet scattered around his feet are a shattered skull and dried-out bone pieces, signs that suffering's imprint on his life remains very real, even in death. There are several significant parallels between Job and Christ: Job sits on a granite block, which, like the dilapidated throne chair of Christ, is broken off at the left corner;

like the Hebrew inscription on Christ's throne, which is faded and obscured by the overgrowth of weeds, the Hebrew inscription on two sides of Job's block is darkened by the shadows of Job's body and barely legible. By identifying two Hebrew words, *gōʾălî ḥāy*, Hartt has definitively connected a part of the inscription with Job 19:25, "My redeemer lives," the same passage Jerome interprets in the passage cited above. From this he concludes, as do other interpreters, that Carpaccio intentionally draws attention to Jerome's view of Job as one who prefigured Christ's suffering and prophesied his resurrection.[113]

Job's posture and gestures as he sits on the block are, however, tantalizingly ambiguous. He sits with his legs crossed; his left elbow is on his knee, and with his left hand he supports his head as he stares with glazed eyes not at Christ, who is slumping in his direction, but at the viewer. This is a common representation of Job, and as Gert von der Osten has argued, may well be the typological origin for the conventional depiction of "Christ in Distress."[114] Most representations of Job on the dunghill (*Job in sterquilinio*) show him holding himself erect, supporting his body or his head with one hand and using the other hand either to hold some object that symbolizes his plight (a potsherd, a staff, or a crutch) or to make some gesture, such as the upraised hand that may indicate his rebuke of his wife or his plea/prayer for help from his friends or from God. Von der Osten notes that it is usually only by the gesture Job makes with his other hand that viewers can distinguish him from the related type of the Christ in Distress.[115] Carpaccio shows Job using his right hand, index finger extended, to point to his feet. This is apparently the only example of Job making such a gesture. Of the three figures in the scene, only Job wears sandals on his feet. Jerome's sandals have been removed and placed side by side to his left. Christ is barefoot. By pointing to his feet and in the general direction of the shattered bones lying around them, Job seems to be calling the viewer's attention to the ground upon which he has been walking, perhaps as a reminder where his journey in life, and in death, has taken him thus far.[116] As a righteous sufferer, he endured the death of his children, and by extension the death of a faith that was once undisturbed by doubts and questions. He persevered in hope, as the Hebrew citation on the block bears witness. But this inscription, like the fortitude from which it emerged, has been damaged—not destroyed, but still cracked open. Like the other figures around him, Job is dead. The hope for resurrection hangs in limbo; it is a promise as yet unfulfilled. Even the Christ slumping on a throne inscribed with the word *Israel* must endure the present moment, represented here as utterly exhausting, until the redemption promised becomes reality.

Hartt has described Carpaccio's *Meditation on the Passion* as a "meditative image" in which different historical elements are combined in a new totality that "is endowed with exclusively personal religious meaning."[117] Carpaccio's Job directs the viewer's gaze toward his feet as an invitation to meditation and devotion. The import of the gesture is not clear. Is he offering instruction? If so, then what is the lesson? Is he still the patron intercessor for the sick that we see in the San Giobbe Job? One may imagine that Carpaccio has departed from the conventional depiction of Job with hands clasped together in prayer in order to draw a more intentional connection between Job's own pain and suffering and Venetians who are diseased in body and soul. If so, then Carpaccio may be suggesting that Saint Job is not only the prefiguration of Christ; he is also the prototype of the perfect Christian.[118] Like Job Christians must be both heroic and humble; they must stand fast in faith, especially when they cannot fully comprehend their place in the providence of God.

"And Then a Hero Comes Along"

It is easier to summarize the various characterizations of Job in the didactic tales than to risk drawing definitive conclusions. We have surveyed representative, but by no means exhaustive, readings and rereadings of the "patient Job" who dominated the interpretive tradition of both Jews and Christians from the first century to the beginnings of the Renaissance. From an exegetical perspective, the trajectory moves, in accordance with shifting historical circumstances, from the meager and rather simplistic biblical version of the righteous person who is rewarded for enduring, without complaint, undeserved affliction; to the *T. Job's* depiction of the ethically minded athlete/wrestler who defeats Satan in order to serve the poor; to James's commendation to first-century Christians of Job's endurance; to the Middle Ages, when Job's virtues, allegorized and sacramentalized, become the template for medieval knighthood; to the dawning of the Renaissance, when Job becomes the patron saint of both the afflicted who pray for comfort and the musicians who offer it.

Heroes and saints are exemplary persons who evoke approval, adoration, and emulation. As Bolgar notes, they are important for the history of culture because they show the traits and types of behavior that have enjoyed public favor. In short heroes and saints provide an index of a society's values at given points in time.[119] The critical recognition here is that heroes and saints change with time. In today's world a Google search on "hero" produces 172 million results in a few seconds; type in "saint" and you get almost 500 million results. A quick glance through the first dozen or so entries suggests that the first things the words *hero* and *saint* are associated with in modern culture are pop music, such as the lyrics of Mariah Carey's 1993 hit song "Hero" ("And then a hero comes along / with the strength to carry on"), and global network security, such as the "Saint Network Vulnerability

Assessment Scanner," a downloadable program that for a modest price promises protection against hackers. The name of Job is nowhere to be found in Google searches such as these, except when the computer thinks the searcher is looking for employment opportunities, in which case "job" is everywhere.

It is no doubt the case that we think of heroes and saints differently in the twenty-first century, but we should not overinterpret anecdotal data drawn from random Google searches. A serious view of cultural history suggests there is hardly a time when the Job(s) of the ancient didactic tale has not contributed to the way societies think about the nature of humankind in relationship to God. In response to the wisdom offered through the Delphic oracle, "Know thyself," philosophers from the fifth century B.C.E. centered on three essential characteristics of the *homo verus,* the true man. The *homo verus* is (1) a mortal being who is by nature exposed to suffering and death but (2) possesses virtues, proximate to divine wisdom, which enable moral choices that overcome the weaknesses of human nature. Such virtues (*virtus*), exemplified as intellectual wisdom and spiritual fortitude, enable human beings (3) to complete successfully the journey of life from its divine origin to its divine end.[120] Early Christian writers, as we have seen, from James to Chrysostom to Gregory the Great, interpreted *homo virus* as a virtual homonym for the biblical Job.[121]

Typically the terms *hero* and *saint* are used with reference to a primary virtue, usually based on a single incident in a character's life, which is adequate to summarize his or her legendary existence. In Job's case this virtue is identified as "patience," the fortitude and perseverance he displays especially in chapters 1–2 of the biblical story. And yet, as this chapter has tried to demonstrate, patience is a multivalent virtue that cultures interpret differently at any given point in time. From the biblical world's endorsement of Job's spiritual triumph over Satan; to the affirmation in the Middle Ages of Job as the patron of knights and crusaders who wage physical combat against the enemies of the church; to the Renaissance, when as the patron saint of musicians and lepers, Job in his heroic faith exemplifies true Christianity, the definition of Joban patience is a kaleidoscope of often tenuously connected behaviors.

We have good reason to believe that it was not substantively different for the biblical writers who gave us the final form of the book of Job. The patient Job of the didactic tale, perhaps the oldest part of the story, is redefined in the poetic dialogues that stand at the center of the book, which likely reflect the needs and values of a later and different world. In the aftermath of the Babylonian exile, which brought in its wake a Holocaust-like shattering of traditional affirmations about God and humankind, models of patient submission yielded to the imperatives for exemplars of heroic protest and resistance. In this setting the Job who speaks in Job 7:17 responds to the wisdom in the age-old command "Know thyself" with his own counterquestion: "What are human beings, that you [God] make so much of them?" Job's pursuit of the answer to this question, to which we must now turn, introduces a still different understanding of what perseverance and courage require of those who would be numbered among the "blameless and upright who fear God and turn away from evil" (Job 1:1, 8; 2:3).

2

GOD AND THE SATAN

"Have you considered my servant Job?"

Zuss (God) to Nickles (Satan): Listen! This is a simple scene.
I play God. You play Satan.

Archibald MacLeish, J.B.

The really astonishing thing is how easily Yahweh gives in to the insinuations of Satan. . . . Yahweh has become unsure of his own faithfulness.

Carl Jung, Answer to Job

We have examined the characterizations of Job in the didactic tale. The next chapter will focus on Job's wife. Both characters are interesting in their own rights,
but it is likely that neither would have been considered important enough to remember were they not inextricably linked to the conversation between God and
the satan in Job 1:6–12 and 2:1–6. This conversation is the fulcrum upon which the
whole Joban story rests.

Before God and the satan enter the story, Job, his wife, and his family live
securely in an edenic world. After God and the satan converse, the world they
know vanishes, leaving in its wake the destruction of their possessions, the death
of their children, and the unremitting trauma of psychic turmoil and physical affliction. Job, whose life had once merited recognition as the "greatest of the all the
people of the east" (1:3), now acquires a "greatness" of suffering (2:13) that distinguishes him for wholly different reasons. Before God and the satan spoke with
one another, there was no reason to question the integrity of either Job's piety or
his prosperity. After they spoke, the story cannot find resolution until someone
can satisfactorily answer the question posed by Job's last words in the prologue:
"Should we accept only good from God and not accept evil?" (2:10 [NJPS]). The
rest of the book is driven in one way or another by the effort to explain how those
who are "blameless and upright," by God's own assessment (1:1; cf.1:8, 2:3), can

construct any sort of sustainable affirmation that connects the words *God, good,* and *evil*. We will turn in due course to the various ways the dialogues between Job and his friends and between Job and God grapple with this issue.

The necessary preface to those dialogues is the narrator's constructed dialogue between God and the satan, the first and only recorded conversation between these two parties in the Old Testament. The dialogue between God and the satan unfolds in two exchanges (1:6–12 and 2:1–6), each followed by the narrator's description of the consequent, mutually agreeable effects of these two exchanges on Job and his family (1:13–22 and 2:7–9), who are not privy to any of the heavenly decisions that are about to change their lives. Each exchange is initiated by questions from God, a subtle narrative device that signals that God sets the agenda for the ensuing conversation. To the repeating question "Where have you come from?" (1:7a, 2:2a), the satan twice responds that he has come into God's presence after having gone "to and fro on the earth" (1:7b, 2:2b). Twice God asks if the satan has "considered my servant Job"; in each instance God indicates that such consideration is merited because Job's righteousness exceeds that of anyone the satan might inspect. There is "no one," God twice affirms, "who is like him on earth" (1:8, 2:3). God's words of affirmation are more laudatory than those of the narrator in 1:1–5, but they do not substantially advance what we as readers already know about Job. It is the satan's response to God that adds to the plotline.

In the first round of dialogues, the satan raises two questions that shift the conversation from God's affirmation of Job to Job's motives for loyalty to God. First, a general question, seemingly rhetorical in tenor: "Does Job fear God *for nothing*?" (*ḥinnām* [1:9]). Without waiting for God's answer, the satan follows with a second question, now directed specifically to God, which he answers himself and challenges God to refute: "Have you not put a fence around him and all that he has . . . ?" (1:10), in other words, is it not true that you, God, have so protected Job from adversity that the only response he knows how to make is to bless you? What if, the satan continues, you remove this protective border, stretch out your hand, and allow affliction to "touch" Job and all that he possesses? When blessed by God, the satan does not doubt that Job will bless God in return. But when cursed by God, will Job not curse God in return? God responds to the satan's challenge by agreeing to remove Job's divine patronage,[1] thereby relinquishing Job and "all that he has" to the satan's power. There is one qualification. The satan's hand may extend to all that Job possesses, but it must stop short of touching Job himself (1:11). With an agreed agenda, the satan "went out from the presence of God" (1:12). In rapid succession four messengers announce a series of calamities that suddenly "fall" (1:15, 16, 19) upon Job's world, devastating his oxen, donkeys, sheep, camels, servants, and, finally, his sons and daughters.

Both the satan and God are portrayed as onlookers; both watch to see how Job will respond to his losses. When the narrator reports that Job continues to bless God (1:21–22), it seems that God's confidence in Job has trumped the satan's suspicions.

Or perhaps not. A second round of dialogue between God and the satan (2:1–6) begins by repeating almost verbatim the opening exchange. The redundancy serves rhetorically both to reinforce what we readers already know—God has initiated a conversation with the satan about his servant Job—and to up the ante on what is at stake in the conversation by introducing three new aspects to God's words (2:3). First, God affirms that Job "still persists in his integrity (*tummâ*)," despite what he has experienced. By calling attention to the constancy of Job's virtues (cf. *tām*, "blameless" [1:1, 6]), God announces that nothing the satan has done thus far has altered either Job's fidelity or God's assessment of him. Second, God acknowledges that Job's integrity remains unblemished, "although you [the satan] incited me against him." The verbal construction "incite against" (*sut* + *bĕ*) normally conveys the negative connotation of "provocation," of stirring up someone to an action against another that would not have happened without incitement (e.g., 1 Sm 26:19; 2 Sm 24:1; Jer 43:3). Since Job 2:3 is the only place in the Hebrew Bible where this expression occurs with God as the object of such incitement, it raises the unsettling thought that God exercises something less than complete sovereignty over divine decisions. Can God be provoked by queries not his own (or are they?) to do something he would not otherwise have considered? Third, and still more unsettling, is God's admission that yielding to the satan's provocation, which results in the innocent deaths of seven sons and three daughters (1:18–19), has happened "for no reason" (*ḥinnām* [2:3]). Exegetical details may be parried,[2] but the insertion of these words into God's discourse with the satan now places God's complicity in gratuitous suffering at the center of the interpretive challenge.

Seizing on God's admission that there is no correlation between human behavior and divine action, the satan challenges God once more to extend his hand against Job, this time by permitting the satan to afflict Job's "bone" and "flesh." Once more God accepts the satan's challenge, handing over Job's fate to the satan, with a faint but important caveat: "Very well, he is in your power, only spare his life" (2: 6). Stepping over the narrative borders between heaven and earth, the satan leaves the presence of God and steps directly into Job's world. With God's permission he strikes Job with "loathsome sores" that cover his body "from the sole of his foot to the crown of his head" (2:7). With these words signifying a God-permitted affliction of Job's body, the narrative of God's dialogue with the satan comes to an end. The satan disappears from the story; in the remainder of the book of Job, he is never mentioned again.[3] God's last words to the satan, "Very well, he is in your power" (2:6), mark the last time God speaks until 38:1.

Modern commentators typically identify a number of key exegetical issues that bear on interpreting this dialogue. The satan is associated with the "heavenly beings" (*běnê hā'ĕlōhîm*, literally, "sons of God" [1:6, 2:1]) who "present themselves before the Lord." The concept of a divine council comprising a ruling god and an assembly of gods with delegated responsibilities is well attested in Egypt, Babylon, and Canaan.[4] Numerous references or allusions to such a council in the Old Testament confirm that the concept took root in Hebraic thought.[5] The narrator describes the satan's relationship to this council somewhat ambiguously. By saying the satan "also came among them," the narrator opens the door on a question: is the satan a legitimate member of this council, thus one of God's own chosen attendants, or he is an intruder, thus one who does not belong and has no legitimate role in divine affairs? With few exceptions contemporary commentators generally adopt the former position. Early postbiblical commentators, however, as we shall see, saw these two options as major fault lines in a critical debate about the relationship between God and the devil and, by extension, the cosmic battle between the forces of good and evil.

Commentators also note the importance of the use of the definite article with the word *śāṭān* (*ha* + *śāṭān*), which is the case in each of its occurrences in Job (1:6, 7, 8, 9, 12; 2:1, 2, 3, 4, 6, 7). The definite article indicates that the word should be understood as a title that is descriptive of one's function and responsibility. *Haśśāṭān* is "the accuser," "the adversary," "the doubter," that is, the member of the heavenly council tasked as a kind of prosecuting attorney who seeks to establish the facts of a case in the pursuit of justice.[6] The construction of the word provides another indicator that the satan is not God's opponent, that his intentions are neither evil nor opposed to God's purposes. Rather the satan functions as God's advocate by probing human behavior for truth and faithfulness. *Haśśāṭān* is "the narrative embodiment of a hermeneutics of suspicion." His role is to question all meaning that claims to be transparent and inscrutable. Can anyone's profession of fidelity to God be truly disinterested? Does there not always linger the suspicion that commitment to God is, at least implicitly, a calculation of the rewards and the costs?[7] One instructive analogue, although often applied in ways contrary to its original meaning, is the *advocatus diaboli* (devil's advocate), officially *promotor fidei* (Promoter of the Faith), whose duty in Roman Catholicism since the sixteenth century is to make sure that all possible objections are thoroughly examined before the church acts to canonize a saint.[8]

Most English translations omit the definite article and capitalize the word as *Satan,* thus inviting identification with the devil of later Jewish and Christian literature. While this rendering is demonstrably incorrect on critical grounds, it has nevertheless contributed to a major trajectory of interpretation that sees a genetic connection between Job's encounter with *haśśāṭān* and the *diabolos* (devil [Greek, Latin]) who, according to the New Testament, is Jesus's principal adversary (e.g., Mt 4:1–11; Mk 1:12–13; Lk 4:1–13). This connection is deeply rooted in the public imagination, as the rest of this chapter will demonstrate. From the illuminated manuscripts of Byzantine miniaturists to Goethe's *Faust,* from medieval Jewish philosophers to Milton's *Paradise Lost,* and in the works of modern dramatists of all sorts, the roles of the satan and God in Job's story have been a reservoir for creative interpretation. The reception history of God's dialogues with the satan is an important reminder that scholars inform the public reading and understanding of scripture but do not define it.

Dialogue, whether real or constructed, is a rhetorical device for the examination of contrasting perspectives and thus a lens through which readers may view the moral values of the characters involved. God's dialogues with the satan in Job 1–2 invite questions but do not answer them. Is the satan God's advocate or Job's adversary? Does God know in advance the answers to the satan's questions, or must God test Job's fidelity by suffering to know whether he is who God believes him to be? Is God complicit in gratuitous suffering, or are the deaths of seven sons and three daughters simply a necessary part of the (fictional) drama the Joban story requires? These and other such questions are muted in the final form of the story by the narrator's repeated assertion that faced with adversity he does not deserve, Job continues to bless God. Come what will, he does not curse God, and he "does not sin or charge God with any wrongdoing" (1:21–22, 2:10).

Even so the prologue ends in silence. The friends come to console and comfort Job, but seeing the enormity of his suffering, they cannot (for now) speak a single word. The satan, having done what is in his power to test Job, retreats from the story, never to speak again. God, having initiated a conversation that leaves Job sitting on ashes asking (rhetorical?) questions about good and evil, remains passive before the all-too-evident consequences of divine words.

This silence will of course be broken by Job's curses in chapter 3 and by the ensuing dialogues with the friends. But before addressing how the rest of the book contributes to the questions raised by God's dialogues with the satan, it is instructive to pause here in order to examine how generative this conversation has been for post-biblical interpreters. One caveat is necessary. The objective in what follows is not to construct a history of Satan or the devil in Jewish and Christian literature and beyond.[9] For such approaches extensive resources are available that readers may consult if they wish. The focus in this chapter will instead be on how the conversation between God and the satan in Job 1–2 has contributed to this larger conversation.

"Satan knocked at the Door. . . . Tell Job I wish to meet with him" (*T. Job* 6:4–5)

The LXX rendering of the conversation between God and the satan essentially follows the biblical account. Several linguistic details are noteworthy, more for the subtle nuances they add to the translation than for particularly advancing the story line.

The translator populates the heavenly council with "angels of God" (*angeloi tou theou*), rather than "sons of God" (*bĕnê hā'ĕlōhîm*), then uses the same term, *angelos,* to render the Hebrew term *malāk,* which describes the "messengers" who report the initial calamities that befall Job (LXX 1:6 [cf. 2:1], 14, 16, 17, 18). The LXX consistently translates *haśśāṭān* in the Hebrew text as *ho diabolos* ("the devil"; *A New English Translation of the Septuagint and the Other Greek Translations Traditionally Included under That Title:* "the slanderer"; 13 times in total). It is interesting that the translator chooses not to transliterate *haśśāṭān* as *ho Satanas,* a term used six times in the *Testament of the Twelve Patriarchs* as a synonym for Beliar, the force of darkness/evil (*T. Asher* 6:4; *T. Dan* 3:6, 5:6, 6:1; *T. Gad* 4:7), nor does he ever use the adjective *ponēros* to define the *diabolos* as "evil," an epithet that 1 Macc 1:36 (c.100 B.C.E.) later applies to Antiochus IV, the "evil adversary" of Israel (see also Tobit's [c. 225–175 B.C.E.] use of *to ponēron daimonion,* "the evil demon [Asmodeus]," in 3:17; cf. 6:8, 8:3). The *diabolos* comes into God's presence "with" the angels (*met autōn* [LXX 1:6]), which is perhaps slightly less ambiguous than the Hebrew "among them" (*bĕtôkām*). In all other respects, the role of the *diabolos* in the LXX is essentially the same as that of the satan. Both are heavenly agents with access to God's presence; both have delegated earthly duties; both are engaged by God with questions about Job; both are given God's permission to use their powers in circumscribed ways to afflict Job; and thus both the satan and the *diabolos* are presented as forces that work in consonance with God's will, not in opposition to it. In sum "the demonology of the LXX of Job is rather bland."[10]

The first major literary embellishment of the Hebrew Bible's conversation between God and the satan is in the *Testament of Job* (first century B.C.E.–first century C.E.). The *Testament* devotes approximately 40 percent of its story to the account of Satan's attacks on Job (twenty-one of fifty-three chapters), thus essentially creating a narrative that differs significantly with both the MT and the LXX. The *Testament* omits entirely the biblical version of the heavenly council scenes in which God and the satan discuss Job's fate, thus effectively removing the problematic that God is actively involved in Job's suffering. Indeed God does not figure prominently either as a speaker or an actor in the *Testament.*[11]

Instead the story begins with Job's recounting to his children his consternation upon seeing sacrifices offered to a nearby "idol's temple" (2:2). When he asks if the god worshipped in this temple is the one who made heaven and earth, the answer comes in a "revelation scene"[12] in which an angel appears to him in "a very bright light" saying that the temple belongs to the "devil (*diabolos*) . . . by whom human nature is deceived " (3:3).[13] Having received knowledge that sets him apart from the rest of deceived humanity,[14] Job asks for and receives permission to destroy "the place of Satan (*ho topos tou Satana* [3:6]).[15] He is fully informed of the consequences of such actions—"he [*Satanas*] will rise up against you with wrath for battle"—and assured that if he is "patient" (*hypomeinēs*), then he will win the crown of victory, his losses doubly restored, and "shall be raised up in the resurrection" (4:3–11). After Job has been "sealed by the angel" against defeat (5:2), he carries out his mission, withdraws to his house, and waits for Satan's response. When Satan knocks at Job's door and announces that he "wishes to meet with him" (6:4–5), the confrontation that dominates the first half of the *Testament* (chapters 2–27) begins in earnest.

In the *Testament*'s account of the confrontation between Satan and Job, the following five items merit careful consideration.

First, the *Testament* removes God as a complicit partner to Job's affliction and instead shifts the emphasis from Job's role as a passive victim of inexplicable affliction to his role as an active protagonist who knows in advance the price he will pay for acting on his convictions. It is Job's decision, informed by an angel of God, to enter into combat with Satan. The plotline that follows does not place in question God's ultimate vindication of Job; instead it accents how Job will certainly triumph over Satan, if he perseveres in faith.

Second, whereas both the Bible and the LXX limit the satan's role to Job 1–2, the *Testament*'s Satan is at the center of the action that carries the first half of the book. *T. Job* 2–5 serves in essence as the prologue, setting the scene by describing Job's decision to destroy Satan's temple. *T. Job* 6–26 describes Satan's retaliation against Job. *T. Job* 27 reports Job's defeat of Satan and Satan's shamed retreat. Although Satan does not directly appear again in the text, he continues to have a behind-the-scenes presence in his inspired spokesman, Elihu, "not a human but a beast" (42:2), who speaks "insulting words" to Job (41:5).

Third, a critical strategy of Satan's assault is disguise and deceit. He disguises himself as a beggar (6:4) in order to gain access to Job's goods; as the king of the Persians (17:1) in order to exact revenge on Job's property and children; as a great whirlwind (20:5) in order to overturn Job's throne and to strike him with a severe plague; and as a bread seller (23:1) in order to lead Job's wife astray. Finally through the person of Elihu, the "evil one" (43:5) "inspired by Satan" (41:5), he makes his boldest move. Elihu speaks as if possessed of the "great whirlwind" force that both the biblical text and the *Testament* attribute to God (Job 38:1, 40:6; *T. Job* 42:1). In essence he veils himself as a "counterfeit of the divine presence," "a fake theophany"[16] that evokes God's censure (*T. Job* 43:5, 6, 7, 10).[17]

Fourth, Satan's various disguises enact a contest that is fundamental to the *Testament*'s story: the power of divine revelation versus the powers of earthly deception.[18] From the outset Job is the beneficiary of a revelation that gives him insight into heavenly realities; he knows in advance that, if he perseveres, the powers of Satan cannot overcome the "strength" God gives "to his elect ones" (4:11). For his part Satan knows that humans are susceptible to deception, that they can be tempted by the necessities of life to make choices based on immediate realities rather than heavenly promises. The battle that ensues between these opposing powers is not waged primarily between God and Satan, as in the biblical text, but instead between Satan and Job.

According to the *Testament,* Satan is a formidable opponent. Job's maid does not recognize Satan when he disguises himself as a beggar, and so he "came and took away all [Job's] wealth" (7:1–8:2). Both "rogues" and Job's "fellow country-men" obey Satan's command, disguised as a mandate from the "king of Persians," to destroy Job's possessions and slaughter his children, leaving Job himself, at least temporarily, silenced by despair (17:1–18:5). Disguised as a "great whirlwind," Satan overturns Job's throne and strikes him with plagues from head to toe—even the worms that infest Job's body appear to obey Satan's command (20:1–9). And Satan deceives Job's long-suffering wife, tricking her into shame (the shearing of her hair) in exchange for three loaves of bread (23:1–11).

There are reminders along the way that Job's knowledge of these matters is superior to Satan's. Although his maid is taken in by Satan's disguise, Job is not; he announces that Satan may do what he will but that he is prepared to withstand Satan's assault (7:13). Although numbed by the betrayal of the "cheap and worth-less men" (18:3) who participated in the slaughter of his children, Job "understood what had happened" and continued to bless the name of his God (19:3–4). When Job's wife fails to recognize Satan's deception, Job supplies the discernment she lacks: "Do you not see the devil (*diabolos*) standing behind you, unsettling your reasoning . . . ?" (26:6). Job's victory is achieved when he challenges Satan to abandon his disguises: "Come up front! Stop hiding yourself! . . . Come out and fight!" (27: 1–2). The *Testament* describes the battle that ensues as a wrestling match, with the stronger opponent—Job—eventually overthrowing and pinning his adversary (27:3–5).[19] As J. J. Collins notes, "Job defeats Satan not only by his patient endurance but also by his spiritual insight which enables him to penetrate Satan's disguises."[20]

And, finally, Job's victory over Satan eventuates in his personal ascension to the heavenly realm, where he is able to see his deceased children "crowned with the splendor of the heavenly one" (40:3). In contrast to other testamentary liter-ature (especially the *Testament of the Twelve Patriarchs*), the *T. Job* is not primarily concerned with Job as a model of piety for the people of Israel. Rather the accent throughout is on Job's personal piety, his model for how faithful individuals may persevere against all worldly trials, if they but commit themselves to the superiority of divine wisdom. Job's words in *T. Job* 18, which resonate both the shock of the death of his children and his faint but abiding trust in what has been revealed to him about God's intentions, are the epicenter of the *Testament*'s distinctive eschatology.

Still more striking and worthy of reflection, the *Testament* has no record of Job ever receiving any such promise from the angel of God—yet another telltale reminder that Joblike piety requires not only extraordinary commitment to what is revealed but also creative imagination. In the battle between the power of divine revelation and the powers of earthly deception, the *Testament* reads the biblical story as a summons to each and every individual to defeat Satan and win the victory that only God, in the end, can award.

The *Testament*'s characterization of the roles played by God and Satan goes beyond anything in either the Bible or the LXX. Its embellishments, whether based on haggadic or midrashic archetypes or on an earlier version of the *Testament* itself, are likely the primary source for Byzantine illuminated manuscripts (fourth–fifteenth centuries), which devote proportionally far more illustrations to what had become the Joban narrative—Job 1–2 as retold in *T. Job* 1–27—than to any other part of Job.[21] The evidence is particularly striking in Byzantine manuscripts from the ninth through the twelfth centuries, each of which on average uses four to six miniatures to illustrate all the principal stages in the dialogue between God and Satan: Satan's appearance among the angels; the initial exchange between God and Satan; God's granting Satan permission to destroy Job's possessions; Satan's affliction of Job's body; and Satan's withdrawal.[22] While illustrations in early manuscripts (fourth through early ninth centuries) follow the text closely, these later, middle Byzantine manuscripts often incorporate "legendary" aspects that, following the *Testament*'s example, "paint" both God and Satan into the story in imaginative ways.

The *T. Job* does not have a heavenly council encounter between God and Satan, as noted above. Byzantine miniatures follow suit, typically depicting a separation between God (and the heavenly angels) and Satan's work on earth.[23] Numerous illustrations represent God's role with only a permissive hand extended from heaven in the direction of Satan, who is pictorially separated from both God and God's angels. In a ninth-century folio, the top right of the page depicts God's hand extending from the heavens, with beams of light directed downward and to the left. The accompanying text, to the left of the hand and extending beyond it, creates a spatial separation between the top and bottom of the page. In the bottom left, a black Satan is enclosed in a shadowed aureole. He wears a white girdle and white boots; his feet are in motion, as if he is running to the assignment he has been given. Looking upward and to the right, in the direction of the divine hand that gives him permission to proceed, he sets off, holding in his left hand a long, crooked staff, presumably a weapon to be used in his assault on Job. At the bottom right of the page and separated from Satan, eight haloed angels stand directly beneath God's extended hand. The angel to the farthest left, closest to Satan, looks upward toward God's hand, at the same time exposing a bared buttocks to Satan, a depiction suggesting rude disdain for what is about to happen.[24] The same manuscript, on the following page, depicts the extended hand of God, to the left, directly opposite a similar black representation of Satan, again looking in the direction of the hand. His feet are moving, but he now stands on a serpent, a suggestive connection with the extensive mythology surrounding God (good) and evil (Satan/serpent).[25] An eleventh-century manuscript depicts the spatial distance between God and his heavenly attendants and Satan still more clearly. To the left God's hand from heaven extends directly into the midst of eight angels, divided into two groups. To the far right, Satan, a black, winged figure, extends his right hand, as if waiting for instructions from heavenly deliberations to which he is not privy.[26]

Disguise and deception are primary characteristics of the *Testament*'s Satan. Byzantine miniatures employ three kinds of representations or "disguises" for Satan.[27] Some manuscripts, like those discussed above, depict Satan as a black, sometimes winged, humanlike figure. Others represent him as animal, beastly, or monstrous in form. A ninth-century illumination accompanying the text of Job 2:7 shows a pockmocked, scratching Job sitting on a bench, with his mourning wife standing to his left. Job looks to the right, where a three-headed monster is poised for attack. The bottom third of the monster's torso has a serpent's head, its mouth opened, fangs extended. The middle of the torso has the head of a lion, mouth opened, teeth exposed, its front paws stretched in Job's direction. The top third of the monster has the scaly body of a dragon, its long neck arched over Job's head, its mouth opened, dripping saliva in anticipation of the kill.[28] A third way of depicting Satan is the use of a combination of anthropomorphic and monster forms. This mixed type is present in a twelfth-century miniature, also of Job 2:7, which depicts a prone Job under assault from three directions: a black serpentine figure with two jackal-like heads coils around his midsection and between his legs; an orange lion attacks Job's head from the rear; and hovering above and to the front, a black, winged figure with a human face and human hands drives a sword into Job's chest.[29]

Neither the biblical text nor the LXX describe the satan as directly involved in the destruction of Job's property and children. The Sabeans carry off Job's oxen and donkeys and kill his servants (Job 1:15); "the fire of God from heaven" (LXX: "fire fell from heaven [*ek tou ouranou*]") consumes the sheep and their attendants

(1:16); the Chaldeans carry off the camels and kill the servants (1:17); and "a great wind" from the desert collapses the house and kills Job's children (1:18). The *T. Job* attributes all these acts of destruction directly to Satan (16:2–4, 17:6–18:1). Here again it is the *Testament*'s version of the story that seeds the imagination of the miniaturists. The "great wind" that in the biblical version killed the children is depicted as the work of several of Satan's black minions, who blow through horn instruments with force sufficient to pull down the foundations of the house on top of the children.[30] Other manuscripts depict Satan himself, again as a black, winged figure, leading away Job's herds and pulling Job along the ground with them, his hands tied, by means of a long rope.[31] The *Testament*'s version of the story omits the role of the four messengers who announce the news of Job's losses. A group of Byzantine manuscripts retain the messengers' role but, consonant with at least some versions of the *Testament,* depict them with dark wings[32] and, in one case, with dark skin,[33] features generally characteristic of Satan.

The influence of the *Testament*'s embellishments of the roles of God and Satan in Job's story, especially on Eastern miniaturists from the fourth to the fifteenth centuries, cannot be doubted. Even so the trajectories of both Eastern and Western Joban interpretation among Christians in the Middle Ages (the latter more indebted to Gregory's allegorical and Christological reading of Job, *Moralia in Job,* Rome, sixth century) was by no means limited to either manuscripts or commentaries. The readers of illuminated manuscripts were typically those who lived in monasteries and castles; the readers of commentaries, those who had the leisure, interest, and ability to ponder them. Most commoners would have depended more on the interpretations of Job they could see in public places, especially in the iconography that adorned the capitals and portals of churches and cathedrals and in the frescoes painted on their walls.[34]

The sculptor of the Romanesque capitals on the twelfth-century La Daurade church in Toulouse, France, crafts a series of scenes interpreting Job 1:13–19, mostly consonant with the biblical version. One capital, however, depicting a gleeful Satan with a grotesque head striding across Job's dead children, is attuned to the *Testament*'s version.[35] Two capitals of the twelfth-century church of Saint-André-le-Bas in Vienne, France, show King Job on his throne, surrounded by his wife and a beggar who extends his right hand in the hope of receiving something from Job. The capital on the left adds a fourth figure to this scene. Almost hidden behind the beggar, this figure displays the facial features of Satan. It is an effective way of suggesting, following the *Testament*'s account of Satan disguising himself as beggar (7:1–3), that the beggar is Satan's agent.[36] Of medieval Joban iconography, perhaps the most evocative is located on the north portal of Chartres Cathedral. In the top half of the scene, God, flanked by two angels, looks toward the viewer, as if unaware or disinterested in the scene unfolding below. The scene below places Job's three friends on his left, his wife to his right. In the middle Satan places his right hand on Job's head, his left on Job's feet. The vicelike grip indicates the intent to buckle Job into death. At the penultimate moment, the sculptor freezes the action, focusing the viewer's attention on Satan's grotesque face, tongue extended, turned toward the seemingly implacable God above, as if waiting for permission to finish the job.[37]

Along with the Joban sculptures that often adorned the exteriors of medieval cathedrals and churches, worshippers would be instructed in the interpretation of Job by the frescoes that covered the nave and altar of public worship spaces. Among many examples Bartolo di Fredi's frescoes of biblical scenes in the fourteenth-century basilica of the San Gimignano Collegiata in Tuscany may be singled out.[38] Along the walls of the left aisle, progressing toward the central altar, di Fredi painted a double row of rectangular scenes with a series of lunettes above.[39] The lunettes depict creation scenes, all from Genesis (God's creation of the world, the creation of man, the divine charge to exercise dominion, the creation of woman, and the commandment against eating the forbidden fruit). Immediately below the lunettes, the first series of rectangular frescoes extend the Old Testament story with representations of the killing of Abel, the building of the Ark, the animals entering the Ark, the sacrifice of Noah after the flood, the drunkenness of Noah, the separation of Abraham and Lot, Joseph's dream, and Joseph's betrayal by his brothers. The second row of frescoes continues the Old Testament story with representations from the lives of Joseph (his forgiveness of his brothers), Moses (leading the Israelites out of Egypt, on Mount Sinai with Joshua), and Job. Five scenes, more than those allotted for any other biblical character on the entire wall, including Moses, are devoted to representations from Job 1–2: Satan receiving permission to tempt Job, the killing of Job's servants and animals, the destruction of Job's house and children, Job's blessing of God in the midst of calamity, and the arrival of Job's friends. These frescoes provide yet another indicator that for many ordinary people in the Middle Ages, the major message of the book of Job could be discerned from the prologue.

The first three scenes in the Joban series are particularly instructive for our consideration of postbiblical characterizations not only of Job but also of God and Satan. The first scene represents King Job and his queen sitting at a banquet table. In front of them and to their left, attendants set the table with food, as musicians (two with trumpets, one with a drum, another with a harp) provide accompanying music. To their right a servant holding a basket distributes its contents to a group of others who appear to have come begging for food. Two dogs underneath the royal table help themselves to the scraps on the floor. The depiction of Job as a ruling king, a detail not found in the Old Testament, may be explained by the embellishments in both the LXX (42:17d) and the *Testament* (1:1, 20:4–6, 28:7,

29:4). The depiction of Job's charity toward others, another embellishment to the biblical story (see Job 29:12–16, 30:25, 31:16–23), almost certainly draws upon the *Testament*'s detailed account of Job's philanthropy (9–15, 44:1–45:3, 53:1–4). Di Fredi framed this banquet scene by placing it within a large balconied setting that includes three onlookers who are leaning over the banister as they watch the happenings below them. At the top left, as if they were also included among these spectators, di Fredi painted a heavenly council scene, which sticks more closely to the biblical version. In the center of a golden aureole, God extends his right hand. Immediately surrounding and connected to the aureole, four angels robbed in white, two on each side, form the inner circle of God's confidantes. To the right, slightly removed from these angels, a black, winged Satan stands with his arms crossed over his chest. He looks in God's direction, toward the extended hand that gives the permission to attack Job he has requested.[40] A similar council scene appears in the second fresco of the series, which depicts the killing of Job's servants and animals. In this scene, however, there are two Satans, one standing just outside God's inner circle, arms still crossed, the other, his duplicate in form and color, hovering in the top middle of the scene. While the first Satan is stationary, eyes fixed on God, his double simultaneously wields a sword, a gesture of assault replicated by the soldiers below, who are beheading Job's servants.[41] The third in the series, depicting the collapse of Job's house and the deaths of his children, shows only one Satan, the same black, winged figure from the preceding fresco, now blowing through a horn, thus producing gusts of wind that leave everything below in ruins.

In sum, beginning with the *Testament*'s embellishment of Job 1–2, postbiblical characterizations of God and Satan move in opposite directions. The biblical story, essentially followed by the LXX, connects Job's sufferings to a conversation between God and the satan. The satan's/devil's association with the heavenly council is portrayed somewhat ambiguously in the MT and the LXX: Is he one "among" the heavenly beings (MT)? Is he one who comes "with them" (LXX), perhaps as an intruder? The exegetical difference between the linguistic options seems slight. Either way the satan is involved in heavenly deliberations; either way God is complicit in the sufferings Job experiences. The *Testament* omits the council scenes, thus canceling the interpretive possibility embedded in the biblical story, that "for no reason" or some undisclosed reason, God has targeted a "blameless and upright" servant for misfortune. Instead the *Testament* gives Satan his own story. Satan is the one who deceives humans (2:3). A deceiver he may be, but in the *Testament*'s version it is Job, fully informed of the consequences, who decides to attack Satan, not the satan who asks God for permission to attack Job, as in the biblical account. The battle that ensues is between Job and Satan—not Satan and God—and because Job's defeat of Satan is never in doubt, God's primary role in the drama is reduced to awarding the crown when Job's predetermined victory is complete (4:10; cf.43:13–17).

The *Testament*'s account becomes the primary repository for Eastern, and to a lesser extent Western, Joban interpretive strategies. In the East, Byzantine illuminated manuscripts, especially ninth- through twelfth-century manuscripts, draw upon the *Testament*'s embellishments to depict Satan as one whose disguised powers on earth have no connection with God's intent or will. Satan is other than God; he is black, monstrous, and hostile to the God who sits in heaven and confers with his angelic attendants. Satan's disguises, as winged humans and as animals, underscore the Byzantine conceptualization of Satan as God's always defeatable, demonic opponent. Joban iconography and frescoes from the Middle Ages, some indebted to Eastern influences, others to commentaries and expositions on Job that are more likely drawing upon Western sources (especially Gregory's *Moralia*), extend the embellished interpretation of Job to commoners, whose access to Job's story is primarily restricted to what they can see in the sculptured capitals and portals that adorn the exteriors of their churches and cathedrals and the frescoes that fill up the interior walls of their public worship spaces. An ordinary worshipper entering the sanctuary and approaching the high altar would, according to the evidence surveyed here, have walked through a pictorial reminder of the major Old Testament and New Testament exemplars of faith who illumine the path for those who would be obedient to God. Among these exemplars is Job, whose story, reduced to the major episodes of Job 1–2 and as interpreted and reinterpreted, encourages the faithful to remember that despite all trials and temptations, God can and will secure the ultimate victory for all believers.

Medieval Jewish Commentary on Job 1–2 from Saadiah Gaon to Maimonides: Reading Job as a Divine Test or Wager

Jewish commentators were also keenly interested in the book of Job, especially during the medieval period. By one estimate no less than seventy-six Jewish commentaries were produced between 900–1500.[42] Of these I single out two works for discussion here: Saadiah Gaon's (882–942) *The Book of Theodicy*[43] and Maimonides's (1138–1204) *The Guide of the Perplexed.* Although these works are similar in some aspects of their treatment of the book, they represent two quite different readings of the roles played by God and Satan in Job 1–2. At the center of their disagreement is whether Satan's role is part of a *divine trial,* which confirms God's providential care of Job (Saadiah), or part of a *divine wager,* which intentionally raises philosophical questions about God's wisdom and knowledge (Maimonides).

Saadiah is widely recognized as the first major Jewish thinker to compose a systematic account of the concepts of Judaism. The aim of this work, *The Book of*

Beliefs and Convictions, was to establish the coherency of Mosaic thought when tested against philosophical reasoning.[44] Among the issues Saadiah addresses is the problem of evil as discussed in Jewish and Islamic treatises of his day.[45] If the moral teaching of the Torah is both absolute and universal, Saadiah argues, a defense of God's moral governance of the world, especially when measured against human suffering, is necessary. Toward this end he devotes considerable attention to explaining the reasons for suffering in a world created by a good and gracious God. First, suffering is a means by which a righteous God punishes sin; punishment in this lifetime, Saadiah says, makes it possible for sinners to be rewarded fully in the world to come. Second, God uses suffering as a trial, again for the benefit of the righteous, in some cases so that they may demonstrate the integrity of their devotion, thereby earning extra reward in heaven, in other cases so that they may demonstrate their worthiness of having been favored with God's blessing.[46] Both these explanations for suffering lay the conceptual groundwork for Saadiah's commentary on Job, aptly titled, from this perspective, *The Book of Theodicy*—the book in defense of God's justice.

In the introduction to *The Book of Theodicy,* Saadiah cites three reasons why the "Lord God of Israel" merits praise and thanksgiving: the "beneficence and bounty" God manifests in creating the world; the "grace and beneficence" God displays in revealing "divine commandments and prohibitions"; and God's "beneficence" in "creating suffering, sickness, and injury . . . in the interest of humanity."[47] The last of these reasons, the divine gift of suffering, is always purposive, always consonant with God's goodness and grace, for it serves to discipline and instruct, to purge and punish sin, and to test "the upright servant, whose Lord knows that he will bear sufferings loosed upon him and hold steadfast in his uprightness."[48] In none of these reasons for praising God, including, especially, God's "creation" of suffering, can God be accused of the "least injustice."[49]

To reinforce this assessment, Saadiah turns to the "prophet Job," the "one righteous person who was tested and bore the test with fortitude that was acknowledged."[50] Setting up the commentary that follows, Saadiah announces in advance the conclusion toward which careful exegesis of the text will lead:

> Therefore the Allwise caused [the account of Job] to be written for us and set out as a paradigm for us to learn from and adapt ourselves to patient acceptance, that we might know, when sufferings and calamities befall us, that they must be of one or two causes: either they are to be called punishments, and we must search out the relevant shortcomings and remove them and improve our actions. . . . Or they are a trial from the Allwise, which we must bear steadfastly, after which He will reward us. Thus, if we have searched ourselves and found nothing requiring such punishments, we know that they were unprovoked and we call them a test and

bear them patiently. . . . In neither case do we ascribe any injustice to the Creator. Rather we confirm the description He gave of Himself in His Scripture, *The Lord is just in the midst thereof,* etc. (Zeph 3:5). And that is why this book is given the title *The Book of Theodicy.*[51]

The commentary proper comprises a close, philologically informed, interpretation of the "plain" sense of the text. The commentary on Job 1 begins with "the truth about . . . the *land of Uz.*" In Saadiah's reading Uz is the home of both Job, a historical descendant of Abraham[52] who lived during the period of the exodus from Egypt, and of Satan, a human being and the leader of a group of human beings in the land of Uz who are envious of Job's wealth and claim that he only serves God for the reward. Satan cannot be an angel or heavenly being, Saadiah asserts, because "all monotheists agree that the Creator made his angels, who minister to Him, in the knowledge that they would not disobey Him. . . . [Satan's opposition to God] is among the most egregious acts of rebellion."[53] Knowing that suffering will redound to Job's benefit, God executes Satan's wishes and afflicts Job in order to prove that Job is worthy of divine favor. Saadiah sums up as follows: "I would say that for any prophet or upright servant of God defamed by slanderers as Job was, it would be fitting for God to try him so as to clear him of their outrageous charges."[54]

A final observation concerning Saadiah's Job commentary is in order. While he affirms Job as a universal model of faithful endurance for all people—as he puts it, Job is a "lesson to all creation"[55]— Saadiah also sees Job as addressing the specific plight of Jewish people, whose experience of exile raises acute questions about the "rewards" for faithful obedience to divine commandments. If the reward for obedience to God's word is suffering that threatens extinction, then how can the costs of fidelity to God ever be justified? In response Saadiah argues that "God has brought humiliation on the Jews in order that they not be accused of obeying Him for the wrong reasons."[56] As we shall see, Saadiah's assertion that Job is both a theological and ethical model for faithful Jewish suffering throughout history seeds a significant trajectory of postbiblical Jewish commentary.[57]

Maimonides represents a major shift in Jewish thinking during the Middle Ages. Writing some two hundred years after Saadiah, Maimonides does not so much abandon the plain reading of the text that remained prominent during his day as subsume it under a larger synthesis of biblical, rabbinic, and philosophical wisdom. While Saadiah and other Jewish commentators were not averse to philosophical reasoning, Maimonides drew upon Aristotelian thought to develop a comprehensive framework for addressing philosophically problematic biblical texts and issues. The culmination of this effort, *The Guide of the Perplexed,* is aptly named. Here Maimonides addresses those who "remain in a state of perplexity and confusion" as to whether the validity of the Law is to be established by religious conviction or by the intellect, by an internal "divine science" of the soul or an external "natural science" of the mind.[58] The objective is to explain both the public teaching of the Law, which is addressed to every Jew, and the "secrets" of the Law, which can only be apprehended by those whose intellects have been perfected.[59] The *Guide* is structured in three parts: part 1, "Account of the Beginning," considers views regarding God and the angels; part 2, "Account of the Chariot," considers views regarding prophecy (subsumed under the imagery of Ezekiel); and part 3, "Providence," considers views relating to divine providence, the problem of evil, and the rationality of God's commandments and actions. Maimonides places Job at the center of his discussion of divine providence (3:22–23). Almost half of this section on the book of Job—nearly the whole of chapter 22—is devoted to Maimonides's views on the prologue, specifically the roles played by God and Satan. As Maimonides puts it, within the "extraordinary and marvelous" story of Job, and especially through the discourse between God and Satan, "great enigmas are solved, and truths than which none is higher become clear."[60]

Maimonides begins by asserting that the story of Job is a "parable intended to set forth the opinions of people concerning providence" (3.22.486). Two issues present themselves immediately: the affirmation of the widely held Talmudic view that Job is fictional literature and the assessment that the story is an authoritative treatment of divine providence. The latter should be discussed before proceeding, because Maimonides's discussion of Job in 3.22–23 assumes the primary discussion of providence in 3:17–18, in which Maimonides reviews and assesses five opinions about providence (3.17.464–74). (1) The Epicurean view is that there is no providence at all, because "there is no one who orders, governs, or is concerned with anything" (3.17.464). Whatever happens in the world happens by chance. (2) Aristotle's view is that God exercises general providence over certain things—the spheres and what is in them, which remain "permanent in a changeless state"— but not over the circumstances of individual species of plants, animals, or human beings, whose existence is always subject to chance (3.17.465). (3) The Ash'ariyya school of Islamic thought understands divine providence to be absolute; everything is determined by God's inscrutable will and purpose. The righteous may suffer, the wicked may prosper, and in this there is no injustice, for everything is permissible in divine governance. (4) The Mu'tazila school of Islamic thought understands all of God's commandments, prohibitions, rewards, and punishments to be determined by wisdom. There can be no divine injustice, even when a righteous person suffers, for in such cases, consonant with God's wisdom, the reward in the world-to-come will be greater. (5) "The Law of Moses Our Master" is that God's providence is executed through a just distribution of rewards and punishments: "all the calamities that befall men and the good things that come to men . . .

are all of them determined according to the deserts of the men concerned through equitable judgment in which there is no injustice whatever" (3.17.469).

While affirming the Law of Moses as "our opinion," Maimonides nonetheless adopts a revised Aristotelian distinction between general and individual providence. God's general providence is stable and unchanging, as Aristotle says, but God also exercises a general providence in the realm of human beings, based on the perfection of intellect (3.17.474). In 3:18 Maimonides explains how God's providence watches over human beings according to the measure of their perfection and excellence. Divine providence is calibrated to different grades of human perfection, that is, "to their nearness to or remoteness from God. . . . Those who are near to him are exceedingly well protected . . . whereas those who are far from him are given over to whatever may befall them" (3.18.476). To reinforce his argument, Maimonides cites exemplars from Israel's ancestral history—Abraham, Isaac, and Jacob—each of whom attests to divine providence watching over them "according to the measure of their perfection" (3.18.475). None of these however equals the witness of Job, whose story, as Maimonides endeavors to make clear in 3:22–23, is "one to which extraordinary notions and things that are the mystery of the universe is attached" (3.22.486).[61]

The discussion of Job begins with the assertion that it is a "parable" about divine providence. Thus at the outset Maimonides disagrees with Saadiah on the historicity of the book. The fictional aspect of the book is reinforced by Satan, a clearly allegorical figure "in the view of everyone endowed with intellect" (3.22.486). Maimonides then offers a number of cryptic comments about Satan's role, a summation of what he has understood from reading the Sages. (1) Satan presents himself before God only *after* the sons of God ("The sons of God came to present themselves before the Lord, and the Satan came also among them" [Job 1:6]), a way of speaking "only used with regard to one who has come without having been for his own sake the object of an intention or having been sought for his own sake." (2) Because Satan is said to have roamed all over the earth, Maimonides concludes that "there is no relationship whatever between him and the upper world, in which there is no road for him" (3.22.487). (3) God delivers Job into the hands of Satan, and Satan, not God, causes Job's suffering. Concerning why God did this, there are different opinions put forth in the story itself by Job and his friends, though all assume that God was culpable. Even so "the most marvelous and extraordinary thing about this story is the fact that knowledge is not attributed in it to Job. He is not said to be wise or a comprehending or an intelligent man. Only moral virtue and righteousness in action are ascribed to him. If he had been wise, his situation would not have been obscure for him" (3.22.487). (4) In the second encounter between Satan and God (Job 2:1–6), Maimonides reports insights that come to him "through something similar to prophetic revelation":

The words "And Satan came also among them" (Job 2:1) reaffirm the distinction between Satan and God's attendants but also indicate that Satan "has a certain portion," inferior though it may be, in contributing positively to the perfection of Job's intellect (3.22.488). (5) Satan may roam over the earth accomplishing certain actions, but "he is forbidden to gain dominion over the soul" ("Only spare his soul" [Job 2:6]) (3.22.488). (6) For those who understand the teachings of the Sages, Satan is the "evil inclination," the "angel of death." Thus, as the Sages say, "every man is accompanied by two angels, one to his right and the other to his left. . . . one is good and the other evil" (3.22.487–88).

The remainder of Maimonides's comments on Job (3.23) deal with the general agreement between Job and his friends that God has caused Job's misfortunes. The purpose of the story, Maimonides says, is not to show their agreement but to invite reflection on their differences. Among the friends Maimonides identifies Bildad with Saadiah's view that Job's afflictions are but a divine test; if one passes the test, the rewards will be increased. This is an incorrect view of God's providence, Maimonides asserts. The differences between Job and his friends "ha[ve] perplexed people," Maimonides observes, but the opinion attributed to Elihu, the friend whose counsel is "superior," trumps all others. "The notion of His providence is not the same as the notion of our providence; nor is the notion of His governance of things created by Him the same as the notion of our governance of that which we govern" (with reference to Job 34:21–22) (3.22.496). A crucial part of Job's learning process is the lesson that his imperfect intellect, informed by only a literal reading of the Law, must be and could be transformed into perfection by suffering. Once Job learns this lesson, he becomes the central character in a story that supersedes even the Torah in explaining the import of divine providence.[62] Maimonides ends his discussion of the book of Job with an exhortation:

> This is the object of the Book of Job as a whole; I refer to the establishing of this foundation for the belief and the drawing attention to the inference to be drawn from natural matters, so that you should not fall into error and seek to affirm your imagination that His knowledge is like our knowledge or that His purpose and His providence and His governance are like our purpose and our providence and our governance. If man knows this, every misfortune will be borne lightly by him. And misfortunes will not add to his doubts regarding the deity and whether He does or does not know and whether He exercises providence or manifests neglect, but will, on the contrary, add to his love. (3.22.497)

To whom is Maimonides's exhortation addressed? Two centuries earlier Saadiah argued that Job's sufferings, historically anchored to the period of Israel's exodus from Egypt, have more than a universal significance. They are also a particular model for Jews, in any time place and time in history, who experience inexplicable suffering. Maimonides reads Job differently. Although he agrees that Job's (fictional) story has both a universal and particularistic trajectory, he limits the latter to the uneducated masses of Jews in his own time, who must become philosophically educated, like Job, if they are to attain the intellectual perfection that enables them to comprehend the truth of God's providence.[63]

In sum medieval Jewish commentary on Job 1–2 revolves around two axes, which can be generally distinguished by the conventional labels "conservative" and "liberal."[64] The conservative approach is represented by Saadiah, who interprets Job as a historical figure confronted by Satan, a fellow human being who is envious of his prosperity. Gifted by God with the experience of suffering, Job demonstrates for Jews of all times the virtue of patient endurance of whatever God commands in a test whose end results are known in advance. The liberal approach is represented by Maimonides, who interprets the "fiction" of Job's story as a philosophical summons to enlightenment; the intellect of the righteous must be perfected, and to this end suffering is the agent of the inscrutable journey toward union with God. Trial by divine testing (Saadiah) assumes that God's providence, ultimately, is beyond question. Trial by divine wager (Maimonides) renders God's ultimate providence vulnerable to human apprehension, which requires a decision on whether to heed the angel on the left or the angel on the right, one good, the other evil. The final decision on God's providence, Maimonides says, rests on how human beings respond to this challenge.

"Give the Devil His Due"

The debate during the Middle Ages between a literal interpretation of Job 1–2 (Saadiah) and a parabolic or fictional assessment (Maimonides) was by no means limited to Jewish commentary. One needs only consider Aquinas's literal interpretation, advanced significantly by Calvin, to be reminded that both Christian and Jewish interpreters during the Middle Ages remained preoccupied with these issues.

Johann Wolfgang von Goethe's (1749–1832) *Faust,* the first serious literary attempt to "give the devil his due," signals a radical departure from this intraclerical debate.[65] Goethe clearly models his principal characters, Faust and Mephistopheles, on the biblical version of Job and the satan, but his genius is to construct them not as single-issue theological spokespersons for good and evil but instead as genuinely complex persons whose perspectives on the realities of life leave no presumed truth unexamined—or unmocked.[66] Faust is no righteous sufferer who endures whatever God decrees; he is an unscrupulous scholar who will do whatever it takes to discover "what secret force / Hides in the world and rules its course" (lines 386–87).[67] Goethe's Mephistopheles, widely recognized as "one of the most inspired characters in the whole of world literature,"[68] relentlessly exploits the human quest for happiness by exposing the questionable motives hidden behind even the most noble efforts to escape dismay and disappointment. Mephistopheles may be "a spiritual lunatic," but "like many lunatics, he is extremely plausible and cunning."[69]

Goethe recasts Job 1–2 as a "Prologue in Heaven" between God, three archangels (Raphael, Gabriel, and Michael), and Mephistopheles. The archangels praise God's creation. Mephisto, a "menial" who concedes that he cannot speak as "nobly" as God's angelic "staff," offers a dissonant, albeit sympathetic, appraisal of creation's burden for human beings that includes a pointed gibe at the creator, who he describes as a "small god of the world . . . more brutish than is any brute" (276–86). In bringing Mephistopheles on stage before God, Goethe reverses the sequence of the Joban prologue by transferring the initiative for the conversation in heaven about Faust, like Job, God's "servant" (299), to God's interlocutor. In response to God's questions—"Do you come only to accuse? / Does nothing on the earth seem to you right? . . . Do you know Faust?" (294–95, 297)—Mephistopheles engages God as follows:

MEPHISTO: He serves you most peculiarly, I think . . .
    His spirit's ferment drives him far,
    And he half knows how foolish is his quest:
    From heaven he demands the fairest star,
    And from the earth all joys he thinks best;
    And all that's near and all that's far
    Cannot soothe the upheaval in his breast.

THE LORD: Though now he serves me but confusedly,
    I shall soon lead him where the vapor clears.
    The gardener knows, however small the tree,
    That bloom and fruit adorn its later years. (300–311)

Following this exchange Mephisto makes a wager with God: "You'll lose him yet to me / If you will graciously connive / That I may lead him carefully" (312–14). God responds by granting Mephisto permission to "clasp" Faust and "lead him down . . . your own abysmal course" (325), ever confident that Faust, "a good man in his darkling aspiration," will "remember the right road throughout the quest" (327–29). The last words in the "Prologue in Heaven" are Mephisto's:

    I like to see the Old Man now and then
    And try to be not too uncivil.
    It's charming in a noble squire when
    He speaks humanely with the very Devil. (350–53)

For the remainder of Goethe's account, God is a nonfactor, never speaking and never represented, except obliquely (with reference to the "Spirit" [483, 1447, 1607], the "choir of angels" [738; cf. 2133, 3798–99, 3813–14, 3825–27, 3833], and, especially in part 2, the "circle of spirits"). Unlike the satan, his counterpart in the Joban prologue, Mephisto is, however, a constant presence in Goethe's play. In Goethe's view God not only tolerates Mephisto's role in the heavenly court but also confesses a special fondness for this "knavish jester" (337–43).

Part 1 of the drama begins on Easter eve, with a despondent Faust sitting in his book-lined study. Even though he knows himself to be smarter than "all the shysters, / the doctors, and teachers, and scribes" (366–67), he concedes that after ten years of study, he "knows nothing"; he remains "the wretched fool [he] was before" (359). He "yields" (377) to magic in the hope that some unknown spirit may reveal what "secret force / Hides in the world and rules its course" (382–83). The chiming of church bells announce the dawn of Easter, a chorus of angels proclaims the resurrection message—"Christ is arisen . . . Leave behind prison / fetters and gloom! . . . For you the Master is near" (737, 796, 798–99, 806)—but Faust remains unmoved: "Although I hear the message, I lack all faith or trust" (765). Walking outside the city on Easter morning, Faust sees the resurrection joy others experience, but he complains to Wagner, his assistant, that he is conflicted by two brotherly souls fighting within him for supremacy: one clings to the world in "grossly loving zest"; the other "rises forcibly in quest / Of rarified ancestral spheres" (1112–17). When Faust returns to his study, a black dog he has encountered along the way follows him inside. As he resumes his quest for revelation concerning the mysteries of the world, the dog begins to snarl, distracting Faust from his ruminations (1202–9).

Faust gradually recognizes that the black dog is but one of several disguises Mephisto assumes during the course of the unfolding drama (a fiery phantom, 480–512; a traveling scholar, 1321–1525, a noble squire, 1532–1867). Once he "sees" Mephisto as the "spirit that negates" (1338), as "part of the darkness which gave birth to light" (1350), and as the "peculiar son of chaos" (1384), Faust suggests a pact by which he hopes to gain access to Mephisto's occult powers. The pact is triggered by his Joblike curses on human existence, capped off by a curse on love, hope, faith, and, above all, Joban patience, which is for him "a weight . . . a life I hate" (1587–1606).

Goethe lays out clearly the conditions of the pact Faust initiates with Mephisto:

> Mephisto: If you want to make your way
> Through the world with me united,
> I should surely be delighted

To be yours, as of now,
Your companion, if you allow;
And if you like the way I behave,
I shall be your servant, or your slave. . . .

Here you shall be master, I be bond,
And at your nod I'll work incessantly;
But when we meet again *beyond,*
Then you shall do the same for me.

Faust: Of the beyond I have no thought . . .
My joys come from this earth, and there,
That sun has burnt on my despair:
Once I have left those, I don't care:
What happens is of no concern. . . .

Mephisto: So minded, dare it cheerfully.
Commit yourself and you shall see
My arts with joy. I'll give you more
Than any man has seen before.
      (1642–48, 1656–59, 1660, 1663–65, 1671–74)

Faust signs the pact in blood (1737), an affirmation that signals he will not abort the contract with Mephisto under any circumstances. When he reiterates his commitment by saying "Let our passions drink their fill! . . . Let every wonder be at hand!," Mephisto responds with an invitation to proceed. "You're welcome to whatever gives you pleasure / Help yourself and don't be coy" (1751, 1753, 1764–65).

Goethe turns the Joban wager between God and the satan on its head. He recasts the bet between God and the satan that suffering would subvert Job's piety into a wager between Faust and Mephisto that understands unrestrained joy and pleasure as the highest desire of human beings. The pursuit of happiness, not the avoidance of suffering, Goethe's Mephisto suggests, is the greatest temptation of all to those who would conform their lives to the directives and promises of God. As Mephisto says to Faust after their bargain is struck, "Follow the ancient text and my relation, the snake . . . / We'll see the small world, then the larger one. / You will reap profit and have fun / As you sweep through the course with ease" (2049, 2053–54). Forgoing Easter's promise, Faust agrees to join Mephisto on a magic carpet ride through various pleasures that promise he can at last "cast dusty knowledge overboard, / And bathe in dew until restored" (396–97). In consort with Mephisto, he experiences the "joy" of drinking in "jolly company" with those who know "life can be fun" (2159–60); the freedom and fun of imbibing the witch's elixir of life (2347–2601); and the sensual pleasure of relationship with a young maiden named Gretchen (or Margaret), a love affair so torrid and true that Faust is willing to commit murder to sustain it (3703–14).

Faust learns to love. This achievement, taken solely on its own, may suffice as evidence that Mephisto has won his wager with God. Faust affirms that one glance from Gretchen "gives far more pleasure / Than all the wisdom of the world" (3079–80); he commends Mephisto for giving him happiness that makes all desire languish (3240–50); he affirms that "feeling is all"—to attribute such bliss to any other name, like "God," is but "sound and smoke / Befogging heaven's blazes" (3456–58). These and other such affirmations hint that Faust, with Mephisto's help, has successfully "cast dusty knowledge overboard, and bathe[d] in dew until restored."

Does Mephisto "save" Faust from a misplaced trust in God's providence? Goethe's answer seems to be a strategically qualified yes. Mephisto enables Faust to be "enlivened once again" by his "many-hued reflection" on love and strife (part 2, 4679, 4727), though this reflection is but another iteration of the reflections that, according to part 1 of Goethe's drama, Faust had sought to escape. Furthermore, despite God's confident prediction that Faust would in the end remember and choose the "right road" toward the attainment of God's promises ("Prologue in Heaven," 329), Faust remembers but does not choose the path God had ordained (part 2, 11403–7). In the end Faust is "saved," but not in the conventional Christian sense.[70] In his old age, he affirms that Mephisto, not God, has enabled him to attain the "highest wisdom that I own / The best that mankind ever knew" (part 2, 11573–11574). God had earlier asserted that "man errs as long as he will strive" ("Prologue in Heaven," 317). In the end, however, God seems now to be instructed (or overruled) by angels who carry Faust's soul to heaven (part 2, 11934–37).

Goethe's characterization of Mephisto is still more complex and thus more evocative. Mephisto, observing Faust's last breaths, concedes that in one way he has "resisted all my toil" (part 2, 11591). Even so, as Faust is laid in his grave, Mephisto watches over him, lest grave robbers "rob the Devil of his soul" (part 2, 11612–15), thus denying him the ultimate reward his pact with Faust had assured. Despite Mephisto's vigilance, angels come and take Faust's soul to heaven, leaving Mephisto to complain about the injustice done him: "Who will enforce the rights I possess?" (part 2, 11834).

This turn of events reinforces the supreme irony in Goethe's recasting of the Joban story. Faust may be a distant reconfiguration of the biblical Job, but Goethe construes Mephisto—the quintessential devil—as the most authentic Joban figure in the drama. Mephisto has entered into a contract with Faust; he has scrupulously fulfilled the conditions of this contract; and now he is the one who suffers—like the biblical Job—when the terms of the agreed-upon contract are violated. The most telling and instructive lines of Goethe's Mephisto are these: "How do I

[Mephisto] feel! Like Job, with boil on boil, / I see myself, I shudder and recoil" (part 2, 11809–12).

Mephisto is clearly no candidate for sainthood. He is cynical, unscrupulous, diabolical in the most literal way. Nevertheless Goethe constructs him as thoughtful, introspective, even sympathetic to the human struggle to live and prosper. "Man moves me to compassion," he says to God at the outset, "so wretched is his plight. / I have no wish to cause him further woe" ("Prologue in Heaven," 297–98). And in the strictest terms, he acts with a certain integrity, a fidelity to stated commitments, demonic though they are, that renders him vulnerable to betrayal, loss, and despair. Goethe's humanization of both God's affection for Mephisto ("It's charming . . . when He [God] speaks humanely with the Devil ["Prologue in Heaven," 353–54]) and Mephisto's self-incriminating ruminations on grief (part 2, 11835–43) are, as Kaufmann discerns, "acidly penetrating."[71] In Goethe's rendering Mephisto takes his initial cue from the lines spoken by the satan in Job 1–2. But in the remainder of the drama, Mephisto gradually comes to understand himself as Job.

We began this survey of Goethe's Mephisto with a reference to Orleans's words to Constable in Shakespeare's *Henry* IV, *Part I:* "Give the devil his due." In pondering what we may possibly owe to Goethe for his characterization of the devil, it seems apt to conclude with another Shakespearian quote, this an inviting query from Banquo to Macbeth, who claims to have all knowledge about things evil: "What! Can the devil speak true?" (*Macbeth* 1.3.108).

Carl Jung: "God Is at Odds with Himself"

A number of twentieth-century readings accent the dark side of God as revealed in Job 1–2.[72] For my purposes here, I single out Carl Jung's (1875–1961) *Answer to Job.*[73] As a practicing psychiatrist, Jung took issue with Sigmund Freud by advocating a theory of collective unconsciousness, based on his reading of the Bible, especially the book of Job, that subjects God—"an antimony," "a totality of opposites" (10)—to psychological analysis. He effectively puts God on the couch.

Jung describes the Joban prologue as the moment when God recognizes that he lacks sufficient self-reflection to make moral judgments. Had God "taken counsel with his own omniscience" when the satan first introduced a "doubting thought" into his consciousness, he would not have exposed a faithful servant such as Job to such a gratuitous moral test (19–20). Yet, as Jung notes, "the really astonishing thing" is that God gives in to the satan's insinuations without thinking (44). God never rebukes the satan, never expresses disapproval of his murderous actions. Why? Because God "projects his own tendency to unfaithfulness upon a scapegoat" (44). Jung explains God's behavior by suggesting that Job's moral superiority forces a jealous God to acknowledge that "man possesses an infinitely small yet more concentrated light than he, Yahweh, possesses" (21).

Jung argues that the ramifications of the prologue drama are consequential for both Job and God. To his horror Job discovers that God "is not human but, in certain respects less than human" (32). Confronted by Job with the moral superiority of "man's godlikeness," God becomes "unsure of his own faithfulness" (45) and thus is forced to recognize antinomies in the divine nature that require deep reflection on God's part. From Jung's perspective God's inner struggle is not finally resolved until God decides to "catch up" to "morally higher" (68) creatures by becoming fully human—in Christ's life and suffering. God "must become man precisely because he has done man a wrong" (69).

Jung's prefacing comments to these discernments are worth noting. He says at the outset that he is not concerned with how ancient readers may have read the book but instead with how modern readers "come to terms with the divine darkness which is unveiled in the Book of Job, and what effect it has" on them. Jung's objective is "to give expression to the shattering emotion that the unvarnished spectacle of divine savagery and ruthlessness produces in us" (4). Near the end of his book, he is more explicit concerning the moral and ethical challenges that the book of Job presents contemporary readers:

> Everything now depends on man: immense power of destruction is given into his hand, and the question is whether he can resist the will to use it, and can temper his will with the spirit of love and wisdom. . . . This involves man in a new responsibility. He can no longer wriggle out of it on the plea of his littleness and nothingness, for the dark God has slipped the atom bomb and chemical weapons into his hands and given him the power to empty out apocalyptic vials of wrath on his fellow creatures. Since he has been granted an almost godlike power, he can no longer remain blind and unconscious. (161, 164)

Jung finds the God who hands over Job willy-nilly to the satan to be a flawed character. Such a God is less than the God human beings expect and deserve. As the "face of boundless evil," as H. G. Wells puts it, this God endorses and inspires inexplicable cruelty among those who tune their moral compass to divine behavior.[74] Such a God is not only not acting like God; this God is actually less than human, for any reasonable human being would necessarily recoil at the thought of killing innocent children just to show off divine powers. As Robert Frost's Job says about God's treatment of him: "'Twas human of you," but "I expected more."[75]

Such readings of God's character effectively turn upside down a central tenet of the Old Testament's moral vision. It is no longer God as creator of the world who models the justice and righteousness upon which the covenantal relationship depends; now human beings must teach God how to be God. Instead of setting their moral compass to the words of the one who says, "I am your God . . . and you shall be my people" (Jer 30:22), God's people, Jung insists, must now reverse the logic, reply back that they are his people, and he must therefore be a God in whom the best of their virtues are writ large.

The ethical dilemma presented by God's characterization in Job 1–2 confronts us with the imperative of dealing with the "dark side" of a God who submits the righteous to suffering "for no reason."[76] It is and should be difficult for readers to accept without question that such acts are compatible with what we expect of divinity. Does the characterization of God in Job 1–2 provide a moral compass that enables modern readers to decide, then act upon, what is right, righteous, and worthy of our highest ethical aspirations? First readings require second and third readings.

In the interim the response to this question by John Barton may be instructive. "I hope the answer is yes, but the Old Testament [and the book of Job] does not make it an easy question to answer; and it gives plenty of ammunition if we want to fight on the other side."[77]

3

THERE WAS ONCE A WOMAN IN THE LAND OF UZ

Job's Wife

> The woman of pride and splendor.
>
> *T. Job* 40:13

> I suppose his [Job's] wife suffered. But whoever wrote the story made nothing of her.
>
> Muriel Spark, *The Only Problem*

> The strength which belongs with faith was no longer hers, and gradually she was also losing the strength which is needed to despair.
>
> Joseph Roth, *Job: The Story of a Simple Man*

The story of Job is primarily about the ordeals of a righteous *man,* and as such it genders the roles of belief and doubt, perseverance and vacillation, as they are enacted within a patriarchal culture of the ancient Near East. Women are also part of Job's life, but they are relegated to the margins of his story.

The prologue merely mentions Job's three daughters (1:2, 4, 13, 18). They are not named, and they do not speak. From the perspective of the narrator, they are little more than props in the story. They are part of the list of "possessions" that establishes Job's prosperity, and like the sheep, camels, oxen, donkeys, and servants, they will be erased from this list as part of a plan to test Job's fidelity that they know nothing about. The epilogue confirms Job's ultimate restoration by providing another list of his possessions, now doubled in number (42:12), including three new daughters. Once again, they do not speak, but they are named with terms signifying their natural beauty—Jemimah ("dove"), Keziah ("cinnamon"), and Keren-happuch ("horn of eyeshadow")—and they are given "an inheritance along with their brothers" (42:14–15), a telltale but undeveloped clue that may suggest a modification of conventional practices in which daughters inherit only when the father has no sons (cf. Nm 27:1–11, 36:1–12). Apart from Bildad's argument that Job suffers because his children sinned (8:4), the dialogues at the center of the book do not mention either Job's daughters or his sons.

Job's wife also plays a minor role in the story, but her characterization is more complex.[1] According to the narrative, she and Job are the sole survivors of calamities that decimate their family. As Job sits in the ashes scratching his sores (2:8), his wife, unnamed and until now unmentioned, speaks the only line she has in the entire book. The New Revised Standard Version's translation represents a conventional rendering: "Do you still persist in your integrity? Curse God, and die" (2:9). This rendering, especially when coupled with Job's rebuke in the following verse—"You speak as any foolish woman would speak" (2:10a)—leaves little doubt that we should read her contribution to the story as wholly negative. She is simply another trial Job must bear.[2]

The Hebrew text contains, however, a number of complexities. First there is no interrogative marker in the text; thus from a grammatical standpoint the wife's first words convey an assertion—"and yet you *still persist in your integrity*" (*'ōděka maḥăzîq bětummātekā*)—not a question. Moreover she uses almost the same words that God uses to express unwavering confidence in Job's ability to withstand any assault on his convictions the satan might try. "He [Job] *still persists in his integrity*" (*wě'ōdennû maḥăzîq bětummātô*)," God says to the satan, "although you incited me against him, to destroy him for no reason" (2:3). A literal reading therefore suggests that Job's wife has watched him withstand every temptation to compromise his integrity, and now she, like God, affirms that he remains the truly righteous person she knows him to be.

Second, the words "*curse God and die*" are curiously ambiguous. This part of the verse in Hebrew reads "*bless (bārēk) God and die*." The prologue and epilogue contain seven occurrences of the verb *bārak*. Three are routinely translated with the normal meaning, "bless" (1:10, 21; 42:12); four, including this statement by Job's wife, are widely read as a euphemism for "curse" (*qālal* [1:5, 11; 2:5, 9]), on the assumption that the author (or a later editor) regarded a text that spoke of cursing God as blasphemous and unacceptable. To discourage this notion, the author supposedly substituted the word *bless* for *curse* and expected readers to recognize that the text had been altered and to resubstitute *curse* at the appropriate place. In 2:9, for example, we are meant to read that Job's wife encouraged him to continue blessing God (cf.1:21), even if he must do so with his dying breath. But we are meant to understand that what she really means is that Job should curse God, which is what the satan has (euphemistically) predicted he would do (1:11, 2:5). We may weigh the merits of this argument—whether to interpret what is said but not meant or what is meant but not said—but the text itself does not linger over such issues.³ Instead it reports that Job dismisses his wife's words, whatever they meant. He concludes that she speaks like a "foolish" (*nĕbālôt* [2:10]) person, a characterization elsewhere applied to those who renounce God (Ps 14:1) and scorn the righteous (Ps 39:8 [MT 39:9]).

Despite his seemingly unqualified rejection of her words, Job's own next words subtly reflect the imprint of his wife's counsel. His first verbal response to loss and brokenness was a simple declarative that echoes traditional affirmations about God's providential oversight of the creaturely journey from mother's womb to earth's grave: "Naked I came from my mother's womb, and naked shall I return there; the Lord gave, and the Lord has taken away; blessed be the name of the Lord" (1:21; cf. Gn 3:19; Pss 104:27–30, 139:13–15; Eccl 5:15; Sir 40:1). After his wife speaks, Job's response shifts from an assertion to a question that strains to remain merely rhetorical: "Surely, (if) we receive the good from God, should we not also receive the bad?" (2:10). With these freighted words, tensively balanced between what Job has affirmed and what he may now be less certain about, the prologue winds its way toward silence, "when no one spoke a word" (2:13).

After seven days and seven nights, the words that break the silence hanging over the ash heap are Job's curses, not blessings (3:1–10). Though his wife has exited the scene, her presence lingers. She has spoken only six Hebrew words. With the first three, she has echoed God's confidence in Job's integrity, which he has exemplified by blessing God in the midst of his suffering. With the next three, she has echoed the satan's prediction that Job will curse God, which seems to be the objective of his words in chapter 3. Her words thus bring together in one speech both sides of the heavenly debate between God and the satan on how Job will respond to undeserved suffering. Job has now both blessed and cursed; like his wife he has combined two seemingly incompatible options in one response. This turn of events would appear to deny a clear victory to either God or the satan, neither of whom, supposedly, had expected that a "blameless and upright" man could both bless and curse God and still maintain his integrity.

By (unwittingly?) enacting his wife's counsel to bless and curse, Job not only stalemates the game in heaven; he also seems to change the rules by which it will be played from this point forward. Victory was to have been determined by testing Job's fidelity to God; when God's blessings are removed, will Job "fear God for nothing (*ḥinnām*)" (1:9; cf. 2:3)? Now the tables are turned, and victory, from Job's point of view, is to be determined by testing God's fidelity to him. Will God affirm that Job "fears God and turns away from evil" when Job's blessings are withdrawn from God? We can sharpen the question by placing God's words on Job's lips: will God remain faithful to Job "for no reason"? Perhaps this is making too much of the contribution of Mrs. Job's one-line, six-word speech. Then again, it is the very ambiguity of the way she speaks, combining antonyms—blessing and cursing—to make an assertion about integrity that prompts Job to combine the antonyms *good* and *bad* (*raʿ*; literally, "evil") with the word *God* into what is arguably the single most important question of the entire book. "Should we accept only good from God and not accept evil?" (2:10 [NJPS]).

After her address to Job in 2:9, Job's wife never speaks again. Job speaks about her only twice more in the rest of the story; in both instances he refers to her as little more than an incidental presence. In 19:17 he says that his wife, along with other persons who now exclude him from their company (19:13–20), finds his breath, or perhaps his very existence, "repulsive." In 31:9–10 he takes an oath, swearing he is innocent of any imaginable crime or misdeed, including adultery (vv. 9–12). If anyone can present evidence of his infidelity, then he will offer his own wife's violation as compensation: "If my loins were seduced by a woman . . . let any man take my wife and grind between her thighs!"[4] Modern sensibilities should cause readers to wince at these references, the first Job's unsupported assertion that his wife has forsaken him, the second his willingness to abandon her if it will advance his claim to innocence, but here again the text passes over them without comment. For the biblical authors, it seems, what Mrs. Job thinks and does is unimportant, and so, apart from her brief appearance in the prologue and these passing words about her in the dialogues, she silently disappears from the story. God does not address her in the speeches from the whirlwind (38–41). The epilogue makes no mention of her in its final report of Job's blessing and restoration (42:7–17); it offers no assessment of her relationship to God or Job; it says nothing about her relationship to her new children or grandchildren; it does not record how long she lived or how she died.

Beyond these references to Job's daughters and his wife, there are only a few scattered and mostly generic statements about the women in Job's world. Both Job and his friends use being "born from a woman" or from a woman's womb as a trope for the burdens and limitations of mortality (3:11–13, 10:18–19, 14:1, 15:14, 25:4; cf. 17:14; 24:20, 21). In the speeches from the whirlwind, God uses similar imagery to question whether Job understands the intricacies of the cosmic birthing processes that God oversees (31:8, 29; cf. 39:1–4). The friends accuse Job of neglecting "widows" and "orphans" (22:9); Job cites his care for "widows" and "orphans" as evidence that he uses his wealth to assist those who are most at risk in his world (29:12–13, 31:17–18, cf. 6:27; 24:3, 7; 27:15).

Altogether these various references to Job's wife, daughters, and other women constitute less than .1 percent of the verses in the book. By any measurement we are justified in concluding that this is a book written by men and primarily for men. It tells a story about undeserved suffering and the possible ways those who "fear God and turn away from evil" may respond to it from a man's perspective. Job is, however, not just any man; he is, as the narrator tells us, the "greatest of all the people of the east" (1:5). God's assessment is still more expansive: "there is no one like him in all the earth" (1:8, 2:3). Against the backdrop of the patriarchal assumptions that shape the biblical writers and their world, Job is therefore an incomparable *pater*, a father who is unequaled in his capacity to provide for the dependents in his household. His children, his wife, their extended families, and his servants are cued by their place in the hierarchy of this world to accept his decisions as requisite for their survival and prosperity. The presenting question of the book—"Have you considered my servant Job?" (1:8, 2:3)—which the narrator attributes to God himself, reflects and reinforces this culturally encoded understanding of Job's importance for those who live in his world. The narrator presumes that anyone who ventures to answer his/God's presenting question knows in advance that they are being summoned to conform their lives to the truth established by this story about the "man in the land of Uz whose name was Job."

Contemporary readers of the book can be expected to respond to the narrator's presenting question with a counterquestion formed by concerns biblical authors did not anticipate. Was there once also a *woman* in the land of Uz? With a fraction of its content, the story acknowledges that the answer is yes, but its affirmation is thinned by the absence of corroborating details. How much can we know about the women in Job's world from his wife's ambiguous one-line speech or from three named daughters who do not speak at all? Should we subordinate our curiosity to a contextualized reading, which privileges the values of the patriarchal culture that shapes this story? Should we learn and value what we can about this culture but insist on pressing its settled perspectives for answers to questions it has missed or dismissed? These and other questions linger for contemporary readers of the book of Job, but before we move to our various ways of answering them, we should pause to consider how the "first" translators and commentators on this book dealt with Mrs. Job's contribution to this ancient story about a righteous man.

There Was Once a Woman in the Land of Uz

The first translators of and commentators on the story of Job as received in the Hebrew text appear to have been fascinated with its brief mention of Job's wife. As rereaders and retellers of the story, they both expanded and transformed the wife's role in ways that had far-reaching consequences for later readers, both Jewish and Christian. Two important exemplars of this approach are the LXX, the Greek translation of the Old Testament that served the early church, which likely dates to the second half of the second century B.C.E., and the pseudepigraphical *Testament of Job*, which dates to the first century B.C.E.–first century C.E.

The Greek book of Job substantially follows the story line in the Hebrew text. An opening prologue is followed by an introductory lament by Job, which leads in turn to an alternating sequence of dialogues between Job and his three friends; a lengthy monologue by Elihu/Elious; two speeches by God, each followed by a response from Job; and a concluding epilogue. The primary differences can be characterized as "abridgments," especially in the dialogues, which are approximately 20 percent shorter than in the Hebrew version, and as "extensions," which occur in both the prologue and the epilogue.[5] Most important for our purposes here is the extension of the prologue by the addition of a substantial speech by Job's wife.

At 2:9 the Greek text expands the wife's speech from one line to a full lament that significantly reshapes what she says to Job.

> Then after a long time had passed, his wife said to him, "How long will you persist and say, 'Look, I will hang on a little longer, while I wait for the hope of my deliverance?' For look, your legacy has vanished from the earth—sons and daughters, my womb's birth pangs and labors, for whom I wearied myself with hardships in vain. And you? You sit in the refuse of worms as you spend the night in the open air. As for me, I am one that wanders about and a hired servant—from place to place and house to house, waiting for when the sun will set, so I can rest from the distresses and griefs that now beset me. Now say some word to the Lord and die!"[6]

In this presentation we learn that Job's wife did not speak impulsively but only "after a long time had passed." The chronological reference, though imprecise, places her by Job's side throughout the ordeal, and thus positions us as close as words can get us to the grief of a mother whose womb has delivered children to lives snatched away prematurely. We look through her eyes at the gruesome sight of her husband's affliction—worms eating their way through a body rotting from the inside out—and feel the effect not only on him but also on her, for as he wastes away night by night, she spends her days roaming like a hired servant from place to place, from house to house, until the setting sun offers the only rest she can find. Her final words are perhaps even more ambiguous than those she speaks in the Hebrew account. She does not urge Job either to "curse" or "bless" God, nor does she speak of how any response he makes might affect his integrity. Instead, on the heels of describing her own weariness and sorrow, she implores Job to "say some word to the Lord (*eipon ti rhēma eis kyrion*), and die!" Death, it seems, would be welcomed relief for them both.

This description of a mother's grief concerning what befalls her children is similar to an account in the apocryphal book of Tobit, also dated to the late third or early second century B.C.E. The plotline focuses on Tobit, a righteous Jew living in exile, his wife, Anna, and their son, Tobias. Like Job, Tobit's exemplary piety leads to his loss of property and physical affliction, in this case blindness, and like Job (cf. Job 3), Tobit prays in a moment of despair that God will take his life. As the story unfolds, Tobit remembers some money he had left in his homeland, and against Anna's wishes he sends Tobias to retrieve it. Two interchanges between Tobit and his wife provide commentary on a mother's grief when her husband's decisions put her children in jeopardy. In the first, after Tobit sends Tobias away with a kiss, saying, "Have a safe journey," "his mother began to weep, and said to Tobit, 'Why is it that you have sent *my child* away? Is he not the staff of our hand [that is, the person they both rely upon[7]] as he goes in and out before us?' . . . Tobit said to her, 'Do not worry; our child will leave in good health and return to us in good health. Your eyes will see him on the day when he returns to you in good health. Say no more!' . . . So she stopped weeping" (5:17–21, 6:1 [NRSV]; emphasis added).

When Tobias's return takes longer than expected, both Tobit and Anna begin to worry. Tobit remains cautiously confident; but as their next exchange indicates, Anna's worries are deeper than his assurances:

> "*My child* has perished and he is no longer among the living." And she began to weep and mourn for her son, saying, "Woe to me, *my child,* the light of my eyes, that I let you make the journey." But Tobit kept saying to her, "Be quiet and stop worrying, my dear; he is all right. Probably something unexpected has happened there. . . . Do not grieve for him, my dear; he will soon be here." She answered him, "Be quiet yourself! Stop trying to deceive me! *My child* has perished." She would rush out every day and watch the road her son had taken, and would heed no one. When the sun had set she would go in and mourn all night long, getting no sleep at all. (10:4–7 [NRSV]; emphasis added)

In both the LXX and Tobit, we can detect initial moves to expand upon the book of Job's template for a wife's role. In different ways both provide clues to a woman's/wife's point of view on the notion that fidelity to God equates with the deaths of innocent children. Both profile the wife of a righteous man as a faithful companion who not only shares in his suffering, but also feels his pain in ways that only a mother can. In the LXX Job's wife laments the loss of sons and daughters, "my womb's birth pangs and labors," with words that mirror God's response to the satan in 2:3. As God concedes that Job's destruction has been carried out "for no reason" (*dia kenēs*), she now sees that she has birthed her children "in vain" (*eis to kenon*); for no reason they are born to death, not life. In Tobit, Anna weeps and laments for "my child"; in an interesting reversal of the biblical account in which Job rebukes his wife for speaking foolishly, Anna rebukes her husband for trying to deceive her with false comfort.

The roles of Job's wife, his daughters, and of women in general, are even more extensively developed in the *Testament of Job*.[8] Written in the genre of a testament or farewell address from a father to his children, this account recasts the biblical story as the last words of "Job, the one called Jobab" (1:1), who was once "the king of all Egypt" (28:8).[9] He gathers his children around him to tell them the story of his life—the challenges he faced, the virtues that enabled him to overcome them, and the lessons he wants to impart before he dies. As the story unfolds, significant aspects of the biblical account are both embellished and rewritten, including the cause and consequences of Job's suffering, the roles of Satan, God, the friends, and his daughters, and Job's restoration and vindication. I will explore these matters in subsequent chapters, but at this point I focus on the retelling of the story about Job's wife, which is split into two lengthy segments, *T. Job* 21–25 and 39–40.

In the first segment, Job continues narrating his life story by saying that during the forty-eight years (21:1; some manuscripts specify seven years) he spent on the dung heap, he saw his wife, Sitidos (from *sitizō*, "to give bread"),[10] working as a slave for a rich man in order to earn bread for Job and herself. After eleven years, her master reduced her supply of bread, and Job recounts how she willingly divided her meager portion with him, "saying with pain, 'Woe is me! Soon he will not get even get enough bread!'" (22:2). She resorts to begging in the marketplace, and when Satan disguises himself as a bread seller, she agrees to exchange her hair for three loaves of bread, saying to herself, "What good is the hair of my head compared to my hungry husband?" (23:8). Once the exchange has been completed, and Sitidos has delivered the bread to Job, he recalls what she said to him, "crying out with tears":

> Job, Job! How long will you sit on the dung heap outside the city thinking, "Only a little longer!" and awaiting the hope of your salvation? As for me, I am a vagabond and a maidservant going round from place to place. Your memorial has been wiped away from the earth—my sons and the daughters of my womb for whom I toiled with hardships in vain. And here you sit in worm-infested rottenness, passing the night in the open air. And I for my part am a wretch immersed in labor by day and in pain by night, just so that I might provide a loaf of bread and bring it to you. Any more I barely receive my own food, and I divide that between you and me—wondering in my heart that it is not enough for you to be ill, but neither do you get your fill of bread.
>
> So I ventured unashamedly to go into the market, even if I was pierced in my heart to do so. And the bread seller said, "Give money, and you will receive." But I also showed him our straits and then heard from him, "If you have no money, woman, pay with the hair of your head and take three loaves. Perhaps you will live for three more days." Being remiss, I said to him, "Go ahead, cut my hair." So he arose and cut my hair disgracefully in the market, while the crowd stood by and marveled. (24:1–10)

At this point Sitidos's speech is interrupted by a third-person lament. The speaker is not identified, but the location of the lament hints that it conveys the perspective of the crowd in the marketplace that looked on as she exposed herself to the humiliation of having her hair cut. The repeating refrain, "Now she gives her hair for loaves" (with slight variations), accentuates the price she has paid—public shame and disgrace—on Job's behalf.[11] It also anticipates the repeating refrain in Eliphas's lament for Job, "Where then is the splendor of your throne?" (32:2, 3, 4, 5, 6, 7, 9, 10, 11, 12), thus creating a structural and thematic parallel between the losses suffered by both Job and his wife (cf. 25:1–8).

Sitidos resumes her lament in the following verses, which expand upon her only line in the biblical book (Job 2:9): "Job, Job! Although many things have been said in general, I speak to you in brief. In the weakness of my heart, my bones are crushed. Rise, take the loaves, be satisfied. And then *speak some word against the Lord and die.* Then I too shall be freed from weariness that issues from the pain of your body" (25:9–10; emphasis added),

As in the biblical account, Job responds to his wife's words immediately, although in this account he speaks at greater length and with considerably more sensitivity. He does not accept her counsel to "speak some word against the Lord," but he does not accuse her of speaking foolishly, as he does in both the Hebrew and Greek versions (LXX Job 2:10), for he recognizes that the devil has confused her thinking in order to make her look like "one of the senseless women." Instead he encourages her to remember their past blessings and to be patient until God shows mercy (26:1–6).

Sitidos makes a second appearance in chapters 39–40. After the three friends, portrayed here as kings, appear, she throws herself at their feet, imploring them to remember the woman she had once been, before Job's misfortunes changed her life. "But now," she says as she weeps, "look at my debut and my attire!" (39:5). Eliphas takes off his purple robe and wraps it around her (39:7). She pleads with the kings to order their soldiers to dig through the ruins of the house that had collapsed on her children so that she can retrieve their bodies and give them a proper burial. Job intervenes, saying that his children will not be found there, because they have already been taken up into heaven by their creator (39:11–12). When the kings interpret this as a sign of his madness, Job invites them and his wife to look toward the east, where they see a vision of his children "crowned with the splendor of the heavenly one" (40:3). Seeing this, Sitidos prostrates herself in worship and says, "Now I know that I have a memorial with the Lord," following which she lies down in a manger and dies "in good spirits," the animals weeping around her (40:4–6, 11). She is buried near the house that fell on her children, her eulogy provided by the city's poor, who tune their laments to the honor they perceive Sitidos deserves but has not received: "Look! This is Sitis

[Sitidos], the woman of pride and splendor! She was not even considered worthy of a decent burial!" (40:13).

These two segments in the *T. Job* provide a fuller description of the wife's role than we find in either the Masoretic text or the LXX. The *Testament* characterizes her more sympathetically by accentuating the length of time she suffered alongside her husband, the wrenching grief she bore for the loss of her children, the poverty that drove her into servitude, and the humiliation she accepted by selling her hair, perhaps the last vestige of her dignity, in order to secure enough food to extend the miserable existence that she and Job shared. Like the LXX the *Testament* tempers the one-line version of her biblical speech by omitting any reference to cursing God and reporting simply that she urged Job to speak "some word" against God.

At the same time, the *Testament* retains and expands upon the negative characterization embedded in the biblical story. It links Job's rejection of his wife's counsel to her lack of discernment. She does not recognize that Satan has disguised himself as a bread seller; she does not realize that by agreeing to Satan's terms she becomes a willing—and foolish—accomplice in his plot to deceive Job; she does not understand that her children are in heaven and need not be buried. In all of these matters, her knowledge is inferior to Job's. What she does not understand, Job can explain, because God has revealed to him, not her, the truth about things seen and unseen. For all its attention to the virtues of Job's wife, a "woman of pride and splendor" (40:13), the *Testament* continues the tradition of using her "as a foil to show off Job's superior handling of the situation."[12] The last move the *Testament* makes in this direction is the way it contrasts her death with Job's. She dies as the "wife of Job" (25:1) who was "not even considered worthy of a decent burial" (40:13); despite her extraordinary loyalty to her husband, she is more pitied than honored. Job dies as a "man of God" (53:4) whose soul ascends to the heavens in gleaming chariots (52:7, 11). Because of his extraordinary loyalty to God, he "received a name renowned in all generations forever" (53:8; cf. 4:6). In sum the *Testament* effectively widens the gap readers must negotiate when assessing the differences between the contributions of the "wife of Job" and the "man of God."

The more developed presentation of the wife of Job in the *Testament* is likely connected, in part, to the historical context that shaped its authors and readers. Although an exact provenance cannot be established, a number of scholars have proposed that the *Testament* was composed among the Therapeutae, a first-century Jewish monastic group living in Alexandria.[13] In this group, as described by Philo in *De Vita Contemplativa,* women played a prominent role in the religious life of the community, including meditation on scripture, prayer, and hymn singing. Philo speaks positively of the Therapeutae women, who are so devoted to the "verities of wisdom" that they "have spurned the pleasures of the body and desire no mortal offspring but those immortal children which only the soul that is dear to God can bring to birth unaided."[14] It is difficult to judge how prevalent this view of women might have been among Jewish communities in the Hellenistic and Roman periods, for elsewhere Philo, Josephus, and other Jewish sources describe women in more conventionally subordinate and negative ways.[15]

However culturally conditioned the *Testament*'s description of Job's wife may have been, we cannot discount the very real possibility that it is simply expanding upon a derivative tradition that is deeply rooted in Jewish folklore. In *The Legends of the Jews,* Louis Ginzberg collects haggadic embellishments, ranging from the second to the fifteenth centuries, which in his judgment preserve authentic and persistent undercurrents in Jewish interpretations of the book of Job. Two excerpts from this legendary material about Job's wife show striking similarities with the accounts contained in both the LXX and the *Testament.*

The first reports that Job's wife urged him to "pray to God for death" because she feared that he could not bear his suffering without forfeiting his piety. Job rejects her counsel, because he understands that his wife is "not strong enough to bear her fate with resignation to the will of God." The following addendum to their interchange, also reflected in the LXX and the *Testament,* seems to have circulated widely:

> Her lot was bitter, indeed, for she had had to take service as a water-carrier with a common churl, and when her master learnt that she shared her bread with Job, he dismissed her. To keep her husband from starving, she cut off her hair, and purchased bread with it. It was all she had to pay the price charged by the bread merchant, none other than Satan himself, who wanted to put her to the test. He said to her, "Hadst thou not deserved this great misery of thine, it had not come upon thee." This speech was more than the poor woman could bear. Then it was that she came to her husband, and amid tears and groans urged him to renounce God and die. Job, however, was not perturbed by her words, because he divined at once that Satan stood behind his wife, and seduced her to speak thus. Turning to the tempter, he said: "Why dost thou not meet me frankly? Give up thy underhand ways, thou wretch." Thereupon Satan appeared before Job, admitted that he had been vanquished, and went away abashed.[16]

The second reports that after the three friends arrived, profiled in legendary lore as kings, Job's wife, Zitidos, threw herself at their feet saying, "Remember what I was in other days, and how I am now changed, coming before you in rags and tatters." Here again the similarities with the LXX and the *Testament* suggest that their embellishments of the biblical account were widely known.[17]

These early Jewish expansions on the biblical account of Job's wife were of great interest to Christian interpreters, especially artists, in the Greco-Roman period. Beginning in the third century, artists painted scenes from the Joban story on the walls of the Roman catacombs, typically above the niches where Christians were buried. Against the backdrop of persecutions suffered by Christians, especially in Rome, these paintings provide visual exegesis of the promise that those who lived and died with the fidelity exemplified by Job—and his wife— would ultimately be rewarded and restored by God. Many of these depictions draw their inspiration not from the biblical version of Job's story but from the postbiblical rereadings and retellings that accentuate his wife's contribution to his legacy. A painting in the Via Latina catacomb depicts Job's sitting on a collection of rocks as he looks over a field of green grass.[18] His legs are crossed in a way that foregrounds the pockmarks of affliction that run from his left thigh to his left ankle, but his pose suggests serenity more than despair. He leans slightly to the right, his right hand resting on a supporting boulder, his left draped over his scarred left knee. His wife stands immediately behind him. She wears a long robe with open sides and wide sleeves, perhaps suggestive of the dalmatic garments associated with priests and bishops. Her head is tilted to the right, her eyes looking at Job below. Her left arm bends at the elbow, and she extends her hand, now hidden behind Job's head, in a gesture that indicates tactile support and comfort. Her head is tilted to the right as she lowers her gaze to the slightly elevated stick with a piece of bread that she offers Job with her right hand. Similar depictions of Job's wife giving bread to her husband on a stick appear frequently in sculptures and manuscript illustrations from the fourth century onward.[19] In some the wife is shown giving Job bread with one hand and covering her nose with her other hand, a representation that apparently conveys her reaction to the stench associated with Job's "worm-infested rottenness" (T. Job 24:3–4; cf. Job 19:17).[20] In others she offers bread with the mark of a cross, a suggestive representation for Christians that invites association with the Eucharist and the bread of life.[21]

Early Christian artists often grouped depictions of Job and his wife with other biblical figures in sculptures and paintings that telescoped central events of scripture. The frieze of the fourth-century sarcophagus that commemorates the death of the Roman prefect Junius Bassus is divided into two horizontal panels, each containing five biblical scenes.[22] Both pentads are centered on the third in the sequence, which on the bottom panel depicts Jesus's entry into Jerusalem and on the top panel, Jesus in resurrected glory, sitting between Peter and Paul. The ten scenes are juxtaposed both horizontally and vertically, which suggests that viewers are to look for thematic parallels and connections among them. Viewed from left to right and from top to bottom, the sequence is as follows: (1) the sacrifice of Isaac, which stands above (2) Job and his wife; (3) the arrest of Peter, which stands above (4) the temptation of Adam and Eve; (5) the resurrected Christ, which stand above (6) the scene of Jesus's entry into Jerusalem; (7) Jesus before Pontius Pilate, which stands above (8) Daniel in the lion's den; and (9) Pontius Pilate sitting in judgment, which stands above (10) Rebekah pondering the judgment of her sons, Esau and Jacob.

At the far left end of the lower panel, scene 2 shows Job seated on stones that form a bench and a footstool. To the right stands a second figure, often identified as one of the friends, and Job's wife. With her left hand, his wife holds her robe to her nose. Her right hand rests on Job's left hand. The location of this scene immediately below the one depicting Abraham's sacrifice of Isaac (with Sarah noticeably absent) offers a suggestive link to the "tests" both Job and Abraham endured and, more important from a Christian perspective, to human acts of sacrificial love and devotion that prefigure God's sacrifice of Jesus on the cross. It also perhaps subtly reflects the tradition that traces Job's genealogy to Abraham (cf. *T. Job* 1:6; LXX Job 42:17c). A second interpretive context is suggested by placing Job and his wife immediately next to the scene of Adam and Eve in the garden. Separated by the tree in the garden that bears the forbidden fruit, the serpent coiled around its trunk, Adam and Eve cover their naked bodies with their hands and look away from each other in shame. Job and his wife, by contrast, are both clothed and unashamed, an indication that Job and perhaps also his wife in a different way have withstood the temptation to abandon each other and God. As a sign of the mutual need and support that continues to unite them, they extend their hands to each other, bridging the gap created by the figure (possibly Satan in disguise) that stands between them.

At a Byzantine gravesite in Arles in the Provence region, a similar depiction of Job and his wife is placed directly below one of Jesus and the Samaritan woman at the well (Jn 4:1–30).[23] The figures in the two reliefs are positioned in parallel places, Jesus and Job on the right, the Samaritan woman and Job's wife on the left. In the upper relief, Jesus stretches out his hand to the woman with a request for water; the bucket for drawing the water and the well are between them. In the lower relief, Job sits on a Roman-style chair, his right foot and right hand extended to his wife, who stands opposite him. With her left hand, she holds the folds of her robe to her nose; with her right she extends a long stick holding a piece of cross-marked bread to Job. The juxtaposition of the two reliefs invites viewers to make connections between the Samaritan woman's gift of water to Jesus and Job's wife's gift of bread. In both instances the women, for different reasons objects of shame in their respective communities, are depicted as agents of compassion. They both offer tangible gifts that sustain the life of a person in need.

Demonizing Job's Wife and Feminizing Job

These early expansions upon the role of Job's wife in the LXX, the *T. Job,* and in haggadic legends generally present her more sympathetically than in the biblical account. While preserving the tradition that she is used unwittingly by Satan to deceive her husband, these early retellings portray her actions as motivated by compassion, not malevolence. Beginning in the fourth century, however, and continuing through most of the Middle Ages, Christian interpretation of Job's wife gradually rigidified.[24] With a few important exceptions, she was viewed either as a temptress, like Eve, or as the devil incarnate. In sum Job's wife was demonized. Commentators interpreted her words and actions as the essence of the evil that the faithful, like Job, must reject and defeat. Numerous artists drew upon this commentary and added visual exegesis that depicted her as verbally abusing Job or physically striking him.

An early move in this direction can be found in the *Apocalypse of Paul,* a fourth-century pseudepigraphal work that provides an account of Paul's rapture to the "third heaven" (2 Cor 12:2–4). When an angel brings him to the gates of Paradise, Paul sees two golden tablets inscribed with letters. When he asks what this means, the angel explains that these are the names of the righteous who served God with a whole heart while they lived on earth (chap.19). Among the righteous who greet him are Abraham, Isaac, Jacob, Moses, the prophets Isaiah and Ezekiel, and Job (chap 49).[25] Various aspects of this recounting of Job's life draw upon embellishments already present in the LXX and the *T. Job* (e.g., the worms associated with his suffering and the length of his ordeal, here said to be thirty, not forty-eight, years, as in the *Testament*). One important difference signals a move we have not seen in earlier retellings. In the *Testament* it is Job's wife who says, "Speak some word against the Lord and die" (25:10), although Job realizes that she has been influenced by the devil, who is standing behind her. The *Apocalypse* now attributes the wife's words directly to the devil. In essence Job's wife and the devil have become one and same person.

The Latin fathers of the church, Ambrose, Augustine, Jerome, and Gregory the Great, followed a similar exegetical approach, each drawing a connection between Eve's temptation of Adam and Job's wife's temptation of her husband. The most elaborate and most influential exposition is Gregory's *Moralia in Job,* a six-volume, thirty-five-book treatise on the biblical book that was completed in Rome in 595. Gregory's objective was to interpret every verse in the book of Job from three perspectives, the literal or historical meaning of the text, the allegorical meanings that disclose the deeper truths beneath the text, and the moral lessons that are to be learned and appropriated by the church. With these objectives, inherited mainly from Augustine, Gregory develops a thick explanation of Job's wife's words in Job 2:9, "Dost thou still retain thine integrity? Curse God, and die" (3.8.12).[26]

To unfold the literal meaning of the wife's words, Gregory begins by explaining that the devil usually tests human beings in two ways. First he "tries to break the hearts of the stedfast by tribulation." If this fails, he tries "to melt them by persuasion." Because the devil could not break Job with suffering, he "betakes himself to subtle appliances of temptations . . . and because he knows by what means Adam is prone to be deceived, he has recourse to Eve" or, as Gregory explains, to Eve's counterpart in this story, Job's "wife and helpmate" (3.8.12).

Gregory interprets the conversation between Job and his wife as a repetition of Eve's temptation of Adam in the garden. The analogy between Eve and Job's wife builds on the intimacy of the relationship between a wife and her husband to show how a woman's affection can be used to lead her husband astray.[27] Her heart is like a ladder that Satan can climb to breach Job's heart, the citadel of his own emotions. Her words have "the force of love" (3.8.13) that can penetrate the heart like "a javelin," which Satan hurls "as if from a place of ambush" (3.8.14). Gregory observes that Satan "shewed craftiness" in destroying everything Job possessed but leaving behind his wife as his helper, for temptation is most persuasive when it comes from those closest to us. When his wife says, "Dost thou still retain thine integrity?" Gregory equates her words with Eve's old way of speaking. "For what is it to say, 'give over thine integrity,' but 'disregard obedience by eating the forbidden thing?' And what is it to say, Bless God and die, but 'live by mounting above the commandment, above what thou wast created to be?'" (3.8.14). It takes a "strong Adam" to resist the passionate but misdirected urgings of Eve, and, as Gregory says, it takes Job's "manly reproof" to discipline his wife's "looser mind" (3.8.12).

Having posited a connection between Job's wife and Eve and between Job and Adam, Gregory turns to "the mystical sense of the allegory" (3.8.25) disclosed in Job's wife's words. He argues that the "mispersuading woman" represents the weak members of the church. By extension Job's reproof of his wife teaches the church to beware worldly members who urge wickedness, whether by fear or love. In support of this allegorized reading, Gregory turns to the New Testament story of the woman with a hemorrhage who, from the midst of a pressing crowd, reaches out to touch the hem of Jesus's garment (3.20.36; cf. Lk 8:43–48, Mt 9:18–26, Mk 5:25–34). Gregory identifies Job's wife with the crowd harassing Jesus and by extension with church members who tempt the faithful with worldly ideas. The woman with the hemorrhage could touch Jesus because she displayed true humility, but the crowd who press upon him are a burden and should not be allowed to come close because in their hearts they are really very distant from Jesus's teachings. According to this logic, Job's wife is a burden, perhaps an inevitable one, since he has allowed her into the inner chambers of his faith, and it would be better if he had no contact with her at all. A few lines later, Gregory extends his exposition by referencing Jesus's rebuke of Peter for trying to dissuade him from pursuing the journey of obedient suffering that would lead to the cross: *"Get thee behind Me, Satan"* (3.20.38; cf. Mt 16:23, Mk 8:33). "When any of the Elect encounter evil within coming from carnal men, what a model of uprightness they exhibit in themselves," Gregory concludes, when they "learn from the words of him [Job], wounded and yet whole, seated yet erect," who says to his wife, "Thou speakest as one of the foolish women speaketh" (3.20.38–39).

In the third part of his exposition, Gregory turns to the moral lessons to be learned from the story of Job and his wife. He begins by saying, "The illadvising wife is the carnal thought goading the mind." The battle between fleshly thoughts and the "holy mind" (3.32.62) represents the spiritual warfare between the "reprobate" and the "Elect" (3.32.63).

Gregory's *Moralia* is widely regarded as the most important work on Job in the Middle Ages. It is hardly surprising, therefore, that his exposition of Job's wife as an Eve-like temptress who was instigated by the devil exerted influence on virtually every Christian commentator on the book from the seventh to the fifteenth centuries. As Nahum Glatzer has noted, after the publication of the *Moralia,* "the book of Job proffered no message beyond the one that the Gregory commentary saw in it."[28] The influence extends not only to epitomes, translations, and commentaries based on the Gregorian reading of Job and his wife, but also to poems, plays, paintings, sculptures, and carvings that drew their inspiration from the same source.

A fourteenth-century manuscript illustration shows Satan holding Job with his left hand and beating him with a rod that he holds in his right hand.[29] At Job's right his wife looks on. Her dress could suggest innocence,[30] but her stern facial expression, accented by the placement of her hands firmly on her hips, betrays a rebuking "I told you so" attitude. The caption alludes to Gregory's exegesis: "Satan beats him with whips and his wife beats him with words." The Middle French mystery play, *La Patience de Job,* perhaps "the most significant medieval vernacular composition on the Job theme,"[31] offers a similar exegesis. Beginning with a prologue in which the speaker invites "corrections by those clerics here present who are familiar with the lives of the fathers" (319–21), this play rewrites the biblical story by assigning Job's laments to his wife, who complains that she would rather die than beg bread for her survival (3222–64; cf. Job 3).[32] When Satan appears, he announces that he will try to defeat Job by using his wife against him, as he did with Adam (4731–5543). Ultimately Satan's plot fails, but Job concedes that he has felt besieged on all sides: "On the one hand I am hunted by the devil, / on the other I am menaced by my wife" (5718–19). A seventeenth-century Flemish painting extends the commentary.[33] Here Job is positioned between three demonic figures, who flail away at him with serpents, and his wife, who places her hands on her hips, bends at the waist, and juts out a wrinkled, shrewlike face, mouth opened, as if adding her words to the beating that causes her husband to tumble backward. In other examples Job's wife not only looks on as he is beaten, she strikes him herself with a rod, a bundle of keys, or with a spoon.[34]

Numerous works juxtapose Job, his wife, and the devil with depictions of Jesus being beaten or tempted by the devil. Two woodcarvings on a fourteenth-century altarpiece at Doberan Abbey in Mecklenburg, Germany, place Job and his wife side by side with a scene depicting Roman soldiers preparing Jesus for crucifixion.[35] In the scene on the right, Jesus wears a royal robe and sits in silence as two soldiers behind him weave a crown of thorns on top of his bowed head. In the left foreground, a miniature devil, dressed as a street entertainer, taunts Jesus by dancing and making faces. The scene on the left shows Job sitting on a bed of stones. He wears a monk's hood and crosses his arms and hands over his chest, perhaps in meditation or prayer. He beard is trimmed in the same manner as Jesus's in the adjacent scene. His wife stands opposite him, her hands raised in what appears to be a clapping gesture. To her right, and just above her hands, a black devil looks on. In both scenes the devil works his way, in the one through Job's wife, who mocks her husband's piety, in the other through the soldiers who prepare a mock crown for Jesus.

A particularly gruesome depiction of the demonization of Job's wife is on the central panel of the fifteenth-century altarpiece in the Chapel of St. Job in Chieri, Italy.[36] The picture is a complex presentation of thirty-three characters, with various animals moving in and around multiple scenes. The bottom half of the painting is, however, focused by two scenes of Job's wife and two of Job. They are arranged in an X-shaped parallelism. The scene in the top left, which shows Job's wife talking to a group of musicians, is connected to the scene in the bottom right that shows these same musicians serenading Job. The scene in the top right, which shows Job's wife talking to him as he sits on a mound of dirt, is diagonally parallel to the scene in the bottom left, which shows Job sitting on a mound, now being whipped by a demonic figure who appears to be a composite of the devil and Job's wife. The upper half of her body shows sagging breasts; in the lower part, in place of her genitals, there is a face with a grossly long, protruding tongue, a graphic representation, no doubt, of the way Job's wife used her tongue to berate him.

Demonizing Job's wife is by far the dominant approach of medieval exegetes and artists. There is, however, a subtle but significant departure in several works that feminize either Job or his virtues. Prudentius's poem *Psychomachia* (fifth century) uses the story of Job to describe the victories of the virtues over the vices. Patience, the virtue traditionally associated with the biblical portrait of Job in chapters 1–2 and especially accentuated in the *T. Job* (e.g., 1:5; 4:6; 26:5; 27:4, 7), is feminized as Patientia, who, protected by her corselet, endures the vicious attacks of her rival, Ira (Wrath). Once Ira exhausts herself in futility, she commits suicide, and Patientia walks unharmed through the battlefield to lend her support to other virtues. She is accompanied by the noble warrior Job, "her earthly exemplification," who had fought by the side of "his invincible mistress."[37]

The Qur'an contains four references to Job (Suras 4:163, 6:84, 21:83–84, 38:41–44), none of which mentions his wife. The first two list Job (Ayyub), along with Abraham, Isaac, Jacob, and Jesus, as a prophet who was guided in righteousness and recompensed for his goodness by Allah. The third and fourth suras add brief narrative details about Job's suffering and restoration, which post-Qur'anic interpreters expand upon by citing Islamic traditions about the role of Job's wife.[38]

The reference in Sura 21:83–84 occurs in the context of questions about the proper attitude of those who face suffering. "And Job—when he called unto the Lord, 'Behold affliction has visited me, and Thou art the most merciful of the merciful.' So we answered him, and removed the affliction that was upon him, and We gave his people, and the like of them with them, mercy from Us, and a Reminder to those who serve."[39]

With some variation in detail, later commentators represent Job's wife, Rahma ("compassion"), as the Islamic ideal of "those who show mercy."[40] When others deserted Job, "she was patient along with him, serving him and bringing him food, and praising God with him when he praised Him."[41] She physically carries Job from one village to another and asks for help, but she is constantly turned away. She builds a hut for Job where he rests on a bed of ashes and stones she has collected. When Iblis, the Enemy of God, sees Rahma crying over her husband's misery, he thinks she is complaining and seizes the opportunity to trick her into offering Job a way out of his ordeal: if Job will offer a sacrifice to Iblis and not speak the name of God, then he will be healed. Job recognizes the plot, rebukes Rahma, and drives her away, swearing that if God would heal him, then he would whip her with a hundred lashes. Instead of urging Job to curse God, as in the biblical story, she pleads with him to "call upon the Lord to relieve you."[42] Job says that he is too ashamed to pray; anticipating death, he tells Rahma that God will provide her another husband when he is gone. She tearfully rejects this idea—"By God, no one after you shall ever have me, Job"[43]—and continues to beg food for her husband. She sells her hair to a baker for two loaves of bread. When she brings the bread to Job and shows him where her hair had been cut, Job weeps bitterly, for it had been her hair that had supported him when he used to get up to pray. This is the incident, according to later interpreters, that explains the meaning of Sura 21:83: "Verily evil hath afflicted me: but thou art the most merciful of those who show mercy. Yea, adversity afflicts me indeed when my wife sells her hair."[44] Because of her unending compassion for Job, it is said that "God Most High had compassion upon Rahma, the wife of Ayyub, for her patience along with him in his trial."[45] The audience for these post-Qur'anic stories would surely have understood the connection between Rahma and the same Arabic term, *rahma,* most often associated in the Qur'an with Allah's compassion for those who suffer (Suras 10:21; 11:9; 30:33, 36; 41:50), the same compassion extended by human agents such as Jesus (Sura 19:21), Muhammad (Sura 21:107), and Job's wife.[46] Sura 38:40–44 provides an additional detail in explanation of how Job was healed.

> Remember also Our servant Job; when he called to his Lord, "Behold Satan has visited me with weariness and chastisement." "Stamp thy foot! This is a laving-place cool, and a drink." And We gave him his family, and the like of them, as a mercy from us, and a reminder unto men possessed of minds; and, "Take in thy hand a bundle of rushes, and strike therewith, and do not fail in thy oath." Surely We found him a steadfast man. How excellent a servant he was! He was a penitent.

Later commentators report that when Job stamped once on the ground with his foot, a spring of water burst forth, and he washed away the sores that afflicted his body. When he stamped a second time, another spring appeared, and when he drank from it, he stood up sound and fully restored. The angel Gabriel brought him new clothes to wear and gave him a piece of fruit from Paradise. Job ate half and left the other half for his wife, a gesture that indicates she shared equally in his restoration. When she arrived, she did not recognize him at first, so changed was his appearance, but when Job addressed her, she ran to him and they embraced. The command that Job take "a bundle of rushes, and strike therewith" is interpreted to mean that he took a bundle of a hundred delicate branches and struck his wife with a single blow, thus fulfilling his vow.

Islamic manuscript illustrations from the twelfth to the sixteenth centuries add visual commentary to this story by depicting Job standing in a stream of holy waters. A sixteenth-century illustration of *Qisas al-Anbiya* (*Legends of the Prophets*) by al-Nishapuri shows Job standing ankle-deep in waters that flow through a bank covered with flowers and budding trees. On one side of the bank, the angel Gabriel holds Job by the hand; on the other Rahma, regally adorned in a red dress that matches the colors in Gabriel's robe, extends a bowl of food to her husband.[47] Such an image stands in stark contrast with those we have reviewed above. Instead of the devil who beats Job, there is an angel who restores him; in place of a wife who berates him, an attendant Rahma stands by his side, an earthly manifestation of divine grace.

For Spanish Muslims in the sixteenth century who were forced to convert to Christianity, these legends about Rahma provided more than a story about a compassionate wife. They offered a "subversive text of resistance."[48] As Christian officials moved to suppress all expressions of Muslim culture by burning their texts, imposing heavy taxes, and forcibly relocating those who resisted, Moriscos, as Christians called these converted Muslims, concealed an Aljamiado version of

Job's story.[49] It portrays Rahma in much the same way as the other post-Qur'anic stories, although it enhances her role with a number of important embellishments. When Eblis (Satan) bargains with God for permission to afflict Job, God warns him not to harm his wife, "because she is his aid and support with my help."[50] Once Job is stricken, Rahma carries him on her back as she moves from village to village begging for food. She uses a hoe to build a shelter for herself and Job, a wayside from which she cries out for mercy, but Eblis instructs the villagers to drive her away: "throw that woman out of your village and do not let her work for you nor give her anything; because she will poison your food and ruin your goods from venom, and you will all come to the evil of her husband."[51] When she returns to the shelter with the little food that she has been able to get for Job but cannot find him, she tears at herself and cries out, "Oh, Job! I have suffered for you seven years and seven months; now at the point that I had hope of Allah, that Allah would have mercy on you, the wild beasts have come and eaten you; you are my consolation, oh my love, oh Job, what devil has stolen you and carried you away?" When she finds Job healed and restored, she embraces him, then sees that he is weeping. She asks why, and he explains that he is crying out of compassion for her, because he has sworn that if God would heal him, he would beat her with a hundred lashes. Instantly she replies, "Oh, my beloved Job! If you have sworn, of course, then give me 2,000 [lashes], so that you fulfill your oath."[52]

M. E. Perry has argued that Moriscos read this story not only because it reminded them that the faithful must endure suffering, but also because they saw in Rahma a model of courage, determination, and intelligence that inspired them to take action to assure their survival. As Rahma, with God's help, was essential to Job's survival, so Moriscas played a critical role in the survival of their families. When husbands perished in rebellion or were taken away into captivity, their wives became heads of households. They assumed primary responsibility for preserving their Islamic culture and identity; in the privacy of their homes, they secretly observed the holy days, read to their children from the forbidden texts, taught them prayers and Islamic beliefs, and hid them from the compulsory schools that were established to Christianize them. In sum "Rahma offered these women not only an example of the strong active woman working to assure the survival of her family; she also provided a deeper understanding of their power as women."[53]

Perry argues that Rahma's gendered depiction of strength in perilous times was empowering not only for the women in the Morisco community but also for the men.[54] Men continued to see themselves in conventionally patriarchal ways, and they would have assumed that their status and power required their wives to remain loyal and obedient in all circumstances. Job's story did not overturn this view of their dominant role in the family, but it would likely have tempered it with the understanding that when they were most vulnerable to expulsion and death, they, like Job, could draw strength from their wives, who were using every means available to protect and defend their families.

Thus far we have surveyed two approaches to the interpretation of Job's wife in the Middle Ages. By far the dominant approach is the demonizing of her as an Evelike temptress, as the devil's helper's in striking Job, or as a she-devil who physically beats Job herself. Less prominent but sufficiently attested is what may be described as a feminization of Job or his virtues, as in Prudentius's Patientia, represented as Job's mistress, or in post-Qur'anic characterizations of Rahma as an agent of divine compassion to Job. In the late fourteenth century, Geoffrey Chaucer appropriated both these approaches to Job's wife by attributing them to two different characters in The Canterbury Tales: Alisoun, the "wicked wife" of Bath; and Griselda, the long-suffering wife of Walter.

In "The Wife of Bath's Prologue," Alisoun asserts that she is an "expert" (3.174) when it comes to mastering the "misery" and "woe" of marriage (3.3).[55] Her expertise has been honed through five marriages that have taught her how to "whip" (3.175) any husband into submission. "First put them in the wrong, and out of hand," she says, for "No one can be so bold . . . at lies and swearing as a woman can" (3.226–29). She "tortured them without remorse" and "launch[ed] complaints when things were all [her] fault." "In the end," she says, "I always ruled the roost" by "keeping up a steady grumble" (3.384–85, 404–6). When her husbands grow weary with her insults, she compares herself to Job's wife, who taught him the time-honored truth that the husband's role in marriage always requires patience (3.433–37, 440–42).

Alisoun betrays the conventional "misogynist reading of Job's wife,"[56] which Chaucer represents as having been passed down by the clerics from generation to generation in the "book of wicked wives" (3.685). Alisoun knows this "cursed book" (3.789), for her fifth husband reads it to her every night. Beginning with Eve, "whose wickedness brought all mankind to sorrow and distress," (3.715–16), he would continue reading through the long history of other wicked women, concluding with the lesson he took from it for Alisoun: "Better to share your habitation / With lion, dragon, or abomination / Than with a woman given to reproof" (3.775–76). Rather than deny this representation of women as wicked, Alisoun embraces it as critical for her self-understanding. Her reading of herself agrees with her husband's reading of her. As Ann Astell puts it, "She embodies the book her husband reads."[57] She reads herself as adding yet another important chapter to the book of wives, which now concludes with the story of how she struck her husband in the face, causing him to fall backward into the fire (3.792–93). Her husband yields in submission and tells Alisoun, "Do as you please for all the rest of life" (3.820). After she had mastered him once again, she celebrates the sovereignty in marriage she had pursued and won with a final word: "From that day forward there was no debate" (3.822). In sum Alisoun "presents herself as a nightmare of the antifeminist imagination, a woman who not only exemplifies every fault of which women have been accused but pre-empts the very language of accusation."[58]

In addition to the "book of wicked wives," Chaucer also constructs his tales from a second source, the legends of "women saints" ("hooly seintes lyves" [3.690]). In "The Clerk's Tale," he adapts a legendary story about Griselda and her husband, Walter, that offers an alternative view of women in relation to their husbands.[59] With good reason Griselda's story is often identified as the "wife testing plot,"[60] for the storyline follows the brutish schemes Walter devises to test her obedience. When he proposes marriage, he insists that Griselda swear to his conditions (4.351–55). Griselda agrees; thinking herself unworthy of marriage to such a noble man, she says simply, "if it seems good to you it is to me" (4.361). Soon afterward Griselda gives birth to a daughter, and Walter, still suspecting her fidelity, demands that she summon her patience and let him send the child away. Griselda yields to Walter's demands without complaint: "My child and I are your possession / And at your pleasure, on my heart's profession / We are all yours . . . do therefore as you will" (4.501–4). The same thing happens four years later when Griselda has a son. Again she agrees to let Walter send him away, now extending her promise to absolute fidelity by adding that if Walter should demand her own death in order to prove her constancy, then she would gladly die to please him (4.664–65). As a final test, Walter tells Griselda of his decision to divorce her in favor of a younger wife; he sends her home to her father and orders that she prepare the wedding for his new bride. Once again Griselda agrees, now using Job's own words to declare her unwavering commitment: "Naked out of my father's house, I went / And naked I return again today" (4.871–72; cf. Job 1:21).

Chaucer's Griselda, as Astell notes, is "Job in female form."[61] "Perfect in [her] constancy" (4.1146), Griselda not only withstands Walter's trials with Joblike patience and humility, she seems even more heroic than Job. After seven days and nights of silence, Job rose up from the ash heap and began to curse (Job 3). Chaucer attributes Job's curse not to Griselda, who never utters a word of complaint, but to her father, Janicula, who takes Job's words as his own (4.901–2; cf. Job 3:1). By attributing Job's patience to Griselda and Job's impatient curse to her father, Chaucer effectively depicts Griselda as "a new and more perfect Job."[62] We may extend this assessment still further. Multiple references in "The Clerk's Tale" attribute to Griselda characteristics normally associated with the Virgin Mary or Christ himself.[63] She is described, for example, as the "grace" sent from God into a "little ox's stall" (4.207), "her heart so equitable and her hand / So just they thought that Heaven had sent her down / to right all wrongs" (4.440–41). Her patient endurance of undeserved suffering is more than a feminine virtue, it is Christlike; in the end she effects Walter's repentance and conversion (4.1044–57).

The Clerk of Oxenford, who tells Griselda's story, adds a further word that invites reflection. On the one hand, the Clerk appears to be offering an internal critique of the clerical interpretation of Job's wife, as represented by Alisoun, who accuses clerics of always speaking negatively about women: "Take my word for it, there is no libel / On women that the clergy will not paint" (3.688–89). On the other the "Envoy" of the story, whether the Clerk or Chaucer himself, warns both men and women that Griselda's virtues are unrealistically ideal and cannot be replicated in other persons. Husbands should not hope to find the equal of Griselda in their wives, and no woman should aspire to Griselda's virtues (4.1177–87). By splitting Job's wife into two personae, Chaucer's likely intent was to frustrate any one single reading. Readers during the Middle Ages may have grown comfortable with the dominant negative view of Job's wife, as represented by Alisoun, but Chaucer's Griselda offers another story, which he insists should be included among the tales that shape the pilgrims' journey to Canterbury.

"Nice and Womanish"

Astell has argued that Chaucer presents Griselda as "a woman fit to be Job's wife, a Marylike Eve at the side of a New Adam." Whether Chaucer wished to commend Griselda to his readers as the exemplary wife or to suggest that her "Marylike" virtues exceed what any ordinary woman can realistically attain remains for Chaucer scholars a matter of ongoing debate. Nevertheless it is instructive to think of the search for "a woman fit to be Job's wife" as an important legacy of Joban interpretation during the Middle Ages. Two medieval representations of Job's wife compete for the prize of orthodoxy. The biblical text, embellished by deeply engrained postbiblical interpretation, supports understanding Job's wife either as demonic or as saintly—in Chaucerian terms, either as Alisoun or Griselda. Given such stark options, it is not surprising that Griselda emerges as the preferred option. Artistic representations of Job from the sixteenth century on follow suit. To adapt a phrase from John Calvin's *Sermons from Job,* Job's wife becomes "nice and womanish."[64]

In his early fifteenth-century *Jabach Altarpiece,* Albrecht Dürer uses two side panels, now separated, to depict how Job was comforted in the aftermath of the losses he suffered.[65] The background of the left panel shows Job's house being consumed by fire. In the left foreground, Job sits on a mound, his scarred body naked except for the cloth that covers his waist and drapes between his legs. He supports his slumping head, eyes and mouth closed, with his left hand. His right arm is crossed over his right knee, his fingers hanging limply between his legs. To his right his wife stands over him and pours water from a bucket over his neck and shoulders. The train of her red dress rests on the ground and extends into the right panel, which suggests that the two panels originally depicted a continuous scene. The background to the right panel shows the Sabeans and Chaldeans driving away Job's flocks and herds; in the foreground two minstrels, one playing a flute, the other, perhaps a representation of Dürer himself, playing a small drum.

While some have argued that Job's wife pours water on her husband as a threatening or mocking gesture, a strong case can be made that the cooling water she offers, like the soothing music of the minstrels, is a positive gesture intended to relieve Job's pain.[66] In support of this understanding, Terrien notes that Dürer himself combines the two gestures in an earlier lithograph in which he depicts a despondent man holding his head while standing in a pool of water in a bathhouse; to his right two musicians try to raise his spirits by playing their instruments.[67] We may speculate that Dürer's depiction of Job's wife as a comforting and devoted spouse was also influenced by his appreciation for Geoffrey de La Tour Landry's *Le Livre du chevalier de La Tour Landry.* Published in the late fourteenth century, this book was widely known throughout Western Europe; at least twenty-one copies of the French manuscript are still in existence, along with translations in English (1484) and German (1493). The German translation, *Der Ritter vom Turn,* was illustrated with forty-six woodcuts, most of them done by Dürer himself.[68] La Tour Landry's book was a compilation of moral precepts, drawn in large part from biblical examples, which he produced for his daughters in the hope of teaching them how good women should behave. Among the biblical models he selected was Job's wife, who in this story comforts Job with food that sustains his life. Although not without her faults, Job's wife, La Tour Landry concludes, was the kind of woman his daughters should take as a model: there was not "so lyke a good woman as she was."[69] It is reasonable to conclude that Dürer's depiction of Job's wife in the *Jabach Altarpiece* represents a similar assessment.

Georges de La Tour's *Job and His Wife* (c.1635) also accentuates the feminine virtues represented by Job's wife's comforting her husband.[70] To the right of the painting, La Tour shows Job sitting on a bench with a nightcap on his head. His midsection is covered, but his exposed neck, chest, arms, and legs depict a frail, older man whose bones protrude through his skin. He clasps his hands together over his knees as he looks into the eyes of his wife, who stands over him. His mouth is open as if he is asking his wife for help. On the ground below his knees, a broken piece of pottery reminds the viewer of the potsherd the biblical Job used to scrape his sores (Job 2:8); at the same time, it evokes the traditional symbol of diminished virility. His wife wears a floor-length red dress and a neatly folded kerchief on her head. Pearl earrings, along with the embroidered stones in the cuffs of her gown, indicate the attire of a woman who keeps up with the fashions of the day. As she bends her head toward Job's, she gracefully extends her left hand over his head. Her palm is turned upward; three fingers are gently curled, while the thumb and index finger point out. The gesture is the same as the one La Tour gives to the angel in *The Dream of St. Joseph* and similar to his depiction of the Virgin Mary in *The New Born Child* and in *The Adoration of the Shepherds*.[71] With her right hand, she holds a burning candle; its steady flame simultaneously illuminates the square apron covering her womb and Job's right shoulder, right arm, and his interlocked fingers. The gaze of her eye, her slightly parted lips, and the flame that transfers light from her womb to his impaired body suggest that she tenderly provides the strength that sustains their love for one another, even when Job himself is unable to reciprocate. Here again La Tour uses symbols he employs in other paintings, such as *St. Sebastian Tended by St. Irene Holding a Lantern*,[72] to depict the extraordinary capacities of a wife to nurse her husband back to health. The connection between Job and St. Sebastian, the patron saint of those who suffer, was often made by Baroque and Renaissance artists who saw their towns and villages ravaged by the Black Plague. La Tour would no doubt have had a deep personal interest in reflecting on a wife's role during such hard times, since his own wife died in 1652 from the plague that struck his hometown in Lorraine.[73]

William Blake's *Illustrations of the Book of Job* (1818–25) provides another example of depicting Job's wife as "nice and womanish."[74] Blake uses the King James Version of Job's story, but he freely diverges from the biblical account in order to offer his own re-creation of both Job and his wife. As the title page to the 1825 edition indicates, this is a version of Job's story "*Invented* and Engraved by William Blake." The twenty-one illustrations are sequenced in three groups of seven, which provides an overall structure that generally follows the biblical storyline: plates 1–7 are illustrations of events described in the prologue (Job 1–2); plates 8–14 illustrate aspects of the dialogues between Job and his friends and Job and God (Job 3:1–39:30); and plates 15–21 represent Blake's version of the resolution of the story, beginning with God's second speech about Behemoth and Leviathan and concluding with the epilogue and Job's restoration (Job 40:1–42:14). In an important departure from the biblical account, Blake includes Job's wife in all but two of the illustrations (plates 3 and 11), an indication that he wishes to portray her as standing by her husband's side through virtually every part of the story. Moreover Blake always distinguishes Job's wife by placing her with Job and either opposite to or clearly separated from the friends, who do not equal the compassion and loyalty she demonstrates.

Plates 1–7 illustrate the prologue's account of Job's suffering. Blake places Job's wife by his side at the very outset, as the two of them sit surrounded by their family (plate 1). Both have open books resting on their laps, a representation of their mutual reliance on the scripture that guides their lives. Job's hands are placed on the book; his wife's hands are raised in prayer, as she directs her gaze toward her husband. The caption beneath the picture—"Thus did Job continually"—is taken from the biblical narrator's summation of Job's piety (1:5); in Blake's depiction this affirmation clearly applies to Job's wife as well. Subsequent scenes in this first group extend this depiction. As the satan appeals to God in heaven for permission to test Job, Job and his wife remain side by side below, still holding on to the scriptures. The satan is shown as asking for permission to afflict not only Job but also his wife; as the satan raises his hands to God, Blake draws two disembodied shadows of Job and his wife underneath his arms (plate 2). Once the satan begins his assault on Job, his wife participates in his suffering. In plate 6 Job lies prone on a bed of palm fronds, his back arched and his head thrown backward, as the satan stands on top of him. With his right hand, he hurls flaming arrows at Job's midsection; with his left he pours a vial of poison on Job's head and shoulders. Job braces his feet on his wife's knees. In the biblical account, this marks the moment when his wife urges him to curse God (Job 2:9). Blake ignores this part of the story and instead shows Job's wife hiding her face in grief. She feels, but cannot look upon, her husband's misery.

In the biblical account, Job's wife exits the story after the prologue. In Blake's version she remains by his side to the very end. Plate 10 shows Job kneeling as his three angry friends point accusingly at him. To his right, opposite the friends, his wife scrunches up beside him. Her hands are crossed over her knees, her fingers spread apart in a gesture that suggests she cannot comprehend what the friends are doing. Blake adds a detail that accents the anguish she shares with her husband: tears are streaming down the cheeks of both Job and his wife. Plate 13 shows Job and his wife kneeling before the divine revelation from the whirlwind (Job 38:1). Both see the vision God imparts; both receive a blessing from the right hand God extends over their heads. The friends, by contrast, kneel at the feet of Job and his wife and bow in terror.

In the final sequence of seven illustrations, Blake shows that Job's wife is also included in his ultimate restoration. She is by his side when he recognizes that he has seen God "face to face" (Job 42:5; plate 17), when he intercedes for his friends (42:8–9; plate 18), when friends bring them gifts to express their sympathy and compassion (42:11; plate 19); and when, in one of several departures from the biblical account, Job tells his three daughters the story of his life (cf. Job 42:14–15; plate 20).[75] The last illustration (plate 21), a counterpart to the first, shows Job and wife once again surrounded by their family. Instead of holding sacred texts, they and their children now greet the dawn of a new day, symbolized by the sun rising in the east, by playing musical instruments. For the first time, a female figure stands between Job and his wife, although there is no separation between her body and theirs. She holds in her hands an unrolled scroll, perhaps the score for the music everyone is making. She is Blake's personification of the arts, including his own, through which, he insists, the human spirit can be created and re-created.

There may be various reasons why Blake gave such prominence to Job's wife. Some have suggested that his appreciation for a good wife reflects his relationship with his own wife, Catherine, "who so faithfully shared the tribulations, the poverty, and also the visions of her husband."[76] Others see a connection between Blake's accentuation of the feminine and the sensuality of poetry, which he fervently believed, along with other romantic poets of his era, was the necessary antidote to the Age of Reason.[77] I am inclined to believe that these suggestions are essentially connected to a larger and overarching possibility. Blake depicts Job's wife subjectively, not objectively; he sees her as Job sees her.[78] And since Blake portrays God and Job as mirror images of each other,[79] he hints that not only Job but also God sees Job's wife as the epitome of the good and faithful wife.

Center Stage: The Compassionate Rebel

Modern novelists and playwrights have also noticed the sparse details in the biblical account about Job's wife. Why did she say "Curse God, and die"? Was she an embodiment of the evil that tempted her husband to abandon his piety? Was she motivated by compassion for her husband or anger? Was she a faithful and dutiful wife, or was she the epitome of the shrew who makes her husband's life miserable? As Ruth, a character in Muriel Spark's Joban novel, *The Only Problem,* observes, "I suppose his wife suffered. But whoever wrote the story made nothing of her."[80] Modern writers have tended to magnify Job's wife's suffering as an explanation for the harsh words the biblical account attributes to her. As we have seen, other postbiblical interpreters have taken a similar approach. What distinguishes contemporary writers from these earlier explorations is their characterization of Job's wife not simply as a compassionate woman who faithfully attends to a suffering spouse but also as a woman whose compassion for the suffering is motivated by righteous anger. Righteous anger that seeds a quest for justice is a virtue biblical interpreters often see in the Job of the dialogues. Modern writers see this quality in Job's wife. In their creative retellings of the story, Job's wife is often depicted as the stronger and more courageous of the two. She is the compassionate rebel who stands on center stage demanding justice, while her husband sits on the ash heap paying useless homage to an immoral God.

In *Job: The Story of a Simple Man,* Joseph Roth replaces the exemplary Job of the biblical prologue with Mendel Singer, who is "pious, God-fearing, and ordinary, an entirely commonplace Jew."[81] He earns a meager living by teaching children who come to his home to read and memorize the Bible. His life has always been hard. There seems never enough income to support his wife and three children, and with a fourth child on the way, the future promises little relief. Still Mendel is at peace with himself and with God. When he rises in the morning, he thanks God for the gift of the day; when he goes to bed at night, he prays "with tired but zealous lips." He is, quite simply, a man with a pure conscience and a chaste soul; "he had nothing to regret, and he coveted nothing" (4).

Mendel's wife, Deborah, reflects the indomitable spirit of her biblical namesake, the prophetess, judge, and "mother in Israel" (Jgs 5:7). When her fourth child, Menuchim, is born with a crippling deformity, she becomes a one-woman army determined to fight for his recovery. Mendel insists that the poor are always powerless and must bear whatever God gives or takes away, but Deborah no longer calls upon God. She seeks advocates for her child wherever they may be found (13). When all her efforts fall short, she determines to secure a blessing from a rabbi. She knows there will be many petitioners waiting in line, but she clears a way through the mob with an impassioned frenzy that will not be thwarted (14).

She receives the blessing she sought, but "blessings need a longer time for their fulfillment than curses" (25), and she grows weary and more despondent as her child continues to languish. Mendel cautions her to remember that "against the will of heaven there is no power." "Thus it is written" (41), he says, and thus it shall be. She should quiet herself and wait for God to do what God will do. Powerlessness is, however, something Deborah is unwilling to accept (41). Her rebuke eats away at Mendel, slowly kindling his indignation. He begins to think of her as a "disease," a "faithful enmity" (42) that is targeting him for destruction.

Deborah's frustration with her husband's inaction multiplies day by day. Mendel decides to move the remnants of the family from their hometown in Russia to America, leaving Menuchim in the care of their neighbors. By this time Deborah's persistence has begun to crumble beneath the weight of crushing realities. The rabbi's blessing will not be fulfilled. God does not want to heal her son. There is nothing she could have done to change the situation. As she prepares for the departure, the narrator of the story observes that "the strength which belongs with faith was no longer hers, and gradually she was also losing the strength which is needed to endure despair" (106). Shortly after their arrival in America, Deborah dies; her last words, spoken in a "deep male voice," a dark, Jewish lullaby for dead children (153).

Roth follows the biblical version by providing a "happy ending" for the story,[82] but not before chronicling Mendel's own belated affirmation of his wife's righteous rage and despair. When his friends urge him to follow the example of Job's patience by trusting in God's providence, Mendel laughs at their naïveté. Emboldened by the memory of his wife's resolute pursuit of justice, he realizes that he too is too angry with God to pray. When Jews assemble to sing the Kol Nidre, Mendel's lips remain closed; his heart is like stone. Mendel "hated God"

(177). He concludes that "the Devil is kinder than God. Since he is not so mighty, he cannot be so cruel" (171).

In *J.B.* Archibald MacLeish presents J.B.'s wife, Sarah, as a person who is acutely aware that God may require more in return for life's blessings than anyone could or should be willing to pay. Scene 1 begins with Sarah, J.B., and their children sitting down to a sumptuous meal on Thanksgiving Day. She asks J.B. to say grace, which he does with an abbreviated version of the Lord's Prayer: "Our Father which art in Heaven / Give us this day our daily bread."[83] The words are familiar, of course, and almost before J.B. can finish, everyone around the table provides the ritualized ending—"Amen!"—that signals the eating can begin. Thanksgiving, however, always makes Sarah nervous. She worries that "God doesn't give all this"—a good home, good food, a healthy, happy family—"for nothing" (30). She knows instinctively that they owe God something for their good fortune (33), and because she is not sure what the price may be, she is frightened that happiness is an impending danger (35, 38). "God rewards and God can punish" (39), she reminds J.B., which means that they and their family are inextricably "caught . . . in Heaven's quandary" (43). J.B. dismisses Sarah's worries by reassuring her that God's blessings are a "free gift" that requires nothing more than "thanks . . . paid like love" (40).

In subsequent scenes MacLeish essentially follows the biblical story line. A series of messengers inform J.B. and Sarah that their children have been killed in a car accident and that their home and community have been destroyed by an unspecified "natural" calamity. Through it all J.B. clings to his faith in God's mysterious justice. He cannot conceive that God could be guilty of punishing people without cause; in his theology humans standing before the bar of divine judgment "have no choice but to be guilty. God is unthinkable if we are innocent" (111). Like his biblical counterpart, J.B. presses Sarah to repeat after him the credo that sustains his unquestioning piety. "Say it after me," he says to Sarah, "The Lord giveth . . . The Lord taketh away." Sarah balks at the word *taketh*—"Takes! Kills! Kills! Kills! Kills!" (89)—and she rejects her husband's defense of God.

> Does God demand deception of us?—
> Purchase His innocence by ours?
> Must we be guilty for Him?—bear
> The burden of the world's malevolence
> For Him who made the world? (109)
>
> I will not stay here if you lie—. . .
> Not if you betray my children . . .
> They are
> Dead and they are innocent! I will not

> Let you sacrifice their deaths
> To make injustice justice and God good! . . .
> If you buy quiet with their innocence—
> Theirs or yours . . .
> I will not love you. (110)

MacLeish does not criticize Sarah when finally she says to J.B., "Curse God and die" (110). Instead he presents her as both more honest and more compassionate than her husband. Sarah understands that no assertion about God or God's justice can fill the void created by the death of innocent children. "Cry for justice," she says, "and the stars / Will stare until your eyes sting" (151). There is "only love" (152), Sarah says in the last scene, and for that people must cling to one another when the lights go out and the way ahead grows dark and God is nowhere to be found.

In *A Masque of Reason,* Robert Frost imagines a forty-third chapter to the book of Job in which Job, his wife, Thyatira, and God meet a thousand years after their biblical drama concluded to review what had happened. Frost envisions the biblical story as entertainment, a staged comedy that invites a contemporary audience to laugh at the farce of both human and divine reason. None of the characters are exempt from a comedic undercutting, which allows Frost to explore the serious questions at stake in the biblical story without privileging any particular perspective concerning how they should be resolved.

At the outset there is someone caught in the braches of a tree, described as both a "burning bush" and a "Christmas Tree," which is lighted with "the ornaments the Greek artificers made for the Emperor Alexius." Once this figure gets loose, Job's wife recognizes him immediately: "It's God. I'd know Him by [William] Blake's picture anywhere. Now what's he doing?"[84] God apologizes to Job "for the apparently unmeaning sorrow / You were afflicted with in those old days." "It was the essence of the trial," he continues, that "you shouldn't understand it at the time. It had to seem unmeaning to have meaning" (474). God also thanks Job for releasing him "from moral bondage to the human race," claiming that in pre-Joban days, he had no choice but to prosper good and punish evil; otherwise he would have "suffer[ed] loss of worship." Because Job freed God to be God, God now promotes him to the level of a saint (476).

Neither Job nor his wife accepts God's explanation for what happened to them, but it is Thyatira who takes the point in questioning God. "I stood by Job," she says to God, implying that God did not: "all You seem to do is lose Your temper / When reason-hungry mortals ask for reasons." She presses the protest (478), as she believes only a woman can, asserting that Job should have raised when it might have made a difference.

Frost suggests that both Job and God are guilty of patronizing Thyatira. Job dismisses her concerns as typical of those a woman might raise; after all, since she is a woman, "she's not interested in general ideas and principles" (479). God responds to Thyatira's questions by saying that "she's beautiful" (479) and "I'm charmed by her" (480), a subtle but telling clue that in Frost's retelling of this biblical story, God considers Job's wife to be an enchanting but harmless figure. The final words of Frost's addendum to the biblical story, which he assigns to Job's wife, seem to reinforce both the importance of her contribution and how easily it may be erased from the memories of those who, like Job and God, may be inclined to dismiss her as merely a charming, even comic, supporting character. After listening to God and Job talk back and forth about the reasons why Job had suffered so, Thyatira asks God, Job, and the devil to pose for a picture to commemorate the event. She positions the three beside God's throne, the same prefabricated plywood throne that God stood beside when he first got loose from the tree (474). She takes out her Kodak camera, and just before snapping the shot, she ends the play with these words:

> There, that's just the right arrangement.
> Now someone can light up the Burning Bush
> And turn the gold enameled artificial birds on.
> I recognize them. Greek artificers
> Devised them for Alexius Commenus.
> They won't show in the picture. That's too bad.
> Neither will I show. That's too bad moreover.
> Now if you three have settled anything
> You'd as well smile as frown on the occasion. (489–90)

There's Always Someone Playing Mrs. Job

If it is true that "there's always Someone playing Job," as Zuss, the God character, says in *J.B.*, then we should not be surprised that there is also always someone reading themselves into the story of Mrs. Job. From the one line attributed to her in the biblical account, translators, commentators, artists, playwrights, and poets have extrapolated various stories about Job's wife. Some have demonized her, others have sanctified her. Some have seen her as a profile in courage, others as a "typical" woman whose passions, commendable though they may be, lack the intellectual heft that only a strong man can provide. Some have seen her as an ardent feminist, a fearless champion for those who suffer innocently; some have feminized her, accentuating her beauty, grace, charm, even her fashionable attire. Such different readings of Job's wife can be connected to a range of shifting historical, cultural, and political factors, but it is clear that few interpreters have been willing to follow the lead of the biblical script and simply dismiss her from the story. The trajectory of postbiblical readings moves, by fits and starts, to reposition Job's wife on the stage of this ongoing drama. From being little more than a prop in the original staging, she emerges as a major character, sometimes speaking her words just outside the spotlight of center stage, sometimes assuming center stage herself.

Contemporary interpreters extend this trajectory still further. Some recast the biblical account as Job's wife's first-person account of their life together.[85] The story is Job's story, told from his wife's perspective. Anna Ruth Henriques has taken a different approach. In *The Book of Mechtilde,* she demonstrates that a woman might tell her own story and use Job's story to illustrate it.

Henriques explains in the introduction to *The Book of Mechtilde,* that although the book is based on the book of Job, the main character, Mechtilde, "replaces Job."[86] Mechtilde is Sheila Mechtilde Henriques, née Chong, of Kingston, Jamaica. After nine years of battling breast cancer, she died in 1978. She was the author's mother. Henriques notes that she had wanted to create a memorial of some sort for her mother. The book of Job helped her conceptualize how to do so. Like Job her mother was a good person who had suffered misfortune and sickness. Unlike Job, who was rewarded for his patience and faith with the restoration of his health and family, Mechtilde's reprieve from suffering came with death.

Henriques's memorial takes the shape of an illuminated manuscript. On each left-side page, she tells her mother's story, beginning with a brief narrative that resembles the opening words in Job (2). Henriques proceeds, sometimes in prose, sometimes in poetry, to describe major episodes in her mother's life: drinking and laughing with her husband and daughters; her affection for the land, people, and rituals in Jah; the satisfaction she and her husband shared when their hard work was rewarded with modest prosperity; and beginning with the words "Then misfortune struck" (24), her long illness, death, and final peace.

Each right-side page is a tightly packed series of concentric illuminations. At the outer edge of each page, a gold border of loosely sketched flowers, fruits, and animals creates a pastiche of nature teeming with life in the face of death. Inside these borders Henriques uses a calligraphic script with gold lettering to cite passages from the book of Job, which begin near the center of the page and expand in widening circles until they reach the inner edges of the framing borders. She does not cite any passages from the prologue or epilogue, choosing instead to begin with Job 3:1–26, Job's opening curse and lamentation from the ash heap (3), and to end with Job 42:1–6, Job's final response to God about what he has learned from his ordeal (81). In between she cites a lengthy portion from every chapter. There is no apparent effort to link these passages directly to the story of Mechtilde's life as it unfolds on the opposite pages; instead Henriques simply wraps the

Joban story, figuratively and literally, around the colorful paintings of Mechtilde that stand at the center of each page.

The format of these three concentric circles invites different ways of interpreting the composition. On the one hand, we may view the passages from Job as the lens through which we interpret Mechtilde's Joblike journey. On the other Henriques suggests that Mechtilde's life journey leads us to reread Job. It is not Job who shows us how to read her; it is she who teaches us how to read him.

In one of these pictures, Mechtilde lies in a hospital bed as her three daughters look at her through the opened slats of a louvered door. Her face is a mask of gold; her head is haloed with a nimbus of light (77). The same face, eyes downward, appears elsewhere at the base of a wild ginger blossom (67) or within the scarlet petals of a hibiscus (33, 35, 37). Some pictures show her in scenes from everyday life, climbing the stairs of the family house past photographs of her three daughters (11) or fishing in a boat while her daughters sit on the banks (51). Others are infused with multiple cultural and religious symbols—Christian and Jewish, Chinese and Creole, European and African—that celebrate the diversity of the family's heritage: a shofar lies behind a great teardrop, inside of which is a small tree of life with green sprigs (27); a baby swaddled (or shrouded) in a tightly wrapped white cloth lies between a serpent and a red apple (39), a hand and a seeing eye (41), and an egg and a fish (43). From first picture to last, it is the image of Mechtilde that focuses the reader's attention. From pictures of her as healthy young woman with a tilaka painted on her forehead and a sequence of hairstyle changes (45, 47, 49, 61, 63), she is slowly transfigured by cancer and chemotherapy into a hairless woman (65) whose final resting place, in the last picture, is a coffin (81). On the opposite page of this last image is Henriques's poem about the journey of life, which ends in the "Duppy Kingdom," in Jamaican folklore the place of the restless dead:

> Jesus Peace
> Is this what you die for
> Part of what one must become
> Duppy Kingdom
> Where no one
> Can sleep
> Fright-filled
> Of themselves and
> Their hapless heads
> Chests beating
> Breaths rising
> Breasts falling

> For Duppy
> Duppy Kingdom
> Done come? (80)

It is of course a long way from the land of Uz, the biblical home of Job, to the mango groves of Jamaica, where the story of Mechtilde begins and ends. And yet perhaps Henriques provides an appropriate place to conclude this chapter on the ever-widening reach of the mere six words the biblical account records for the unnamed wife of Job. A minor character she may have been for the Joban author, but she has left a large footprint in the imagination of those who have sensed that she had a story of her own to tell. The various embellishments provided by post-biblical readers do not carry the imprimatur of holy scripture accorded to the canonical story, but they do invite interpreters to reread the text with an enlarged sense of its generative power. The question they pose, if we may rephrase the words from God that set the original story in motion, is "Have you considered my servant, Job's wife?"

PART II

Center Stage

The Wisdom Dialogue (Job 3:1–42:6)

4

JOB'S WORDS FROM THE ASH HEAP

The Scandalous Voice of Defiance

After this, Job opened his mouth and cursed.

Job 3:1

Submission, thou dost know I cannot try;
For what submission but that fatal word,
The death-seal of mankind's captivity . . .
would he accept
Or could I yield?

Prometheus, in Percy Shelley's *Prometheus Unbound*

The prologue to the book of Job ends in seven days and nights of silence during which no one—neither Job, his friends, nor God—speaks a word, "for they saw that [Job's] suffering was very great" (2:13). The silence is both rhetorically and theologically significant;[1] it requires readers to pause, to contemplate the vexed gap between first words about innocent suffering and other ones yet unimagined, inarticulate. Inside this gap multiple and typically competing options vie for dominance. On one end of the spectrum, willing submission to what is, however destructive it may be, may trump every compulsion to protest. This appears to be Job's first response in 2:10: "Shall we accept only good from God and not accept evil?" (NJPS). On the other end of the spectrum, as the Polish poet Czeslaw Milosz writes in reflecting on the extermination of Jews in the Warsaw Ghetto, "rage will kindle at a poet's word."[2] Susan Neiman extends the analogy from Warsaw to New York and Washington, D.C., and to reflection on the silence imposed on language by the events of September 11, 2001: "For a day or so after the catastrophe, language itself seemed useless. At midday on September 12, CNN showed silent pictures above a running band of caption: NO COMMENT NO COMMENT NO COMMENT NO COMMENT NO COMMENT NO COMMENT. By nightfall there was ordinary newscasting discussing everything from economic losses to the appropriateness of discussing anything at all. . . . Terror is meant to strike us dumb. *Finding words with which to face it is an act of reconstruction.*"[3]

After seven days and nights of silence, when suffering seems to have rendered all words "useless," Job speaks again. His words from the ash heap set the agenda for everyone—the friends, God, we readers—who will follow him into the abyss of the search for an answer to a question that ultimately refuses silence: "Why did you [God] bring me forth from the womb?" (Job 10:18; cf. 3:11).

"Counter-Cosmic Incantations" (Job 3)

"There is little in literature as black as the opening verses of Job's curse" in Job 3:1–10.[4] "Black" is an apt descriptor, for Job uses five different words to buttress his call for a deep and impenetrable darkness to eclipse the light of his world.[5] With seven curses—three against the day of his birth (3:3–5) and four against the night of his conception (3:6–9)—Job expresses a death wish. His language clearly parallels Jer 20:14–18, but more important, it appropriates the language and imagery of Genesis 1 in ways that suggest he is cursing not only the particular day of his beginnings but also the primordial day of creation that set in motion all beginnings. In this respect Job's first words from the ash heap constitute a "counter-cosmic incantation"[6] that has the rhetorical effect of nullifying the hopes and promises attached to each day of the seven-day creation scheme in Genesis 1. The clearest example is Job's opening curse of "that day" when he was born—"let that day be darkness" (3:4: *yĕhî ḥōšek*)—which rhetorically reverses God's first creative act, "let there be light" (Gn 1:3: *yĕhî 'ôr*). The parallels are not exact, but they are sufficient to suggest that Job calls for a systematic reversal of God's primordial design for life.

Genesis 1: "And God said . . ."[7]	Job 3: And Job said . . .
v. 3 Let there be light	v. 3 Let there be darkness
v. 7 [Let there be] waters *above* the firmament	v. 4 Let not God *above* seek it . . .
v. 2 [Let there be] darkness was upon the face of the waters	v. 5 Let gloom and deep darkness claim it . . .
v.14 [Let there be] lights to separate day and night . . . for seasons and for years	vv. 6–7 Let thick darkness seize that night Let it not rejoice among the days of the year Let it not come into the number of months Let that night be barren
v. 21 [Let there be] great sea monsters	v. 8 Let those whose curse it curse the Sea those who are skilled to raise up Leviathan
v.15 [Let there be] lights to give light upon earth	v. 9 Let the stars of the dawn be dark Let it hope for light, but have none v.15 Let it not see the eyelids of the morning[8]

Three aspects of what it means to curse are important for understanding Job's words. First, in the Hebrew Bible, to curse is to refuse to bless. To curse is to withhold approval of the status quo, to deny its inevitability, to evoke a reversal of what is in order to speak different alternatives into existence. On the other side of silence, when Job decides to curse, not bless, his life, he places himself in opposition to God's evaluation that a world in which seven sons and three daughters die "for no reason" remains "very good" (Gn 1:31; Job 2:3). Second, to speak a curse (or a blessing) is to set in motion the very action the words convey. When Job curses the day of his birth, he seeks to effect the death that his misery has forced him to contemplate but has not allowed him to experience. Third, curses (and blessings) are effective only when spoken by authorized persons (e.g., kings, prophets, priests, elders) within circumscribed conditions (e.g., in times of personal or national crisis or in the liturgies of the cult). The power of the utterance rests not in the words themselves but rather in the authority and status of the one who speaks them. Job has no such status in the biblical story. He has no official title; his standing in his community depends on God's affirmation—he is "blameless and upright, one who fears God and turns away from evil" (1:8, 2:3; cf. 1:1)—and this affirmation has been replaced by another that seems to diminish rather than enhance his status. The one acclaimed as "the greatest of all the people of the east" (1:3) is now one whose "greatness" is defined by suffering (2:13), by what he has lost by fearing God, not by what he has gained.

Job's curses create an abiding tension within the ongoing drama. How should readers evaluate one who curses what God blesses? Is opposition to God a viable option for a mere mortal or only an absurd one? How can words, even those spoken in earnest by a recognized righteous and blameless person, reverse what has already happened? Can Job unbirth himself? How can one who sits on the ash heap, where no person of status would normally be found, command attention and respect? What authority, what power, does Job have to effect change in the status quo? I pose the questions but defer their contemplation, which requires more than one reading.

In the second segment of chapter 3 (vv.11–26), Job moves from curse to lamentation. The key word throughout is "Why?" (*lāmmâ*, vv.11, 20; and with different words or by implication in vv.12, 16, 23). The question, typically addressed to God, is heavily laden with protest and accusation (e.g., Ex 32:11–12; Pss 10:1, 22:1, 74:1; Jer 20:18; Lam 5:20). The lead question, "Why did I not die at birth?" (3:11), moves Job deeper into the solitude of his personal suffering and into the realm of his contention that settled religious or cultural orthodoxies must not, cannot, erase the voice of the first-person singular, the voice of the individual sufferer for whom the norms of collective judgment become no more than tautologies. Job's view from the ash heap of suffering is that death and consignment to Sheol, where there is no distinction between the righteous and the wicked, is preferable to a life deprived of justice (3:13–19).[9] In 3:20–26 Job extends the lament. If he could not die at birth, why then must he continue to live? His question, best translated as active not passive (as in NRSV), is "Why does [God] give light to the sufferer?" (NJPS). When the most one can say about life in the world God has created is that there is no "ease," no "quiet," no "rest," only "turmoil" (rōgez, NRSV: "trouble" [3:26]), what is the incentive for continuing?

Job's curses and laments in chapter 3 set the agenda for everyone who decides to engage him. As the story unfolds, the friends (Eliphaz, Bildad, Zophar [Job 4–27], and Elihu [Job 32–37]) will respond to the challenge. So too, eventually, will God (Job 38:1–41:34). We will deal with these responses in subsequent chapters. For now it is instructive to focus on Job's opening words, which in the rich and variegated history of interpretation become a trope for the scandalous voice of defiance.

Antecedent Voices

In the world of ancient literature, Job is of course not the first to protest innocent suffering. Texts from Mesopotamia, Egypt, and Canaan confirm that the social, cultural, and historical situations that gave rise to questions about suffering, divine justice, and the meaning of life were present at least as early as the second millennium. A brief overview of major Mesopotamian exemplars suffices to illustrate the similarities and the differences with the biblical Job.[10]

"A Man and His God," also known as the "Sumerian Job," is a second-millennium copy of a text that may be centuries older. It records the lamentations of a righteous sufferer who has inexplicably lost his health, wealth, and respect. The burden of the sufferer's lament is a god who appears indifferent to his plight:

> My companion says not a true word to me,
> My friend gives the lie to my righteous word.
> (And) you, my god do not thwart him.
> You carry off my understanding,
> The wicked has conspired against me.
> Angered you, stormed about, planned evil,
> . . . .
> I, the discerning, why am I counted among the ignorant? (lines 35–41, 43)
>
> How long will you neglect me, leave me unprotected?
> . . . .
> (How long) will you leave me unguided? (98, 100)[11]

Unlike his biblical counterpart, the Sumerian Job accepts the counsel of the sages, who instruct him to give up his lament and conform to the truth of conventional wisdom: all suffering is the consequence of sin.

> They say—the sages—a word righteous (and) straightforward:
> "Never has a sinless child been born to its mother,
> ... a sinless workman has not existed from of old" ...
> My god, now that you have shown me my sins ... ,
> I, the young man, would confess my sins before you. (101–4,113)

The end of the text reports that when the sufferer confessed his sins, the god was pleased and rewarded him by turning his "suffering into joy" (125).

"I Will Praise the Lord of Wisdom" (*Ludlul bēl nēmeqi*), also known as the "Babylonian Job," comprises four tablets from Ashurbanipal's library in Nineveh. The extant texts date to the seventh century B.C.E., but they are likely copies of texts composed in the second millennium. A noble person who has experienced a reversal of fortunes complains that his fidelity counts for nothing, because the gods have abandoned him.

> I called to my god, but he did not show his face,
> I prayed to my goddess, but she did not raise her head. ...
>
> Like one who has not made libations to his god.
> Nor invoked his goddess at table,
> Does not engage in prostration, nor takes cognizance of bowing down;
> From whose mouth supplication and prayer is lacking,
> Who has done nothing on holy days, and despised sabbaths, ...
>
> Like one who grown torpid and forgotten his lord,
> Has frivolously sworn a solemn oath by his god,
> (like such a one) do I appear.
> For myself, I gave attention to supplication and prayer:
> To me prayer was discretion, sacrifice my rule.
> The day of reverencing the god was a joy to my heart; ... (2.4–5, 12–16, 21–25)[12]

Here again lament gives way to compliance, as the sufferer concedes that Marduk's justice is simply inscrutable ("Who knows the will of the gods in heaven?" [2.36]). The only thing this sufferer can know with certainty is that there will be no relief until he appeases Marduk, who has the power to heal (*bēl nēmeqi*), with praise and thanksgiving (4.42). Although the "blasphemous implications"[13] in the Babylonian Job's wonderments about innocent suffering are similar to the biblical Job's, the poem's dominant concern is the sufferer's eventual restoration. There is no attempt to explain the problem or to offer a solution, other than to affirm that the deity makes all things right in the end.

A third Mesopotamian text, "The Babylonian Theodicy," anticipates the impact of Job's personal suffering on the principles of justice that undergird world order. Cast as a dialogue between a sufferer and his companion, the sufferer complains that he was abandoned as an orphan and left vulnerable to oppression and violence. The friend assures him that while suffering is common to all, those who remain steadfast will ultimately be better off for the experience (lines 12–13, 18–19, 21–22).[14] The sufferer counters that his friend has not understood. The dialogue continues through repeated exchanges. The sufferer asserts the inexplicable reality of his plight. The friend responds with disputations and counterarguments. By the end of the poem, the two reach a resolution of sorts. The sufferer thanks his friend for his companionship and asks that he join him in petitioning the gods for mercy.

> You are kind, my friend; behold my grief.
> Help me; look on my distress; know it. . . . (287–88)

> May the god who has thrown me off give help,
> May the goddess who has [abandoned me] show mercy . . . (295–96)

There are parallels between "The Babylonian Theodicy" and Job, but again there are also clear differences. Two deserve comment. First, the sufferer in "The Babylonian Theodicy" implies that the gods have failed him, but he never directly challenges them. He is satisfied to air his grievances before his friend and to wait in contrition for the merciful return of the gods who have inexplicably abandoned him. Job, by contrast, becomes increasingly determined to address his complaints and accusations directly to the God he holds responsible for his misfortune (e.g., 7:7–21, 10:1–17, 13:20–28, 30:20–31, 31:35–37). In the end Job speaks of a change of heart (42:5–6), but it is far from clear that his words express contrition. Second, the "dialogue" in "The Babylonian Theodicy" is between the sufferer and his companion. The gods never speak, never intervene, never have more than a spoken-about presence in the debate about pious suffering. By contrast the *first* and *last* "character" to speak in the biblical Job's story is God (1:7, 42:7). Moreover although the dialogue between Job and his friends is extensive (Job 4–27), the dialogue on which the book turns is the one between Job and God (38:1–42:6).

A fourth Mesopotamian text, "The Dialogue of Pessimism," deserves mention. In a dialogue between a master and his slave, the master contemplates the benefits of suicide, reminiscent of Job's death wish in Job 3.

> "Slave, listen to me." "Here I am, sir, here I am."
> "What then is good?"

"To have my neck and your neck broken
And to be thrown into the river is good.
'Who is so tall as to ascend to the heavens?
Who is so broad as to compass the underworld?'" (lines 79–83)[15]

The slave responds with sympathy for the master's considerations, but in the end he says, perhaps satirically, that his master would not last three days without the dialogue he provides (86). The master's weariness with life is more akin to Ecclesiastes than to Job, who despite his death wish, refuses to relinquish the faint hope that those who dare to argue their case with God (cf. Job 13:3) will ultimately get a hearing.

In sum none of the ancient Near Eastern antecedents exemplifies the persistent defiance that characterizes the Job who speaks in Job 3–27. In terms of genre, most of these Mesopotamian texts are praises and thanksgivings for the relief of suffering, not protests.[16] The Joban author certainly engages conventional genres, motifs, and ideas concerning righteous suffering, but his purpose seems aimed more at challenging normative assumptions than at sustaining them. Bruce Zuckerman makes the point well.

[The] Job in the Poem does not come to praise God but to provoke him. And when God does appear, He does not do so because He has been moved to pity by an abject supplicant, as would be expected according to convention, but rather because He has been greatly angered by the unflinching demands of an antagonist who is anything but abject. . . .

The departure from the expected correspondences here could not be more dramatic. . . . The Righteous Sufferer is careful not to become so strident as to provoke his god, lest that god turn a deaf ear as a result. But in Job precisely the opposite happens: Job has broken this taboo, and conversely (if not perversely) God's response may be characterized as direct reaction to this flouting of convention.[17]

The defiant Job who flouts ancient Near Eastern convention does not escape the critical notice of early translators and interpreters. LXX translators depart from the Hebrew at points throughout the dialogues to introduce changes that mitigate Job's contentious remarks. Some changes alter Job's speeches by subtly removing God as the object of his questions and complaints. In Job 3:20, for example, Job asks, "Why does he [God] *give* (*yittēn*) light to one in misery . . . ?" The Greek translator renders this question with a passive verb—"Why then is light *given* (*dedotai*) to those in bitterness . . . ?"—thus removing the implication that God is the agent of Job's affliction.[18] In 9:22 Job charges that God makes no distinction between the innocent and the guilty: "It is all one. . . . he [God] destroys both the blameless and the wicked." The LXX avoids the implication that God's justice is capricious by attributing a different assertion to Job: "Therefore I said, 'Anger destroys the great and powerful.'" Job's speech in 16:7–17 describes God as a brutal enemy who attacks hapless victims without restraint. The translator does not eliminate the accusation altogether, but he does redirect it, for example in 16:13–14, by substituting plural pronouns and verbs that shift the blame away from God and on to Job's unnamed enemies.

Hebrew: His archers surround me. He slashes open my kidneys, and shows no mercy; he pours out my gall on the ground. He bursts upon me again and again; he rushes at me like a warrior.

Greek: They surrounded me with spears, hurling them into my kidneys, without sparing; they poured out my gall on the ground. They threw me down, fall upon fall; they rushed at me powerfully.

In other places the translator changes Job's complaints about God's injustice to expressions of confidence in God's justice. In 19:6 Job complains that "God has put me in the wrong." The Greek Job does not accuse God of wrongdoing; he says only that God "troubles" him. In 27:2a Job says, "God . . . has taken away my right." The translator effectively turns Job's complaint into an affirmation of the God "who has judged me so." In the epilogue the narrator reports that Job's friends and family showed him sympathy and comfort "for *all the evil (kol-hārā'â)* that the Lord had brought upon him" (42:11b). In the Greek version, the narrator says that when Job's friends came to comfort him, they were "amazed at *all those things (ethaumasan epi pasin ois)* that the Lord had brought upon him" (LXX Job 42:11b; author's translation). They are amazed not at the evil God had inflicted upon Job, but rather at the surplus of God's beneficence, which is reported in the preceding verse: "The Lord gave Iob twice as much as he had before so that he had double" (LXX Job 42:10). These and other such changes in the LXX "construct a character for Job that is more saintly than that seen in the Hebrew text."[19] The motivation for these changes may be debated,[20] but it is clear that the LXX effectively tones down Job's rebelliousness and highlights his confidence in God's justice and his ultimate vindication by God.[21]

The *Testament of Job* goes even further by significantly recasting the dialogues between Job and his friends. With the LXX (2:11) the *Testament* depicts Job's friends, Eliphas, Baldad, and Sophar, as kings. They enter the scene some twenty years after the onset of Job's affliction, and initially, as in the biblical account, they sit beside him in silence for seven days and nights (*T. Job* 28:4). How to break this silence, however, is their quandary, not Job's, for they have to be convinced that the tragic figure before them is in fact Job. Only after extensive interrogation, including a three-day incense ritual that enables them to withstand Job's stench (31:2–4), can they come close enough to verify their friend's identity.

From this point on, the *Testament* essentially reverses the biblical account by attributing doubts and questions about innocent suffering to the friends, not to Job. Eliphas speaks a lengthy "royal lament" concerning Job's loss of wealth and status, which is accented by a repeating refrain: "Where then is the splendor of your throne" (32:2, 4, 5, 6, 7, 9, 10, 11, 12).[22] Job responds by affirming that his "throne is in the upper world, and its splendor and majesty come from the right hand of the Father" (33:3, cf. 33:5). Baldad worries that Job's hope and trust in God's justice are signs of mental instability, "For who would not be driven to senselessness and imbalanced when he is sick?" (35:5). Job responds by saying that sanity in the face of suffering inspires praise of God's inscrutable wisdom, not doubt: "Why then should I not speak about the magnificent things of the Lord?" (38:1). Sophar, earnestly seeking a way to help Job ("What then do you wish us to do for you?" [38:7]), offers the help of physicians that he and his fellow kings have brought with them. Job responds by saying that he will be healed by the God who created the physicians (38:6–8).

In the book of Job, Job's dialogues with the friends culminate in God's appearance to Job in the whirlwind. In the biblical version, God's speech is a litany of questions, to which Job responds first with silence, then with a confession that his knowledge is inferior to God's (38:1–42:6). The *Testament* omits this speech entirely and replaces it with the words God speaks in the biblical epilogue (42:7–9). Thus God's appearance serves not to question Job but to expose the sins of the friends, who "have not spoken truly regarding my servant Job" (*T. Job* 42:4–5). The three friends, who have heard these words along with Job, recognize their sins and offer atoning sacrifices to God. Elihu, "inspired by Satan" (41:5), remains unforgiven; in the end his only compensation is Eliphas's dirge for "the evil one" who will have "no memorial among the living" (43:5, 17).

Both LXX and the *Testament* effectively censor the defiant Job who has such prominence in the biblical account. It can be argued that the biblical account itself encourages such censoring, that by framing the story with a prose account of Job's piety and his ultimate reward it neutralizes the portrait of defiance that dominates the poetic center of the book. If our assessment of the tension between the two contrasting portraits of Job were to be governed solely by lectionary readings, which focus on the patience of Job, or by the disproportionate attention postbiblical artists and other interpreters give to the Job who submits in contrition to God's will for his life,[23] then we might well wonder whether the Job who speaks in Job 3–27 has left any discernible footprint at all, in culture or religion. In consideration of this issue, it is instructive to reflect on the connections between the Hebraic portrait of the Job who curses and laments life in relation to God, however his words may have been muted, and the Greek repertoire of tragedy.

Prometheus: "A Spectacle That Shames the Fame of Zeus"

In his survey of *The Vision of Tragedy,* Richard Sewall notes both the difference and the similarity between Job and the Greek tragedian vision. On the one hand, "tragedy" is an inapt characterization of Hebrew literature.

> Although the Hebrews had their recalcitrant figures, capable, like the Poet of Job, of deep penetration into the realm of tragedy, they are rightly regarded as the people of a Covenant, a Code, and a Book. This is one reason, perhaps, why they never developed a tragic theater, where their beliefs and modes of living would be under constant scrutiny. Their public communication was through synagogue and pulpit; their prophets and preachers proclaimed the doctrine of obedience to divine law, and the rabbis endlessly proliferated the rules for daily life. The rebellious Job was not typical. For the most part, their heroes were lonely, God-summoned men whose language was that of witness to the one true light.[24]

On the other hand, Sewall demonstrates that even though the Greeks invented the term *tragedy,* we can see in the book of Job "the basic elements of the tragic form."

> The cultural situation, the matrix out which *Job* came, is the very definition of the "tragic moment" in history, a period when traditional values begin to lose their power to comfort and sustain, and man finds himself once more groping in the dark. The unknown Poet's "action," his redoing of the orthodox and optimistic folktale of the pious and rewarded Job, is (as we can say now), a classic example of the dynamics of tragedy, of vision creating a form. And the greatest figure of his creation, the suffering, questioning, and unanswered Job, is the towering tragic figure of antiquity. More than Prometheus or Oedipus, Job is the universal symbol for the western imagination of the mystery of undeserved suffering.[25]

Sewell's ambivalence concerning the connection between Job and the Greek tragedies, especially the Promethean myth, is characteristic of Joban studies. There is a long trajectory of work, beginning with Bishop Theodore of Mopsuestia (d. 428), that speculates on the connection between Job and Greek tragedians (Aeschylus, Sophocles, and Euripides).[26] Perhaps the most ambitious is H. M. Kallen, who argues that the Joban author created a Hebraized form of Euripidean tragedy, with each round of the dialogue between Job and his friends followed by a choral ode.[27] Kallen's conclusions are now mostly dismissed or ignored. Nevertheless the evocation of Job as a tragic, Promethean figure is deeply embedded in public discourse. To cite Lamartine again as but one example: "*Job is the Prometheus of the word,* raised to the heavens still shrieking, still bleeding, in the very claws of the vulture gnawing at his heart. He is the victim become judge, by the sublime impersonality of reason, celebrating his own torture and, like the Roman Brutus, casting up to heaven the drops of his blood, not as an insult, but as a libation to a just God!"[28]

I am not concerned here to advocate the Joban author's dependence on either the Greek tragedies generally or on the Promethean myth specifically.[29] I submit, however, that the defiant Job who challenges God, like other "titanic" figures in ancient literature, has become a touchstone for authors, composers, artists, poets, and others whose aspirations for justice, both political and religious, have moved them to "rebel passion."[30]

The essential features of the Promethean myth originate with Hesiod (eighth century B.C.E.), who describes Prometheus as a Titan who stole fire from the heavens and gave it to humanity, against the wishes of the gods, thus provoking Zeus to punish him by chaining him to a pillar where he endured the daily torture of an eagle consuming his liver.[31] Some two centuries later, Aeschylus (c. 525–426 B.C.E.) wrote the most influential version of the myth, *Prometheus Bound*, the second part of a trilogy whose first and third parts are not extant.[32]

Prometheus Bound comprises seven scenes. A brief overview sets the table for the discussion that follows.

Scene 1 (lines 1–87)

As the play opens, Kratos (Power), Bia (Force), and Hephaestus, the god of fire, come to execute the decreed punishment on Prometheus, whose offense (*hamartias,* "sin" [9]), conferring fire on mortals, "brooks the sovereignty (*turannida;* literally, "tyranny") of Zeus."[33] Hephaestus is reluctant to enforce the divine decree ("Alas, Prometheus, I groan over thy pangs" [66]), but he eventually submits to Kratos's argument that Prometheus is "but a dullard compared to Zeus" (62), and as such he deserves the punishment Zeus has ordered, otherwise Hephaestus himself may be guilty of negligence ("Haste thee then to cast the fetters about him, lest the Father behold thee loitering" [53]).

Scene 2 (lines 88–127)

Abandoned to his suffering, Prometheus delivers a soliloquy in which he invokes the four elements of the cosmos—heaven, earth, waters, and sun—to hear his lament. Prometheus vows to endure the "evil from the gods" (92), for as his name (Forethought) indicates, he knows in advance what his destiny will be. Nevertheless, like Job, Prometheus must decide whether to endure in silence or to complain that his penalty is harsh beyond expectation. Pain compels speech, for as he says, the "might of Necessity brooketh no resistance" (105).[34] Before he speaks, however, he hears the sounds of approaching visitors and wonders whether they come to comfort or to condemn (117–23).

Scene 3 (lines 128–285)

The entrance of the chorus of Oceanides (daughters of Oceanus) marks the beginning of a series of conversations between Prometheus and various visitors. The Oceanides have heard the "the clang of iron" (132) as Hephaestus chained him to the rocks, and they race to his side on winged chariots. Like Hephaestus the chorus is initially frightened by the arbitrary implementation of Zeus's "new-fangled laws" (150–51), and they raise their voices in lamentation ("Who feels not with thee the pang of thy woes—save only Zeus?" [161–62]). The chorus asks Prometheus to explain what has happened to him, and when he does, they are shocked by his accusation that Zeus, in stubborn wrath, acts like a tyrant toward those who challenge his authority.

> Of wretched mortals he took no heed, but desired to bring the whole race to nothingness and to create another, a new one, in its stead. Against this purpose none dared make a stand save I myself—I only had the courage; I saved mortals so that they did not descend, blasted utterly, unto the house of Death. Therefore I am bent by so grievous tortures, painful to suffer, piteous to behold. I that gave mortals first place in my pity, I am deemed unworthy to win this pity for myself, but am thus mercilessly disciplined, a spectacle that shames the fame of Zeus. (233–43)

To no avail Prometheus implores the chorus to participate in his suffering ("'Tis easy for him who keeps his foot free from harm to counsel and admonish him who is in misery. . . . Take part in the trouble of him who is now in sore distress" [265–66, 276]).

Scene 4 (lines 286–398)

The second visitor is Oceanus, who also claims to come in friendship and sympathy. He urges discretion, lest Zeus overhear Prometheus's blustering words, and he promises that Zeus will grant freedom from suffering if Prometheus will but cease from his rebellion. Prometheus refuses the counsel and resolves instead to "drain to the dregs my present lot until such time as the mind of Zeus shall abate its wrath" (377–78).

Scene 5 (lines 399–500)

The chorus returns in scene 5, now affirming that the "whole earth crieth aloud in lamentation" (406) with Prometheus because "Zeus, holding thus direful sway by self-appointed laws," displays such an "overweening spirit" (403–5). Prometheus responds that he has acted only out of compassion for humankind: mortals were blind, mute, and ignorant until he gave them sight, speech, and knowledge: "every art possessed by man comes from Prometheus" (505–6). Like their father, the chorus of Oceanides cautions Prometheus against any further defiance of Zeus ("This thou must learn as yet; be not importunate" [519]). Their conclusion, which resonates with the counsel of Job's friends, is that Prometheus has but one option: fear Zeus, "the dispenser of all things," and never transgress what he decrees ("Never shall the counsels of mortal men transgress the ordering of Zeus" [527, 550–51; cf., e.g., Job 22:21]).

Scene 6 (lines 561–943)

The entrance of Io changes significantly the tonality of the drama. She is the first figure in the tragedy who is not a god. A beautiful and chaste maiden, she was forced by her father, Inachus, to satisfy Zeus's sexual desires. Hera, Zeus's jealous wife, turns her into a half-cow, half-human figure, who is chased through the world by a gadfly. When her flight drives her into the Scythian wilderness, where Prometheus has been banished, she presents herself to him, sufferer to sufferer, as a hideous example that mirrors his own situation. Io recounts her story to Prometheus, emphasizing Zeus's cruelty toward her, and confesses that she has lost her will to live ("Better it were to die once for all than linger out all my days in misery" [750–51]). Prometheus foresees that there will be no relief either for Io or for himself "till Zeus be hurled from his sovereignty (turannidos)" (756). This will happen, Prometheus explains, because Zeus's "own empty-headed purposes" (762) will lead him into a marriage with one of Io's descendants that will produce a child, Hercules, "a son mightier than his sire" (768). Prometheus alone has the power to check Zeus's will and save him from this fate, but he cannot be coerced to give up his secret until Zeus, wrecked upon his own evil, learns "how different it is to be a sovereign (archein) and a slave" (926–27).

Scene 7 (lines 944–1093)

In the final scene, Zeus sends Hermes, his "underling" (984), to demand that Prometheus reveal what he knows about the future ("Bend thy will, perverse fool, oh bend thy will at last to wisdom in face of thy present sufferings" [999–1000]), failing which, Hermes warns, Zeus will inflict upon him still greater suffering. Prometheus is obstinate in his refusal: "There is no torment or device by which Zeus shall induce me to utter this until these injurious fetters be loosed" (990–91). Hermes instructs the chorus to dismiss any sympathy it may have for Prometheus ("never deem stubbornness better than wise counsel" [1034–35]). Instead the chorus dramatically decides that it is better to perish with a rebel who speaks truth than to survive by affirming the tyranny of Zeus, of which they are now convinced. The chorus, in a way "unparalleled anywhere in Greek literature," has been "converted to the rightness of his [Prometheus's] cause."[35]

The last lines of the play belong to Prometheus. As Zeus unleashes the full fury of his wrath, he ends as he began, by invoking the cosmos to bear witness to the truth of his defiance. "Behold, this stormy turmoil advances against me, manifestly sped of Zeus to make me tremble. O holy mother mine, O thou firmament that dost revolve the common light of all, thou seest the wrongs I suffer!" (1091–93).

The basic plotline of *Prometheus Bound* is sufficient to make clear, if only on a first reading, that Prometheus and Job are literary characters linked by a common struggle. Both endure suffering that exceeds explanation; both must decide whether silent acquiescence or defiant resistance is the faithful response to divine decree; both debate the options with visitors, would-be comforters all, who advise first caution, then compliance with the deity's inscrutable decision; both refuse such counsel by insisting that the deity can be converted to the cause of the righteous; and both complete their journeys with a vexed combination of reward and consequence: for Job the loss of seven daughters and three sons, coupled with the ultimate restoration of his family; for Prometheus his savage overthrow by Zeus, coupled with the support of the cosmos. There are differences between the two accounts, to be sure—Prometheus is a god, Job a mere mortal—but at the core of both accounts is an audacious quest for justice, sustained by the conviction that the deity cannot be absolved of responsibility for the suffering of the righteous.[36] Prometheus, like Job, refuses the conventional counsel that when it comes to questioning the deity's wisdom, "mortals must be mortal-minded."[37]

When mortals such as Job or Titans such as Prometheus refuse to be mortal-minded when it comes to divine authority, then we may be sure that their defiance has "cultural-critical implications."[38] Georges Méautis, for example, makes a strong case for understanding Aeschylus's depiction of Zeus as a tyrant and Prometheus's defiance of such tyranny as an indictment of the subversion of democracy that he witnessed firsthand during his sojourn in Sicily at the court of Hiero of Syracuse (478–67 B.C.E.) during the Persian wars.[39] Scholars debate whether there is one specific historical character or one identifiable political era that underlies Aeschylus's critique of regnant political theories.[40] Even so there can be little doubt that when he introduces the play by having Kratos say that Prometheus must "be lessoned" ("learn to love" [10–11]) in the tyranny of Zeus, Aeschylus casts his vote for Prometheans who refuse to "be lessoned" into silence. To be silent in the face of tyranny, Prometheus says, is to feign worship and flattery to whoever happens to be ruling at the time. This Prometheus refuses to do, as he makes clear in a response to the chorus: "Worship, adore, and fawn upon whoever is thy love. But I care for Zeus less than naught. Let him do his will, let him hold his power for his little day—since not long shall he bear sway over the gods" (937–40).

Later Greek and Roman writers seem not to have made much of Prometheus's defiance, focusing instead on the women in his genealogy, especially Pandora, the Evelike woman thought to have introduced sin into the world.[41] The myth continued to be largely neglected during the medieval period, perhaps because of a general antipathy toward pagan literature, perhaps because the Titan's rebellion against Zeus was connected with a blasphemous assault on papal authority, or perhaps simply because vernacular translations of Aeschylus did not appear until the sixteenth century.[42] A revival of the Promethean myth begins to gain traction in the seventeenth and eighteenth centuries, especially with the onset of the Romantic era, foregrounded by the Sturm und Drang that swept across Germany and most of Western Europe, including England, during the time.[43] Two examples must suffice: Goethe in Germany and Lord Byron in England, both of whom accent the heroic aspects of Promethean defiance.[44]

Goethe's first treatment of Prometheus was a fragmentary play in 1773, which he subsequently abandoned. He took up the myth again in what became an epoch-defining poem, "Prometheus," completed in 1775. By his own account, the catalyst was in substantive measure the enduring and conflicted impact on him of Napoleon and his double identity as both liberator and rebel.[45]

Goethe renders Aeschylus's play in eight stanzas that track Prometheus's growth from childhood to maturity, a poetic parallel to the Enlightenment's view of humanity's progress from tyranny to freedom.[46] David Wellbery, noting Goethe's early legal training, interprets the poem's structure as a three-part "juridical thrust"—accusation, narration, call to judgment—that prosecutes the case for emancipation from Zeus."[47] Stanzas 1–2 indict Zeus and the gods for wretchedly nourishing themselves on the sacrifices, prayers, and false hopes of children and beggars. Stanzas 3–7, a narration of Prometheus's sufferings, are a lament and interrogation. When Prometheus was a child and turned his "erring eyes" heavenward in the hope of finding a sympathetic hearing, why was there no response?[48]

> Who helped me
> Against the Titans' wanton insolence
> Who rescued me from death,
> from slavery?. . . .
>
> I honor you? For what?
> Have you ever eased the suffering
> of the oppressed?
> Have you ever stilled the tears
> of the frightened?

With a final question, Prometheus chides Zeus for believing that suffering would cause him to retreat ("Did you fancy perchance / that I should hate life / and fly to the desert / because not all my blossom dreams ripened?"). Stanza 8 conveys the verdict by evoking, then subverting, the *imago dei* affirmation in Genesis 1:27.

> Here I sit, forming men
> in my own image,
> a race to be like me,
> to suffer, to weep,
> to delight and to rejoice,
> and to defy you,
> as I do.

Within a decade after its publication, Goethe's "Prometheus" ignited a controversy that extended far beyond eighteenth-century German philosophical thought.[49] Goethe's denial of divine providence, his affirmation of human beings as independent creators who suffer, rejoice, and refuse homage to religious authority, became part of the Pantheism Controversy, out of which emerged the word *nihilism*.[50] Regnant philosophical, political, and religious orthodoxies were subjected to severe scrutiny, as thinkers such as Heinrich Heine, Immanuel Kant, Friedrich Schelling, G. W. F. Hegel, Karl Marx, and Friedrich Nietzsche pushed Goethe's unorthodoxies one way and another. As Blumenberg notes in his assessment of Goethe's impact on the eighteenth century, "his fundamental idea is that God would have had to arrange the world differently if he had been concerned about man."[51] Nietzsche's appropriation of Goethe's rendering of the Promethean myth by advocating the Übermensch (superman) as both the goal and the burden of humanity pushes the debate still farther.

> That man should freely dispose of fire without receiving it as a present from heaven, either as a lightning bolt or as the warming rays of the sun, struck these primitive men as sacrilege, as a robbery of divine nature. Thus the very first philosophical problem immediately produces a painful and irresolvable contradiction between man and god and moves it before the gate of every culture, like a huge boulder. The best and highest possession mankind can acquire is obtained by sacrilege and must be paid for with consequences that involve the whole flood of sufferings and sorrows with which the offended divinities have to afflict the noble aspiring race of men. This is a harsh idea which, by the dignity it confers on sacrilege, contrasts strangely with the Semitic myth of the fall in which curiosity, mendacious deception, susceptibility to seduction, lust—in short, a series of preeminently feminine aspects was considered the origin of evil. What distinguishes the Aryan notion is the sublime view of active sin as the characteristically

Promethean virtue. With that, the ethical basis for pessimistic tragedy has been found: the justification of human evil, meaning both human guilt and the suffering it entails.[52]

In 1922 the Danish biographer Georg Brandes (1842–1927) assessed Goethe's "Prometheus" as "the greatest revolutionary poem of all time."[53] In his autobiography Goethe himself seems to have anticipated that his poem would have a similar impact. "*Prometheus* was the priming powder for an explosion that revealed and brought into discussion the most secret relations of estimable men: relations unknown to those men themselves, slumbering in an otherwise highly enlightened society."[54]

Goethe's "priming powder for an explosion," which triggered the Romantic interest in a more humanistic depiction of Promethean defiance, is also manifest in Byron's poem "Prometheus" (1816). The first stanza equates Prometheus's suffering with the "suffocating sense of woe" that comes to all whose pain is "echoless."[55] In the second stanza, Prometheus denounces the gods' "deaf tyranny of Fate" and their "ruling principle of Hate." In the third and final stanza, he declares the lesson mortals must learn from the "sum of human wretchedness."

> A mighty lesson we inherit:
> Thou art a symbol and a sign
> To Mortals of their fate and force;
> Like thee, Man is in part divine,
> A troubled stream from a pure source;. . . .
>
> And his sad unallied existence. . . .
>
> Triumphant where it dares defy,
> And making Death a Victory.

Even as Goethe, Byron, and other romantic poets[56] viewed Prometheus as a heroic champion who inspires human beings to defy authority, they were engaging, and stretching, lingering Joban-type questions. Is it noble or scandalous for mortals, even if they are "part divine," to contest the will of the gods? Is it an act of courage to claim that mortals can convert the gods to justice, or is this merely hubris cloaked in poetic imagination? What is the line between being created "in the image" of the gods and being "mortal-minded"? No one exploited such questions more than Milton in *Paradise Lost* (1667), where Prometheus is Satan writ large.[57]

Milton initially depicts Satan as a rather sympathetic figure who is plagued by doubts and uncertainties about his role. He resolves the doubts by concluding that he can "subdue the Omnipotent" (4:85–86), that ultimately "evil" will be his good.[58]

> Horror and doubt distract his
> Troubled thoughts, and from the bottom stir
> The Hell within him, for within him Hell
> He brings. . . .
>
> His grieved look he fixes sad. . . .
>
> Me miserable! which way shall I fly
> Infinite wrath, and infinite despair?
> Which way I fly is Hell, myself am Hell;
> And in the lowest deep a lower deep
> Still threatening to devour me opens wide,
> To which the Hell I suffer seems a Heaven. (4:18–21, 28, 73–78)

When Satan makes his final appearance (book 10), Milton makes clear that his defiance of divine decree is a "heinous and despiteful act," which a just God will curse, not bless.

> Meanwhile the heinous and despiteful act
> Of Satan done in Paradise . . .
>
> Was known in Heaven; for what can escape the eye
> Of God all-seeing, or deceive his heart
> Omniscient?
>
> Fallen he is; and now
> What rests but that the mortal sentence pass
> On his transgression. . . . (10:1–2, 5–6, 47–49)

The debate concerning whether Prometheus should be condemned as a blasphemous Satan (Milton) or praised as a champion (Goethe, Byron) is manifest in the work, and in a sense in the marriage, of Mary Wollstonecraft Godwin and Percy Bysshe Shelley. Mary Shelley's *Frankenstein* (1818) is subtitled "The Modern Prometheus." The protagonist of the novel, Victor Frankenstein, is a well-intentioned but tragically misdirected Promethean figure who creates life in his own image. The creature he animates from discarded human body parts is strong and eloquent, but his appearance is so extraordinarily horrifying that Victor abandons him immediately. The creature in turn wanders about, seeking revenge on his creator by killing his brother, his best friend, and his wife. One night, while scavenging in the woods for food, the creature discovers a cache of books, among them Milton's *Paradise Lost,* likely intentionally left for him by Victor. From reading Milton the creature identifies himself with Satan, "wretched, helpless, alone" and filled with "the bitter gall of envy" (92).[59] Of the two major characters, however, the monster, rather than Victor, is more human, despite his murderous ways, and he elicits compassion and sympathy. In trying to convince Victor to let go of his rage and hatred and listen to his story, the creature says, "I am thy creature, and I will be even mild and docile to my natural lord and king, if thou wilt also perform thy part, the which thou owest me. Oh, Frankenstein, be not equitable to every other and trample upon me alone, to whom thy justice, and even thy clemency and affection, is most due. Remember, that I am thy creature: I ought to be thy Adam, but I am rather the fallen angel, whom thou drivest from joy for no misdeed" (69). Shelley turns the Aeschylean tragedy on its head by exploiting the implications of its romanticized view of human creativity. Victor, the Promethean figure, is a god-like Zeus who creates life only to destroy it "for no misdeed." The creature created in the image of his creator accepts the master-slave relationship, which consigns him to a life of malignant opprobrium from which there can be no redemption.

Two years after the publication of *Frankenstein,* Percy Shelley's "Prometheus Unbound" (1820) returns to a more conventional Romantic rendering of the hero. In the preface to this four-act play, Shelley explains that his inspiration is the lost sequel to Aeschylus's *Prometheus Bound,* which he envisions as the vindication and restoration of Prometheus by Jupiter (Shelley's Zeus). He singles out Milton's equation of Lucifer and Prometheus in *Paradise Lost* for particular criticism. Milton's Lucifer is tainted by "ambition, envy, revenge, and a desire for personal aggrandizement"; Shelley's Prometheus, by contrast, is a "type of the highest perfection of moral and intellectual nature, impelled by the purest and the truest motives to the best and noblest ends" (133).[60]

In act 1 Prometheus repents of the curse Jupiter has placed on him (1:303–5) but refuses submission, "that fatal word, / The death-seal of mankind's captivity" (1:396–97). In act 2 Pantheia and Asia descend to the realm of Demogorgon, off-spring of Jupiter and Thetis. When Asia questions Jupiter's "omnipotent but friendless" reign (2:48–49), Demogorgon explains that the hour is coming when he will dethrone Jupiter, because "all things are subject but eternal love" (2:120). Act 3 shifts to heaven, where Jupiter boasts to the gods that that his omnipotence prevails over all but Prometheus, whose insurrection, like "unextinguished fire," threatens to make "our antique empire insecure" (3:5, 9). Demogorgon drags Jupiter into the abyss of chaos; Hercules releases Prometheus; and the "thrones, altars, judgment seats and prisons" that once fated human beings to wretched existence become "the ghosts of a no more remembered fame" (3:164, 170). Act 4 comprises a hymn of rejoicing, which ends with Demogoron's final assessment of the moral of the play.

> To suffer woes which Hope thinks infinite;
> To forgive wrongs darker than Death or Night;

> To defy Power which seems Omnipotent;
> To love, and bear; to hope, till Hope creates
> From its own wreck the thing it contemplates;
> Neither to change nor falter nor repent:
> This, like thy glory, Titan! is to be
> Good, great and joyous, beautiful and free;
> This is alone Life, Joy, Empire and Victory. (4:570–78)

The End of the Promethean Myth?

By the end of the nineteenth century, the myth of Prometheus, generative of "indefatigable explication,"[61] seemed to reach its end in satire. André Gide's *Prometheus Misbound* (1899) transforms the poetic account into a burlesque narrative.[62] Zeus is a "Meglionaire" banker in Paris, who gratuitously gives a five-hundred-franc note to a stranger, Cocles, whom he encounters on the street. Zeus explains that his passion is gambling, specifically lending money to strangers as an experiment in proving that those who become rich for no reason cannot help but inflict suffering on others. The "other" in this case is named, suggestively, Damocles. Prometheus is a modern Parisian, who, having once been chained to a rock in Caucasus, became uncomfortable, simply stretched out his arm, and freed himself. "Between four and five o'clock on an autumn afternoon, [he] walked down the boulevard which leads from the Madeleine to the Opéra" and ordered a beer in a sidewalk café (105). There he meets Cocles and Damocles. When he tells them his name, Damocles says, "Excuse me, sir, but it seems to me that this name has already. . . ." Prometheus interrupts him, "Oh! . . . that is of no importance whatsoever" (119). As far as Prometheus is concerned, he has no history, no identity, and nothing to contribute to the conversation with Cocles and Damocles save for the fact that his sole possession is an eagle (or vulture) that survives by eating his flesh.

These essentials contribute to the absurdity of the narrative, which ends with Prometheus offering a "totem meal"[63] to Cocles and other mourners at Damocles's funeral. The entrée is the eagle, fattened by its feeding on Prometheus. The narrative concludes with these words from Prometheus, written, as he says, with a pen made from one of the eagle's feathers. "Its flesh has nourished us. . . . I eat it with no animosity; if it had made me suffer less, it would have been less plump; if it had been less plump, it would not have been delectable" (173).

Blumenberg argues, I believe correctly, that by turning the tragedy into a "grotesque" deformation of itself, Gide signals that the myth of Prometheus has reached its hermeneutical end.[64] The realties that generated it are now forgotten; like the name "Prometheus," they no longer have any importance. In a "brief moment of culinary enjoyment," the "old seriousness" of the myth has been, literally, consumed.[65] Zeus, Prometheus, and those who visit with him have become little more than aesthetic caricatures in a story of benign entertainment. To support this assessment, Blumenberg cites Kafka's reflections on the Promethean myth, with which I conclude this chapter.[66]

Kafka's "Prometheus" (1918), a sequence of four legends each stated in two lines, takes up less than a page. He begins by informing the reader that these are the four interpretive options and concludes by saying that everything ends "in the inexplicable."[67] The first two legends essentially correspond with the conventional myth: Prometheus was chained to a rock for betraying the secrets of the gods to men; the gods sent eagles to feed on his liver, which was perpetually renewed; and so Prometheus "pressed himself deeper and deeper into the rock until he became one with it." The third legend emphasizes that Prometheus's act has been forgotten by all over the course of thousands of years: "forgotten by the gods, the eagles, forgotten by himself." The fourth legend resembles the third but substitutes the word *weary* for *forgotten:* "Everyone grew weary of the meaningless affair. The gods grew weary, the eagles grew weary, the wound closed wearily." All that remains, Kafka says in the concluding lines, is "the inexplicable mass of rock," and it is utterly unaffected by the pain of the one chained to it. In the end the myth, like the "substratum of truth" that grounds it, is "inexplicable."

What happens, Blumenberg asks, when "myth can no longer take place, because 'too little' happens?"[68] If the "substratum of truth" that gives rise to the myth is forgotten by all, if the search for its meaning becomes wearying to all, if the inexplicable no longer compels a search for the meaning of the inexplicable, then what more is there left to say? If all that remains of the Promethean myth is at the most aesthetic enjoyment, at the least "eschatological melancholy," then "why," Blumenberg goes on to ask, "should the world have to continue in existence if there is nothing more to say?"[69]

Similar questions may be asked of Job's curses from the ash heap. If the substratum of truth that grounds righteous defiance and the refusal to bless the world God has created become a forgotten footnote to a story that is simply a good read, then why bother to wrestle with inexplicable questions such as "Why?" If there is nothing more to say about the Joban story than what can be summed up in a Brothers Grimm truism—"In the beginning . . . and they all lived happily ever after"—then defiance may remain an aesthetic curiosity, but it will not likely translate into a culture-critical consciousness.

Early Joban interpreters and commentators, as noted above, move in the direction of muting, minimizing, or omitting Job's scandalous voice of defiance. LXX translators soften Job's complaints and denude his indictments of God. The *T. Job* omits altogether Job's curses and transfers his doubts and questions about innocent suffering to the friends, whose sins God exposes. The structure of the book of Job itself no doubt provides some license for such interpretive moves. It frames and rhetorically neutralizes Job's seven curses in 3:1–10 with seven occurrences of "bless" in the prologue and epilogue (1:5, 10, 11, 21; 2:5, 9; 42:12). Further the New Testament reduces the complexity of the Joban story to a single maxim, the "patience of Job" (Jas 5:11), which may not be the equivalent of burlesque but is nonetheless vulnerable to being fossilized as little more than cliché. In short the reception history of Job's curses, like that of Prometheus, might appear to end by suggesting that Job's defiance has been forgotten, by God, by Job himself, and by his readers. To paraphrase James 5:11, all that we see and remember of the Joban story is its affirmation of a merciful and compassionate God.[70]

The concluding line of Blumenberg's magisterial study of the Promethean myth ends with a final question: "But what if there were still something to say, after all?"[71] The question returns readers to Blumenberg's first chapter, where he lays out his argument that myths never simply evaporate into thin air. Even when jettisoned to aesthetic imagination or simply forgotten, myths linger and against all odds demand ongoing work, because they are "indispensable aspects of the comprehensive efforts that make human existence possible."[72] As Blumenberg puts it, "Cultures that have not yet achieved mastery of their reality continue to dream the dream and would snatch its realization away from those who think they have already awakened from it."[73]

Is there still something more to say about Joban defiance? I submit that there is. The first clue is that Job's words from the ash heap do not end with curses. They reach beyond defiance to lament (Job 3:11–26), which presses the "Why?" question to and perhaps beyond Hebraic convention into litigious argumentation. Unlike Aeschylus's Prometheus, the biblical Job does not simply quake at God's thunder and lightning and vanish from sight. Instead he presses his case, demanding that when it comes to seven daughters and three sons who die, by God's admission, "for no reason," it is God's injustice, not human sin, that merits indictment. To Job's laments, and his desire to put God on trial for crimes against humanity, we must now turn.

5

GOD ON TRIAL

"Who ever challenged Him and came out whole?" (Job 9:4)

I insist on arguing with God.

Job 13:3

The revolt of the believer is not that of the renegade; the two do not speak in the name of the same anguish.

Elie Wiesel, *Souls on Fire*

We thank thee, Father, for these strange minds that enamor us against thee.

Emily Dickinson, quoted in Kazin, *God and the American Writer*

Peter Shaffer's play *Amadeus* focuses on the conflicted lives of Antonio Salieri and Wolfgang Amadeus Mozart.[1] Salieri was a bright and promising young musician who pledged to honor God with his virtue and his talent, on the condition that God grant his dream to become the greatest composer of his time. He rose swiftly through the ranks of his peers and was rewarded by being appointed court composer for Joseph II, emperor of Austria. Mozart was a brash, immoral, undisciplined virtuoso who at the age of ten was already touring Europe and winning distinction with music of divine beauty. When Salieri realized that he was about to be eclipsed by Mozart's rising star, he felt betrayed by God. It seemed as though God had decided to reward the unworthy and punish the one whose only desire was to serve him. With righteous indignation Salieri sets out on a collision course with Mozart and, more important, with God. In the closing speech of act 1, he lays down a Joblike gauntlet. He will teach God the true meaning of justice or die trying.

> *Capisco*! I know my fate. Now for the first time I feel my emptiness as Adam felt his nakedness. . . . Tonight at an inn somewhere in this city stands a giggling child who can put on paper, without actually setting down his billiard cue, casual notes

which turn my most considered ones into lifeless scratches. *Grazie, Signore!* You gave me the desire to serve You—which most men do not have—then saw to it the service was shameful in the ears of the server. *Grazie!* You gave me the desire to praise You—which most men do not feel—then made me mute. *Grazie tanti!* You put into me the perception of the Incomparable—which most men never know!— then ensured that I would know myself forever mediocre. [*His voice gains power.*] *Why?*... *What is my fault?*... Until this day I have pursued virtue with rigor. I have labored and worked the talent You allowed me. [*Calling up*] *You know how hard I've worked!* Solely that in the end, in the practice of the art, which alone makes the world comprehensible to me, I might hear Your Voice! And now I do hear it—and it says one name: MOZART!... Spiteful, sniggering, conceited, infantine Mozart—who has never worked one minute to help another man!... *Him* You have chosen to be Your sole conduct! And *my* only reward—my sublime privilege—is to be the sole man alive in this time who shall clearly recognize Your Incarnation! [*Savagely*] *Grazie e grazie ancora!* [*Pause*] So be it! From this time we are enemies, You and I! I'll not accept it from You—do you hear?... They say God is not mocked. I tell You, *Man* is not mocked!... They say the spirit bloweth where it listeth: I tell You *no!* It must list to virtue or not blow at all! [*Yelling*] *Dio ingiusto*—You are the Enemy! I name Thee now—*Nemico Eterno!* And this I swear: To my last breath I shall *block* You on earth, as far as I am able! [*He glares up at God. To audience*] What use, after all, is man, if not to teach God His lessons? (73–75)

Salieri's decision to call God to task for injustice is a radical, perhaps even absurd idea. Who can question the justice of the judge of the world? To name God as "the Enemy" is surely an act of treason, a blasphemy that must by any definition constitute an impermissible breach of faith. Who dares talk to God in such a way? And yet, as the Duke of Albany observes at the end of *King Lear,* there are times when the silence from the heavens we hear as we cry for justice is so deafening, that we must speak "what we feel, not we what we ought to say" (5.3.322–23).

Between Job 2 and Job 38, there is a gaping chasm of divine silence. On one side there is God's painfully permissive address to the satan: "Very well, he is in your power" (2:6). On the other side, there is his blustery but enigmatic response from the whirlwind (38–41). Between relinquishment and revelation, Job is on his own, surrounded by what may be described as nothing more than God's "ontological stammer."[2] He has, of course, the "comfort" of his friends, who try to explain God's silence with two recurring arguments: (1) they read Job's affliction as a metaphor for sin and divine judgment, and they urge him to repent so that God may be present for him once more (8:3–6, 11:13–19, 22:23–28); (2) they read silence as a metaphor for God's inscrutable wisdom, which is necessarily too deep and too high for mere mortals such as Job to comprehend (8:8–9, 11:7–9, 15:7–8; cf.

33:12–14). Job should not misread silence as absence, they insist. If he will only submit obediently to what God gives and withholds, then he can be "at peace" with God and with himself (22:21).

Job is not persuaded. Against the notion that affliction is a metaphor for sin, he insists that the reality, the very physicality of his pain shatters every attempt to give suffering a name that belongs to something else. "*Look at me,* and be appalled," he says to the friends, "and lay your hand on your mouth" (21:5; cf. 6:28). If they would but look into his eyes, red and raw from weeping, if they would but touch his body and feel the hurt that has been stitched like sackcloth into his very skin (16:15–16), then they would know that moralisms can never bandage physical pain. Against the notion that silence is a metaphor for God's benevolently mysterious transcendence, Job insists that it is instead a sinister ruse (10:13–17) for God's malignant abandonment of good to evil and justice to injustice (10:1–17, 16:6–17, 19:6–12, 27:7–12, and especially 24:1–17). Like Salieri, Job takes his stand against any God who cannot be bothered to intervene on behalf of the righteous. In Salieri's words, "They say the spirit bloweth where it listeth: I tell you *no*! It must list to virtue or not blow at all. . . . What use, after all, is man, if not to teach God His lessons?"

"I would lay my case before him, and fill my mouth with arguments" (Job 23:4)

Job's first words from the ash heap in Job 3 are curses. His curses move toward lamentation, undergirded by the repeating question "Why?" The lament is deeply embedded in Hebraic tradition, as its prominence in the Psalms confirms, and has long been recognized as a major genre in the book of Job.[3] Lament typically comprises four elements: *invocation* of God; *lament,* generally questions directed to God about what has gone wrong in one's personal life or in the community; *petition* for God to redress and resolve the situation; and a *concluding note of confidence,* which indicates God has heard and will answer. In Job 3 Job appropriates the language but stops short of engaging fully the spirit of lament. He refers to God only indirectly, does not petition for relief or restoration, and does not expect there to be any response from heaven or earth that will make a difference to his plight. He does not end on a note of hope; instead he yields to the painful solitude of grief, searching for an answer that does not come. Job addresses God for the first time in 7:7–21 but here only to mock lament's invitation to hope and confidence by offering a doxology of sarcasm, not praise. "What are human beings that you [God] make so much of them?" (7:17). For the psalmist (Ps 8:4; cf. Ps 144:3), the question evokes awe and astonishment; for Job the question only deepens his despair that God has exalted him in order to make him a better target for destruction. His only petition is that God leave him alone (7:19). In Job 9–10 Job begins to push the conventional language of lament still further by imagining a radically litigious faith partnership with and against God. Like Abraham he determines to stand face to face with the creator of the world and ask, "Shall not the Judge of all the earth do justice?" (Gn 18:25).

Legal metaphors that connect human suffering with divine trial law are common to ancient Near Eastern and Hebraic traditions. F. Rachel Magdalene has argued, based on her assessment of some 340 Neo-Babylonian litigation texts (mid-seventh to fifth century B.C.E.), that the Joban author most likely developed his legal metaphors from a conventional ancient Near Eastern trial procedure. Human suffering, the cause for which may be known or unknown, becomes part of a routine "inquisitorial system of adjudication" that assumes claims and counterclaims against the gods can be satisfactorily resolved.[4] Because biblical trial accounts give such an incomplete picture of Israelite trial law,[5] Magdalene's work provides depth and context for biblical scholars who have long discerned that the trial motif is prominent in the book of Job.[6]

Legal language describing God and people as litigants in a trial occurs frequently in the Hebrew Bible. A variety of terms convey the idea, especially the word *rîb,* "strive, contend" (e.g., Job 9:3, 10:2), which is used in both verbal and nominal forms to describe the process by which two opposing parties settle a dispute. The process envisions a lawsuit in which one person presents charges against another. The case proceeds through examination and cross-examination until the charges are proven true or false. Normally God is depicted as the plaintiff (and judge) in such cases, and God's adversaries (e.g., individuals, Israel, foreign nations) are the defendants. Prophetic judgment speeches (e.g., Is 3:13–15; Jer 2:4–13; Hos 4:1–3; Mi 6:1–4; Mal 3:5), for example, use the trial metaphor to describe the process by which God indicts, examines, and ultimately judges Israel for failing to obey the covenant.

Unlike the prophets, Job dares to imagine filing a lawsuit in which he is the plaintiff and God is the defendant. He would question God about the actions that have been taken against him. Did God hand him and his family over to affliction? What are God's motives in consigning innocent children to death and innocent parents to bereavement and torment? Can these motives be justified? Is God right to deal with human beings in this manner? As the defendant God would be expected to answer the questions and explain divine actions. At the end of the court hearings, Job will have put his life on the line to argue his case against God (13:13–28); he will have summoned heaven and earth as his witnesses against God (16:18–22); he will have named God as his enemy (13:24); he will have indicted God for cruel and bestial crimes against humanity (10:1–17, 16:6–17, 19:6–20); and he will have demanded that if God cannot answer his charges, then the jury has no recourse but to declare the creator of the world guilty and unworthy of creation's respect (31:35–37).

Magdalene argues that Job's charges and countercharges against God have a legal basis that would be widely recognized in the legal world of his time.[7] Job's basic claim is that God has abused divine authority and obstructed justice. This claim comprises three arguments: (1) Job claims that God has abused the legal process by initiating a false suit against him. Though he is "innocent" and "blameless," God has determined "without cause" that he is guilty (9:20, 17);[8] though there is no "violence" in Job's hands, though his "prayer is pure" (16:19), God crushes him with a savage violence (10:1–17, 16:6–17, 19:6–12, 27:7–12) motivated by hate (16:9). God treats Job like an enemy who deserves only to be harassed, then driven away (13:25–26). (2) Job claims that God violates basic principles of social justice, that he actively perverts justice by exonerating the guilty and condemning the innocent. Job describes himself as an eyewitness to God's corruption (13:1: "My eye has seen all this") and claims that even the animals, birds, plants, and fish corroborate his charge (12:7–9). Why do the wicked prosper while the righteous suffer (21:7)? Job asserts that it is not only because God makes no distinction between them (9:22: "It is all one . . . he destroys both the blameless and the wicked"), but also because God "mocks the calamity of the innocent" and "smiles on the schemes of the wicked (10:3). (3) Job claims that the world God has created is morally chaotic from its genesis. There is no justice for Job because God has created human beings for a life of slavery, not freedom; for harsh, unrewarding labor, not fulfillment, less still for happiness (7:1–6). Like a flower that rises then withers, all mortals come forth from the womb as a shadow that cannot last (14:1–2). Born into a world that runs amok without divine direction (21:7–26, 24:1–12), the great equalizer is death, not God. And even death is no more than a flawed aspiration. On the one hand, death is to be desired, for it brings a merciful end to a life full of misery (10:20–22, 14:14–17). On the other life inevitably delays the mercies of death, leaving its victims to "grope in the dark" and "stagger like a drunkard" (12:25) toward a goal they can cannot reach, until God clears the way. In sum Job's three arguments, especially the third, return us to the presenting question of Job 3, now strategically revised. The question is no longer "Why did *I* not die at birth?" (3:11). It has now become an accusation directed against God: "Why did *you* bring me forth from the womb?" (10:18).

Can a mortal such as Job sue God? There may be legal precedent for doing so, but Job knows all too well that putting God on trial is impossible. God is the creator of the world. Who dares to say to God, "What are you doing?" (9:12). God is the "Judge of all the earth" (Gn 18:26). Who can summon the judge into court? The idea of filing charges against God is transparently absurd, for God is no mere mortal who can be questioned and held accountable for answers that will not wash. Anyone who takes up the challenge must bear the cost (13:14–15).[9]

A visual image invites us to ponder the cost of contending with God. Francis Gruber's *Job* is an oil on canvas painted for the Salon d'Automne in 1944, just after the liberation of Paris from German occupation. Gruber depicts Job as a thin young man sitting on a backless chair. His right leg is crossed over his knee, a resting place for his right elbow, which supports his drooping head. His left arm hangs limply by his side. The posture is a graphic illustration of the cost of one who has protested German bombardment to no avail. The red-brick wall opposite Job abuts a makeshift construction of wooden planks that shores up a bombed-out wall. Through the window one sees apartment buildings with broken windowpanes. Job looks forlornly at a paper on the floor. It reads "Maintenant encore, ma plainte est une révolte, et pourtant ma main comprime mes soupirs" ("Even now my complaint is a revolt, and yet my hand restrains my sighs"). The first half of the inscription appears to be from Job 23:2 ("My complaint is bitter"). The latter half is difficult, but it may echo Job 23:11 ("My foot has held fast to his [God's] steps; I have kept his way and not turned aside"). Gruber's intentions are open to debate, but his splicing together of these two Joban texts offers a suggestive interpretation of Job as both a rebel and a loyal follower. The critical link is the conjunction "and yet," which signals Job's resolve to "revolt" against God while still holding on to God.[10]

With Gruber I submit that Job knows that putting God on trial is impossible yet morally imperative. Without justice there can be no relationship with God. Job's fraught decision to file a case against God echoes the clear-eyed discernment of Dorothee Soelle: "In the face of suffering you are either with the victim or the executioner—there is no other option."[11] In the game of life, God must take sides. So what will it be God, Job dares to ask, are you with me or against me? From Job's perspective the hapless cries of every victim of injustice in the world are screaming for an answer. In the words of the Jewish poet Nelly Sachs (1891–1970), a contemporary witness to the atrocities at Auschwitz and Hiroshima, "when dying proceeds to sever all seams" in the "landscape of screams," when from tortured and "bleeding eyes" there flow "tears [that] open the black bandage," then the silence of God is indictable.[12]

We may get our bearings on Job's daring quest for justice by entering into his preliminary ruminations about putting God on trial in chapters 9–10.[13] He begins with what seems to be an unqualified affirmation of Eliphaz's argument in 4:17 that it is impossible for mortals to be righteous (*ṣdq*) before God: "Truly, I know that this is so; how can a mortal be just (*ṣdq*) before God?" (9:2). Job agrees that is impossible to be *ṣdq* before God, but his affirmation is different, and it is made on other grounds. Eliphaz interprets "righteous" in a moral and religious sense (cf. Gn 38:26). His argument is that no human being can be considered righteous in relation to God, because mortals are by definition sinful, morally flawed creatures (cf. 4:7–5:7). In the words of Wallace Stegner, Job is simply "born struck out," and it is silly for him to stand in the batter's box demanding that the pitcher throw a fourth strike.[14] No mortal, certainly not Job, can stand before a perfectly righteous God and raise questions about who suffers and why. Job, however, interprets *ṣdq* to mean "innocent" in a legal sense (cf. Ex 23:7; Dt 25:1). His affirmation is that human beings could not obtain a legal verdict of "innocent" if they were so bold as to enter into a lawsuit with God. The sense of Job's statement is captured by the Revised English Bible: "no one can win his case against God" (9:2; cf. NJPS, Today's English Version). The impossibility of being innocent before God, Job contends, is not because humans are morally imperfect, but because God skews the legal processes for obtaining justice. As David J. A. Clines notes, commenting on God's violations of standard investigative procedures, God behaves "like a gangster."[15]

Having defined his claim, Job nevertheless concedes that two fundamental characteristics of God present any would-be litigant with insurmountable problems. First, if one were to "contend" (*rîb*, "hold a trial") with God, "one could not answer him once in a thousand times" (9:3). Because the Hebrew text uses pronouns (*one, him*) rather than proper nouns, it is possible to interpret Job's words in different ways. NRSV understands the phrase to mean that a *person*—such as Job—could not answer one of the charges that God would bring against him. Such a rendering depicts God as the plaintiff in the case, Job as the defendant, a view that is consonant with the dominant use of the trial metaphor elsewhere in the Hebrew Bible. But it is also possible, and in this case more likely, to interpret the phrase as meaning that *God* would not answer the charges that Job would bring (cf. Revised English Bible). While Job is keenly aware that he would be hard-pressed to respond to God's cross-examination (cf. 9:14–15), his greater concern is that God will not answer him when he pleads for justice.[16] Of course Job cannot be faulted for believing that the odds in favor of his words having any impact on God are slim and none, perhaps one in a thousand. Even so it is that "fraction of one percent," as Robert Frost puts it, that stays his tenuous hold on humanity, on God, and on the justice he believes must bind the two together in common cause.[17]

The second obstacle to bringing God to trial is God's superior wisdom and strength: "[God] is wise in heart and mighty in strength—who has resisted God and succeeded?" (9:4). Under normal circumstances one might expect that wisdom and strength are precisely the characteristics one looks for in a just God, but Job's suffering has left him vulnerable and fearful of an encounter with a God such as this. He suspects that God will use these attributes not to redeem him but to destroy him. Faced with the prospect of such an overwhelming adversary in court,

Job wonders what chance he has to prevail. The force of Job's rhetorical question may be rendered thusly: "Who can oppose God and survive to tell about it?"

The divine attributes of wisdom and power trigger Job's doxology of praise (9:5–10), which on first impression seems to conform to the response that Eliphaz has modeled for him (5:9–16). On close inspection, however, it becomes apparent that the characteristics of God that evoke praise from Eliphaz prompt something very different from Job. Job's doxology adopts the hymnic form that is common in the Psalter. It is composed of seven participial verbs (rendered in English by relative clauses beginning with *who*) that suggest Job's review of God's way of dealing with the world intends to be complete and comprehensive. The twin themes of wisdom and power, which Job treats in reverse order, provide the basis for his characterization of the God he believes he will encounter if he persists in going to trial. Verses 5–7 focus on God's awesome power, which Job perceives to be destructive and brutal. God overthrows mountains, shakes the earth from its place until the pillars upon which it rests threaten to collapse, commands the sun not to rise in the day and the stars not to shine in the night. That God has the power to shake the foundations of the cosmos and convulse nature is not in itself a reason for dread. Indeed such a description normally signals the coming of God to save the oppressed from their enemies (Na 1:1–6; Hb 3:3–13) and to deliver the afflicted from their distress (Ps 18:6–16). Job, however, can discern nothing positive in such raw demonstrations of divine force. He can see that God is empowered to turn creation upside down and to replace order with chaos, but like the mountains (v. 5a) he does not know what God is doing or why. He senses that God's power is motivated by anger (v. 5b; cf. v. 13), but that such anger should be used to destroy creation, with no hint of compassion or redemption, offers little reason to believe that an encounter with this God will effect his restoration.

Verses 8–10 shift the focus from God's destructive power to his inscrutable wisdom. God "stretches out the heavens," "tramples on the waves of the Sea," and makes the constellations that provide the temporal rhythms of creation. Each of these acts comprises a conventional reason for a doxology praising the creator (Am 5:8; cf. Job 38:31–32), and yet from Job's perspective they are great and marvelous acts that are utterly "beyond understanding" (v. 10). When Job looks from his ash heap at the world and the God the friends insist he praise, he does not see what the friends want him to see. When Job applies the conventional reasons for praising the creator to his own life, he concludes that God can neither be comprehended nor resisted (vv. 11–13). God "passes by," but Job cannot see; God "glides past," but Job cannot discern who it is that has come and gone. Both verbs are used elsewhere to describe experiences of revelation in which God's presence is made available in extraordinary ways (Ex 33:18–23 [Moses], 1 Kgs 19:11–12 [Elijah]; cf. Job 4:15). For Job such experiences disclose only that God is more absent than present. And yet Job has felt a divine presence that is all too painfully real. God snatches things away at will, and there is no one who can intervene to say "What are you doing?" (cf. Eccl 8:4; Dn 4:35 [MT 4:32]).

When Job looks at the world he is expected to praise, it seems to demand a doxology of terror. God is powerfully destructive and relentlessly powerful. Praise may be adequate for Job's friends, who seem untroubled by the mysterious ways in which God governs the world. But for Job, whose pain makes the quest for justice imperative, such praise is incomprehensible. It would be roughly equivalent to rising at the beginning of a Sunday morning worship to sing with gusto the words "Praise God from whom all destructive power comes; Praise God who comes to savage the world arbitrarily and without restraint."

How does one bring charges against an adversary who will not be bound by reason or logic, whose way of dealing with persons is motivated by caprice and malevolence? If justice is determined on the basis of power, then who can match the invincible strength of God? As Job puts it, "there is no umpire" (v. 33) between him and God, so who is going to throw the yellow flag when God violates the rules? Moreover if Job's case is to be settled on the merits of law, who will summon God into court (vv. 19–21)? Even if God were to appear in court, Job is convinced that he could never effectively argue his case. Truth would not win out, because God would prove him wrong, even though he knows, and he knows that God knows, that he is "blameless" (vv. 20, 21; cf. 1:1, 8; 2:3). If indeed Job were to go to court with God, he would lose more than a legal case. He would lose his identity and his self-worth; in essence he would lose himself. He would cease to be the righteous person that God knows him to be and would become instead someone that he could no longer recognize (v. 35). Job's encounter with God would leave him a shell of his former self. If to be in the presence of God means one must live a lie, then life itself becomes a thing to be despised (v. 21b; cf. 7:16).

In the face of such overwhelming odds, it would not be surprising if Job simply yielded to despair. That he does not do so is a measure of his resolve to cling fast to his integrity come what may. He determines to let the bitterness of his soul, which will not be quieted, run its course, even if it means that he must address an absent God in an empty courtroom (10:1–17). In that courtroom he imagines himself beginning with two imperatives that would lay the groundwork for his suit (10:2). He will say to his absent adversary "Do not condemn me," that is, do not declare me guilty without evidence. And he will insist that God give him a statement of the alleged charges against him, which he stands ready to dispute.

Like a plaintiff interrogating a defendant, Job rehearses three questions he insists God must answer (10:3–7). Under normal circumstances he might assume that the questions are only rhetorical, that the response to each is obvious and beyond dispute. But since Job is no longer clear about God's character or intent, the questions are now open-ended. First Job asks if God has decided that it is "good" to be an agent of oppression (v. 3). That God should oppress (ʿāsaq) should be unthinkable, for such behavior involves a cruel mistreatment of others that God routinely condemns (Am 4:1; Mi 2:1–2; Jer 7:6; Ez 22:29; Zec 7:10) and promises to judge harshly (Pss 103:6, 105:14, 146:7). This is the only instance in the Hebrew Bible where God is the subject of this negative verb. Yet when Job considers the evidence before him, he is no longer certain that God is acting like God. What is God's rationale for rejecting the careful designs of divine handiwork and smiling with approval on the designs of the wicked?

With a second (v. 4) and third (v. 5) question, Job presses this interrogation by asking if God is limited by the same conditions that apply to humans. Does God have the imperfect vision of human eyes so that what he sees is only partial and subject to error? Is God's life span fixed by days and years so that, like humans, he has only a limited time in which to accomplish a task? The questions *ought* to be absurd. Surely God "does not see as mortals see" (1 Sm 16:7). Surely the one who is "from everlasting to everlasting" (Ps 90:2; cf. Gn 21:33, Dt 32:40, Is 40:28) is not bound by the normal constraints of the calendar. Why then does God act as if there is not enough time on the calendar to hear and respond to Job's case (vv. 6–7)?

Job's sense that God is acting in ways that are contrary to the divine nature leads him once more to question God's intentions as creator (10:8–12; cf. 9:5–10). He opens with two statements that invite God to respond to the incongruity he discerns in the creative design for human life. God's own hands formed and shaped him, and yet now God has turned to destroy (bālaʿ; literally, "swallow"), not sustain, the very creature that he worked to bring into being (v. 8). According to the prologue, God has already acknowledged to the satan that destroying Job "for no reason" is not beyond what the creator is willing to do (2:3). Job of course was not privy to that admission, but without realizing it he now presses God to speak with a similar candor. Job also calls on God to remember that he has been fashioned out of clay (v. 9), an image that recalls the potter who molds a vessel with great care from beginning to end. Job suspects, however, that his end is to be returned to dust, like a vessel that is flawed and cannot be fixed (cf. Jer 18:1–4). The NRSV treats the expression as a question—"Will you turn me to dust again?"—but the Hebrew renders it as a simple declaration. God has decided to discard him, although there is no evidence that he is blemished or sinful. What kind of creator destroys the creation without bothering to check if it is worthy of the initial investment?

Job completes his interrogation by charging that God's meticulous attention to him masks sinister intentions (10:13–17). Hidden within God's heart is a strategy to seek and destroy the very life that he has so carefully wrought. Job knows that this is so, and he would present the evidence that compels his adversary to agree with him. God "watches" his every move, not to find ways to love and uphold him, but to spy out each and every misstep he might make (cf. 7:20). If he should sin, which he denies having done, God will not forgive him. If he is innocent (ṣādaq; NRSV: "righteous"), which he insists he is, God will ensure that his affliction is so heavy, his shame so overwhelming, that he cannot lift his head to assert his integrity or to defy his mistreatment (cf. Jgs 8:28, Ps 83:2 [MT 83:3], Zec 1:21 [MT 2:4]). The imagery of 10:16 suggests that God stalks Job for royal sport, like the hunter who delights in tracking and killing the lion. Job's sense of God's violent intentions toward him spill over into his description of the adversary that will confront him in court. God will send witness after witness to testify against him. Like a general whose passions for defeating the enemy have reached fever pitch, God will order fresh troops against him until he succumbs.

Job's decision to put God on trial represents a dramatic shift in his understanding of how he must engage God. Silence before divine decree is inadequate. Defiance may be necessary, even courageous, but saying no to God does little to change present circumstances. To lament is to give voice to questions that are restless for change, to make an authentic claim on God's justice, to refuse resignation, even if it means that in speaking *to* God, Job must also speak *against* him. For Job, however, lament is more than simply an aggressive speech-act. It is a means for imagining new ways of encountering God. Like all mortals Job realizes that "mere" human beings cannot possibly have equal footing in a relationship with God. Nonetheless he envisions a face-to-face encounter with God in a courtroom where the rules of law negate all inequalities between the litigants. They would be free to argue their positions without threat of intimidation or violence. At least in the eyes of the court, the two parties would engage one another as if they were equals. It is a radical thought that enables Job to imagine, hence to live like, he has something to contribute to this relationship that matters. In thinking that he might stand before God as a near equal partner, Job is emboldened to live as if the impossible were possible. It is a daring way of imagining that humankind really is created in the image of God.

"Either He is responsible or He is not. If He is, let's judge Him; if He is not, let Him stop judging us"

Job's decision to put God on trial was of comparatively little interest for early Joban commentators, whose hermeneutical and theological predilections generally shaped and conformed to a conventional view: Job was wrong to question God's justice and repented of the hubris that emboldened him to put God "in the wrong" (Job 40:8; cf. 42:3). While the LXX mutes Job's complaints, the *Testament of Job* omits them altogether. Gregory's *Moralia in Job* (sixth century), the touch-stone for interpretation of Job in the Middle Ages, contrasts Job's curses and laments with Paul's restraint in 1 Corinthians 10:23: "All things are permitted to me, but not all things are useful" (5.11.17). The reformers (Luther, Calvin, Beza) generally followed suit by arguing that God sent afflictions on Job as pedagogical chastisements for sin. As Susan Schreiner says of Calvin's sermons on Job, for example, "Calvin was irresistibly drawn to the arguments of the friends, which extolled the justice of God."[18]

For my purposes here, I fast-forward to twentieth-century Jewish literature, where the notion of putting God on trial for crimes against humanity seeds re-flection on the horrors of the Holocaust.[19] Two very different Jewish renderings of Job and the trial motif, Elie Wiesel's *The Trial of God* and Franz Kafka's *The Trial,* merit reflection.

Elie Wiesel explains the genesis of his play *The Trial of God* with these words: "Inside the kingdom of night, I witnessed a strange trial. Three rabbis—all erudite and pious men—decided one winter evening to indict God for allowing his chil-dren to be massacred. I remember: I was there, and I felt like crying. But there nobody cried."[20] The setting is 1649 at an inn in Shamgorod, a fictional city that represents villages in the Ukraine and Poland that were devastated by pogroms associated with the Khmelnytsky Uprising in the 1920s. In Wiesel's rendering only two Jews survived: Berish the innkeeper and his daughter, Hanna. Both are scarred victims. Berish's two sons, Hayim ("Life") and Sholem ("Peace"), were killed. Hanna ("Grace"), was tortured and raped. One night three minstrels arrive at the inn. They have come to perform a play for the holiday of Purim, a carnival time when people retell the story of Esther, Haman, and Mordecai by playing games, wearing masks, and pretending. Berish makes it clear that he is not inter-ested in celebrating anything that has to do with God (15).

As the night wears on, Berish finally agrees to participate in a play, provided the minstrels allow him to choose the subject. He insists that they stage a mock trial in which the master of the universe will have to answer for the shameful silence that hovered over Shamgorod while innocent people were slaughtered. Berish states his intentions clearly: "Listen: either He is responsible or He is not. If He is, let's judge Him; if He is not, let Him stop judging us" (54). The idea seems cold and frightening to the minstrels. They are understandably hesitant even to pretend that God can be treated as a defendant, charged with a crime, and possi-bly indicted. What if the verdict is guilty, they ask.

Berish pushes them to agree to his idea. Of course it will take courage to enact such a drama, but Berish argues that Purim, like all high holy days, is an invitation to believe that at least on some occasions it is permissible to reverse roles with the supreme judge of the world (56). At first reluctantly, then with growing enthusiasm, the minstrels take up the challenge. As the curtain falls on act 1, one of them, Mendel, announces their resolve: "Tonight we will be free to say everything. To command, to imagine everything—even our impossible victory" (56).

As the trial proceeds, Berish puts his questions to God, each one more daring, more accusatory, more dangerous. The minstrels grow increasingly uneasy. One of them, Yankel, warns Berish: "Questions are like trips: *we must know when to stop*" (89; emphasis added). Berish presses on. He insists that he is willing to pay the price for a quest for justice that cannot be relinquished. "I—Berish, Jewish innkeeper at Shamgorod—accuse Him of hostility, cruelty and indifference. Either He dislikes His chosen people or He doesn't care about them—period! But then, why He has chosen us—why not someone else for a change? Either He knows what's happening to us, or He doesn't wish to know! In both cases He is . . . He is . . . guilty!" (125).

Sam, one of the customers at the inn, agrees to play the part of God's defense attorney. He defends God's justice with arguments reminiscent of Job's friends: "If God chooses not to answer, He must have his reasons. God is God, and His will is independent from ours—as his reasoning" (132). On the strength of this argument, Sam insists that Berish has but one viable option: "Endure. Accept. And say Amen" (132; cf. Job 8:3, 11:7–10, 22:21–23).

Berish refuses this option and chooses another:

He [God] annihilated Shamgorod and you want me to be for Him? I can't! If He insists upon going on with His methods, let Him—but I won't say Amen. Let Him crush me, I won't say Kaddish. Let Him kill me, let Him kill us all, I shall shout and shout that it's His fault. I'll use my last energy to make my protest known. Whether I live or die, I submit to Him no longer. . . . I'll demand justice. For the widows of Jerusalem and the orphans of Betar. For the slaves of Rome and Cappadocia. And for the destitute of Oman and the victims of Koretz. I'll shout for them, against Him I'll shout. To you judges, I'll shout, "Tell Him what he should have not done; tell Him to stop the bloodshed now." (133–34)

Wiesel notes that his play was designed to be performed as a "tragic farce: a *Purimschpiel* within a *Purimschpiel*."[21] Suspended in temporary revelry, people laugh because they are tired of crying. Berish, Wiesel's Joban figure, exemplifies the bleak reality. On the one hand, he concedes that putting God on trial, however serious, is nothing more than a game (86).On the other, when he looks at his beloved Hanna and thinks of her silenced screams, even temporary laughter cannot mitigate his anger (104). Wiesel's Joban protagonist lives and participates in a world "inhabited by assassins and clowns" (104); any entertainment the reader derives from the story is only crassly comedic. Everyone who laughs wears a mask that cannot hide irreparable shame.

Near the midpoint of the play, Mendel says, "Purim signifies absence of knowledge." Indeed the whole purpose is to drink until one can no longer "distinguish between good and evil, between Mordechai the Just and the wicked Haman, between light and shadow, life and death" (91). To reinforce the point, Sam brings the play to its end with this "explanation": "I'm His [God's] servant. He created the world and me without asking my opinion; He may do with both whatever He wishes. Our task is to glorify Him, to praise Him, to love Him, in spite of ourselves. . . . Faith in God must be as boundless as God Himself. If it exists at the expense of man, too bad. God is eternal, man is not" (157).

Literary critics and biblical scholars have long recognized Kafka's *The Trial* as one of the most important—some would argue the most important—commentaries on Job's dispute with God in contemporary Judaism.[22] Kafka wrote the book in Prague in 1914–15, during the collapse of the Austrian-Hungarian Empire. It was published in German as *Der Prozess* in 1925, a year after his death, and in English in 1935. Kafka did not live to see the horrors of World War II, but two of his sisters died in the Lodz ghetto and another at Auschwitz in 1943.

The protagonist of the story is Joseph K., a respected bank official contentedly enmeshed in the bureaucracy of mercantilism. Kafka begins with these words: "Someone must have been telling lies about Joseph K., for without having done anything wrong he was arrested one fine morning."[23] Thus begins his entry into a legal system that both promises and problematizes the pursuit of justice. Kafka never directly refers to Job, but his use of the trial metaphor echoes the biblical antecedent.[24] Both Job and K. are consumed with the effort to defend themselves against a charge about which they can get no information. Both experience a reversal that tests their attitude and their character. Both repeatedly proclaim their innocence. Both believe they are victims of injustice. Friends counsel both to trust the legal system; both find the system to be as corrupt on the inside as it appears to be from the outside. Both have opportunities to understand and to conform to how the system works. Job's instructions come from God's speeches in Job 38–41; K.'s from a painter and a prison chaplain, who convey the essence of Kafka's vision: in the words of Walter Benjamin, "a sort of theology passed on by whispers."[25]

Acting on the advice of a colleague, K. visits Titorelli, a painter commissioned by the court, in the hope that he might tell him something that explains how the legal system works. When he arrives at Titorelli's studio, he finds him working on a portrait of what he takes to be a judge rising menacingly from his chair. Behind the judge's seat, Titorelli had painted a large, hovering figure that K. cannot identify.

"It is Justice," said the painter at last. "Now I can recognize it," said K. "There's the bandage over the eyes, and here are the scales. But aren't there wings on the figure's heels, and isn't he flying?" "Yes," said the painter, "my instructions were to paint it like that; actually it is Justice and the goddess of Victory in one." "Not a very good combination, surely," said K., smiling. "Justice must stand quite still, or else the scales will waver and a just verdict will become impossible." "I had to follow my client's instructions," said the painter. "Of course," said K., who had not wished to give any offense by his remark. (146)

As Titorelli adds his finishing touches to the picture, K. sees a reddish glow like a halo emerge around the head of the judge. The shadow exaggerates the brightness of the judge's portrait, which now seems to be flying right into the foreground, toward K. "It no longer suggested the goddess of Justice, or even the goddess of Victory, but looked exactly like the goddess of the Hunt, in full cry" (147).

In the penultimate scene, K. visits the Prague cathedral. The bank has asked him to host an Italian client on a tour of places of cultural interest. The client does not show up, so K. fills time by wandering around in the cathedral, which seems to him unusually deserted, dark, and prisonlike (205). He notices a priest ascending a pulpit in a small side chapel. The pulpit's structure, too low and curved for an ordinary man to stand in upright, seemed "designed . . . to torture the preacher" (207). Instead of preaching a sermon, the priest calls K.'s name. "'You are Joseph K. . . . You are an accused man,' said the priest in a very low voice. 'Yes,' said K., 'so I have been informed.' 'Then you are the man I seek,' said the priest. 'I am the prison chaplain. . . . I had you summoned here,' said the priest, 'to have a talk with you. . . .' 'Do you know your case is going badly?' asked the priest. 'I have that idea myself,' said K." (210).

The priest proceeds to tell K. a parable about the doorkeeper who stands before the Law.[26] An ordinary man from the countryside asks for admittance to the Law. The doorkeeper explains that he cannot permit this at the moment and gives the man a stool to sit on as he waits. He waits for days, years; "the Law, he thinks, should be accessible to every man and at all times" (213), but each time he requests that the door be opened, the doorkeeper refuses. When the doorkeeper sees that the man is about to die, he says to him: "No one but you could gain admittance through the door, since the door was intended for you. I am now going to shut it" (214–15).

The priest and K. discuss multiple interpretations of the parable, each one adding possibilities that subtract from clarity. The priest advises K. that "it is not necessary to accept everything as true, one must only accept it as necessary." It is a "melancholy conclusion," K. says. "It turns lying into a universal principle" (220). "You have to leave now," said the priest (221). As K. gropes his way out of the cathedral's darkness, the priest reminds him that he is but the servant of the court, then adds these words: "The Court wants nothing from you. It receives you when you come and it dismisses you when you go" (222).

What does the parable mean? What is K. meant to learn from it? The priest's parable resonates with Jesus's instructions on prayer: "Ask, and it will be given you; search, and you will find; knock, and the door will be opened for you. For everyone who asks receives, and everyone who searches finds, and for everyone who knocks, the door will be opened. Is there anyone among you who, if your child asks for bread, will give a stone? Or if the child asks for a fish, will give a snake? If you then, who are evil, know how to give good gifts to your children, how much more will your Father in heaven give good things to those who ask him!" (Mt 7:7–11).

The priest's doorkeeper, however, seems more a caricature of the God of Jewish law than an example of Christian grace and charity. K. takes the story to mean that the doorkeeper is either deceptive or cruel (215). Some interpreters claim, the priest counters, that "the story confers no right on anyone to pass judgment on the doorkeeper. Whatever he may seem to us, he is yet a servant of the Law; that is, he belongs to the Law and as such is beyond human judgment" (220). Is there some truth in the parable about the relation of the individual citizen to the law? Some truth about the claims of the innocently condemned on institutional systems of law and governance? K. is caught in a bureaucracy whose justice invites his knock at a door that remains inexplicably closed. George Steiner suggests a "naïve gloss" on the conundrum Kafka presents his readers: "*The Trial* is translucent, it stands open to our apprehension as do Biblical parables and narrations. If we remain baffled and rebellious to the light of meaning—a light which may well be inhuman in its indifferent purity—if we do not enter a door open and intended for each and every one of us, the guilt, the consequences are ours. Or to put it simply: it is not so much we who read Kafka's words, it is they who read us. And find us blank."[27]

The novel ends much like it begins, only now the two men who knock on K.'s door have come not to arrest him but to execute him, in accordance with the court's decision. Sizing them up by their appearance, K. says, "Tenth-rate actors they send for me. . . . They want to finish me off cheaply" (224). They place his arms in an irresistible grip and walk him to a deserted stone quarry near a "still completely urban house" (227). They strip him to the waist, prop him against a boulder, and begin arguing among themselves about who will complete the deed. As they pass a butcher knife back and forth between them, K. turns his head away. He sees a person emerge from a nearby house. This person leans forward and stretches out his arms. "Who was it? A friend? A good man? Someone who sympathized? Was it one person only? Or was it mankind? Was help at hand?

GOD ON TRIAL

Were there arguments in his favor that had been overlooked? Of course there must be. . . . Where was the Judge whom he had never seen? Where was the high Court, to which he had never penetrated? He raised his hands and spread out all his fingers" (228).[28]

There is no time for more thinking. One of the men grabs K. by the throat; the other drives the knife into his heart. With failing eyes K. sees his executioners standing cheek to cheek as they complete the final act. The last words belong to K.: "'Like a dog!' he said; it was as if the shame of it must outlive him" (229).

"O that my words . . . were inscribed in a record, incised on a rock forever" (Job 19:23–24)

From these second readings of the Joban trial metaphor by Kafka and Wiesel, I return to the archival source. In preparing for his trial against God, Job makes two important declarations. In the first (19:23–24), he voices the hope that his complaint will be incised in stone, a permanent record that will last beyond his despair, beyond his friends' rebuke of his aspiration for divine justice, beyond even the silence of God. In the second (31:35–37), Job adds his signature to a formal indictment of God and expresses the hope that God will respond in kind with a written account of the charges against Job. The first declaration informs the second. Job seeks an inerasable record of the trial and its outcome that can be read and evaluated by future generations. The book of Job is the reality of his yearnings. We readers become not only stewards of his record; we also become, in the imagery of the trial metaphor, the adjudicating judge in Job's trial against God.[29]

Job's trial against God is a trope for the contest between public law and private plea. On the plenary side is the "law-as-sentence," which provides broad and established legal precedent for instruction, admonishment, and exemplary correction. On the other side is the supplementary breakout session, the often anomalous "complaint as plea,"[30] which presses the legal system to address particularities for which there may be no precedent or parallel. The jury must decide which voice to empower, the voice of legal orthodoxy that sustains civic solidarity or the voice of individual complaint that signposts the borderland between consensus and dissent. From Kafka's perspective the legal bureaucracy is and should be impermeable to the particulars of Joseph K.'s case. As the priest in the cathedral tells him, "You are held to be guilty. Your case will perhaps never get beyond a lower Court. . . . Your guilt is supposed" (210). From Wiesel's perspective Berish's case against God must go forward, futile though it may be. As Berish says, God may be merciless, but "He will not succeed in stifling my truth" (42). These and other "fictions of the law," as Jonathan Lamb argues, require readers to see "'I' to 'I' with Job, if they are to see 'eye to eye'" with the judge who renders the verdict.[31] Lamb goes on to note that "this association has a long history." He cites Calvin as one sixteenth-century example. In support of Lamb's thesis, I add another from the nineteenth-century poet James Russell Lowell.

> Once to every man and nation comes the moment to decide,
> In the strife of Truth with Falsehood, for the good or the evil side;
> Some great cause, God's new Messiah, offering each the bloom or blight,
> Parts the goats upon the left hand, and the sheep upon the right,
> And the choice goes by forever 'twixt that darkness and that light. . . .
> Careless comes the Avenger; history's pages but record
> One death-grapple in the darkness 'twixt old systems and the Word;
> Truth forever on the scaffold, Wrong forever on the throne;
> Yet that scaffold sways the future, and behind the dim unknown,
> Standeth God within the shadow, keeping watch above His own.[32]

To suggest that we readers are to make a decision about the fate of one who stands on the "scaffold" of death may be excessive. Then again verdicts depend on perspective, on whether one sees the issues from the vantage point of the principles of the law or "I" to "I" with the aggrieved who appeal to the law for justice; from the perspective of Job and Joban figures such as Berish and Joseph K. or from Sam and the priest, who convey the court's opinion. How should readers, belated jurors and judges of Job's suit against God, decide the case?

Martha Nussbaum argues that justice requires more than simply an assessment of the facts in a legal case. Justice requires the wisdom of the "'judicious spectator,' whose judgments and responses are intended to provide a paradigm of public rationality (whether for the leader or for the citizen)."[33] Those who pass judgment on others must be a "spectator," because judicial neutrality requires detachment. If decisions are to be rendered without bias, they must not be compromised by personal interests. But the spectator must also be "judicious," by which Nussbaum means that justice requires judges who demonstrate more than a technical mastery of the law. Above all judges must possess the moral capacity for sympathetic identification with those who are being judged. "To be able to assess judicially another's pain, to participate in it and to ask about its significance," she writes, "is a powerful way of learning what the human facts are and of acquiring a motivation to alter them."[34] Conversely if judges cannot imagine what it feels like to be the persons who come into their courts, if they have no emotional triggers that cause them to flinch in the presence of another person's pain and loss, their desperate need for restitution, then it is unlikely their verdicts can promise anything more than a determination of guilt or innocence that alters nothing.

How might judges acquire the requisite balance between "empathetic participation and external assessment"?[35] Nussbaum takes a clue from Stephen G.

Breyer's confirmation hearings before the Senate Judiciary Committee upon his nomination to the United Sates Supreme Court.

> I read something that moved me a lot not very long ago. I was reading something by Chesterton, and he was talking about one of the Brontës, I think her *Jane Eyre*. He says you go and look out at the city—I think he was looking at London—and he said you, you see all the houses now, even at the end of the nineteenth century, and they look all as if they're the same. And you think all those people are out there going to work and they're all the same. He says, but what Brontë tells you is they're not the same. Each one of those persons in each one of those houses and each one of those families is different, and they each have a story to tell. Each of those stories involves something about human passion. Each of those stories involves a man, a woman, children, families, work, lives—and you get that sense out of the book. And so sometimes I've found literature very helpful as a way out of the tower.[36]

Breyer speaks of literature as a source of moral guidance; it sharpens sensitivities and enlarges imagination. To be sure, as Nussbaum cautions, literature may also distort and misrepresent facts: its "truth" may be biased; its perspective will almost always be fallible. Thus reading literary works, like judging a legal case, requires one to be a judicious reader/spectator, to be both immersed and detached, both skeptical and sympathetic. Nussbaum's term for this is the "literary judge"[37] or, to invoke the language of Walt Whitman, the "poetic judge."

"For the great idea . . . the bard walks in advance, leader of leaders"

In "By Blue Ontario's Shore" (1867), Whitman reflects on what America most needed to restore itself after the Civil War had wreaked havoc on a young nation's aspirations for democracy. He encounters a "Phantom" that calls for a poet who will embody justice that speaks across the great divide of winners and losers. He describes the characteristics of the poet judge as follows.

. . . the poet is the equable man,
Not in him but off from him things are grotesque, eccentric, fail of their full returns,
Nothing out of its place is good, nothing in its place is bad,
He bestows on every object or quantity its fit proportion, neither more nor less,
He is the arbiter of the diverse, he is the key,
He is the equalizer of his age and land,
He supplies what wants supplying, he checks what wants checking . . .
He judges not as the judge judges but as the sun falling around a helpless thing,
As he sees the farthest he has the most faith . . .
He sees eternity in men and women, he does not see men and women as dreams
    or dots.[38]

The "equable" judge, the Phantom insists, must be the arbiter of diversity. He must be the "equalizer," the one who adds what is lacking, who checks what is excessive, who sees and understands more because he sees differently. Men and women are not mere "dots"; they are more than abstractions of life, more than a sum of facts to be ciphered and sifted. They have within them something of eternity, complex measures of the immeasurable. For the equable judge, therefore, it is not enough to judge "as the judge judges." He must judge instead "as the sun falling around a helpless thing." This analogy is thick with poetic and forensic imagination. Nussbaum's exegesis is instructive:

> This bold image suggests, first, enormous detail and particularity. When the sun falls around a thing it illuminates every curve, every nook; nothing remains hidden, nothing unperceived. So, too, does the poet's judgment fall, perceiving all that is there and disclosing it to our view. . . . In particular, the sun illuminates the situation of the helpless, which is usually shrouded in darkness. But this intimacy is also stern and rather pitiless: by comparing judgment to sunlight rather than gentle shade, Whitman indicates that the poet's commitment to fairness and fitness does not yield to bias or favor, that his confrontation with the particular, while intimate, is unswerving. There is a certain ideal of judicial neutrality here—a neutrality, however, linked not with remote generality but with rich historical concreteness, not with quasi-scientific abstractness but with a vision of the human world.[39]

Beyond Nussbaum's cogent discussion, it is important for my purposes to note how the poem continues. Whitman imagines himself interrogating those who might offer themselves as candidates for the role of the "equable man." If one is to embody norms of judgment that counter conventional modes of justice, then these are the questions that must be answered satisfactorily:

Are you he would assume a place to teach or be a poet here in the States?
The place is august, the terms obdurate.
Who would assume to teach here may well prepare himself body and mind,
He may well survey, ponder, arm, fortify, harden, make lithe himself,
He shall surely be question'd beforehand by me with many and stern questions . . .
Have you studied out the land, its idioms and men?
Have you learn'd the physiology, phrenology, politics, geography,
    pride, freedom, friendship of the land? its substratums and objects? . . .
Are you faithful to things? do you teach what the land and sea,
    the bodies of men, womanhood, amativeness, heroic angers, teach? . . .
Can you hold your hand against all seductions, follies, whirls, fierce
    contentions? are you very strong? are you really of the whole People?

Are you not of some coterie? some school or mere religion? . . .
Do you hold the like love for those hardening to maturity? for the last-born? little
    and big? and for the errant?[40]

If we consider such questions in light of another of Whitman's poems, "Song of Myself" (1881), we might be justified in thinking that he thought of himself as at least one of those who could pass the test for the poet judge. He describes himself as a "kosmos," as the "acme of things accomplish'd" and "an encloser of things to be," as the "teacher" whose words "itch at your ears till you understand them."[41] Because "agonies are one of [his] changes of garment," he does not have to ask the wounded person how he feels; he "becomes the wounded person."[42] Someone must have the courage to speak for the "many long dumb voices" of those disfigured and trivialized by agony. Whitman sees himself as one who is willing to rise to the challenge.[43]

Judicious readers must decide whether Whitman, like Job who decides to file a suit against God, exemplifies more hubris than wisdom in his aspirations to be an agent of justice. Whitman concedes that the poetic judge best keep silent in the dispute with God about the distinction between the eternal and the immediate.[44] Nonetheless he determines that when standing face to face with the mystery of God's justice, he will not be "tamed," he will instead "sound [his] barbaric yawp over the roofs of the world."[45] Job's decision is similar: "He [God] may kill me; I have no hope; but I will defend my ways to his face" (Job 13:15). Emily Dickinson, a contemporary of Whitman, may well have approved of both his and Job's audacity. As one poetic judge to another, she says, "The abdication of Belief / Makes the Behavior small."[46]

Job's friends and Job's God also have a voice in this case. They might well concur with Dickinson's assessment, but their assent may mean something completely different. They, too, deserve the presumption, at least on first reading, of "judicious spectators."

6

JOB'S COMFORTERS

"Do not despise the discipline of the Almighty" (Job 5:17)

> Come, ye philosophers, who cry, "All's well,"
> And contemplate the ruin of a world.
>
> Voltaire, "Poem on the Lisbon Disaster"

> All Nature is but art, unknown to thee
> All chance, direction, which thou canst not see;
> All discord, harmony not understood;
> All partial evil, universal good:
> And, spite of pride, in erring reason's spite,
> One truth is clear, Whatever is, is right.
>
> Alexander Pope, "Essay on Man"

Afflicted with inexplicable sufferings, Job sits in silence for seven days and seven nights. Three friends who come to "console and comfort him"—Eliphaz, Bildad, and Zophar—respect this need for silence before suffering that is "very great" (Job 2:13).[1] With Job they too must think deeply about what words merit interruption of the silence. Their task is made more difficult and more important because Job speaks first. His curses and laments in Job 3 define their role as friends. How should they comfort one who curses life and the God who created it? How should they console one whose "why?" questions demand answers that may exceed, and perhaps nullify, conventional affirmations? Inside the gap between silence and speech, the friends, like Job, contemplate multiple responses.

The friends' response comprises three cycles of speeches (Job 4–14, 15–21, 22–27). The general theme in the first cycle is God's moral governance of the world, especially his unfailing care for the righteous and his equally unfailing punishment of the wicked (4:7–11, 8:8–19, 11:11). Like kind and sympathetic counselors, they each gently raise a series of rhetorical questions, questions they trust will nudge Job to answers they already know. Eliphaz, always the lead spokesperson, sets the tone the others will follow (4:2, 6–7). With varying measures of comfort and encouragement, the friends are confident that if Job will heed their counsel, if he "will seek God" (8:5), if he will put away all iniquity (11:13–14), then God will reward his righteousness (5:24–27, 8:20–21, 11:16–17).

Job, however, sees his world differently. He is innocent (6:28–30, 9:21, 10:7), and he accuses the friends of "whitewashing the truth" (13:4) in order to insulate themselves and God from scrutiny. He charges that God is more absent than present (9:11, 13:24), more hostile than compassionate (6:4, 9:17–24, 12:17–25). God exercises power, without restraint and without purpose, to destroy the very world the friends claim he has so wondrously and justly created (10:8–12). From Job's perspective God's moral governance of the world is very much in question. One needs only ask the animals; even they know the world is more complicated than the friends allow (12:7–9).

The second cycle of speeches (Job 15–21) follows the same general pattern as the first. The friends begin with rhetorical questions that set the agenda for their concerns (15:2, 18:2, 20:4–5), then proceed with observations about the world as they understand it. There are, however, noticeable differences in both the tone and substance of their address to Job. Initially they argued that God punishes the wicked and rewards the righteous. Now they trim their focus to one part of this argument—the punishment of the wicked (15:17–35, 18:5–21, 20:6–29)—with no parallel assertions about the fate of persons, such as Job, who claim to be righteous. Initially they addressed Job with deference; now they are more aggressive, and their tone is sharper (15:7–9, 18:3, 20:3), an indication that their resolve is stiffening. They offer no word of encouragement to Job; instead they increase their warning, rebukes, and opposition. Once again Eliphaz leads the way (15:4–6; cf. 18:4, 20:4–11). In the friends' view, Job has crossed the line by turning his "spirit against God" (15:13). If he is not stopped, then he will jeopardize the "fear of God" upon which they believe the whole enterprise of religion rests.

Job, however, continues to focus on God's violence toward him (16:6–17, 19:6–12). In his last speech in this cycle, he confronts directly the friends' retribution theology (21:17–26), once again questioning its claim to truth: "How often is the lamp of the wicked put out? How often does calamity come upon them?" (21:17). Job continues to insist that he is innocent (16:17), thus his question is this: is there any place in heaven or on earth where the cries of the innocent are heard and addressed? To pursue the question, he presses the idea of a courtroom trial in which he may file his grievances against God and obtain the justice he seeks and deserves (16:18–22; cf. Job 9–10).

The symmetry of the speeches breaks down in the third cycle. Eliphaz once again takes the point with rhetorical questions (22:2–5) that lay the foundation for his final address, but Bildad's speech (25:1–6) is unusually short, and Zophar's speech is missing altogether. Various explanations may account for the apparent disarray in this cycle, and various attempts to restore a supposed original form have been proposed.[2] However these issues may be resolved, it is clear that the friends' approach in the third cycle takes yet another turn. They give up all efforts to coerce a confession from Job. Now they simply pronounce him guilty: "Is not your wickedness great? There is no end to your iniquities" (22:5). The friends' notion of an orderly trial, with evidence so strong Job can only yield and agree to guilt, has not worked. But inasmuch as the friends claim the right to be both judge and jury in the case of *Job v. God*, they can adjust the facts to fit their presumptions. Toward that end Eliphaz proceeds to invent the crimes that justify the verdict. He finds Job guilty on two counts. The first is moral failure (22:6–11), defined as Job's gratuitous abuse of the poor and needy. The second is theological error (22:12–20), defined as Job's accusation that God is too remote from the human condition to render the justice required. Eliphaz calls no witnesses; he produces no evidence. He bases his case on a priori conclusions: if Job suffers, then sin must be the cause (22:21–27). In Eliphaz's court Job has but one option: "Agree with God, and be at peace; in this way good will come to you" (22:5). This counsel anticipates Kafka's reading of the Joban story in *The Trial*. When Joseph K., arrested "without having done anything wrong," seeks redress in the courts, his lawyer's maidservant gives him this warning: "You can't defend yourself against this court, all you can do is confess."

Job refuses the friends' counsel, as before. In his seventh and last speech in the cycle of dialogues (Job 23–24), he complains once again about the absence of God (cf. 9:11, 13:24), now with a scathing interrogation of divine justice that exceeds anything else in the book. Why do those who rely upon God never see the judgment he promises (23:1)? Why do the wicked run free, leaving their victims to cry out for help to a God who sees nothing wrong with the way the world is working (23:2–12)? Why do those who rebel against the light have license to subvert the moral order of the cosmos by using darkness as a cover for their criminality (23:13–17)? By any reasonable definition of justice, Job claims, such evidence requires God's intervention, yet the abuses pile up, and God remains silent. When there are no visible signs of either God or God's justice, the moral order that sustains society collapses (24:13–17), and the wicked are free to co-opt justice for sinister and selfish purposes. As the friends become more and more irrelevant to this debate, Job becomes more and more resolved to press the case for justice. His last words in chapter 27 end with yet another unanswered question: "Will God hear their [people who have been labeled wicked] cry when trouble comes upon them?" (27:9).

Upon their arrival on the scene of Job's suffering, Eliphaz, Bildad, and Zophar are identified as "friends" (*rēʿê* [Job 2:11]). They are not detached "messengers" (*mal'āk* [1:14–19]) who merely report calamity; they come to express genuine sympathy (to "console" means to share grief by nodding the head; cf. Jer 15:5, 22:10) and to show compassion (to "comfort" means to share in another's sorrows; cf. 2 Sm 12:24, 1 Chr 19:2; Ru 2:13; Job 19:25). The epilogue uses the same two verbs, *console* (*nûd*) and *comfort* (*nḥm*), to describe the friends and family members who offer Job concrete expressions of sympathy and support ("a piece of money and a gold ring" [42:11]). Moreover Job's three friends base their counsel on truths deeply embedded in Hebraic traditions that address the issue of suffering and divine justice. They adhere to time-honored precedent, which they firmly believe is always adequate for adjudicating any particular circumstances that may call it into question.

Nonetheless God's evaluation of the friends—"My wrath is kindled against you . . . for you have not spoken of me what is right" (42:7, 8)—typically nullifies any sympathies readers may have for the friends. To set the table for the subsequent discussion, I place two of William Blake's nineteenth-century etchings of Job's friends side by side.[3] In the first depiction of Job's comforters (plate 7), Blake positions Job on a mound of straw, his head resting on his wife's chest. His hands, palms downward, extend by his side. His wife kneels beside him, her body providing a pillar of support, her uplifted hands gesturing the prayer Job himself seems too exhausted to offer. The three friends, to the left of Job and his wife, raise their own hands in consonance with Job's wife, although their reach heavenward is more extended and their facial expressions convey more intensity and emotion. It is as if they wish to lift Job out of distress and deliver him safely into the arms of God. At the top and bottom of this frame, Blake inscribes the words from Job 2:11: "When they lifted up their eyes afar off and knew him not they lifted up their voices and wept." To these words Blake adds a quotation from James 5:11, which provides the catchword—*patience*—that conveys not only the popular understanding of Job's exemplary faith but also the reason for the friends' sympathetic support: "Ye have heard of the patience of Job and have seen the end of the Lord, that the Lord is very pitiful, and of tender mercy."

In the second etching (plate 10), Blake's Job has moved from the ash heap to a kneeling position. No longer leaning backward, he now holds himself upright, his stomach muscles taut, as if in anticipation of a negative response to the curses he has spoken in Job 3. His disease-spotted torso is wrapped from the waist down with the traditional sackcloth. His head is tilted backward. His tear-stained eyes are fixed on the God above, whom he cannot see but will not cease to trust. Blake exegetes Job's solemn misery with three scripture citations added to the top of the frame (Job 23:10, 19:21, 13:15).

The juxtaposition of these two etchings is Blake's way of showing that Job's three friends have ceased to play the role of comforters. They have now become his inquisitors. With outstretched hands they point fingers of ridicule toward him.[4] In contrast with Job, the friends' expressions are cold and hard, as is particularly clear in the face of the friend to the forefront, presumably Eliphaz. Job's wife, whose right hand is also partially extended, seems now to have joined in the reproach. Two further citations in the bottom of the frame, both from Job's last speech in the first cycle (12:4, 14:3), convey what has drawn the friends' ire.

The figures in the border add to Blake's reading of the bleakness of the friends' perspective. Two angels, each weighed down with chains, appear to be holding on with some difficulty to the picture of Job. In the bottom left-hand corner, a bird (a raven? a cuckoo?), perhaps a symbol of slander, steps on a serpent. In the bottom right-hand corner, an owl, perhaps a symbol of false wisdom, grasps a helpless mouse in its talons.[5]

Well-intentioned friends they may be, but second and third readings of Eliphaz, Bildad, and Zophar, as Blake's exegesis suggests, tilt toward negative assessments. At issue is more than simply a reading of the friends' counsel to Job. Their reliance on a priori truths, which in their judgment trump all particular anomalies, seeds an extended debate about primary and contingent truths. To get our bearings on this debate, we turn to the eighteenth century and the traumatic aftershocks of the earthquake in Lisbon on November 1, 1755.

Job as Lisbon; Job's Friends as Leibnizian Theodicy Makers

On All Saints' Day, 1755, a massive earthquake struck Lisbon, population 275,000, then the fourth largest city in Europe. Approximately 30,000 people died; more than 100,000 were injured. The effect of the quake reached as far south as Morocco, as far west as the Caribbean. Tremors were felt in Switzerland, Italy, and France.[6] Voltaire's *Candide* (1759) describes the devastation Candide and Pangloss witness as they walk through Lisbon:

> Hardly have they set foot in the city . . . when they feel the earth tremble under their feet; the sea rises boiling in the port and shatters the vessels that are at anchor. Whirlwinds of flame and ashes cover the streets and public squares, the houses crumble, the roofs are tumbled down upon the foundations, and the foundations disintegrate; thirty thousand inhabitants of every age and of either sex are crushed beneath the ruins. . . . Said Pangloss: "What can be sufficient reason for this phenomenon?" "It is the end of the world," exclaimed Candide.[7]

"What can be sufficient reason for this phenomenon?" In his 1710 publication, *Theodicy,* G. W. Leibniz anticipated and attempted to answer the question. Leibniz coined the term *theodicy* as part of his effort to construct a defense of God's justice in the face of metaphysical, natural, and moral evil. His defense of God rests on his distinction between primary truths and contingent truths.[8] Primary truths are a priori propositions; insulated from critique, they presuppose causal connections between deed and consequence. Everything in the world God created happens for a reason, even if the reason cannot be identified. "Everything is as it is,"[9] and there is always an ultimate divine equity between means and ends. In response to the arguments by Pierre Bayle[10] and others that life's uneven mixture of good and evil necessarily brings God's justice into question, Leibniz counters that we must judge God's intentions *ab effectu,* "since God has chosen this world as it is. We know, moreover, that often an evil brings forth a good whereto one would not have attained without that evil. Often indeed two evils have made one great good."[11] Contingent truths are first-person experiences that interrupt a priori assertions with anomalous, but necessarily partial, complaints alleging the dominance of evil over good. Leibniz cites Job as an example of one who makes a partial complaint about divine injustice without understanding the difference between primary and contingent truths. "The Lord took away Job's substance," Leibniz says with reference to Job 1:21, "although that was done through the malice of the brigands." This contingent truth suggests "only that the things God has done are used as occasion for ignorance, error, malice, and evil deeds, and contribute thereto, God indeed foreseeing this, and intending to use it for his ends, since superior reasons of perfect wisdom have determined him to permit these evils, and even to co-operate therein."[12] After the earthquake in 1755, which in the words of Voltaire's Candide seems to confirm "the end of the world," the tautologies of primary truths are stretched to, perhaps beyond, their limits. Jonathan Lamb's assessment aptly frames the ensuing eighteenth-century debate: "Leibnizian providentialists are the comforters, Lisbon is Job."[13]

We may enter this debate by focusing on representative eighteenth-century works. On the side of Leibnizian providentialists, Alexander Pope argues for the primacy of unassailable truths to unanswerable questions. On the side of Lisbon/Job, Voltaire repeatedly challenges what he perceives to be little more than trite axioms. Pope's "Essay on Man" (1734) is widely regarded as having been inspired by Leibniz's *Theodicy.* The essay is addressed to Henry St. John, Lord Bolingbroke, who served as Queen Anne's secretary of state and prime minister. The two were friends who discussed and generally agreed upon a range of philosophical, ethical, and political principles. As Pope writes to Bolingbroke in the introduction to the essay, "Together let us . . . laugh where we must, be candid where we can; but vindicate the ways of God to Man."[14]

Pope's defense of God is double-pronged. First he reiterates Leibniz's maxim that universal good smoothes out all paradoxes of partial evil (4:36–39, 48–50). The conceit of humans is to imagine themselves as better, more just, than God.

But this impiety, Pope cautions, is a prime example of the false equivalency of the immediate and permanent. Because humans see only a "part . . . not a whole" (1:60), it is a sin to contest the "Eternal Cause" (1:114–16, 121–23, 128–30).

Pope draws one major lesson from God's "Eternal Cause." Humans must "cease" importunate demands and "submit" to God's "Disposing Power" (1:280, 287). In sum, as Eliphaz says, there is but one faithful option for the Jobs of this world: "Agree with God, and be at peace; in this way good will come to you" (Job 22:21).

> Safe in the hand of one Disposing Power . . .

> All Nature is but art, unknown to thee
> All chance, direction, which thou canst not see;
> All discord, harmony not understood;
> All partial evil, universal good:
> And, spite of pride, in erring reason's spite,
> One truth is clear, Whatever is, is right. (1:289–94; cf. 4:398)

Pope's second line of argumentation is anthropological. To Job's question "What are human beings?" (Job 7:17), Pope responds that they are "vile worms" (1:257) whose questions about divine providence betray the limitations of their knowledge and the folly of their aspirations. Caught between partial knowledge and infinite weakness, human beings are adrift in a "middle state," somewhere between "glory" and "jest" (2:4–10, 17–18). Human beings may complain that God has created a world in which "sometimes virtue starves, while vice is fed" (4:150), but in doing so they can scarcely conceive how God's equitable justice distinguishes between the whole and the parts. Pope replaces Job's question—"What are human beings?"—with another, rhetorical in form but authoritative in its expectation of one and only one correct response: "Has God, thou fool! work'd solely for thy good, thy joy, thy pastime, thy attire, thy food?" (3:27–28). Pope answers his own question (3:29–42) with a litany of examples that demonstrate creation's complexity. In doing so he follows a strategy similar to Job's fourth friend, Elihu (Job 36:22–37:24), who provides a prelude to God's own questioning of Job in the whirlwind speeches (Job 38–41).

Pope acknowledges that primary truths must parry contingent, sometimes unanswerable, questions. So when the "vile man mourns" (1:77), Pope turns to the rhetoric of Job's friends to buttress a fundamental admonition: "Know then thyself, presume not God to scan, / The proper study of mankind is man" (2:1–2; cf. Job 4:17–19, 15:14–16, 22:2–5). When mere mortals presume to know the secrets of divine providence (cf. 1:130–31), Pope counters with a question that echoes Elihu: "Who knows but He, whose hand the lightning forms?" (1:157; cf. Job 37:3). When mortals demand that "this dread order" of God's cosmic plan be broken, or at least informed, by particular cries for justice, Pope responds with a free translation of Bildad's counsel to Job: "Vile worm!—oh madness! pride! impiety" (1:257; cf. Job 25:4–6).

A final observation merits attention. Pope compares the "vile man that mourns" to marginal figures in society, the mad (e.g., 4:71), women (e.g., 2:59, 79), and, at length, the Indians (1:100–102, 109–13; 4:74). These "untutored" ones, such as Job, Pope not only marginalizes but also disparages. Their inferior status is a necessary part of the symmetry of gains and losses that harmonize divine providence.[15] Like Job they are consigned to the ash heap outside the city, where particular cries for justice ricochet back and forth in a world attuned to larger, more important issues.

Theodicies such as Leibniz's and Pope's are interregnum reflections. The catalyst is typically some past event that has raised deep questions about divine justice. From the vantage point of hindsight, theodicy makers review, revise, and when necessary correct regnant explanations for why and how God should be declared not guilty. The objective is not only to provide a way of comprehending the past but also to lay a sure foundation for the future, which, inevitably, will bring new challenges. Theodicies are always tested by on-the-ground realities. They survive as primary truths only as long as they can satisfactorily minimize contingent interruptions. As Job embodies the test for his friends' assertions about God's justice, so Lisbon becomes the test for Leibniz's contention that "everything is as it is."

Voltaire's response to the Lisbon earthquake was almost immediate. By the end of November 1755, he had begun working on the "Poème sur le désastre de Lisbonne," which he delivered to the publisher by the end of the year. The subtitle, "Examen de cet axiome: Tout est bien" ("Examination of This Axiom: 'All Is Well'"), announces Voltaire's intent to challenge Leibniz and Pope.[16]

Voltaire begins by registering the "eternal lingering of [Lisbon's] useless pain" and segues immediately to a challenge aimed directly at Leibniz: "Come, ye philosophers, who cry, 'All's well,' / And contemplate this ruin of a world" (lines 3–5). He particularizes the "expiring murmurs of distress" of Lisbon victims, then asks how philosophers can possibly believe this is the will of a just God (6–17). Identifying with the victims, Voltaire switches to first-person language, now drawing freely on Job: "My plaint is innocent, my cries are just . . . indulge me my lament" (29–33; cf. Job 9:21; 10:1–2, 7; 19:6). Parodying Pope's assertion that mortals who protest God's injustice are "vile worms," Voltaire turns directly to refute Pope's source, Bildad, who comforts Job by reminding him that he is but a "maggot" and a "worm" (96–99, 101–3; cf. Job 25:6). In the remainder of the poem (165–214), he specifically confronts the theodicean arguments of Leibniz, Plato, Epicurus, and

Bayle and concludes that the universe "belies" and "refutes" the conceit of the argument that "all's well" in the world of Lisbon's victims. How can one "conceive a God supremely good, / Who . . . scatters evil with so large a hand?" (132, 134). "The human race," Voltaire says, "demands a word from God" (161).

By the end of the poem, Voltaire limps, "lowly sighing" (217), toward a conflicted hope. All may be well one day, as the philosophers say, but in the interim this is more an "ideal dream" (215) than a present reality. Instructed by the "deepening gloom" that occludes the dream, Voltaire hears no word from heaven, only what he calls "une foule de theologiens de toutes les communions" (a mob of theologians of all sorts of persuasion). He concludes by quoting and commenting on an anonymous caliph's deathbed prayer to the one he revered (228–31).

Two years later, in 1758, Voltaire pressed his case against Leibniz's theodicy in *Candide,* a story that views the destruction of Lisbon and other atrocities through the eyes of Candide and his tutor, Pangloss. Voltaire sketches the basic plotline for the story in the first six chapters, then recycles the major motifs through successive recountings that add to the particulars of an eighteenth-century world "as it is." Candide is the illegitimate nephew of a German baron. Pangloss, his tutor, teaches "metaphysico-theologo-cosmolo-nigology." He has demonstrated to his own satisfaction that "there is no effect without a cause and that, in this best of all possible worlds . . . things cannot be otherwise, for everything . . . is necessarily for the best end" (2). All this Candide "believed innocently." When the baron catches Candide flirting with his daughter, Cunégonde, he expels him from the castle. Thus begins Candide's lesson in the primary truths of cause and effect.

Candide soon finds himself conscripted into the Bulgar army, where he witnesses firsthand the carnage of the Seven Years' War (6–7). Subsequently he encounters a beggar covered with sores, his nose eaten away. He coughs so violently that teeth fly out of his mouth as he talks. The beggar is Pangloss, who explains that he contracted syphilis from a tryst with Paquette, an attendant at the castle, who was herself infected by a long line of companions leading back to a man who sailed to America with Columbus. Pangloss insists that syphilis is "an indispensable thing in the best of worlds, a necessary ingredient" (10); if Columbus had not brought back the disease, then Europeans could not have enjoyed many wondrous discoveries from the New World, such as chocolate. "Private misfortunes make up the general good," Pangloss says, "so that the more private misfortunes there are, the more good as well" (11). Even as he speaks, however, the skies begin to darken and the winds strengthen. The ship on which he and Candide have now booked passage arrives in the port of Lisbon. It is November 1, 1755. The ship splits open and all aboard drown except Pangloss, Candide, and one sailor. Once the three men are on shore, they observe everywhere the wreckage the earthquake has made of Lisbon. Pangloss consoles the victims with the comfort of his learning: "Things could not be otherwise. All is for the best. For if there is a volcano in Lisbon, it could not be anywhere else. For it is impossible that things should not be where they are. For all is well" (13).

The remainder of the tale follows Candide and Pangloss on their journeys to other places: Buenos Aires, Eldorado, Surinam, Paris, Venice, Constantinople. At every stop they confront victims who have experienced horrendous brokenness and loss. At every stop Pangloss is unwavering in his response. "Leibniz cannot be wrong," he insists, "pre-established harmony is the finest thing in the world, like the plenum and subtle matter" (90). Despite the repetition one of the subtleties in Voltaire's narrative is that neither Candide nor Pangloss is immune to the suffering they witness. Candide is repeatedly flogged and imprisoned. Pangloss is disfigured by disease, half-hanged, and dissected. The more Pangloss talks like Job's friends, the more he looks like Job, "his body as it were erupting in protest against the composure of the language of justification. The matter leaking through an instrument no longer fit to contain it."[17]

Voltaire brings *Candide* to a conclusion with a garden scene. Candide, Pangloss, and others who have joined and survived this journey with them—Cunégonde, a woman whose sexual exploits have left her ugly; Martin, a scholar whose pessimism is invincible; Cacambo, a prudent optimist who nonetheless has concluded that killing one's neighbor is sometimes justified; an old woman, born the daughter of a pope but literally raped into cynicism by her life experiences; and a dissatisfied monk, Brother Giroflée, who has been forced to take his vows by his parents—have come to their final destination. But this garden, located just outside the city of Constantinople, seems little different from the other places they have been. Two viziers and a mufti, along with others, have been murdered, and the city is in an uproar. When Pangloss asks a local dervish, "the best philosopher in Turkey" (93), what such atrocities mean, the dervish replies, "What does it matter . . . whether there is evil or good? . . . Hold your tongue" (94). At this point in the story, it is no surprise that Pangloss (Greek, "all tongue") does not comply. When Martin implores the garden group to "work without reasoning," because this "is the only way to make life endurable" (95), Pangloss reiterates the rationale that sustains his conviction: "All events are linked together in the best of all possible worlds" (96).

Voltaire does not explicitly connect this garden scene to Job. He does, however, subtly suggest that when God placed man and woman in the Garden of Eden (95) and when God placed Job in the "garden of Uz" (Job 1–2), the one and only option was to cultivate the garden of the world as it is. Wheat and tares, good and evil, all in God's inscrutable providence are indispensable for the best of all possible worlds. Voltaire's critique of this tautological truth remains the same as in his "Poem on the Lisbon Disaster": "Come, ye philosophers . . . contemplate the ruin of a world. . . . Think ye to cure our ills by denying them?" (lines 4–5, 79).

Voltaire's garden scene marks how far humans have traveled since they were placed in the primordial Garden of Eden, where the world as created, according to God's assessment, was "very good" (Gn 1:31). From the calamities that befell Adam and Eve because they transgressed the prohibition against knowing what God knows about good and evil (Gn 2:17) to the calamities that fell upon Job, by God's admission "for no reason" (Job 2:3), the particular "problem of evil," from Voltaire's eighteenth-century perspective, has escalated from one couple and from one individual to a public and universal contingent truth that continues to beg Candide's question: "If this is the best of all possible worlds, then what are the others?" (15). To underscore the lingering question, I end this section with a quote from a contemporary writer, James Wood, who echoes Voltaire's question: "God could have created heaven on earth! Why then did God create earth before heaven? Why the fallible rehearsal for perfection rather than perfection itself?"[18]

"My friends, don't leave me alone with God!"

Leibniz introduced the word *theodicy* to the lexicon of philosophical thought in the eighteenth century. We may wonder why the word and the discussion it prompted—from Pope and other advocates, from Voltaire and other critics—survived the century. In his 1791 essay "On the Failure of All Attempted Philosophical Theodicies," Kant rebuts Leibniz's vindication of God point by point. Kant hypothesizes a trial before the tribunal of philosophy. The author of the theodicy must successfully argue one of Leibniz's three defenses of God: either that God's world is purposeful, even when human reason cannot discern it; or that any contradictions to purposefulness are an inevitable part of a universal harmony in which there is more good than evil; or that human beings, not the creator, must take responsibility for causing suffering, whether physical (pain) or moral (crime). If the trial is to proceed fairly, then the attorney for God cannot simply declare arbitrarily that human reason is incompetent. Complainants may concede that God's wisdom is superior, but by doing so they do not automatically relinquish their right to question God's justice.[19] The result of this trial, Kant concludes, is that "no theodicy proposed so far has kept its promise; none has managed to justify the moral wisdom at work in the government of the world against the doubts which arise out of our experience of the world."[20]

Like Leibniz, Kant turns to Job to buttress his argument. In the trial between Job and his friends, the friends are spokesmen for "doctrinal theodicy"; Job advocates "authentic theodicy."[21] The friends explain all suffering in the world according to the doctrine of divine retribution: if there is suffering, then there must be a cause, some sin that justifies divine punishment. Although the friends cannot name Job's failure, they can render an a priori judgment that he must have done something wrong; otherwise God would not be punishing him. Job speaks not of doctrines but instead of authentic firsthand experience. In doing so he insists his conscience is clear; he speaks in good faith, confessing his imperfections while maintaining the integrity of his protests. Kant assesses the merits of both sides in this debate—the friends' doctrinal theodicy versus Job's authentic theodicy—as follows:

> The ratiocinations which both sides produced either for or against are not re-markable. But the character which the men exhibited while they reasoned is more worthy of attention. Job spoke as he thought, as he felt, and as every man in his position would feel. His friends, however, spoke as if they were overheard by the Almighty whose behaviour they were judging, and as if they cared more for win-ning his favours by passing the right judgement than for saying the truth. The dishonesty with which they affirmed things of which they should have confessed that they had no knowledge and with which they feigned convictions which in fact they did not have, contrasts with Job's free and sincere outspokenness, which is so removed from lying flattery that it almost borders on temerity. This contrast puts the friends in an unfavourable light: "Do you want," asked Job, "to defend God with unjust arguments? Do you want to make considerations for his person? Is it really his cause you want to plead? He will punish you if you make consider-ations for persons! No hypocrite can stand before him."[22]

In a prescient conclusion, Kant adds the following comment: "If Job were to ap-pear before some tribunal of dogmatic theologians, some senate or inquisition, some worthy presbytery or some high consistory of today (with the exception of one), he probably would have met with a worse fate."[23]

Kant's refutation of Leibniz notwithstanding, theodicy making did not end with the eighteenth century. Contemporary writers, especially post-Holocaust writers, have identified Job not only with Lisbon but also with Auschwitz and other concentration camps and Job's friends with the inquisitors and execution-ers who participated in such atrocities. On this point, at least, Kant's assessment of the lingering liabilities of the friends' theodicy rings true: if Job were to appear before a court of his "friends" today, his fate might well have been worse. To il-lustrate I turn to two twentieth-century Job plays, Michael Gelber's *Job Stands Up* and Hanoch Levin's *The Sorrows of Job*.

Gelber, a prominent North American Jewish educator, published *Job Stands Up* in 1975. The play is a contemporary adaptation of the biblical story, which includes musical scores and lyrics, a manual for those who want to study or pro-duce the play, and an extensive set of prefacing essays from the author about why and how he has scripted this ancient story as a modern drama. Gelber notes that as a producer the most challenging aspect of the biblical story is how to render the dialogues between Job and his comforters, thirty-six of forty-two chapters, roughly 85 percent of the book, since there seems to be little or no "action" to be dramatized here.[24] The solution, Gelber says, is to tune oneself to what he perceives to be the worst of the afflictions Job suffered—his "festering friendships" (5)—and how they advance stage by stage to a climatic end. The friends are "inquisitors," kindred spirits to Torquemada and Joseph Goebbels, and they employ techniques that move from interrogation to torture. Each step in the process is part of a calculated strategy to coerce a confession from the accused. The first stage (cycle one of the dialogues, Job 4–14) is the "soft-sell" (10) approach; the friends use words of kindness to ingratiate themselves with Job. In the second stage (Job 15–21), the friends "lay it on the line" (10) by spelling out the consequences for a refusal to confess. The third stage of interrogation (Job 22–27) resorts to physical abuse, analogous, Gelber suggests, to "torture in Spain, the stake in Massachusetts, Siberia in the Soviet Union, the concentration camp in Hitler's Germany" (10). "The methods are severe and justice is arbitrary" (11).

Gelber's script basically follows the biblical text, but to dramatize the friends' strategy, he includes directorial suggestions for actions and gestures that accompany their speeches. In the first cycle, Eliphaz tries "to play pattycake with Job" (65). When Job refuses to play, Eliphaz moves in the second cycle to stage a political rally in which he publicly accuses Job, "like a tub-thumbing campaigner" (76), of being unworthy of the claims he makes for himself. Finally, in the third cycle, Eliphaz and the friends appear as British judges, appropriately dressed in wigs and collars. They take their place on the judges' bench, the book of the law before them; music set to the lyrics of "Man Is Born to Trouble" (Job 5:7) plays in the background. The decorum of the setting, however, belies the intention of the court. Eliphaz ceremoniously approaches Job, then punches him, steps on his toes, pulls his hair, tweaks his nose, slaps him, kicks him until he falls, and demands once again that he confess his crimes (83–84). Bildad seizes Job's cane, loops it through a rope, and squeezes Job painfully (85). Zophar puts his foot on Job and twists it, a final effort to force him to sing compliantly with the music now providing the background for torture: "The Fear of the Lord Is Wisdom" (87; cf. Job 28:28). At every stage in this inquisition, Gelber's Job resolutely refuses to submit to his victimizers. When the play ends, "the actors scatter, exit into the audience and mingle," to which Gelber adds the following comment: "They may or may not open the discussion to the audience, for sometimes audience discussion is enlightening, sometimes not" (97). This implicit invitation to the audience to say what it has learned from the dramatic reenactment of the biblical debate between Job and his friends comes with a litany of thirteen "study-guide" questions. The last question presses the still lingering theodicean issue: "Is God unethical in having created a universe where unethical behavior is tolerated?" (131).

Hanoch Levin (1943–99) was born in Tel Aviv to Polish parents who immigrated to Palestine. After studies in philosophy and Hebrew literature at Tel Aviv University, he devoted himself to satirical works highly critical of authority, human and divine, which drew public acclaim but political rebuke. His play *The Sorrows of Job* is case in point. Levin's Job is a modern-day man of wealth, with iron mines in Lebanon, shipping interests in Alexandria, and a bank account in Rome. "Messengers of poverty" report that Job has lost all his business ventures due to unforeseen disasters. Moreover Rome's emperor has been killed in a political coup, and the new emperor has decreed the confiscation of all Job's possessions and all his remaining assets. When the new emperor's bailiffs come to execute the decree, they strip Job's house, remove his clothes, and extract his gold teeth with pliers. "Messengers of death" report that all his children have died in tragic accidents. Such is the setting for the arrival of the friends.

One by one the friends play their expected roles. Eliphaz begins: "God chose you to suffer / And us—to bring you consolation."[25] Bildad rebukes Job for pretending that he suffers innocently; such is the "the demagoguery of the contented man" (22). Zophar urges Job to repeat after him the words of a prayer of a supplication: "Our father who art in heaven. . . . Into your hands I commit my sprit . . . you are good and forgiving and merciful" (27). As Job haltingly repeats the last words of Zophar's prayer—"God of all the world" (28)—the emperor's soldiers arrive. They have come to demand that all Jews swear an oath of allegiance to the emperor: "You shall have no other gods / Except me, the Emperor." The penalty for refusing to denounce the god of the Jews is "a spit stuck up their rear" (28). From this point on, the soldiers subject both the friends and Job to rigorous interrogation. The friends comply with the order. When the soldiers turn their attention to Job, Zophar urges him to save his life by following their example: "Bark, bark at the empty skies, / Bark as before 'There is no god!' . . . remember the spit!" (33). Job refuses. "The soldiers spread Job's legs and bring the spit" (34). Levin scripts the next scene with lurid clarity. Once Job is impaled, the stage falls silent. As in the biblical story, all the friends can do is look at him. Bildad is the first to break the silence. Job, half-dead, seems to be looking down on him, both literally, from the height of the spit, and figuratively, with a sense of moral superiority. "Why do you look at me . . . with such pride . . . [such] arrogance?" Bildad asks. "Does somebody owe you something?" Bildad answers his own question.

> Take those pleas out of your eye!
> I told you: You are you and I am—I!

You hear? You are you and I am—I!
You are you and I am—I!
Shut your eyes! Or lift them to the sky,
Villain! . . .
Go weep in the bosom of your god. (36)

Bildad and the friends make their exit. As they leave Job calls out to them, "My friends, don't leave me / Alone with god!" (36).

The ending of the play shifts the focus from a private to a public affair. The officer in charge of the execution negotiates the sale of Job's half-dead body to the circus. Based on the officer's calculations, Job should live another six or seven hours before the spit pierces his heart, long enough to sell tickets and make a profit from those who will pay to see "an hour of inner agony" (37), especially if it is accompanied by a little singing, a stripper, and some clowns. Two clowns, one solemn, the other cynical, climb a ladder on either side of Job and paint his face like a clown. Both clowns ask the same question, Job's own, according to the biblical story: "What is man?" (Job 7:17). The solemn one muses, "Where is the thread that binds it all, / Where is the thread and what is meaning?" The cynical one responds, "Don't search for a meaning, / Don't ask for a moral. Why try? / Just watch: a man falls, soon he'll die" (41). Job whispers his last words, a reformulation of the clown's question, now with his own death-full answer:

What is a man on a spit?
A man who is finished, done for it.
Can I describe such despair?
Darkness like that can't be found anywhere. (43)

Levin resists giving Job the last words of the play. The first to respond to Job's dying words is the Ringmaster, whose interest in this circus act is purely economic. "Anywhere!" he says angrily. / You couldn't have waited another hour?! / Anywhere! Phooey!" Levin adds directorial comments: the Ringmaster "spits on Job's corpse and exits. The circus and the audience disperse and exit" (43). The final voice in the play belongs to the "Dead," a postmortem reflection from those who, now with Job, can only speak from the grave (44).

The intent of dramatists such as Gelber and Levin is necessarily an open question. Is their scripting of the Joban story an invitation to join God in rebuking the theodicy of Job's friends (Job 42:7–9)? This certainly seems to be the case. Perhaps all those who would be Job's friends should reflect on what it would mean if Levin had reversed the words of Job's plea for help: "God, don't leave me alone with my friends!" Even so a lingering question remains. What can, what should a friend of Job do if the objective is to "console and comfort" (Job 2:11; cf.

42:11) one who suffers, by God's admission, "for no reason" (Job 2:7)? Theodicy makers draw a line in the sand; one must side either with primary truths about God, whose decisions are always just and righteous, or with the Jobs of the world, whose countertestimony cannot be disqualified and will not be silenced. To cite Voltaire once more, when God inserts the words "for no reason" into the requisites of faith beleaguered by innocent suffering, then the "human race demands a word from God." The book of Job provides a word from God, to which we will turn in the next chapter. In the meantime we may note that Job's three friends, Eliphaz, Bildad, and Zophar have exited the scene. To paraphrase W. H. Auden, each has left to his own mistakes.[26]

"Listen to me and let me also declare my opinion" (Job 32:10)

The dialogues with the three friends climax with a closing speech from Job in which he issues a formal challenge to God: "Let the Almighty answer me!" (31:35). When "the words of Job are ended" (31:40), the stage is set for God's response to the challenge. Instead Elihu, a fourth friend elsewhere unmentioned, preempts God's appearance with his own discourse on the meaning of suffering (Job 32–37). Both Elihu's narrator (32:1–5) and Elihu as a character in his own right (32:6–22 + 33–37) insist that what this story needs is someone who can definitively answer (32:1, 3, 5, 6, 12, 17, 20) Job's questions. Toward this end Elihu speaks for 159 uninterrupted verses; apart from Job he has more lines than any character in the book, including God. Although length alone does not guarantee the importance of Elihu's words—the numbers may add up to little more than bluster and banality—it does invite, at the very least, a "deliberately generous curiosity."[27]

The history of interpretation of the Elihu speeches is complex. A number of historical-critical arguments, both stylistic and substantive, support the near scholarly consensus that Elihu's speeches are a late addition to the book, most likely composed by a different author.[28] The judgment that the speeches are secondary has long been accompanied by a negative assessment of their importance. At best, some would argue, Elihu provides comic relief, an easing of the tensions that may be compared to the roles of the *alazōn* or buffoon in classical Greek comedy or the fool in Shakespearian tragedies.[29] At worst Elihu is an unexpected, unneeded, and unwanted intruder who adds nothing to the story but boring pomposity. Like "someone who has defaced a cultural monument with his graffiti,"[30] he can be dismissed to the sidelines. Nothing would be lost by ignoring everything he says. Recent commentators, somewhat more charitably, have argued that Elihu's speeches, even if secondary, contribute significantly to the final form of the book's intentional literary structure.[31]

The negative assessment of Elihu likely begins with the *Testament of Job* (first century B.C.E.– first century C.E.), which depicts him as an "evil one" who is "inspired by Satan" (41:6; 43:5, 17). According to this account, Elihu listened to the debate between Job and his friends for twenty-seven days, after which he sought to discredit them all with "insulting words" and "arrogant speech" (41:2, 6; 42:1). The biblical text contains no response to Elihu's words either from Job, the friends, or God; the *Testament,* however, reports that God not only rebuked Elihu but also refused to forgive him (42:2, 43:1). When the three friends gather at the altar to receive the forgiveness mediated to them through Job's sacrificial offerings, Eliphas directs toward Elihu an "excommunicative curse" (43:5–6, 7, 10, 11, 13).[32]

A late Byzantine illuminated manuscript shows another facet of the traditionally negative attitude toward Elihu. The artist positions Job on the left side of the miniature; he is naked and pockmarked; he sits slumped over on a mound, eyes cast downward. Seated opposite Job on the right is a youthful, clean-shaven Elihu dressed in a full–length, royal blue robe. Both figures are drawn rather conventionally. A telltale but prominent addition to the scene likely contributes more than simply an aesthetic touch. On the ground between Job and Elihu is an inflated skin bag, toward which Elihu gestures with his right hand. The illustration accompanies the Greek text of Job 32:19: "my belly is as a skin of sweet wine bound up and ready to burst."[33]

Medieval commentators, both Jewish and Christian, are more positive in their assessment of Elihu, generally regarding him as a pivotal figure who steers the Joban debate about innocent suffering in the right direction. Saadiah Gaon (882–942), Maimonides (1138–1204), and Gersonides (1288–1344) give extended attention to Job 33, each one affirming Elihu's explanation of suffering as a divine test the righteous must pass if they are to enjoy God's reward.[34] Maimonides, for example, argues that Elihu provides the correct view on providence by introducing the notion that God provides "the intercession of an angel" who can rescue and restore an afflicted person who is truly righteous, if he will but seize the opportunity.[35]

Maimonides leaves unclear the identity of the angel/intercessor—is it a human or a divine figure?—but his reading of Job 33, and of Elihu's entire speech generally, confirms that he regards Elihu as the only friend who correctly understands Job's situation. In different but consonant ways, both Saadiah and Gersonides make the same argument: Job's suffering is providential, and only Elihu, who understands "the how of prophecy"—"God speaketh once, yea twice, yet [man] perceiveth not"—discerns the course Job must follow.[36]

Medieval Christian "exegetes," both clerical scholars and "ordinary" artists and iconographers, are also generally positive in their assessment of Elihu's contribution. The twelfth-century sculptor of the capitals of Notre-Dame de la Daurade in Toulouse, France, for example, crafts a number of scenes depicting Job and his friends. In one capital the left side shows Job and his three friends engaged in a debate that leaves Job, supporting his head with his right hand, in contemplation.

The right side of the capital shows an angel. With the left hand, the angel extends to Job a jar (of salve or ointment?); the angel places its right hand on Job's knee, as if to anoint and heal his affliction. Job's right hand is open and raised toward the angel, an indication that what the angel offers has moved him from indecisive contemplation to glad acceptance of Elihu's promise of a heavenly intercessor who will redeem and restore him (Job 33:23–28).[37]

The Italian artist Mattia Preti, known as Il Calabrese (1613–99), was also drawn to Elihu's account of the interceding angel. In a large canvas, he places Job and his wife on the right side, the three friends and Elihu on the left. Between them a reclining satan figure looks in Job's direction, as if considering how this debate will end. The three friends raise their hands and look at each other, an indication that they do not agree among themselves about how to respond to Job. Behind them stands Elihu. His body and his hands are not visible, but he alone turns his face upward toward the winged *putto,* unseen by the others, who holds on to one of the crumbling palatial columns that provide the backdrop for this scene.[38] Il Calabrese exegetes the moment before Elihu enters the dialogue, the tensive gap between what he has heard the friends say and his decision to speak, now informed by what he sees and what they have missed.

The book of Job generally, and the Elihu speeches in particular, were of particular interest to John Calvin (1509–64). Given the importance of providence in Calvin's thought,[39] his attention to Job is not surprising; no other biblical book provided so many of the requisite arguments for understanding suffering within the context of God's providential justice. A primary resource for Calvin's exegesis of Job are his 159 *Sermons from Job,* in which he preaches Job's truths about divine sovereignty, nowhere so clearly and persuasively articulated, Calvin believed, than in the speeches of Elihu.[40] As Susan E. Schreiner notes, Elihu is the "mouthpiece" for Calvin's theology.[41]

Calvin sees Elihu's zeal for defending truths about God as an example for the way the reformed church must defend true doctrine against "the poor Papists . . . [who] know not what they do" (220). Commenting on Job 32:1–4, Calvin notes that Elihu's zeal is manifest as "laudable indignation." Ordinary anger is typically self-serving. Elihu's wrath, by contrast, is inspired by the Holy Spirit; it is triggered by his feeling that others have offended God (220, 224–25). What Elihu models, therefore, is the zeal the reformed church should rightly express against the villainies of the Papists, "the dogs and swine who . . . infect everything, who come to poke their snouts into the Word of God, and only try to upset everything" (227). When Christians see how heretics sow their poison, they, like Elihu, are right to respond with righteous indignation.

As a model for preachers, Elihu is critically important for Calvin because his understanding of the doctrine of providence is correct. In his sermon on Job

34:21–26, Calvin endorses Elihu's assertion that God has neither "handled us un-justly" nor "afflicted us unreasonably" (265). Instead God sends prophets such as Elihu "to enlighten us in order that we may properly think of our sins" (263). God "breaks the mighty without asking questions" (Job 34:24), which means that he does not always disclose the reasons why. As Calvin reads Elihu, God punishes without asking questions that might be required by human standards of justice, because "He does not need to trouble Himself with a long trial against us; we shall have no leisure to breathe or to languish in distress until we are entirely ruined by His hand; but we shall be confounded quickly, as if heaven fell upon our heads" (268). What should we learn from Elihu's words in 34:21–26? Calvin makes his point as follows.

> We should always fear God's justice and not come to imagine that He uses any tyranny or cruelty. Therefore let us keep from thinking of such a power in God as He might display without reason. It is true that the reason which He holds is un-known to us, and we must be contented with His only and simple will as with the only rule of uprightness; and whatever comes to pass, let us not wickedly imagine that God goes crookedly or obliquely or that He judges otherwise than with rea-son: on the contrary let us be fully persuaded that, although His judgments seem strange to us, yet they are ordered according to the best rule that can be: namely, according to His will which surpasses all justice. This is what Elihu declares in this passage. The same ought to serve chiefly for us. Then, if any man is afflicted in his own person, he ought to consider that God is just, in order that he may re-pent of his faults; for we shall never have true repentance, unless we know that God afflicts us uprightly; neither can we glorify God, and confess that He is just, unless we have first condemned ourselves. (269)

A major challenge to divine providence is the frequent inexplicability of hu-man suffering. Here too Calvin affirms the correctness of Elihu's response to Job and his friends. Commenting on Job 36:6–14 ("God gives judgment to the af-flicted"), Calvin notes that when there are contrary indications, we should "wait in patience, and we shall know that God will make such afflictions to do us good and that they tend to a good end" (276).[42] The purpose of affliction is to "make us feel our sins" (276). Because people "cannot feel their sins if they are not driven by force to know themselves" (277), God uses affliction to open their eyes and touch their hearts. Elihu rightly discerns the "profit" of (inexplicable) affliction (279–84).

There is no discernible overarching structure to Calvin's sermons on Elihu's contributions to the book of Job, apart from the fact that each one begins with reference to a specific text in Job 32–37. Like other medieval Christian commen-tators, he follows Aquinas in focusing on the simple or natural meaning of the text, eschewing allegorical interpretations. Calvin's admiration for Elihu as a spokesman for the doctrine of divine providence is nonetheless unmistakable. Each sermon ends with the same exhortation: "Now we shall bow in humble reverence before the face of our God."

Job's "Fifth Friend:" The "Belated Reader"

A final comment concerning how we read Elihu (and the three friends) reading Job.[43] Drawing upon the modern literary critic Harold Bloom's notion of the "belatedness of all reading," Carol Newsom suggests that as a reader of Job, both Elihu, the fictional character, and the author of the Elihu speeches are compelled by their changed historical and cultural contexts not only to comment on the story they have received but also "to write [themselves] into the text."[44] They are belated readers who come to a conversation that began without them. The conversation between Job and his friends has stalled in indecision. The friends are "dismayed"; they can speak no more because all words have left them (Job 32:15). Elihu is angry (32:5) because they have yielded prematurely to silence. He is himself "full of words" (32:18), and the spirit within compels him to keep the conversation going. In so doing Elihu "represents the position of all readers, most significantly through his belatedness": "The reader always comes to a conversation that has begun without him and yet at which he finds himself present, a conversation that engages him and yet has no place for him. Hence the need to interrupt, if not by such direct means, then by interpretive commentary or criticism."[45]

At issue for Elihu, even though he may not be fully aware of it, is the "exhaustion and renewal of human discourse." "How is it that human culture never finishes what it has to say about perennial issues of existence? There are, to be sure, moments of pause, when it seems that everything that can be said has been said, but those moments do not last. The inexhaustible source of human discourse lies in the fundamentally perspectival nature of claims to truth."[46] To explicate, Newsom suggests that "the sheer historicity of human existence would suffice to renew speech," which is manifest in Elihu's "usurpation" of the conventional wisdom of his elders. "For Elihu's generation, the moral world has tilted, perhaps ever so slightly, on its axis. That tilt, however, is sufficient for moral and religious issues to be configured differently and to require the words that Elihu so urgently wishes to speak. The modern interpretive difficulty is that the axis of our own moral world has tilted considerably more."[47]

Because the modern world has shifted considerably more than Elihu's world, whatever date we may assign to his speeches, the debate about Joban suffering requires constant engagement. It cannot end in silence, unless we ignore the very process of dialogue—between Job and his friends, between Job and God—that the book of Job models. To return to the words of Archibald MacLeish, "there's always Someone playing Job," and because this is so, the ongoing question is "who will be Job's friend . . . and how?"

David Clines makes a similar argument, although his focus is somewhat different than Newsom's. He suggests that the book of Job invites a "fifth friend" to critique the ethical integrity of all the arguments presented against Job. Although this fifth friend may be "unseasonably late," she or he should take the measure of the book "so that it should not lie forever in the hands of timid and sugary theologians."[48] For all who would be "fifth readers" of this book, Clines poses this question: "If Job is an innocent man, what justice is there in God making him suffer?"[49] He contends that there is "something ethically questionable" about readers who remain undisturbed by the responses of all Job's biblical friends.[50] He therefore writes himself into the book by offering his own critique of its ethical problems.

Once the story of Job attains written form, in whatever time and to whatever degree of finality, then all of us become "belated readers." Like Elihu we come to a conversation that began without us but nonetheless summons our contribution. Given that the biblical story in its seminal form begins with a question from God, "Have you considered my servant Job?" (1:8), Elihu's response may be understood as the model for all who have dared to follow his lead: "Listen to me; let me also declare my opinion" (32:10).[51]

7

"THEN THE LORD ANSWERED JOB OUT OF THE WHIRLWIND . . ." (JOB 38:1, 3)

It is as if God appears in a tie-dyed T-shirt emblazoned with the words "Because I'm God, That's Why."

William Safire, *The First Dissident*

So the poet, through the whirlwind's answer, stills Job. But can the poet still the Job who lives in us? God's majesty is eternal, manifest in cell and star. Yet Job's questions toil on, manifest in death camp and hatred, in tyranny and anthrax, in bomb and bloodshed. Why do the wicked thrive? Why do the innocent suffer? In brutal times, the whirlwind's answer tempts, if not atheism, then the sorrowing conviction of God's indifference.

Cynthia Ozick, "The Impious Impatience of Job"

I now know that thy right worship is defiance.

Herman Melville, *Moby-Dick*

According to the final form of the book, the last time God speaks is in the prologue: "Very well, he is in your power" (Job 2:6a). With these words he hands Job over to the satan to do with him as he will. Only a porous caveat—"spare his life" (Job 2:6b)—stands between Job and his vulnerability to undeserved pain and suffering. Between Job 2:6 and 38:1, God is silent. The three friends, Eliphaz, Bildad, and Zophar, offer their answers; Job refuses them. Elihu attempts to provide the answers the friends could not; Job does not respond, his silence a loud declaration that Elihu's answers are no more adequate than anything he has already heard. The answers Job yearns for come from a God he cannot find (Job 23:3), a God whose beckoning wisdom remains beyond his reach (Job 28:12, 20). To this invincibly silent God, Job makes a final appeal: "Answer me" (Job 31:35). Job's appeal is both ancient and abiding.

If "silence is the only Voice of our God," Herman Melville writes in *Pierre,* then "how can a man get a Voice out of Silence?"[1] The words are those of Melville's protagonist, Pierre Glendinning, a noble young man born into a family of wealth and Christian idealism in Albany, New York. A number of "ambiguities" (hence the book's subtitle) open Pierre's eyes to the vacuousness of Christian teaching about good and evil, the cumulative effect of which turns his pursuit of wisdom into a dispiriting pipe dream: he learns that his late father, whom he revered as a model of human virtue, had an affair that produced an illegitimate daughter, Isabel, now a social outcast; when Pierre decides to be Isabel's protector, he learns that his mother, in collusion with the local minister Reverend Falsgrave, has spearheaded the community's decision to ostracize Isabel; when Pierre flees with Isabel to New York City, he offers Christian charity to another young woman in distress, Delly Ulver, which prompts his mother to disinherit him, a penalty for having disgraced the family name. Melville fingers these ambiguities like the beads of a "wounded rosary,"[2] hoping against hope that the next one will bring clarity. The more deeply Pierre ponders his situation, the more his doubts increase and his determination wanes. His disillusionment reduces him to but one certainty: God's silence is a malicious consecration of an immoral universe where the loudest proclamations of truth come from the "mere moonshine of the Christian Religion."[3] There is no key, Pierre concludes, to unlock the "Talismanic Secret" of God's "profound Silence."[4] Though "the earthly wisdom of man be heavenly folly to God," Pierre now concedes that the "heavenly wisdom of God [is] an earthly folly to man." Who among us has not considered "a sort of infidel idea, that whatever other worlds God may be Lord of, he is not the Lord of this; for else this world would seem to give the lie to Him; so utterly repugnant seem its ways to the instinctively known ways of Heaven."[5] Melville's novel concludes with the triple suicide of Pierre, Isabel, and Lucy (Pierre's fiancée). In the penultimate scene, Pierre stretches out his arms toward his two compatriots, a tableau of Christ on the cross, "life's last chapter well stitched into the middle! . . . Its last lettering . . . is ambiguous still."[6]

This segue to Melville's *Pierre,* representative of his lifelong quarrel with God's silence,[7] sets the stage for what follows. Job's quest for an answer from God begins with a death wish (Job 3), but unlike Pierre he does not execute it. Job *does* get a voice out of the silent God, and it is this divine response out of the whirlwind that sets the compass for understanding the "last letterings" of this book. We may parse the structure and substance of God's response, but before doing so it is instructive to note that in ancient literature the response of the gods to a sufferer's demand is without parallel. Ancient Near Eastern antecedent texts record multiple appeals from the righteous sufferer to the deity, as we have noted above; none of these texts, however, contains a direct reply by the deity.[8] When the author of Job dares to compose a response from God to Job, he breaks rank with all precedent literature. The voice from the whirlwind is, as Newsom rightly says, "something of a tour de force."[9]

The "Dialogue" with God (Job 38:1–40:6)

The words "Then the Lord spoke out of the whirlwind" (38:1) introduce the answer that Job and his readers have long awaited. The outline of the dialogue is clear.[10] God has two speeches (38:1–39:30, 40:1–34 [MT 41:26]); Job offers two responses (40:3–5, 42:1–6). Both divine speeches begin with questions that challenge Job to "gird up his loins" and answer God like the "hero" (*geber* [38:3, 40:7]) he claims to be. The questions in the first speech cluster around God's cosmic "design" (*'ēṣâ* [38:2]), with specific attention to the stability of the world's foundations (38:4–18), the intricate rhythms of meteorological phenomena (38:19–38), and the instinctive habits of five pairs of animals (38:39–39:30). Commentators often note that God's review of creation accents his care and nurture of what humans normally regard as either chaotic or threatening. For example he births the unruly waters of the sea and wraps them in swaddling bands of darkness and cloud (38:8–11); he hunts prey for the lion, a feared human predator (38:39–41), and provides human corpses for the vulture to feed upon (39:27–30). In the second speech, the questions focus on God's governance of the world, the only specific mention of God's justice (*mišpāṭ* [40:8]) in the entire speech,[11] now with a singular focus on a sixth and final pair of animals, Behemoth (40:9–15) and Leviathan (41:1–34 [MT 40:25–41:26]). Following the first speech, God specifically invites Job to respond (40:1–2). He does so by saying "I am small," then placing his hand over his mouth to indicate that he will speak no further (40:3–5). God's second speech ends without repeating the request for a response. Job answers nonetheless, this time with a statement of what he now knows and sees about God and about himself (42:1–6). This "dialogue" is clearly uneven: God speaks for 123 verses, Job for only 9.

The clear structure of this dialogue belies its intractable complexity. What exactly does God's answer teach Job? What do Job's responses disclose about what he has learned? Some commentators, noting that God avoids Job's "Why?" questions, conclude that his answers are no less evasive than those of all Job's friends. What do words about rain, snow, ice, clouds, ostriches, and horses have to do with Job's sufferings? "One is tempted to paraphrase God as saying, 'I may not be much at psychology and human relations, but I am great at meteorology and zoology.'"[12] God's "answer" seems not only benignly evasive but also morally repugnant. At best his words convey an inexplicable indifference to innocent suffering, as Cynthia Ozick says in the epigraph cited at the beginning of this chapter.[13] At worst God seems more fiendish than godlike, a cruel and capricious tyrant who requires Job's forgiveness, not his praise.[14]

Others discern something more substantive in what God says, but there is little agreement on what this is.[15] On one end of the spectrum, some argue that simply by answering Job, whatever the answer may be, God proves that he never forgets or abandons those who suffer.[16] On the other end, some understand God to be teaching Job that he is not confined to human standards of justice.[17] Still others argue that God's nonanswer is *the* answer both Job and his readers need to hear, especially when the question has to do with the "irreducible ambiguities" of innocent suffering.[18] The interpretive challenge is to keep one's expectations open about what God says and how Job responds. As Luis Alonso-Schökel has noted, every assessment of the divine speeches depends on whether the interpreter's expectations are open or closed.

> Closed expectation digs out a channel in advance, and refuses to accept any dénouement which follows a different channel. Open expectation looks in a particular direction, but is prepared to do a detour in order to follow the way out suggested by the text. In the first type of expectation, because the author's final response (through the mouth of one of his characters) does not fit in with my preconceptions, I either reject it, or criticise it, or select what I want from it. In the second type of expectation, although the author chooses a route I was not expecting and so at first disorients me, I nevertheless try to follow him and discover where his trail is leading.[19]

Three observations concerning the form and substance of the divine speeches merit consideration. First, both the rhetoric and the context suggest that God appears to Job in a theophany. Theophanies are special moments of divine disclosure, when the holy God approaches the world in extraordinary ways. They are often located in divine judgment settings, which evoke dread and fear in those who dare to contend with the almighty (e.g., Jgs 5:4–5, Na 1:3–6, Hb 3:5–12).[20] A majority of commentators read God's appearance to Job as having a similar purpose: words spoken with whirlwind force exemplify a terrifying display of divine power that is designed to blow Job away rhetorically, if not also literally. Theophanies almost always trigger a tensive combination of responses, however. Precisely because they are such awesome encounters with the holy, they are both frightening and attractive at the same time. On the one hand, there is danger in coming too close; on the other the attraction of such extraordinary proximity to the sacred is so compelling that the danger is not to be avoided (a classic example is Moses in Exodus 3). God's approach to Job can be read in this light, in which case the objective is to draw him nearer, not to drive him farther away.

Second, God's questions to Job ("Where were you?" "Can you?" "Have you?" "Do you know?") are typically connected with the language of disputation, more specifically with the prophetic lawsuit, in which God, depicted as both prosecuting attorney and judge, cross-examines defendants in a legal case. The objective is to probe for weaknesses in a person's arguments by asking questions they cannot answer adequately or truthfully without incriminating themselves. If one assumes this is the setting for God's questions, then the purpose is not only to dispute Job's charges but also to demonstrate his mendacity in having raised them at all. On close inspection, however, the rhetorical questions in trial speeches function not only to censure persons for their failures. They also serve to encourage them to believe in possibilities that do not seem to exist (a classic example is Is 40:12–31). When God addresses similar questions to Job, therefore, we should leave open the possibility that the objective is to embolden a true servant whose faith is faint but worthy.

Third, a significant part of the discourse focuses on the creatures that inhabit God's world, first the five pairs of animals described in 38:39–39:30, then a sixth pair, Behemoth and Leviathan (40:9–15, 41:1–34 [MT 40:25–41:26]). There is no explicit mention of Job in particular or of human beings in general, an omission that has often been interpreted as a strategic subversion of the assumption that human beings occupy a place of importance in the cosmic scheme. But this survey of creatures also contains clues that invite a more nuanced interpretation. At the center of God's world are two creatures—Behemoth and Leviathan—conventionally regarded as so wild, so hostile, that they must be vigorously confronted and defeated. When God looks at them, however, he sees no cause for opposition.[21] Instead he celebrates their power, pride, and fierce resistance to domestication, for these are God-given virtues of creatures that instinctively confront all challenges without fear of defeat. Moreover when God turns to Behemoth, he invites Job to see a creature "which I made just as I made *you*" (40:15). As the only reference, albeit indirect, to the creation of human beings in the divine speeches, the invitation suggests that when Job looks at Behemoth he should see himself, as God intends him to be.

Expectations should also remain open with respect to the meaning of Job's responses to God. Following God's first address, Job's initial response is "I am small" (*qallōtî* [40:4a]). He does not say "I have sinned," which is what the friends have demanded (8:5–7, 11:30, 22:21–27). He does not say "I am terrified," as he thought he would be if he should ever have to face God (9:34, 13:21). He does not praise God for the mysterious justice encoded in creation, as Elihu has urged him to do (33:14–30, 35:5–13, 37:1–3). Instead he concedes that he is of little account in the eyes of God. He then places his hand over his mouth (40:4b), a gesture that clearly symbolizes silence, but whether a silence that expresses shame, futility, or disapproval is uncertain.[22]

Still more enigmatic is Job's second response in 42:6, which promises at long last to disclose what he has now heard, seen, and understood about God, the world, and himself. It is precisely at this point, however, that the text confronts interpreters with its biggest challenge, perhaps strategically so. NRSV's translation of the verse is but one of many that interpret Job's final words as a confession of sin: "therefore I despise myself and repent in dust and ashes." Although this reading is deeply ingrained in the interpretive history (see below), grammatical ambiguities deny it the certainty it claims. The multiple translation possibilities for 42:6 mean that Job is often "reduced to silence, if not by God, then by interpreters of the text."[23]

Three issues may be singled out. First the verb NRSV translates as "despise myself" (*mā'as*) is ordinarily active, not reflexive, and is almost always followed by a direct object.[24] In 42:6 there is no clearly identified object, although we may reasonably assume that one is implied. Scholars propose a range of possibilities for filling in the blank.[25] Job could be saying "I despise (reject/recant)" his previous words,[26] his lawsuit against God,[27] dust and ashes,[28] or God.[29] Another option, followed by LXX, the Qumran Job Targum, and other commentators, is to read the verb as *māsas* (to melt, flow), in which case the meaning may be that Job "melts," "wastes away," or "yields" before God's words.[30]

Second, NRSV's translation, "repent in," reflects the conventional view that Job engages in the traditional ritual of repentance by sitting *in* dust and ashes.[31] The collocation *niḥamtî 'al,* however, makes this conventional reading highly unlikely for two reasons. First the verb *nāḥam* (*nip'al*), especially when used without a following preposition, is almost always used with reference to God, who changes his mind concerning some previously announced divine judgment. In such cases the inference is not that God has sinned and admits to some guilt, but instead that he "retracts a declared action."[32] A second meaning of *nāḥam,* to be comforted or consoled, is also frequent in the Hebrew Bible, but in such cases the comfort or consolation that occurs is typically self-generated, that is, it conveys a person's decision to move from a period of grieving to more "normal" behavior. The one who has been in mourning is ready to move on with life. Indeed this seems to be the meaning of the verb when it is used elsewhere in Job.[33] Second, the preposition in the collocation, *'al,* normally means "on, upon, concerning," not "in," as in NRSV. At the core of the grammar, therefore, is this question: what does Job change his mind about, having heard God's words? Alternatively, given the flexibility of the verb *nāḥam,* how do "dust and ashes" comfort or console Job?

Third, the phrase "dust and ashes" (*'āpār wā'ēper*) may provide the most telling clue to this exceedingly enigmatic verse. The two words, *dust* and *ashes,* are relatively common in the Hebrew Bible as isolated terms, but as a set phrase they occur together only three times: Genesis 18:27, Job 30:19, and Job 42:6. In each case the phrase conveys something about the human condition in relation to God. In Job 30:19 Job laments that God has thrown him into the mire (*hōmer* [cf. Job 4:19, 10:9, 33:6]) of human mortality, where human existence is "dust and ashes." In the context of his suffering, Job understands this to mean that he exemplifies the way human beings may be banished from society (30:1–8), scorned and terrorized by their peers (30:9–15) and by God (30:16–23). He therefore concludes, at this point in the story, that God has consigned him as a mere mortal of "dust and ashes" to live in a world where those who cry out to the heavens for help should expect no answer. In Genesis 18:27 the phrase applies to Abraham. As he argues with God about the execution of divine justice in Sodom—"Will you indeed sweep away the righteous with the wicked?" (Gn 18:23)—Abraham concedes that as a mere creature of "dust and ashes" he has entered dangerous territory. His recognition of his standing before God is similar to Job's in Job 30:19, with one important exception. Abraham persists with his questioning, which prompts God to reconsider how justice in Sodom should be achieved. The image of God standing before Abraham,[34] inviting, then responding to his demand that the "judge of all the earth do what is just," opens the possibility that Job has now arrived at a new understanding of what it means to be "dust and ashes." When and if human beings live fully into their heritage as descendants of Abraham, which necessarily places them at the dangerous intersection between divine decision and human intervention, then they may know that the creator of the world stands waiting and ready to respond to their input.

I note these grammatical issues not to suggest that they can be resolved but rather to underscore the ambiguity of the text. The assessment of the possible translations of Job 42:6 depends in no small measure on the expectations readers bring to the book. If one construes the objective of the divine speeches to be God's vindication, then interpretive options that stipulate Job's repentance may carry more weight. If one is sympathetic to Job's complaints, then interpretive options that do not sacrifice his integrity on the altar of repentance may command more attention. Alternatively if ambiguity is intentionally encoded in this remarkable exchange between God and Job, then the interpretive imperative may be to yield to its refusal to provide simple answers.[35]

"Remember the battle, and speak no more" (*Moralia,* 6.33.36)

Modern biblical scholars have generally tried to unravel the exegetical complexities of the whirlwind speeches by focusing on their contribution to questions about divine justice—in Leibnizian terms the theodicy question. Pre-Enlightenment commentators, however, were less concerned to defend God's justice than to exalt and affirm his power, exemplified nowhere so forcefully as in his answer to Job.

The most influential of the Latin fathers to pursue this line of interpretation was Gregory the Great, whose *Moralia in Job* was the touchstone for the interpretation of Job in the Middle Ages.

The exegetical complexities of the divine speeches were not Gregory's major concern. His allegorical reading directed him instead to the moral lessons the church should learn from what God taught Job about resisting the assaults of the satan. The foundation for Gregory's extended commentary emerges at the very outset, in his preface to and exegesis of Job 38:1–11.

The God who answers Job out of the whirlwind, Gregory says, shows both "affectionate sweetness" and "dreadful power," the latter more clearly to tame Job's pride (6.28.1).[36] When God challenges Job to gird up his loins, the instruction is to retrain the passions of the flesh, "for by the loins is designated lust, but by lights the brightness of good works" (6.28.12). When Job checks his prideful passions, then he is prepared to hear the truth in God's questions. When God asks, "Where wast thou when I was laying the foundations of the earth?" (38:4), Job hears a history of the church, the prophets, apostles, and preachers who prepared the way for the one foundation that no man can lay, save Jesus Christ alone: "the foundation of the foundations" (6.28.14). The "corner Stone" of the foundation is Christ, who mediates "Divine grace" to the church. Gregory summarizes the moral lesson of Job 38–39 thusly: "But these things which have been said, as descriptive of Holy Church, it seems good to repeat briefly in a moral lesson. For it is right for us to be brought back to our own hearts by those things which we know were said to blessed Job; because the mind then understands more truly the words of God, when it searches for itself therein" (6.28.19). When Job places his hand on his mouth (Job 40:4) after God's first speech, Gregory reads his response as instructive for the church: "Let blessed Job therefore, as typifying the Holy Church, and in what he says alleging his own circumstances, but designating ours, say for us; *I will lay mine hand upon my mouth:* that is, that of my words in me which I consider to have displeased the strict Judge, I conceal before His eyes under the veil of upright conduct" (6.27.2).

Gregory reads God's second speech, which focuses on Behemoth and Leviathan (Job 40–41), as instructions to the church on how to withstand the temptation of Satan and the Antichrist. In a verse-by-verse exegesis, Gregory identifies Behemoth and Leviathan with the fallen angels who defy God and thus are banished to eternal punishment in hell. Behemoth is "the ancient enemy," the "author of wickedness," that God defeats with the "hook of His Incarnation" (Job 40:24).

> Who can be ignorant that in a "hook" a bait is shewn, a point is concealed? For the bait tempts, that the point may wound. Our Lord therefore, when coming for the redemption of mankind, made, as it were, a kind of hook of Himself for the death

of the devil; for He assumed a body, in order that this Behemoth might seek therein the death of the flesh, as if it were his bait. But while he is unjustly aiming at that death in His person, he lost us, whom he was, as it were, unjustly holding. He was caught, therefore, in the "hook" of His Incarnation, because while he sought in Him the bait of his Body, he was pierced with the sharp point of His Divinity. (6.33.14)

Leviathan, the creature that adds the promise of immortality to the temptations of humans, is a similarly fallen and defeated angel, "cast down in the sight of all . . . to the eternal fires of hell" (6.33.37). For example in exegeting Job 41:24, "His [Leviathan's] heart shall be hardened as stone," Gregory writes, "Leviathan will . . . be bound as the anvil of the hammerer, because he will be confined by the chains of hell, in order to be beaten with the continual blows of eternal punishment. . . . We are wrought into shape by his persecutions" (6.34.11).

The moral lesson for the church in God's speech about Behemoth and Leviathan, according to Gregory, is this:

We believe then the sufferings we endure to be weighty, because we see not how severe and irresistible are the assaults of the crafty enemy against us. For every weight would be as nothing to our mind; if it considered the assaults of the secret adversary which might oppress it. But what if Almighty God were to lighten the burdens we suffer, and yet withdraw from us His assistance, and leave us amid the temptations of this Leviathan? Where shall we betake ourselves, when so mighty an enemy is raging against us, if we are not defended by any protection of our Creator? Because, therefore, blessed Job was not conscious to himself of a fault, and yet was enduring several scourges, lest he should haply exceed in the sin of murmuring, let him be reminded what to fear, and let it be said to him, *Remember the battle, and speak no more.* As if it were plainly said to him, "If thou considerest the contest of the secret enemy against thee, thou dost not blame whatever thou sufferest from Me. If thou beholdest the sword of the adversary assailing thee, thou dost not at all dread the scourge of a Father. For thou seest with what scourge I smite thee, but thou omittest to look from how great an enemy I keep thee free by My scourging." (6.33.36)

Job's second response to God moves from silence to confession (42:6), which according to Gregory signifies that he now knows God has saved him not only from the power of the devil (6.35.1) but also from the temptation of pride (6.35.3). Accordingly Job reproaches himself and does penance in sackcloth and ashes. The roughness of the sackcloth symbolizes the wounds of pride. The ashes, the "dust of the dead," symbolize how far he has gone in his sin (6.35.7). Gregory comments as follows: "When holy men, therefore, hear the words of God, the more they advance in contemplation, the more they despise what they are, and know themselves to be either nothing, or next to nothing" (6.35.3). "For the less a person sees himself, the less is he displeased with himself; and the more he discerns the light of greater grace, the more blameworthy does he acknowledge himself to be. For when he is elevated within, by all that he is, he endeavours to agree with that standard which he beholds above him" (6.35.6).

Gregory reads Job's "arduous interior ascent toward God" through suffering as the model for the church's movement through and beyond the travails of this world. Behemoth and Leviathan, Satan and Antichrist, tempt toward tranquil trust in human wisdom, but words from the whirlwind announce grace and redemption. Susan Schreiner makes a cogent connection with God's revelation about Leviathan, "king over all the sons of pride": "Gregory's Job escaped becoming one of Leviathan's sons."[37]

"This is the generation of that great leviathan"

Gregory was not the first to identify Behemoth and Leviathan with the forces of evil. If anything his was a rather conventional view, deeply rooted in ancient Near Eastern mythologies about the primordial forces of chaos the gods subdued in order to create a stable world.[38] In Jewish tradition the rabbis speculated on the connection between Behemoth and Leviathan and "the great sea monsters" (Gn 1:21) God placed in the Garden of Eden on the fifth day of creation. Rabbi Judah comments as follows:

> All that the Holy One, blessed be He, created in his world he created male and female. Likewise, Leviathan the fleeing serpent and Leviathan the twisting serpent he created male and female; and had one mated with the other they would have destroyed the whole world. What [then] did the Holy One, blessed be He, do? He castrated the male and killed the female preserving it in salt for the righteous in the world to come; for it is written: And He will slay the sea monster that is in the sea [Is 27:1]. And also Behemoth on a thousand hills were created male and female, and had they mated with one another they would have destroyed the whole world. What did the Holy One, Blessed be He, do? He castrated the male and cooled the female and preserved it for the righteous for the world to come; for it is written: Behold now its strength is in its loins [Job 40:6]—this refers to the male; and its might is in the muscles of its belly [Job 40:16b]—this refers to the female. (*Baba Batra* 74b)[39]

A ninth-century Codex of Job provides a visual. The artist depicts Behemoth and Leviathan as a single, mixed creature. From the waist up, the creature is a woman. She rests on her right arm and reaches with her left toward the forbidden tree in the Garden of Eden. From the waist down, the creature is serpentine, with male features (beard and horns). The composite depicts Behemoth/Leviathan as the personification of evil.[40] Other medieval manuscript illuminations show the devil or Antichrist riding on or standing royally over Behemoth and Leviathan, sometimes with a full frontal view that depicts him as a winged figure encoiled by a serpent.[41]

Sixteenth- and seventeenth-century Protestant reformers (e.g., Luther and Calvin) resisted Gregory's allegorical interpretation, but they typically used Behemoth and Leviathan as synonyms for the devil, routinely interpreted as a metaphor for the Roman church. Luther's castigation of the Papacy and its supporters is but one example.

> They are bestial people, utterly without the Spirit. They dwell in the reeds, i.e., their own human ordinances, comparable to a reed, which looks like a staff but is empty and hollow within. Human ordinances have similar aspects of solidity. Yet they too have not substance. . . . The type of doctrine is reflected in the people. They will also become inconstant and vacillating and hollow, without faith, swayed back and forth as the teachers choose. Thus we see the pope influencing the world at will with his ordinances. Job also speaks of this beast in the reeds, calling him Behemoth. He adds that he is fond of lying in the court of reeds and in the marsh, i.e., in human doctrines that ignore the cross.[42]

To underscore how deeply embedded was this interpretation of Behemoth and Leviathan in sixteenth- and seventeenth-century culture, we may add the work of John Milton. In *Paradise Lost* Milton depicts "Satan talking to his nearest mate . . . that sea-beast Leviathan."[43]

Thomas Hobbes's (1588–1679) publication of *Leviathan* (1651) and *Behemoth* (1680) marks a radical break with this interpretive tradition. Whereas Gregory and others celebrated God's power to deliver Job from the temptations of Behemoth and Leviathan, Hobbes constructed a political philosophy that advocated total submission to a "common-wealth" he called a Leviathanic state.

Hobbesian scholars widely regard *Leviathan* as one of the most important works of political theory ever composed.[44] Hobbes's contemporaries, however, considered him the bête noire of his time (see below).[45] Hobbes himself seems to have anticipated the paradox that would define his life. In his autobiography he writes that his mother birthed him prematurely when she heard that the Spanish Armada had penetrated the English coastline: she "did bring forth Twins at once, both Me, and Fear."[46] The particular fear that triggered the publication of *Leviathan* was the political turmoil of the English Civil Wars. When Parliament revolted against Charles I, Hobbes, a royalist, fled to Paris, where he remained for eleven years. During this time he served as tutor to the Prince of Wales, who had been forced to flee England, likely in the hope that he would return and assume

the throne. If Prince Charles was to restore the monarchy, however, he would
need to establish a sovereign authority that secured the consent of the governed.
Leviathan was to provide the political philosophy that would enable him to do so.
The objective must be to subordinate all individual will to the common good, to
what Hobbes in his introduction called "that great Leviathan . . . a Common-
Wealth or State, in Latin Civitas which is but an Artificiall Man" (9). Hobbes
published *Leviathan* two years after Charles I was beheaded and nine years before
the restoration of the Stuart monarchy under Charles II. There can be little doubt
that he hoped Charles II would see himself in the picture on the title page.[47] This
visual thus provides a heuristic entry into Hobbes's major thesis.

The top half of the picture shows the crowned monarch as the "Artificiall
Man," the Leviathan, who reigns over the commonwealth. In his right hand, he
holds a sword, symbol of the power of the state; in his left hand, a bishop's crosier,
symbol of ecclesiastical authority. His eyes gaze outward across the vast expanse
of the body politic he governs, both the walled and now peaceful interior of the
state and the potentially chaotic, now subdued, outlying areas. On first sight the
sovereign's upper body appears to be covered by plate armor. On close inspection
the interlocking plates are actually human bodies, individual members of the
polis who are "hammered" together in subservience to the crown. Some turn their
faces inward, some outward, but none look upward; they neither see nor presumably need to see the sovereign who watches over them.

The bottom half of the picture divides into three parts. To the monarch's
right, just below the arm holding the sword, a series of five images illustrate various aspects of the state's power: from top to bottom, a secured city set on a hill,
a crown, a cannon, weapons, trophies and flags, and a battle scene. To the monarch's left, just below the hand holding the crosier, five images symbolize the
church's power: from top to bottom, a church, a bishop's miter, thunderbolts
signifying excommunication, the rhetoric of ecclesiastical debate, and a scene of
disputation in the schools of theology. Viewed as parallels, the two series juxtapose castle and church, crown and miter, cannon and lightning, weapons of war
and weapons of rhetoric, and a battlefield and theological dispute. Between these
two sets of images is the subtitle of *Leviathan,* "The Matter, Forme, and Power of
A Commonwealth Ecclesiasticall and Civil." The subtext of the subtitle is thus
rendered visible: the only one capable of wielding the powers of state and church
with equal justice, and in a way that insures the common good, is the sovereign
monarch of the commonwealth.

Easily overlooked but not to be missed is the small-print Latin inscription at
the very top of the title page: "Non est potestas Super Terram quae Comparetur
ei Iob 41.24." The citation is from God's whirlwind speech about Leviathan: "there
is nothing on earth to be compared with him." It is the first clue that Hobbes

intends to transpose and transform the biblical account of Leviathan into a "grand metaphor of commonwealth."[48]

A picture may indeed be worth a thousand words, but in this case Hobbes's frontispiece invites additional comment. His use of Leviathan as a metaphor for the power of the commonwealth follows a minor but not unprecedented exegetical tradition. The dominant view in the seventeenth century took its cue from Isaiah 27:1, where Leviathan, the fleeing, twisting sea dragon, stands metaphorically for Israel's archenemy, Babylon, whom God will slay with the sword. From Gregory to Milton, this glossing of Leviathan as the personification of evil transposes into the Christian expectation that God, the great fisherman, would use the cross as a hook and Christ on the cross as the bait to capture and defeat Leviathan (Satan).[49] Hobbes would certainly have known this interpretation and may indeed have intentionally confronted it when he drew upon an alternate view. Among the various definitions of Leviathan in seventeenth-century lexicographies were "king," "prince," "association," and "society." These definitions rested on an etymology that derived the word *Leviathan* from two roots: Hebrew *lāwah*, "join, connect, couple," and *tannîn*, "dragon, serpent." The Westminster Assembly's Annotations on the Bible (1641, 1645) explains as follows: "because by his [Leviathan's] bignesse he seems not a single creature, but a coupling of divers together; or because his scales are closed, or straightly compacted together." Schlinder's *Lexicon Pentaglotten* (1637) cites the same derivation and adds a comment about the word's figurative meaning: "*per metaphorum*," Leviathan signifies "princeps" or "rex."[50] The meaning of Hobbes's entire work flows from this metaphorical understanding of Leviathan as a commonwealth and the sovereign monarch as the head or soul that gives life to all.

How specifically does the biblical Leviathan inform Hobbes's political metaphor? In addition to the citation from Job 41:24 on the title page, three references provide clues. The first occurs in the opening paragraph of the introduction, a portion of which I have already cited, where Hobbes signals that the construction of the Leviathanic state is an imaginative act of *imitatio Dei.*

> Nature (the Art whereby God hath made and governes the world) is by the *Art* of man, as in many other things, so in this also imitated, that it can make an Artificiall Animal. . . . For by Art is created that great LEVIATHAN called a COMMONWEALTH, or STATE (in latine CIVITAS) which is but an Artificiall Man, though of greater stature and strength than the Naturall, for whose protection and defense it was intended; and in which, the *Soveraignty* is an Artificiall *Soul,* as giving life and motion to the whole body. (9)

Hobbes then develops the analogy between the human construction of the state and God's creation of humankind with an "anatomy lesson" on Leviathan.[51]

> The *Magistrates,* and other *Officers* of Judicature and Execution, artificiall *Joynts; Reward* and *Punishment* (by which fastned to the seate of Soveraignty, every joynt and member is moved to perform his duty) are the *Nerves,* that do the same in the Body Naturall; The *Wealth* and *Riches* of all the particular members, are the *Strength; Salus Populi* (the *peoples safety*) its *Businesse; Counsellors,* by whom all things needful for it to know, are suggested unto it, are the *Memory; Equity* and *Lawes,* an artificiall *Reason* and *Will; Concord, Health; Sedition, Sickness;* and *Civill war, Death.* Lastly, the *Pacts* and *Covenants,* by which the parts of this Body Politique were at first made, set together, and united, resemble that *Fiat,* or the *Let us make man,* pronounced by God in the Creation. (ibid.)

This opening overview of the Leviathanic state introduces a central idea that Hobbes will pursue: the "Covenants" that create and sustain the consent of the governed. Hobbes understands the covenant that binds monarch and people as a social contract, a "mutuall transferring of Right" (74) in which the monarch promises to protect and defend the people from internal dissension and external threat, in return for which people agree to subordinate individual disagreement to the collective good. So long as the sovereign exercises dominion justly, his power cannot be questioned, and he "cannot be Accused by any of his Subjects" (110). From the peoples' side of this covenantal agreement, the elimination of opposition constitutes true freedom and liberty, "for in the act of our *Submission,* consisteth both our *Obligation,* and our *Liberty*" (119).[52] A monarch's sovereignty is immortal, but in its suppression of protest, it is resolutely godlike.

A second reference occurs in chapter 17, a portion of which serves as the title for this section. When Hobbes turns to the process for constructing the Leviathanic state, he explicates its dependence on power and fear. "The Multitude, so united in one Person, is called a COMMON-WEALTH, in latine CIVITAS. This is the generation of that great LEVIATHAN, or rather (to speak more reverently) of that *Mortall God,* to which wee owe under the *Immortall God,* our peace and defense. For by this Authoritie, given him by every particular man in the Common-Wealth, he hath the use of so much Power and Strength conferred on him, that by terror thereof, he is inabled to [con]forme the wills of them all, to Peace at home, and mutuall ayd against their enemies abroad" (95–96).

The power of the monarch as "Mortall God" and the power of the "Immortall God" is for Hobbes primarily a distinction without a difference.[53] The Kingdom of God is not fully manifest until the end of the world; in the meantime only the civil sovereign has the power to command obedience (chaps. 32–43). Toward this end Hobbes stipulates twelve rights of the monarch, including the power to adjudicate all controversies and to suppress all dissent; to reward fidelity with riches and honor, infidelity with ignominy and death, if necessary; and to keep peace and wage war with military force (96–100). He buttresses his political perspective with scriptural reasoning drawn from both Old and New Testaments, from the requirement of the Israelites' absolute obedience to Moses (Ex 20:19) to Jesus's instruction in the Gospels to "give to Caesar that which is Caesar's" (Mt 22:21 and parallels). Most curious, perhaps also most revealing, is the appeal to 1 Samuel 8:11–17:

> Concerning the Right of Kings, God himself by the mouth of Samuel, saith, This shall be the Right of the King you will have to reigne over you. He shall take your sons, and set them to drive his Chariots, and to be his horsemen, and to run before his chariots; and gather in his harvest; and to make his engines of War, and Instruments of his chariots; and shall take your daughters to make perfumes, to be his Cookes, and Bakers. He shall take your fields, your vine-yards and your olive-yards, and give them to his servants. He shall take the tyth of your corne and wine, and give it to the men of his chamber, and to his other servants. He shall take your man-servants, and your maid-servants, and the choice of your youth, and employ them in his businesse. He shall take the tyth of your flocks; and you shall be his servants. This is absolute power, and summed up in the last words, you shall be his servants. (113)

Hobbes is either unaware of (unlikely) or simply ignores that in context Samuel is presenting a case *against* Israel's fateful move to monarchy. In either case he is unequivocal in his argument that both reason and scripture are in one accord when it comes to commanding absolute obedience to the monarch. As the citation on the title page from Job 41:24 has already anticipated, "there is nothing on earth to be compared with him [Leviathan qua monarch]."[54]

> So . . . it appeareth plainly, to my understanding, both from Reason, and Scripture, that the Soveraign Power, whether placed in One Man, as in Monarchy, or in one Assembly of men, as in Popular, and Aristocraticall Common-wealths, is as great, as possibly men can be imagined to make it. And though of so unlimited a Power, men may fancy many evill consequences, yet the consequences of the want of it, which is perpetuall warre of every man against his neighbour, are much worse. The condition of man in this life shall never be without Inconveniences; but there happeneth in no Common-wealth any great Inconvenience, but what proceeds from the Subjects disobedience, and breach of those Covenants, from which the Common-wealth hath its being. (114–15)

The third critical reference occurs within Hobbes's discussion of the theodicy question. In religious terms the question focuses on divine providence; in the language of Hobbes's political theory, it focuses not only on God's justice but also on the civil sovereign's honor. Here again Hobbes turns to God's answer to Job to make his point.

> This question, *Why Evill men often prosper, and Good men suffer Adversity,* has
> been much debated by the Antient, and is the same with this of ours. . . . And *Job,*
> how earnestly does he expostulate with God, for the many afflictions he suffered,
> notwithstanding his Righteousnesse? This question in the case of *Job,* is decided
> by God himself, not by arguments derived from Job's Sinne, but his own power.
> For whereas the friends of *Job* drew their arguments from the Affliction to his
> Sinne, and he defended himself by the conscience of his Innocence, God himself
> taketh up the matter, and having justified the Affliction by arguments drawn from
> his Power, such as this is, *Where wast thou when I layd the foundations of the earth*
> [Job 38:4], and the like, both approved Job's Innocence, and reproved the Errone-
> ous doctrine of the friends. Conformable to this doctrine is the sentence of our
> Saviour, concerning the man that was born Blind, in these words, *Neither has this*
> *man sinned nor his fathers; but that the works of God might be made manifest in*
> *him.* And though it be said, *That Death entered into the world by sinne,* (by which
> is meant that if *Adam* had never sinned he had never dyed, that is, never suffered
> any separation of his soule from his body), it follows not thence, that God could
> not justly have afflicted him, though he has not sinned, as well as he afflicteth
> other living creatures, that cannot sinne. (182–83)

The intent of this reference to Job is ambiguous, but its location as the lead-in to
Hobbes's argument that the objectives of the Christian commonwealth are consonant with those of the civil monarch suggests an analogy. As Job's escape from
suffering depended on his submission to God's absolute power (symbolized in
Leviathan), so the commonwealth's peaceful survival depends on submission to
its sovereign.[55]

Finally, and by way of summation, I return to the assessment of Hobbes by
his contemporaries and by his subsequent readers. From the moment of its publication, *Leviathan* was severely criticized from virtually all quarters. The clergy,
both Protestant and Roman Catholic, seized on Hobbes's subordination of revelation to reason as grounds for the charge that he was an atheist. Politicians viewed
his theory of a monolithic state that suppresses human passion for the sake of
civil order as not only utopian but also despotic. University teachers, lawyers, and
other professionals, whose expertise Hobbes considered secondary and dispos-
able, vigorously opposed the curbing of their influence on intellectual thought.
There were multiple efforts to suppress the publication. The first English edition
bore a London imprint and a 1651 date; two subsequent and clearly revised editions contained the same information, though it is reasonably clear they were
surreptitiously published in Holland.[56] In 1652 and again in 1655, appeals were
made to Parliament to ban the book. Oxford and Cambridge proscribed teaching
Leviathan and censured professors who failed to comply. In Germany, Italy, and

Holland, critics took similar measures to condemn and diminish the spread of Hobbesism. The pervasiveness of this hostile response is conveyed by an anonymous early eighteenth-century observer: "From a Bishop down to a Country Curate, [Hobbes] was esteem'd for a dangerous and Skeptical Author; and a Parson wou'd as soon visit a House where there's the Plague, or give away the Tithes of his Parish, than let a Parishioner have the Perusal of [his] Book; they have made it a sort of Damnation to speak in his Defence; and who espouses him with the Pen, is liable to the Inquisition of Doctors Commons, and is sure of being trounced for a Heretick."[57]

Whether Hobbes was guilty of the crimes his contemporaries accused him of is a matter for Hobbes scholars to debate.[58] There can be no debate, however, that Hobbes's appropriation of the Joban Leviathan as a metaphor for political hegemony continues to have enormous influence on what we call today the "social sciences" and, more particularly, especially in the university curricula of Western culture, "political science." When constructing institutions that promote civil order based on the consent of the governed, who can disagree with the argument that the most important criterion is *nosce teipsum*—not, as conventionally translated, "know thyself," but as Hobbes renders it, "read thy self,"[59] both in the hopes and fears of other mortals and in the metaphor of Leviathan? More than 350 years after its publication, Hobbes's *Leviathan* remains a critical part of the public discourse on the relative merits of democracy, aristocracy, and monarchy.[60]

"Of thy fire thou madest me, and like a true child of fire, I breathe it back to thee"

The Enlightenment in eighteenth-century England and Germany represented a Joban revival. The "Enlightenment Bible" was attuned to new biblical scholarship that brought attention to the power and beauty of the poetic sections of Job (e.g., Robert Lowth, J. G. Herder), which had largely been subordinated to the narrative about Job's patient suffering at the hands of a just God.[61] Philosophical inquiries into the power of poetry to evoke experiences of the sublime, with the concomitant feelings of elation and fear, drew upon Job's lamentations and God's celebration of creation's extremities as parade examples (e.g., Edmund Burke, Thomas Carlyle).[62] These new approaches fueled more sympathetic readings of Job as a tragic character, more critical readings of Job's God as a less than perfect figure. Both English and German writers during the Romantic period (e.g., Blake and Goethe) advanced this Joban revival in various ways.[63] Within the milieu of the American adaptation of the Romantic movement, Herman Melville's *Moby-Dick* (1851) was the signature work. As the literary critic James Wood notes, "Literature is the new church, and *Moby-Dick* its bible."[64]

Melville's fitful relationship with the strict Calvinism he inherited from his mother is well documented. From at least the age of twenty, when he abandoned a dead-end apprenticeship in a bank for work on a whaling ship bound for Polynesia, he became increasingly disillusioned with the Calvinistic God. Nathaniel Hawthorne, a close friend, described a visit with Melville in 1856 in the English coastal resort of Southport:

> Melville, as he always does, began to reason of Providence and futurity, and of everything that lies beyond human ken, and informed me that he had "pretty much made up his mind to be annihilated"; but still he does not seem to rest in that anticipation; and I think, will never rest until he gets hold of a definite belief. It is strange how he persists—and has persisted ever since I knew him, and probably long before—in wandering to-and-fro over these deserts, as dismal and monotonous as the sand hills amid which we were sitting. He can neither believe, nor be comfortable in his unbelief; and he is too honest and courageous not to try to do one or the other.[65]

In assessing Melville's "quarrels with God," Lawrance Thompson concludes,

> Melville arrived at a highly ironic conclusion: believing more firmly than ever in the God of John Calvin, he began to resent and hate the attributes of God, particularly the seemingly tyrannical harshness and cruelty and malice of God. Thus, instead of losing faith in his Calvinistic God, Melville made a scapegoat of him, and blamed God for having caused so many human beings to rebel. In this sense, then, we might say that Melville became an inverted mystic as soon as he began to be angry with God for being the harsh and logical punisher that Calvinists said he was. Still influenced by the Calvinistic dogma that God did indeed try to exact from mankind a rigid letter-of-the law obedience, and that Adam's fall was indeed the first indication of the unjust ruthlessness of God's punishment, Melville came to view God as the source from whom all evils flow, in short, the "Original Sinner," divinely depraved.[66]

In *Moby-Dick* "Melville slapped at God. . . . but in some way, he could not do without the idea of being slapped by God in return."[67]

Melville used the Bible extensively, especially the Old Testament, in the corpus of his work.[68] Direct references and thematic allusions to the book of Job in *Moby-Dick,* too many to discuss fully in this context, are case in point. Indeed Job may be "the most informing single principle of the book's composition."[69] In what follows I focus on Melville's appropriation of the Leviathan metaphor and its implications for understanding the fraught relationship between God and human beings.

Melville constructs *Moby-Dick*, like the book of Job, as a story within a story. A narrator, Ishmael, provides the frame, his first words an invitation to heed this account of his ventures on a whaling expedition, his last a report that the "the drama's done" (427). Inside this frame Ahab, the captain of this expedition, and his crew, including Ishmael, join forces to hunt Moby Dick, the great white leviathan, "Job's whale" (158). All commit to pull their ship toward its destiny "like god-damn" (279). At the risk of oversimplifying a masterpiece, I suggest that Melville invites reflection on two biblical whales, Jonah's and Job's, and on two quite different responses upon encountering these whales, both metaphors for God, Ishmael's and Ahab's.[70]

Before setting sail Ishmael attends a Sunday service at the Whaleman's Chapel. Father Mapple's sermon comes from the book of Jonah, which he introduces with these words: "Beloved shipmates, clinch the last verse of the first chapter of Jonah—'And God prepared a great fish to swallow up Jonah'" (49). Mapple's exposition stresses two lessons: first Jonah's sin and the divine punishment that brings him to repentance, and second Jonah's deliverance and joy. Woe to the pilot and the shipmates who ignore the dreadful and just punishment of the living God, Father Mapple reminds his congregation: "Sin not; but if you do, take heed to repent of it like Jonah" (52). As the sermon gathers steam toward it conclusion, Mapple focuses on God's agent of rebuke and redemption, the great whale.

> God came upon him in the whale, and swallowed him down to living gulfs of doom, and with swift slanting tore him along "into the midst of the seas," where the eddying depths sucked him ten thousand fathoms down, and "the weeds were wrapped about his head," and all the watery world of woe bowled over him. Yet even then beyond the reach of any plummet—"out of the belly of hell"—when the whale grounded upon the ocean's utmost bones, even then, God heard the engulphed, repenting prophet when he cried. Then God spake unto the fish; and from the shuddering cold and blackness of the sea, the whale came breeching up towards the warm and pleasant sun, and all the delights of air and earth; and "vomited Jonah upon the dry land"; when the word of the Lord came to Jonah a second time; and Jonah, bruised and beaten—his ears like two sea-shells, still multitudinously murmuring of the ocean—Jonah did the Almighty's bidding. And what was that, shipmates? To preach the Truth to the face of Falsehood! That was it! (53)

Father Mapple then offers these final words of exhortation: "But oh! shipmates! on the starboard hand of every woe, there is sure delight; and higher the top of that delight, than the bottom of the woe is deep. . . . Delight,—top-gallant delight is to him, who acknowledges no law or lord, but the Lord his God, and is only a patriot to heaven" (54).

Ishmael's last words come in the epilogue, which is introduced with a citation from Job 1:19: "And I only am escaped to tell thee" (427). The hunt for Job's whale, Moby Dick, has ended in the sinking of the ship and the deaths of the entire crew, save Ishmael. We may read the epilogue against the background of Father Mapple's sermon, in which case Ishmael survives as a Jonah-like prophet, now commissioned to "preach the Truth to the face of Falsehood."[71] But then, what exactly is this truth and what is the falsehood it seeks to dismiss? Perhaps the answer lies in Mapple's Calvinistic doctrine, which views God's justice as sovereign and repentance as the only route to God's saving mercies. This is a possible reading, but Melville's narrator, like the narrator of the Joban prologue-epilogue, invites a more nuanced consideration.[72] Ishmael, who bears the name of the Old Testament's ultimate outcast (Gn 16–17), begins his epilogue not by affirming God's salvific intervention but instead by attributing his deliverance to "chance."

> It so chanced . . . that I was dropped astern. So, floating on the margin of the ensuing scene, and in full sight of it, when the half-spent suction of the sunk ship reached me, I was then, but slowly, drawn towards the closing vortex. When I reached it, it had subsided to a creamy pool. Round and round, then, and ever contracting towards the button-like bubble at the axis of slowly wheeling circle . . . I did revolve. Till, gaining that vital centre, the black bubble upward burst; and now liberated by reason of its cunning spring, and owing to its great buoyancy, rising with great force, the *coffin life-buoy shot lengthwise from the sea, fell over, and floated by my side. Buoyed up by that coffin, for almost one whole day and night, I floated on a soft and dirge-like main. The unharming sharks, they glided by as if with padlocks on their mouths; the savage sea-hawks sailed with sheathed beaks. On the second day, a sail drew near, nearer, and picked me up at last.* (427)

If Ishmael, who now describes himself as but "another orphan," survives by chance, by clinging to a buoyant coffin that defies all reason, what truth and what falsehood does he proclaim?

Inside the frame of Ishmael's narration, the hunt for Moby Dick unfolds. Melville's account of the expedition is thick with masterful characterizations of all the crew members and their mixed motivations for signing on to the adventure. I single out two aspects of the story that have direct bearing on how Melville reads God's speeches and Job's responses: first the multiple and always detailed descriptions of the great leviathan, Moby Dick, whose killing drives the plot; and second the tortured, "monomaniacal" (156) imperatives of Ahab, the one-legged captain of the *Pequod,* whose quest for justice can be satisfied by nothing less than a life-or-death confrontation with the God-whale who has wounded him for life.

First God asks Job a series of questions about his ability to capture Leviathan: "Canst thou draw out Leviathan with an hook?"; "Canst thou put an hook into his nose?"; "Will he make many supplications unto thee?"; "Wilt thou play with him like a bird?"; "Shall the companions make a banquet of him? shall they part him among the merchants?"; "Canst thou fill his skin with barbed irons? or his head with fish spears?" (Job 41:1–7 [KJV]). The questions are likely rhetorical; they assume that the only logical answer Job can give is "No, I can do none of these things."[73] Melville answers differently but complexly. He describes hunting whales as a dangerous, though successful, business enterprise. Whales are a commodity. They can be captured; their bodies can be cut open; their insides can be processed, sold, and consumed. Ishmael describes processing the whale's sperm in terms that make it sound like a sublime experience (322).

For Melville cetology approximates theology. Some attributes of God may be beyond human comprehension; so too some knowledge of whales. But just as theologians can construct systematic accounts of God, so cetologists can identify, classify, and study the whale's behavior. In short God is the not the only one who can understand Leviathan's "parts," "power," and "proportions" (41:12 [KJV]). Here, too, Melville's Ishmael offers a different response to God's "awful tauntings" in Job 41.

> Now the various species of whales need some sort of popular comprehensive classification, if only an easy outline one for the present, hereafter to be filled in all its departments by subsequent laborers. As no better man advances to take this matter in hand, I hereupon offer my own poor endeavors. . . .
>
> To grope down into the bottom of the sea after them; to have one's hands among the unspeakable foundations, ribs, and very pelvis of the world; this is a fearful thing. What am I that I should essay to hook the nose of this leviathan! The awful tauntings in Job might well appal me. "Will he (the leviathan) make a covenant with thee? Behold the hope of him is vain!" [Job 41:4, 9] But I have swam through libraries and sailed through oceans; I have had to do with whales with these visible hands; I am in earnest; and I will try. (116)

Ishmael concedes that his "cetological system" remains incomplete; others will have to fill in the missing details by catching and marking additional whales. Even so the edifice of knowledge he constructs is like the great unfinished "Cathedral of Cologne" (125). Whales, like God, are accessible to human inspection.

While Melville "domesticates and localizes" the Joban Leviathan, he never loses sight of the whale's/God's elusiveness. Melville uses the Leviathan metaphor like "secret ink," which reduces what is known for apprehension, then enlarges the unknown and the unknowable, which annuls comprehension.[74] Ishmael's reflections on "the whiteness of the whale" underscore the point. Whiteness conveys special virtues, such as royalty, innocence, even holiness; yet, as Ishmael says, there "lurks an elusive something in the innermost idea of this hue, which strikes more of panic to the soul than that redness which affrights in blood" (160). "Ghastly whiteness," as for example in the "albino man . . . [who is] more strangely hideous than the ugliest abortion," conveys "transcendent horrors" that shock and repel (160–61). We have not yet solved the "incantation of this whiteness," Ishmael says, which leaves us with more questions than answers (165). Leviathan's whiteness is a "morbid hint" (153) of the consequences that attend the whalers' conceit. They may pursue the great sperm whale, but they can capture no more than the "creamy foam" (155) of its wake as it slips away, unharmed and unaccountable to their best efforts.

As to the second aspect, Ahab bears the name of one of the most notorious kings of Israel. Using royal power, King Ahab confiscated the property of Naboth and thus suffered an ignominious death (1 Kgs 21). From the outset, then, Melville hints that Ahab, his primary protagonist in *Moby-Dick,* is as much an outcast as Ishmael, although for different reasons. Ahab has chased Moby Dick with Joblike curses (143) since the day the great white whale chewed off his leg, leaving him a "poor peggling lubber" (139). His quest for revenge—or justice, depending on how one reads the story—is the imperative that charts the course for the shipmates he enlists on the *Pequod.* When Starbuck cautions that Ahab's rage against an animal that only acted instinctively "seems blasphemous" (139), Ahab responds with unvarnished bravado. "He [Moby Dick] tasks me; he heaps me; I see in him outrageous strength, with an inscrutable malice sinewing it. That inscrutable thing is chiefly what I hate; and be the white whale agent, or be the white whale principal, I will wreak that hate upon him. Talk to me not of blasphemy, man; I'd strike the sun if it insulted me" (140).

When a typhoon from the east threatens to sink the *Pequod,* Starbuck counsels retreat, because God has clearly risen up against their mission. Ahab decides instead to steer directly into the danger; thunder and lightning "lights the way to the White Whale!" He takes his stand on the quarterdeck, his hand raised defiantly toward the "tri-pointed trinity of flames."

> Oh! Thou clear spirit of clear fire, whom on the seas I as Persian once did worship, till in the sacramental act so burned by thee, that to this hour I bear the scar; I now know thee, thou clear sprit, and I now know that thy right worship is defiance. To neither love nor reverence wilt thou be kind; and e'en for hate thou canst but kill; and all are killed. No fearless fool confronts thee. I own thy speechless, placeless power; but to the last gasp of my earthquake life will dispute its unconditional, unintegral mastery in me. In the midst of the personified impersonal, a personality

stands here. . . . Oh, thou clear spirit, of thy fire thou madest me, and like a true child of fire, I breathe it back to thee. (382)

Face to face with the crippling powers of God, Ahab has a revelatory moment. Like Job he learns something about God that changes him. Unlike Job, at least according to the conventional interpretation Melville would have known, Ahab refuses to submit in silence (Job 42:5–6). Instead he "assumes the attitude of a sovereign being who does not quail before these malicious indignities."[75] Like his biblical namesake, he will "own" what in truth he has no power to acquire— the "speechless, placeless power" of God's "inscrutable malice"—even if the effort reduces him to ashes (383). Ahab claims to know more about God than God knows about himself.

> Thou knowest not how came ye, hence callest thyself unbegotten; certainly knowest not thy beginning, hence callest thyself unbegun. I know that of me, which thou knowest not of thyself, oh thou omnipotent. There is some unsuffusing thing beyond thee, thou clear spirit, to whom all thy eternity is but time, all thy creativeness mechanical. Through thee, thy flaming self, my scorched eyes do dimly see it. Oh, thou foundling fire, thou hermit immemorial, thou too hast thy incommunicable riddle, thy unparticipated grief. Here again with haughty agony, I read my sire. Leap! leap up, and lick the sky! I leap with thee; I burn with thee; would fain be welded with thee; defyingly I worship thee! (383)

What exactly is the "unsuffusing thing," which Melville obliquely equates with God's "incommunicable riddle"? What does it mean to be welded in defiance to God's "unparticipated grief"? As usual the answer is likely to be found in Melville's use of metaphor. Several clues invite reflection. When Ahab first sights Moby Dick, the whale's open mouth, with its "two long crooked rows of white, glistening teeth," appears "like an open-doored marble tomb" (410). The metaphor seems to linger in Melville's thinking. In 1857 he visited the pyramids in Egypt. He writes in his journal that he was "oppressed by their massiveness and mystery" and that "a feeling awe & terror" came over him. "By vast pains we mine into the pyramids; by horrible gropings we come to the central room; with joy we espy the sarcophagus; but we lift the lid—and no body is there!—appallingly vacant as vast as is the soul of a man!" "It was in these pyramids," Melville says, "that was conceived the great idea of Jehovah."[76] Melville's two-week stay in the Middle East took him also to Jerusalem. Inside the Church of the Holy Sepulchre, he spent "almost every day" looking at the "spectacle" surrounding the tomb of Jesus. "First passing a wee vestibule where is shown the stone on which the angel sat, you enter the tomb. It is like entering a lighted lanthorn. Wedged & half-dazzled, you stare for a moment on the ineloquence of the bedizened slab, and glad to come out, wipe your brow glad to escape as from the heat & jam of a show-box. All is glitter & nothing is gold. A sickening cheat."[77]

By piecing together these references, we may gain some purchase on the metaphor of Moby Dick's teeth's appearing like an "open-doored marble tomb." As Ishmael ponders Father Mapple's sermon, the mouth of Jonah's whale is God's agent of rescue from death. As Ahab stares into Leviathan's mouth, the tomb awaiting him promises a death that may be defied but not thwarted. As Job would put it, "The Lord gives and the Lord takes away; blessed be the name of the Lord" (Job 1:21). Both whales are God metaphors, and for Melville the great Jehovah's mouth speaks only a "pyramidical silence" (274). Should one gain entrance to God's innermost nature, one finds only an empty sarcophagus or, to extend the metaphor to Jesus's tomb, the "ineloquence of the bedizened slab." Mixed in with these metaphors, a number of descriptors—"horrible groppings," "appallingly vacant," "glitter" not "gold," "sickening cheat"—provide signposts for a journey destined to end in disappointment. For Melville every pursuit of the sacred—Job's whale, the pyramids, the Holy Sepulchre—ends in a fictional substitute for reality. God may be like *x, y,* or *z,* but he is never equal to the imagined alternative. As the final chase for Moby Dick begins, Melville describes "the whale sliding like a metaphor through its fluid of meanings: 'on each bright side, the whale shed off enticings'" (409).[78]

Ahab speaks for the last time on the third and climatic day of the chase for Leviathan. Perhaps because of some "latent deceitfulness and malice" (423), the whale is momentarily subdued. Ahab steers closer. Harpoon in hand, he readies himself for the final assault: "I grin at thee, thou grinning whale" (425). Then the whale rams the ship. As the *Pequod* begins to sink, Ahab speaks his final defiance.

> Death-glorious ship! must ye then perish without me? Am I cut off from the last fond pride of meanest shipwrecked captains? Oh, lonely death on lonely life! Oh, now I feel my topmost greatness lies in my topmost grief. Ho, ho! from all your furthest bounds, pour ye now in, ye bold billows of my whole foregone life, and top this one piled comber of my death! Towards thee I roll, thou all-destroying but unconquering whale; to the last I grapple with thee; from hell's heart I stab at thee; for hate's sake I spit my last breath at thee. Sink all coffins and all hearses to one common pool! and since neither can be mine, let me then tow to pieces, while still chasing thee, though tied to thee, thou damned whale! *Thus,* I give up the spear! (426)

A sky-hawk circling overhead with "archangelic shrieks" seizes the ship's fluttering flag. The ship, "which, like Satan, would not sink to hell till she had dragged a living part of heaven along with her," disappears from sight. Then these final words are given "all collapsed, and the great shroud of the sea rolled on as it rolled five thousand years ago" (427).

Ahab's story, like Job's, is framed by a narrator's account. The Joban narrator, whose perspective is confined to the prologue and epilogue (Job 1–2 + Job 42:7–17), tells an "all's well that ends well" story about a righteous man who suffers unjustly and is rewarded in the end for his patient endurance. Ishmael, Melville's narrator, tells a story about Ahab, the "grand, ungodly, God-like man" (78), who demonstrates that "there is a wisdom that is woe; but there is a woe that is madness" (328). At various points Melville hints that Ishmael, who sees Moby Dick not as good or evil but as the "interlinked terrors and wonders of God" (98), is the model for the conflicted faith in God's justice that he cannot completely abandon.[79] At other points Melville's biography would seem to tilt him toward Ahab's relentless defiance of God, whose malicious justice always eludes accountability. In the end it is Ishmael, afloat on the gratuitous mercies of a "coffin life-buoy," retrieved by a ship named *Rachel,* a final Melvillian metaphor for the unconsoled mother restless for the return of her missing children (Jer 31), who survives to tell the story. However we may read *Moby-Dick,* Melville's epilogue invites readers to return to the beginning of Job's story and start over again. The story that remains to be told, Melville suggests, lies in the hands of those who survive.[80]

EPILOGUE

Job's Children (Job 42:7–17)

There is nothing so whole as a broken heart.

Rabbi Nahman

Though a child of survivors, I am parent to the interpretation of their survival.

C. P. Sucher, "History Is the Province of Memory"

How could they [Job's second children] live in a house filled with tragedy? How could Job and his wife live with their memories?

Elie Wiesel, "Some Words for Children of Survivors"

How does anyone write an epilogue to Job? When a story, whether sacred scripture or fiction, begins with God's confession that innocent suffering happens "for no reason," what conclusion can be constructed that is adequate, let alone convincing? The narrator of the Joban epilogue opts for a "happy ending" that strives to tie up loose ends.[1] In two didactic assessments, the narrator declares that Job, not the friends, has spoken "what is right" about God (42:7–9), and that consequently God rewards Job by restoring his wealth, property, and status (42:10–17). This "all's well that ends well" ending invites reflection on the interchange between Shakespeare's widow of Florence and Helena:

> WIDOW: Lord how we lose our pains!
> HELENA: All's well that ends well yet,
> Though time seems so adverse and means unfit.
> (*All's Well That Ends Well*, 5.1.24–26)

Even if we can settle into this happy ending, Shakespeare's telltale *yet,* and the trailer words *adverse* and *unfit,* may give us pause. David Clines poses the question the epilogue begs: "What, in the end, becomes of Job? After all he has endured, after all his vigor to clear his name, after the encounter with God that has proved so disappointing . . . He steps back into the world of the prologue to the book, the world of the naïve fairytale, and closes the door for ever on the world of intensity, intellectual struggle—lucidity—that he has inhabited since the day of his curse on life (chap.3). Has this been a happy outcome for him? . . . Is this enough to constitute happiness?"[2] A number of subtle clues indicate that the epilogue, whatever closure it may have intended, continues to invite multiple readings that add to the characterizations of God, the friends, Job, and his children.

God

The first clue about God occurs in the narrator's opening statement. The words "After the Lord had spoken these words to Job" (42:7) direct readers back to the divine speeches in 38:1–40:34, not to Job's last words in 42:1–6. Does God accept Job's last words as a worthy response to divine revelation? The narrator does not say, an omission that may be read in different ways. Perhaps God chooses to ignore what Job has said. Perhaps God's acceptance is assumed.[3] The only explicit information we are given is that God is angry. Job feared that God would confront him in anger (14:13, 16:9, 19:11), but it is surprising that God never directly expresses anger toward Job. Instead he is angry with the friends, because they have not spoken "what is right (nĕkônâ)." The term refers to what is "correct" or "truthful," not only in an intellectual sense but also with reference to facts that are established and consistent with reality (cf. Dt 17:4, 1 Sm 23:23).[4] God's anger indicates that the friends' error is not trivial; as Clines notes, "in defending the doctrine of retribution, [the friends] were advocates of a theology hostile to the divine designs."[5] But if retributive justice is not the undergirding moral principle of God's governance of the world, then what is? If blessing the righteous and punishing the wicked is not consistent with reality, then what does justice mean for an innocent sufferer such as Job? God's reaction to the friends subtly returns readers to the prologue, where, by God's own admission, the words "for no reason" (2:3; cf. 1:9) must somehow be factored into a theology that is not hostile to God's intentions.

God's anger is further manifest in his willingness to deal with the friends in distinctly un-godlike ways. Before Job prays for the friends, God is intent on "doing foolishness" ('ăśôt nĕbālâ [42:8]). The word nĕbālâ normally refers to reprehensible or outrageous behavior that subverts acceptable social-ethical norms and brings dishonor and judgment on the perpetrator.[6] The occurrence in 42:8 is the only instance in the Old Testament where God is said to be the one doing nĕbālâ. The conventional view (reflected in NRSV: "to deal with you according to your folly") is that the friends' foolishness, not God's, needs changing or forgiving.

A straightforward reading suggests, however, that Job's unrecorded prayer may have been something like this: "O Lord, do not do anything foolish when you deal with the friends."[7] When the epilogist reports that God "accepted Job's prayer" (42:10), he suggests that God's intentions have changed. In short Job's prayer restores both the friends and God to a relationship that is different than that which would have existed if he had not stepped into the breach between them. Job's participation, which comes at God's invitation, enables God to be more godlike.[8]

Another aspect of God's character is disclosed in the report that he restores Job's fortunes by giving him "twice as much as he had before" (42:10). The doubling may be only a rhetorical flourish designed to connect the epilogue with the prologue (1:3), where Job's possessions are a tangible witness to his piety. Perhaps it is no more than a characteristic feature of conventional stories about the reward that comes eventually to those who remain faithful to God in the midst of hardship.[9] It is nonetheless hard to overlook the connection elsewhere in the Old Testament between double compensation for losses and an admission of wrongdoing. "It is a wry touch," Francis I. Anderson says, "that the Lord, like any thief who has been found out (Exod 22:4), repays Job double what he took from him."[10]

The doubling likely also extends to the epilogist's report that "after this Job lived one hundred and forty years" (42:16). If seventy years is a normal life span (Ps 90:10), then it appears that following this encounter with suffering and with God, Job now begins life again. His former life is over. God grants him a fresh start, as if he can now begin anew unencumbered by what he has experienced and learned about life in relation to God. When he dies, "old and full of days" (42:17), Job, like Israel's revered ancestors—Abraham (Gn 25:8), Isaac (Gn 25:29), and David (1 Chr 29:28)—will be full and satisfied. A number of underlying and unaddressed questions linger. Can a restored Job simply forget his losses? Will replacement children compensate for the deaths of seven sons and three daughters? Can Job, should he, simply resume a life of blessing the God who gives and takes away? What assurance does Job have that his new life will be invulnerable to the same seemingly capricious disruptions of a God who can be incited to act against him "for no reason"? Clines sharpens the question that the epilogue invites but does not answer. "If fire could fall from heaven on his [Job's] flocks and herds one day, who is to know that it will never again in 140 years? It is a little naïve, is it not, to believe that lightning never falls in the same place twice."[11]

Job and His Friends

The epilogue condemns the three friends, represented here by their lead spokesman, Eliphaz, for not having spoken the truth about God. Job alone has done so. The question remains, however: what has Job said about God that is "right"? Was he right to bless God in the face of undeserved suffering (1:21)? If so, then how could he also be right when he cursed the day of his birth and by implication the creator who summons forth all life (3:1-10; cf. 3:11, 10:18)? Was Job right to accuse God of savage indifference to the justice of the wronged (10:1–17, 16:6–17, 19:6–22, 27:2–12)? If so, then why does God criticize Job for questioning divine justice (40:8)? If Job was right to defer in silence to God's first words from the whirlwind (40:5), then why does God continue to seek his response with a second speech (40:6)? If Job's second response in 42:6 is right, then it is at best enigmatic, and readers are left to wonder why God does not say more, either to affirm or explain what Job understands now that he did not before. The transmission history of the prose and poetry of the book may mitigate the contradictory answers these questions pose, but at a fundamental level the different options remain largely irreconcilable. Perhaps we should settle for a minimalist reading: Job is right that God does not govern according to the principles of retributive justice; to claim otherwise, as the friends do, is clearly wrong. But then the price Job pays for being right casts an even more unsettling pall over the story: seven sons and three daughters dead "for no reason," except to teach Job a lesson? How could a righteous God fault Job for refusing to learn such a lesson, even if he is wrong? Dostoevsky's Ivan responds to his brother Alyosha in a scenario that imagines a Joblike refusal to pay the cost obedience to God seems to require.

> I don't want harmony [with God's world], for love of mankind I don't want it. I'd rather remain with my unrequited suffering and my unquenched indignation, *even if I am wrong*. Besides, they have put too high a price on harmony; we can't afford to pay so much for admission. And therefore I hasten to return my ticket. And it is my duty, if only as an honest man, to return it as far ahead of time as possible. Which is what I am doing. It's not that I don't accept God, Alyosha, I just respectfully return him the ticket.[12]

The Joban epilogue does not contemplate such a response, although here again readers may wonder why not.

Instead God instructs Job to pray for his friends, which by all accounts, he does willingly. Two issues emerge. First, why should Job pray for the wrongdoings of Eliphaz, Bildad, and Zophar? The composite story assumes that he has no knowledge of either why he was afflicted or why he has been restored. He knows nothing of God's repudiation of his friends' counsel. He has no evident reason to pray for their forgiveness, apart from what we may assume is his unwavering commitment to be God's faithful "servant" (42:7, 8 [3 times]; cf.1:8, 2:3). What does he owe those who have abused him? Why should he pray for the forgiveness of those who condemn him in the name of God? Perhaps the lesson to be learned is that authentic fidelity to God should be disconnected from every expectation of divine blessing and reward. At least on first reading, this is the implicit connection between the satan's presenting question—"Does Job fear God for no reason (*ḥinnām*)?" (1:9)—and God's decision to explore the answer to the question by submitting Job to suffering "for no reason (*ḥinnām*)" (2:3). The fidelity that binds together God and human beings is, according to this reading, a tensive probing of the limits of divine capriciousness. The underlying and unaddressed question is this: if Job should refuse to pray for his friends, whose fidelity suffers the greater loss, Job's to God or God's to Job?

Second, what does it mean to be an authentic friend of Job?[13] Eliphaz, Bildad, and Zophar try to "comfort and console" (2:11) Job with theological maxims about God's inscrutable justice. They fail. As Job says, they "whitewash" the truth with lies (13:4). The epilogue accents instead the community of "brothers, sisters and friends" who offer the "consolation" and "comfort" Job's other erstwhile friends would not or could not provide. It records no exchange of words concerning "all the evil that the Lord has brought upon him" (42:11). It reports only that these friends share a meal together, an indication that they welcome Job's presence in the routines of everyday fellowship and that they contribute to his material needs with tangible gifts, a modest amount of money and a gold ring.[14] In sum they comfort Job with acts, not words, with communion, not theology. What has become of Job's quest for justice? The narrator leaves open the question, which appears now to be subsumed to the larger imperative of getting on with life—"eating, drinking, begetting, dying"[15]—a blessing that exceeds (and nullifies?) anything Job has experienced thus far.

Job's Children

Job's restoration includes the replacement of his dead children with seven new sons and three new daughters (42:13–16). The narrator names the daughters but not the sons: Jemimah ("dove"; cf. Sg 2:14); Keziah ("cinnamon"; cf. Ex 30:24, Ps 45:8); and Keren-happuch (presumably a reference to the black powder used to beautify the eyes; cf. 2 Kgs 9:30; Jer 4:30). It is unclear what we should make of these names or of the narrator's intention in singling out the daughters.[16] What is clear is that Job bequeaths to his children, specifically the named daughters, an inheritance (*naḥălâ* [42:15]) that requires the stewardship of sustaining the memory of his experiences with God—what God has given and what he has taken away—through four generations (42:16).

"You . . . did not comprehend the extent of your sleeping power"

What is the stewardship required of Job's children? The *Testament of Job,* arguably the first "commentary" on the book, recasts the biblical story as Job's last words of counsel and advice to his children. Before he dies he settles all his affairs with a full account of "the things which the Lord did with me and all the things which have happened to me" (*T. Job* 1:4). The *Testament's* epilogue reports that on his death, Job's new seven sons and three daughters, "accompanied by the poor and the orphans and all the helpless," delivered a eulogy—"Who then will not weep over the man of God?"—then laid him in his tomb, his legacy henceforth to be "renowned in all generations forever" (53:4, 8). Thus begins the stewardship of Job's story by his children.

I have commented on various aspects of this stewardship represented by second, third, fourth, and more readings and rereadings of Job's story. Here I conclude with specific attention to postbiblical Jewish contributions to lessons learned, imperatives considered, and responses that may be authentically faithful for those who believe Job's legacy is alive, not buried. Margaret Susman has argued that the history of the Jewish interpretation of Job is a "seismograph of nations."[17] Emil Fackenheim extends this insight by arguing that everyone in the post-Holocaust generation, Gentile or Jewish, is one of Job's children.[18]

Czar Alexander II was assassinated in 1881. His death, followed by the succession of his son Alexander III, marked a watershed for Russian Jews. Russian officials accused them of conspiring in the assassination and immediately launched a wave of pogroms throughout Russia and beyond. Violence, sustained by anti-Jewish regulations, severely limited their options. Of those who survived, many emigrated. Many turned inward, seeking identity, if not comfort, in biblical history—suffering is validation that God's chosen people had been chosen to suffer.[19] Others creatively explored the imperatives of Jewish themes and traditions in Yiddish literature, which not coincidentally begins to flower in the late nineteenth century.[20] Y. L. Perets (1852–1915) straddled the last two of these options. Unwilling to abandon the pietistic heritage of the Jewish Enlightenment (*Haskala*), Perets exploited Yiddish as a means of religious and social critique.

Perets published the Yiddish text of "Bontsye Shvayg" ("Bontsye the Silent") in 1893. A second edition, published in 1901, contains significant variants. Multiple English translations, including a television rendition and a 1953 Broadway play by Arnold Perl, confirm that a story Perets intended to be timely has proved to be "timeless."[21] Perets makes only one explicit reference to Job in "Bontsye the Silent," but Joban themes are implicit throughout the story.[22]

Bruce Zuckerman reads Bontsye as a "Super-Job."[23] From the day he was born, Bontsye suffers without complaint. Throughout his life he endures one calamity after another, unlike Job, never once raising his voice: he "lived silently and silently he died; like a shadow passing through our world."[24] His life of suffering silence reflects the human condition; it is nothing special, simply a given of life in the world God has created. He is but one "grey particle of sand on the seashore. . . . Mutely born, mutely lived, mutely died and more mutely buried" (183, 185). If his life and death creates no cause for notice on earth, it nevertheless makes a "great impression" (185) in heaven, where a heavenly council convenes to consider Bontsye's postmortem fate: "even God himself knew that Bontsye the Silent was coming!" (185). Father Abraham welcomes Bontsye with a warm-hearted greeting, "Peace be with you" (187). A Defending Angel makes the case for Bontsye's entry into God's presence. The Presiding Judge, God, prepares to render the final verdict.

> My child! . . . you have always suffered and kept silent! There is not a single member, not a single bone in your body without a wound, without a bloody welt, there is absolutely no secret place in your soul where it shouldn't be bleeding . . . and you always kept silent. . . .
>
> There, no one understood all this. Indeed, you, yourself, perhaps did not realize that you can cry out; and due to your cry, Jericho's wall can quake and tumble down! You, yourself did not comprehend the extent of your sleeping power. . . .
>
> In the other world your silence was not compensated, but this is the *Realm of Lies,* here in the *Realm of Truth* you will receive your compensation!
>
> On you the Supreme Assembly shall pass no judgment; on you it will make no ruling; for you it will neither divide nor apportion a share. Take whatever you want! *Everything* is yours! (193)

Bontsye's silence constitutes a moral lien against heaven that Bontsye himself does not understand. One cry for justice from him would require compensation greater than the Realm of Truth could pay. No doubt heaven breathes a sigh of relief when Bontsye speaks for the first time.

> Bontsye, for the first time, raises his eyes! He is just about blinded by the light on all sides; everything sparkles, everything flashes, beams shoot out from everything: from the walls, from the vessels, from the angles, from the judges! A kaleidoscope of suns!
>
> He drops his eyes wearily!
>
> "Are you sure? He asks, doubtful and shamefaced.
>
> "Absolutely!" the Presiding Judge affirms! "Absolutely, I tell you; for everything is yours; everything in Heaven belongs to you! Choose and take what you wish. You only take what belongs to you, *alone*!"
>
> "Are you sure?" asks Bontsye once more with growing confidence in his voice.
>
> "Definitely! Absolutely! Positively! They affirm to him on every side.
>
> "Gee, if you mean it," smiles Bontsye, "what I'd really like is, each and every morning, a hot roll with fresh butter!"
>
> Judges and angels lowered their heads in shame; the Prosecutor burst out laughing. (193, 195)

The ending of the story, like the ending of Job, is oblique. Is Bontsye's request the measure of a simpleton? Is he the ultimate schlemiel, a fool who can imagine nothing better than a hot buttered roll? If so perhaps the Prosecutor laughs because he realizes, with palpable relief, that Bontsye is not a saint with virtuous demands on heavenly justice; he is simply stupid. Is Bontsye's request a poignant testimony to what Jews suffered during the Russian pogroms, to the ravages of hunger that reduce human life to the cravings of the stomach? If so then Bontsye represents the ultimate victim, and what he has been denied, his basic rights as a human being, shames everyone—on earth and in heaven—who stood by in complicit silence.

Zuckerman makes a strong case for reading Perets's story as a parody of nineteenth-century Jewish piety.[25] It unmasks two absurdities.[26] First, it is absurd to believe that anyone could or should endure suffering like Bontsye's without crying out in pain and protest. Many Russian Jews did not acquiesce in silence to their persecutors, and it is they, not Bontsye, who model the virtue of resistance. Silence in the face of unjust suffering is silly, Perets may be saying, and the laugh is on everyone who thinks that patience is an adequate substitute for action. Second, it is absurd that when offered the world, Bontsye asks only for something for himself. What of the suffering of the "thousand million" (183) others who wait for someone to cry out on their behalf? If but one cry can bring down Jericho's walls, what might concerted protest do to collapse the powers of injustice? Perhaps the Prosecutor, the judge of the world, laughs to keep from crying,[27] because Bontsye's request makes the quest for justice—on earth and in heaven—no more important than a breakfast side dish.

However Perets may have intended his story to be read in the nineteenth century, its meaning cannot but be transformed in a post-Holocaust world. In the wake of 1945, "events have robbed Perets' story of its absurdities by turning them into realities, and in doing so, has changed what was originally meant as a parody into history before its time."[28] To read it as a parody would be a sacrilege.[29] "The force of history" demands a rereading and a reevaluation; Bontsye the "silent" must have a voice.[30] Zuckerman discusses multiple rereadings of "Bontsye the Silent." I single out two.

First Elie Wiesel, widely regarded as the most articulate spokesperson for the post-Holocaust generation, interprets Bontsye's silence as a "screaming silence, a shouting silence" that speaks more than words.[31] The most profound truth imposed by the Holocaust is that some suffering cannot be transmitted; it can only be experienced. "In 1945 I felt we cannot really communicate the experience, that all we can do is show the impossibility of communicating the experience—if you take these two facts together, you have a certain need for silence. But the silence is not against language; it is a remedy to language. It tries to purify it, tries to redeem it, to give it back its innocence, its weight."[32] Even a "screaming silence," however, as Wiesel goes on to say, as long as it remains merely metaphorical, is ultimately inadequate: "the generation that is mine could have shouted so loud that it would have shaken the world. Instead it whispered, content with its 'buttered roll.'"[33]

A second example is the Yiddish poet Eliezer Greenberg. His 1946 poem "Y. L. Perets and Bontsye Shvayg in the Warsaw Ghetto" imagines how Perets would have characterized Bontsye had he lived to see him sitting, Joblike, on a pile of ashes in what became of his adopted hometown, Warsaw. Greenberg suggests that Bontsye would have cried out not only to his literary creator, Perets, but also to God. Greenberg's Bontsye would not settle for the role of "the eternally silent one"; he would instead demand a new trial in which he, not the Defending Angel of the original story, argues the case for justice before the heavenly tribunal.

> I want, now, to cry out all the years of silence,
> I want you to give me a tongue, to give me a voice! . . .
>
> To be a witness to how the world kept silent, to how silent the Creator kept
> When our race was mowed down—with kith and kin—the poor just as the rich!
> O my creator, call once more the whole world to a Tribunal,
> But let me—the eternally silent one—be their Defender! . . .
>
> Let me open these eternally sealed lips,
> Which for a lifetime have been locked with silence!
> Let me throw open my heart, which has sobbed for a lifetime
> In silence—locked with a thousand locks.[34]

The case that Greenberg's Bontsye would argue is no longer defined by his own personal need for food; it is has now been enlarged by the imperative cries for justice of a generation murdered, a generation whose voices have been unsuccessfully silenced by unspeakable violence.

> His [Bontsye's] lamentation rises and turns into a wild howling,
> His voice now pounds like a wolf-and-dove roaring.
> Until the morning starts to burn with feverish madness—
> And Perets wails and Bontsye wails—and all is frozen still.[35]

"We won't allow your blood to be covered"

H. Leivick (1882–1962), perhaps the most revered of Yiddish poets, was born Leivick Halpern in Belarus and received a traditional Jewish education in czarist Russia. In 1905, at the age of twenty-three, he joined the Jewish underground and was subsequently arrested and sentenced to four years of forced labor and exile in Siberia. During exile he adopted Yiddish as the language of the people and began composing his first dramatic poems and plays. He escaped to the United States in 1913, where he spent the rest of his life.

As a "poet of conscience," Leivick merged the suffering he experienced during his prison years with traditional Jewish themes and symbols, sin and sacrifice, exile and redemption. In 1957, at the age of sixty-nine, he gave an address titled "The Jew—The Individual" to a conference of writers and intellectuals in Jerusalem. His speech connects the major themes he addressed in the body of his published work, twenty-one plays and ten volumes of poetry, with a traumatic childhood experience. When he was seven years old and walking to the *ḥeder* on the synagogue street, he forgot to take off his hat when he passed a Polish church. A Polish man immediately began to beat him with his fists. Leivick escaped and arrived, crying, at the school. The lesson for the day was the story about Abraham and the sacrifice of Isaac.

> The teacher began the lesson for the day, the verses about the sacrifice of Isaac. Isaac accompanies his father Abraham to Mount Moriah, and now Isaac lies bound upon the altar waiting to be slaughtered. Within me my heart weeps even harder. It weeps out of great pity for Isaac. And now Abraham raises the knife. My heart is nearly frozen with fear. Suddenly—the angel's voice: Abraham, do not raise your hand against your son; do not slay him. You have only been tested by God. And now I burst into tears. "Why are you crying now?" the teacher asked. "As you see, Isaac was not slaughtered." In my tears I replied, "But what would have happened had the angel *come one moment too late*?" The teacher tried to console me with the reassurance that an angel cannot be late. But the fear of coming too late stayed with me.[36]

He concludes by reflecting on his existence, his fate as a post-Holocaust Jew. "I have seen—we all have seen—six million Isaacs lying under knives, under axes, in fires, and in gas-chambers; and they were slaughtered. The angel of God did come too late. Six million slaughtered Isaacs are beyond my comprehension. But I can comprehend one Isaac waiting to be slaughtered and thereby living through the horrors of six million slaughtered, as though he were himself slaughtered six million times. . . . Have we not had enough of sacrificial altars? I ask, have we not had enough?[37]

Leivick's play *In the Days of Job* explores the connections between Isaac and Job. Through most of the play, Leivick basically follows the biblical script, but he splices the conventional dialogues between Job and his friends with an intense, surreal conversation between Job, Isaac, and the sheep offered for slaughter. This dramatic shift begins when Leivick's Job responds to Bildad by citing the words of Job 16:18.

> Let me ask you again:
> Do you really think you know
> Something I do not?
>
> What if I complain?
> My complaint is to God,
> To the almighty; to Him, and not to you.
> I have cried out, nor will I stop complaining.
> O earth. You shall not cover my blood.[38]

The first response comes from "outside" voices, voices Job's friends characterize as the "strange, wild cries" of an ugly mob of the "blind, the leprous, and the diseased" (ibid.).

> Voices: We won't allow your blood to be covered.
> We won't allow. We won't. . . .
>
> It carries everywhere
> It reaches us everywhere.
> Cry louder. Louder still.
> Nor stop your lamentation for an instant. (ibid.)

When Isaac appears on stage, he seems at first little different from Job's other friends. The conversation is casual and cordial, but as it unfolds Job becomes increasingly agitated. "Did you curse when you cried out?" Job asks. Before Isaac can respond, Job answers his own question: "You lay there like a sheep, with no outcry. Like a sheep. Go away . . . away. Out of my sight" (138, 139). Isaac explains that he went to the altar of sacrifice because he was obedient to the temptation God presented Abraham, a temptation, Isaac suggests, not unlike the test God has presented to Job. Job is not consoled; Isaac was tied by his father's hands, Job has been bound by the "hand of God Himself" (140), and he wants to know why. Why did Isaac not cry out with a lamentation that might have stopped the testing of a righteous man? A single cry of protest, Leivick suggests, might have changed the course of history. If Isaac had truly wanted to do something that would now comfort Job, then he would have cried out to God "with my [Job's] voice" (140).

Leivick gives the last words of the play to the sheep, Isaac's replacement sacrifice. It is the voice of the one placed on the altar, the one vulnerable to sacrifice. It is the voice of the one who provides the "first inkling" of the fate of six million Jews who would face the knife and be killed, because the sparing angel came too late.

> Take a good look. See how deeply
> My throat has been carved. Was not

Your father's knife your knife as well?
Or is the blood of a sheep not really blood?
Perhaps I am an incarnation of yourself,
A living prophecy regarding you;
The first inkling of the razor's edge
That must inevitably cut your throat . . .
If not now, then later . . . later.
What if the knife of Mount Moriah missed you?
Has not its sharpness revealed the slaughter
Being readied for you generations hence
By knives as long as the night? (144)

When the sheep exits, Leivick adds a final directorial note: "Abel appears in his place" (145). The ending evokes not only the memory of Job's words in Job 16:18—"O earth do not cover my blood; let my cry find resting place"—but also the generative testimony of Genesis 4:8–10. Murdered by Cain, Abel's blood cries out to God for justice. According to the Genesis account, God responds by punishing Cain for subverting his design for the moral order of creation. In the Genesis account, as in Job's evocation of its abiding legacy, God determines that Cain's violence and Abel's cry for restitution subject the world to the harshest judgment recorded in scripture (Gn 6:11–13), reinforced by God's unconditional promise that the shedding of innocent blood will "never again" (Gn 8 21–22) go without a reckoning from him (Gn 9:5–6).[39] Leivick's conclusion insists that Abel's blood and Job's cries still seek a response—from heaven or earth—that changes the destiny of those who are Job's children.

"We know his story for having lived it"

Because I have decided to focus on post-Holocaust readings and rereadings of Job, I have been from the outset of this chapter inching into sacred territory. I turn now to the writings of Elie Wiesel, which brings me, perhaps, as close to the inner sanctum of Jewish history as a Gentile may be permitted. Wiesel himself presses the caution that itches at my conscience as I try to enter into the world of Joban interpretation post-Auschwitz.

Accept the idea that you will never see what they have seen—and go on seeing now, that you will never know the faces that haunt their nights, that you will never hear the cries that rent their sleep. Accept the idea that you will never penetrate the cursed and spellbound universe they carry within themselves with unfailing loyalty.

And so I tell you: You who have not experienced their anguish, you who do not speak their language, you who do not mourn their dead, think before you offend them, before you betray them. Think before you substitute your memory for theirs.[40]

The caution may be reduced to a simple fact about those who dare to enter into the now fashionable discussion of Holocaust "literature": those who know do not speak; those who speak do not know.[41] Speaking "without knowledge" is what God accuses Job of doing (Job 38:2). Inasmuch as Job was, it seems, a Gentile himself, and given Wiesel's argument that Job is in some sense our "contemporary,"[42] I venture the following comments on Wiesel's reading of Job. At best I hope not to betray the memories that shape Job's children.

Wiesel says that after World War II he was "preoccupied with Job." "He [Job] could be seen on every road in Europe. Wounded, robbed, mutilated. Certainly not happy. Nor resigned" (233–34). The last phrase—"nor resigned"—is critical. Wiesel admires the story of Job's "passionate rebellion," but he is offended by the book's ending and its description of Job's resignation. "The fighter," he says, "has turned into a lamb. A sad metamorphosis" (233). Wiesel imagines and desires a different ending.

> Job's resignation as man was an insult to man. He should not have given in so easily. He should have continued to protest, to refuse the handouts. He should have said to God: Very well, I forgive You, I forgive You to the extent of my sorrow, my anguish. But what about my dead children, do they forgive You? What right have I to speak on their behalf? Do I have the moral, the human right to accept an ending, a solution to this story, in which they have played roles that You imposed on them, not because of them, but because of me? By accepting Your inequities, do I not become your accomplice? Now it is my turn to choose between You and my children, and I refuse to repudiate them. I demand that justice be done to them, if not to me, and that the trial continue. . . . Yes, that is what he should have said. Only he did not. He agreed to go back to living as before. Therein lay God's true victory: He forced Job to welcome happiness. After the catastrophe Job lived happily in spite of himself. (234)

Wiesel is neither a theologian nor a historian. He considers himself a storyteller. If we want to understand how and why he imagines such an ending to Job, how and why such an ending embodies his own story, then we must look to the tales he tells, particularly in the series of six novels he published between 1958 and 1968.[43] Each book, as Wiesel says, is a "kind of testimony of one witness speaking of his own life, his own death."[44] Each book explores the options for speaking after Wiesel decided to break his ten-year vow of silence following his liberation from Buchenwald. The first, probably the most widely read book in all of Holocaust literature, appeared in Yiddish in 1956 with the title *Un di Velt Hot*

Geshvign (*And the World Remained Silent*); a significantly abridged version appeared in French in 1958 under a new title, *La Nuit,* and in English in 1960 as *Night.* A well-known passage marks the beginning of Wiesel's journey.

> Never shall I forget that night, the first night in camp, which turned my life into one long night, seven times cursed and seven times sealed. Never shall I forget that smoke. Never shall I forget the little faces of the children, whose bodies I saw turned into wreathes of smoke beneath a silent blue sky.
>
> Never shall I forget those flames which consumed my faith forever.
>
> Never shall I forget that nocturnal silence which deprived me for all eternity, of the desire to live. Never shall I forget those moments which murdered my God and my soul and turned my dreams to dust. Never shall I forget these things, even if I am condemned to live as long as God Himself. Never. (*Night,* 44)

The words are searing—"flames which consumed my faith forever"; "silence which deprived me . . . of the desire to live"; "moments which murdered my God and my soul." They can be read, but they do not yield to commentary, except perhaps to Wiesel's own. In reflecting on his work some twenty years later, he said *Night* is the "center" for everything else he would write.[45] Each of his subsequent stories circles around the same question: "Where is God now?" (*Night,* 76). In *Night* Wiesel takes the perspective of the victim whose faith in God has been consumed by the inexplicable deaths of the innocent. How should one respond when human barbarity murders the soul, dreams for the future, and the will to live, and God is silent? Wiesel's first probe for an answer is to pray, in spite of himself, "to that God in whom I no longer believed" (*Night,* 104), yet as the conclusion of the book indicates, he wonders if this response is adequate.

> I looked at myself in the mirror. A skeleton stared back at me.
>
> Nothing but skin and bone.
>
> It was the image of myself after death. It was at that instant that the will to live awakened within me.
>
> Without knowing why, I raised my fist and shattered the glass, along with the image it held. . . .
>
> But . . .
>
> Ten years after Buchenwald, I ask myself the question, Was I right to break that mirror?[46]

The subsequent novels explore other options. "In *Dawn* I explore the political action; in *The Accident,* suicide; in *The Town beyond the Wall,* madness; in *The Gates of the Forest,* faith and friendship; in *A Beggar in Jerusalem,* the return."[47] Others have analyzed these mileposts in Wiesel's journey; I need not replicate their assessments.[48] For my purposes here, I single out *A Beggar in Jerusalem,* a story of a "return" to Jerusalem.

The narrator of the story is David, a Holocaust survivor, who has made his way to Jerusalem during the Six-Day War. His alter ego, Katriel, tells him a parable about a man who leaves home in search of a city that promises adventure and fulfillment. By the time he arrives in Jerusalem and joins the Jewish forces that are trying to regain the city, the parable has begun to gnaw at David. It reminds him of a beggar who once told him that the "day someone tells you your life" (*Beggar in Jerusalem,* 159) marks the day when you have not much longer to live. As he stands before the ancient wall of the Temple, David imagines all those who stood there before him, "kings, prophets, warriors and priests, poets and philosophers, rich and poor" (239). He realizes for the first time in his life that the dead have a living presence in Jerusalem, that despite history's evils, remembering, fighting for life can be an ally, not an enemy, in the hope to survive. As Wiesel says in his memoirs, survivors are like the parchments of the Holy Book: "So long as they exist, so long as some of them are alive, the others know—even if they do not always admit it—that they cannot trespass certain boundaries."[49]

At the end of *A Beggar in Jerusalem,* David says that "a page has been turned. The beasts in the heart of man have stopped howling, they have stopped bleeding. The curse has been revoked in this place, and its reign terminated" (252). Jerusalem has been saved, not only because its army won the Six-Day War but also and more important because "Israel . . . could deploy six million more names in battle" (244). David realizes that Jerusalem's victory "does not prevent suffering from having existed, nor death from having taken its toll" (254). Nothing can change the facts of history, but a new vision may keep the future open. "What is important," David says, "is to continue," even when there remain more questions than answers. "The mystery of good is no less disturbing than the mystery of evil. But one does not cancel out the other. Man alone is capable of uniting them by remembering" (254).

Wiesel, like David, may have turned a page when he wrote *A Beggar in Jerusalem.* His personal journey had taken him from his hometown in Sighet to Buchenwald to Jerusalem. From a death camp, where flames consumed his faith in God's justice (*Night,* 56), Wiesel comes to the City of Peace, where David places a note, addressed to the living dead, in the Wall in the Old City. He asks them "to take pity on a world which has betrayed and rejected them." They are powerful enough to do whatever they want. They may "Punish. Or even forgive" (*Beggar in Jerusalem,* 252).[50] And yet. And yet. The words Wiesel gives to David at the close of the book are thick with nuance. The mysteries of good and evil may not cancel out each other, but can they ever be united in an affirmation of God's justice? David suggests that "man alone" is capable of attending to these mysteries, through the act of faithful remembering. If the capacity belongs to man *alone,* then how does Wiesel answer the presenting and still lingering question in *Night:* "Where is God now?"

The question, as Wiesel concedes, stands at the center of everything he has written. He may have turned a page with the publication of *A Beggar in Jerusalem,* but he has spent a lifetime pondering what can be said about God after Auschwitz. Wiesel chooses, ultimately, not to speak *about* God; this is the task of theologians. Instead he takes his cue from the Talmudic account of God's gift of the Ten Commandments.

> On the morning of the day when all Israel was to have gathered at the foot of the mountain, some men were still asleep in their tents. And so God first manifested Himself with thunder and lightning in order to shake, to awaken those who were foolish enough to sleep while time and the heart of mankind opened to receive the call of *Him who lends mystery to all things.* Then, abruptly, there was a silence. And in this silence a Voice was heard. God spoke. What did he speak of? His secret work, His eternally imperceptible intentions? No, He spoke of man's relationship to man, of one's individual duties toward others. At this unique moment God wished to deal with human relations rather than theology.[51]

For Wiesel how we treat human beings is more important than how we theologize about God. As he puts it, "Whoever betrays humanity, whoever torments one's fellow man, denies the existence of God."[52]

Wiesel insists on addressing God, not speaking about God. In this commitment he is compelled to articulate what he calls "the agony of the believer."[53] A selection of Wiesel's comments explicates his journey.

> The Jew in my view may rise against God provided he remains within God. One can be a very good Jew, observe all *mitzvot,* study Talmud, and yet be against God . . . as if to say: You, God, do not want me to be Jewish? Well, Jewish we shall be nevertheless, despite Your will.[54]

> From inside his community [the Jew] may say anything. Let him step outside it, and he will be denied this right. The revolt of the believer is not that of the renegade; the two do not speak in the name of the same anguish.[55]

> I prefer to blaspheme in God than far from him. (*The Town beyond the Wall,* 176)

> I don't believe in art for art's sake. For me literature must have an ethical dimension. The aim of literature I call testimony is to disturb. I disturb the believer because I dare to put questions to God, the source of all faith. I disturb the miscreant because, despite my doubts and questions, I refuse to break with the religious and mystical universe that has shaped my own. Most of all, I disturb those who are

comfortably settled within a system—be it political, psychological, or theological. If I have learned anything in my life, it is to distrust intellectual comfort.[56]

How then does the Jew who revolts against God address God? One of Wiesel's own prayers provides a touchstone for reflection.

I no longer ask You for either happiness or paradise; all I ask of You is to listen and let me be aware of Your listening.

I no longer ask You to resolve my questions, only to receive them and make them part of You.

I no longer ask You for either rest or wisdom, I only ask You not close me to gratitude, be it of the most trivial kind, or to surprise and friendship. Love? Love is not Yours to give.

As for my enemies, I do not ask you to punish them or even to enlighten them; I only ask You not to lend them Your mask and Your powers. If You must relinquish one or the other, give them Your Powers. But not Your countenance.[57]

I conclude this summary of Wiesel's works by returning to his reflections in "Job: Our Contemporary." As noted above Wiesel admires Job's resistance but is offended by his supposed submission as recorded in the epilogue. His first inclination is to wonder if the book's original ending has been lost in transmission. If we had this supposed ending, surely it would confirm that Job did not humiliate himself by repenting, that he died in grief uncompromised by his fidelity to his protest about God's injustice. Since this original ending seems to have been lost, Wiesel imagines its reconstruction. If the reconstruction is unconvincing, then the only recourse is to salvage the biblical ending by reinterpreting it: "In spite or because of appearances, Job continued to interrogate God. By repenting sins he did not commit, by justifying a sorrow he did not deserve, he communicates to us that he did not believe in his own confessions; they were nothing but decoys. Job personified man's eternal quest for justice and truth—he did not choose resignation. Thus he did not suffer in vain; thanks to him we know that it is given to man to transform divine injustice into human justice and compassion" (235).

In what sense then, according to Wiesel, is Job our contemporary? The concluding words of Wiesel's essay on Job are these. "Once upon a time, in a faraway land there lived a legendary man, a just and generous man who, in his solitude and despair found the courage to stand up to God. And to force Him to look at his creation. And to speak to those men who sometimes succeed, in spite of Him and of themselves, in achieving triumphs over Him, triumphs that are grave and disquieting. What remains of Job? A fable? A shadow? Not even the shadow of a shadow. An example, perhaps" (235).

What exactly is the difference between a fable, a shadow, a shadow of a shadow, and an example? We may speculate, but Wiesel suggests that the only ones who can provide definition are Job's children. If, as Wiesel says, Jews are summoned to "celebrate the memory of silence, but to reject the silence of memory,"[58] then breaking silence, even if in protest against God, is the equivalent of obedience to a divine commandment

"Have you considered my servant Job?"

The question that launches Job's story is posed at the outset by God to the satan: "Have you considered my servant Job?" (1:8, 2:3). From a literary standpoint, we may assume that God knows Job's story already. The narrator has sketched its basic outline (1:1–5), and God twice affirms that the basics are correct (1:7–9, 2:3). The satan suggests the basics merit reconsideration; God agrees. Thus begins, at God's invitation, the stewardship of reading and rereading, evaluating and reevaluating the story of "the greatest of all the people of the east" (1:3).

Questions, and the answers they solicit, provide the foundation for conversation that enlarges understanding, even when, perhaps especially when, there is disagreement and debate. The mere existence of the book of Job confirms that the conversation continues. The narrator's prose account is in dialogue with the poetic center of the book. Elihu engages the readings of Eliphaz, Bildad, and Zophar. Job conforms to the words the narrator gives him, then speaks his own very different words to the three friends and to God. God retreats in silence, then reappears with words so forceful that they presumably silence everyone who has spoken thus far. However we may judge the book's compositional history and the canonical process that resulted in the forty-two chapters we now read, we may sure that the "culture of exegesis" it has generated continues long past the "finalization" of the story.

LXX translators add to the prose and nuance the meanings of the poetic dialogues. The *Testament of Job* recasts the story by accenting certain aspects and omitting others. The church fathers, following Gregory's lead, adopted a Christological approach, and medieval Jewish commentators such as Saadiah Gaon and Maimonides, who debated "conservative" and "liberal" interpretations of God's providence, did much the same, for different reasons. Artists, beginning at least in the Greco-Roman period, painted and sculpted their own interpretations of Job. Novelists, playwrights, poets, and musicians—Jews, Christians, Muslims, and secular, from virtually all points on the globe—have added their own distinctive readings. "Have you considered my servant Job?" The first answer to this question, as this book has tried to demonstrate, is "Yes, we have."

Will there ever be an end to the reading of Job? Is it possible to conceive a time in the future when there will be no Jobs in this world, when the imperative to think deeply about innocent suffering will be nullified, either by answers that are so persuasive they silence all complaint or by the universal acknowledgment that justice has eradicated the problem once and for all? All readers of Job's story may hope for such a time. In the fraught interim between now and then, we continue to read and think, to assess and reassess the imperative that comes with responding to the initiating question, "Have you considered my servant Job?" If you have, what can you contribute to the ending of his story that enlarges and enriches it?

The Joban epilogue returns readers to the prologue. In doing so it extends God's presenting question with another. Once we have immersed ourselves in the story of one who, by God's admission, has suffered his reported losses "for no reason," can we ever go back to the beginning and start over again? Job's story begins in Uz, a literary metaphor for Eden, where the "very good" world of God's creation is pristine, seemingly free of any evil that may corrupt or destroy it. His story ends somewhere "east of Eden," to appropriate John Steinbeck's phrase, with the report that he returns to his origins and begins life anew. Perhaps, in the aftermath of Joban-type losses, we can and should build a new life, with the hope and promise that it will ultimately end "old and full of days" (Job 42:17).

The objective in this last chapter, which addresses how we read Job in a post-Holocaust world, is to raise the question whether, east of Eden, we can ever go home again. Our entrance into the "very good" world of God's hopes and expectations is forever barred by the flaming cherubim that God inscrutably places between us and the tree of life (Gn 3:24). In the meantime we read Job's story, and it reads us.

NOTES

Introduction

1. Scripts and videos of episodes of *House, M.D.* can be accessed at http://www .fox.com/house.
2. Wiesel, "Job: Our Contemporary," 211.
3. Lamartine, *Cours familier de littérature*, 2:441, cited in Glatzer, "Introduction," 42.
4. Ibid., cited in Glatzer, "Introduction," 43.
5. MacLeish, *J.B.*, 4. Subsequent citations are given parenthetically in the text.
6. Ibid., 44, 45, 75, 91, 136; cf.135 ("He [J.B.] misconceived the part entirely").
7. See, for example, Levenson, *Book of Job*, 40–54.
8. Besserman, *Legend of Job*, 114.
9. Ibid.
10. Alter, *Canon and Creativity*, 11, 15, 49.
11. Ibid., 16, 77.
12. Levenson, *Book of Job*, 45.
13. Thomas, "To Err Is Human," 561.

Prologue

1. See Spiegel, "Noah, Danel, and Job," 305–55; Sarna, "Epic Substratum," 25. For a recent discussion of intertextual connections, see Joyce, "Even if Noah."
2. Some have speculated that Elihu's Hebrew name indicates that he is not only a character but also the author of these speeches. As Newsom says, Elihu is a "disgruntled reader who quite literally wrote himself into the book" ("Book of Job," 322).
3. Clines regards this phrase in 32:1 ("these three men ceased to answer Job") as evidence that the Elihu speeches, displaced in the final form of the book to their present location, originally stood after Zophar's last speech, that is, after Job 27. Clines, *Job 21–37*, 2:711.
4. F. I. Anderson, *Job*, 50.
5. The presence of the Elihu speeches in the Job manuscripts at Qumran confirms that they had been added at least by the first century B.C.E. A strong case has been made for dating the speeches to the late Persian or early Hellenistic period: Mende, *Durch Leiden zur Vollendung*; Wahl, *Gerechte Schöpfer*.; Müllner, "Literarische Diachronie. The connection with Daniel 4–6, first noted by Duhm (*Buch Hiob*, 159),

continues to draw support from those who see connections between Job and protoapo-calyptic literature. See, for example, T. J. Johnson, *Now My Eyes See You.*

6. See, for example, Mies, "Genre littéraire"; Witte, "Literarische Gattung.

7. For what follows see Newsom, *Book of Job,* esp. 32–89.

8. Ibid., 24.

9. Ibid., 45.

10. Ibid., 45, 47.

11. Tennyson, "In Memoriam A. H. H.," section 96, lines 11–12, p. 171.

12. Sawyer, "Reception History," 12. Sawyer provides a helpful overview, with bibliography, of reception history's emergence as a form of literary studies. His con-tribution provides a methodological apologia for the Blackwell Bible Commentary Series, which adopts the reception history approach. See also Sawyer, "Job." C. L. Seow prefers the term "history of consequences," which includes not only the history of interpretation of the Bible but also its impact and effects. Note especially his overview of the consequences of Job among Jews, Christians, and Muslims ("Reflections on the History of Consequences").

13. Alter, *Canon and Creativity,* 18, 16, 48.

14. Steiner, *Grammars of Creation,* 3.

15. Ibid., 50.

16. Ibid., 158.

17. Ibid., 174.

18. Ibid., 189.

19. Ibid., 257, 281.

20. Ibid., 287.

Chapter 1: The Job(s) of the Didactic Tale

1. Words thematically related to Job's "patience" or more often his "impatience" do appear in the poetic dialogues (e.g., 6:11, 13:15, 14:14, 30:26, all with the Hebrew word *yāḥal,* "wait, hope"; cf. 21:4, with *qāṣar* + *rûaḥ,* "short of breath/spirit" [NRSV: "impatient"]). For discussion of the idiomatic use of *qāṣar* + *rûaḥ/nepeš* as "impa-tience," see Haak, "Interpretation of *qṣr npš.*" For a discussion of Job's "impatience" in the dialogues in comparison to the "patience of Job" commended in James 5:11, see Janzen, *Job,* 157–60. The primary Greek word for patience or endurance, *hypomonē,* which occurs in James 5:11, occurs frequently and with a range of meanings in Job LXX (3:9; 6:11; 7:3; 8:15; 9:4; 14:14, 19; 17:13; 20:26; 22:21; 32:4, 16; 33:5; 41:3), but this word does not appear in the didactic tale.

2. On the narration of Job as a "spectacle" and the "objectified watching" that the didactic tale invites, see Newsom, *Book of Job,* 68–70.

3. For an overview of the compositional issues concerning the didactic tale and the poetic dialogues, see the prologue.

4. There have been surprisingly few studies dedicated to the origin and trajectory of the "patience of Job" theme. The studies by Fine ("Tradition of a Patient Job") and

Ginsberg ("Job the Patient") are often referenced, but both are more concerned to assess the literary distinctions between the prose narrative and the dialogues than to explore the origins and development of the theme in the Bible and beyond. Some studies examine the connections between the patience of Job as exemplified in Job 1–2 and the *T. Job* and the appropriation of this theme in the Letter of James; e.g., Seitz, "Patience of Job"; Garrett, "Patience of Job"; P. Gray, "Points and Lines"; Young, "Patience of Job."

5. Baskin, *Pharaoh's Counsellors*, 26. For rabbinic commentary on the book of Job, see also H. Kaufmann, *Anwendung des Buches Hiob*; Wiernikowski, *Buch Hiob*; Glatzer, "Book of Job"; Glatzer, "Introduction," 16–24.

6. Baskin, *Pharaoh's Counsellors*, 17. Job is frequently compared unfavorably with Abraham. For further discussion of the comparison, see Buchler, *Studies in Sin*, 130–50.

7. See the discussion in Urbach, *Sages*: 1:407–15.

8. Baskin, *Pharaoh's Counsellors*, 9.

9. Ibid., 22.

10. The LXX is approximately 20 percent shorter than the Masoretic text. The "abridgments" occur in five passages: Job 26, shortened from 27 to 11 stichoi; Job 28, shortened and rearranged; Job 31:1–4, omitted; Job 32–37, shortened from 334 to 218 stichoi; Job 40:1–2, omitted. See Witte, "Greek Book of Job," 46–48.

11. See, for example, G. B. Gray, "Additions"; Gentry, *Asterisked Materials*; Witte, "Greek Book of Job."

12. Unless otherwise noted, the LXX translation follows C. E. Cox, "Iob."

13. Baskin, *Pharaoh's Counsellors*, 29.

14. Reed, "Job as Jobab."

15. All translations are from Spittler, *"Testament of Job."* Quotations of the Greek text are from Brock, *Testamentum Iobi*.

16. Haas, "Job's Perseverance."

17. Ibid., 118. The generalized use of *hypomonē* is present in *T. Job* 1:5 and 26:4.

18. All English translations are from NRSV. For the Greek text, see Rahlfs, "Machabaeorum IV."

19. For similar uses of *hypomonē* in 4 Maccabees, see 7:22; 9:6, 8, 22, 30; 16:17, 19, 21; 17:11, 17, 23. For comparable uses of *hypomonē* in other Hellenistic Jewish literature, see, for example, *T. Jos.* 2:7, 17:2; Wis 2:17–20, 16:22; Sir 2:22, 22:18. See also Hauck, "*hypomenō, hypomonē*."

20. For other examples of *hypomonē* in the New Testament and early Christian literature, see Hauck, "*hypomenō, hypomonē*"; Spanneut, "Geduld"; Schrey, "Geduld."

21. Translation from Agourides, "Apocalypse of Sedrach."

22. Cook, "Joseph and Aseneth."

23. In some instances Philo uses *karteria* to describe the virtue of "self-control" or "self-mastery" that the wise call upon to overcome unruly passions (e.g., *Deus* 13; *Agriculture* 97, 105, 152; *De Somniis* 1:120; cf. *De vita Moysis* 1:25).

24. Maccabees, in contrast to 2 Maccabees, which clearly attests a belief in resurrection (e.g., 2 Macc 7:9, 11, 14, 22–23—all passages that 4 Maccabees omits), describes

the reward more in terms of the Hellenistic idea of the immortality of the soul than the Jewish idea of the resurrection of the body. See also Anderson, "4 Maccabees," 539.

25. Cf. Haas, "Job's Perseverance," 134.

26. In the latter half of the *Testament* (chaps. 28–53), *makrothymia* is the only word used for patience.

27. Haas, "Job's Perseverance," 134.

28. See especially P. Gray, "Points and Lines," 415–20.

29. Ibid., 407.

30. Zuckerman (*Job the Silent*, 14) notes that the author of James states that "you have *heard* of the patience of Job" (Jas 5:11; emphasis added). Zuckerman makes the point that this is not the same thing as saying "you have read [in the Bible] of the patience of Job." More likely the author is saying that his readers, whatever they may have read in the book of Job, know of Job's reputation for patience from what they have heard about in the traditions. The only extant composition available to James and his readers that consistently attests Job's patience is the *T. Job.*

31. P. Gray, "Points and Lines," 412–15.

32. L. T. Johnson, "Letter of James," 211–12.

33. P. Gray, "Points and Lines," 420.

34. Ibid., 423.

35. Gordon, "KAI TO TELOS KYRIOU EIDETE (Jas. 5 v.11)."

36. Tertullian, *Of Patience* 14 (*ANF* 3:716).

37. Duensing and de Santos Otero, "Apocalypse of Paul," 728.

38. Origen, "Selecta in Job," in Migne, *Patrologiae graeca*, 12:1033; cf. *Enarrationes in Job*, in Migne, *Patrologiae graeca*, 17:64, where Origen describes Job as "a noble soldier, who knows how to fight in the night . . . and in all kinds of fighting to overcome his adversaries and finally to win." For the English translation, see Lewalski, *Milton's Brief Epic*, 22, 25.

39. Chrysostom, "Fragmenta in Beatum Job," in Migne, *Patrologiae graeca*, 64:521, 525. For the English translation, see Lewalski, *Milton's Brief Epic*, 22. For additional examples of the martial idiom in sources from the Middle Ages to the Renaissance, see Lewalski, *Milton's Brief Epic*, 22–26, and Astell, *Job, Boethius, and Epic Truth*, 70–96.

40. Astell, *Job, Boethius, and Epic Truth*, 84. Astell cites Cassiodorus's (480–475) interpretation of Psalm 37, in which he understands the speaker of the psalm, David, to be playing the role of Job. Thus David, who, like Job, triumphs over his misfortune, becomes the archetype of the "unconquered soldier of Christ." For the text see Cassiodorus, *Exposito Psalmorum*, 343.

41. For the textual difficulties and interpretive issues of this text, see Balentine, *Job*, 296–301.

42. Jerome, *Liber Contra Joannem Hierosolymitana* 30, in Migne, *Patrologiae latina* 23, cols. 381–82.

43. Prudentius, *Psychomachia*, 291.

44. Ibid.

45. Prudentius, *Psychomachia*, 280. See Besserman, *Legend of Job*, fig. 17, 132.

46. Prudentius, *Psychomachia*, 281. See Besserman, *Legend of Job*, fig.18, 133.

47. Astell, *Job, Boethius, and Epic Truth*, 79.

48. Translations from Gregory the Great, *Morals on the Book of Job*, vols. 1–2.

49. Besserman, *Legend of Job*, 55. On Job's characterization as a wrestler, warrior, athlete, *miles Christi*, see Datz, *Gestalt Hiobs*, 135–37, 150–53. On the warrior saint imagery in early Christian exegesis, see Lewalski, *Milton's Brief Epic*, 22–26; Wang, *'Miles Christinus' im 16. und 17. Jahrhundert*, 140–44. On Gregory's Christological approach to Job, see Hester, *Eschatology and Pain*.

50. Astell, *Job, Boethius, and Epic Truth*, 97.

51. Ibid., 159–84.

52. Ibid., 163.

53. Ibid., 165. On Saint Martin see Skeat, *Aelfric's Lives of the Saints*, vol. 2.

54. The legends of Saint Sebastian are recounted in several sources: *Vita B. Agnetis et Acta Sancti Sebastiani*, Codice Laurenziano, 89, supp. 74, 52–53; Tillemont, *Mémoires pour servir à l'Histoire Ecclésiatique*, 4:515–36; Migne, *Patrologia latina* 17, cols. 657ff. My discussion here follows Zupnick, "Saint Sebastian."

55. For discussion of various images of Saint Sebastian and how they change over time, see Zupnick, "Saint Sebastian," figs. 1–22.

56. See, for example, Michelangelo's depiction of Sebastian holding up a cross in the *Last Judgment*; Zupnick, "Saint Sebastian," 246, 256, fig. 15.

57. For the image and further discussion of its complex relationship to Job, see Terrien, *Iconography of Job*, 132–35 and fig. 72. See also Terrien's discussion of Bellini's *Sacra Allegra* (*Iconography of Job*, 128–32 and fig. 71).

58. Bellini's altarpiece, *Pala di S. Giobbe*, now located at the Accademia in Venice, was originally painted for the altar in the Church of San Giobbe, which was part of the San Giobbe hospital in Venice. Bellini's depiction of Job alongside Saint Francis may have been inspired by the fourteenth-century tympanum by Pietro Lombardo that stands over the main entrance. Lombardo shows two figures kneeling in prayer. On the left Saint Francis, wiring the traditional garment of the Franciscan monks, holds a cross with a stigmata-marked hand; on the right Saint Job (San Giobbe), naked except for the cloak that wraps around his waist, clasps his hands together in prayer (the posture is very similar to Bellini's). Both saints direct their gaze toward the rays of sunshine that extend from heaven. For the visual and further discussion, see Balentine, *Job*, 352; Balentine, "Church of Saint Job."

59. Astell, *Job, Boethius, and Epic Truth*, 169.

60. Ibid., 166. The accompanying citation from Bernard ("a new sort of chivalry has appeared on earth"), cited by Astell (167) is from "In Praise of the New Chivalry," 289.

61. Ibid., 167; "In Praise of the New Chivalry," 289.

62. Ibid., 168.

63. Sommerfeldt, "Bernard of Clairvaux."

64. Astell, *Job, Boethius, and Epic Truth*, 171, citing Lull, *Book of the Ordre of Chyvalry*, 76–77.

65. Kennedy, *Knighthood in the Morte Darthur*, 13.

66. Bolgar, "Hero or Anti-Hero?" 123.

67. Ibid., 124, citing A. Pauphilet, ed., *La Queste de Saint Graal* (Paris, 1923), 230, 296.

68. Pauphilet, *Quest of the Holy Grail*, 85.

69. Ibid., 141–42.

70. Ibid., 143.

71. Ibid., 172.

72. Astell, *Job, Boethius, and Epic Truth*, 172.

73. Beecher, "Spenser's Redcrosse Knight," 103.

74. Spenser, *Faerie Queene*, 1.1.1. Parenthetical citations are from this variorum edition edited by F. M. Padelford.

75. Astell, *Job, Boethius, and Epic Truth*, 161.

76. Ibid., 183.

77. Hopkins, *Sinful Knights*; cf. Pearsall, "Middle English Romance."

78. Besserman, *Legend of Job*, 107–11.

79. Eccles, *Castle of Perseverance*, in *Macro Plays*, lines 14–17, 275–91.

80. Eccles, *Mankind*, in *Macro Plays*, lines 229, 286, 288.

81. Ibid., line 321.

82. Lewalski, *Milton's Brief Epic*, 18; Astell, *Job, Boethius, and Epic Truth*, 180.

83. Beecher, "Spenser's Redcrosse Knight," 113–16.

84. Burton, *Anatomy of Melancholy*, 937.

85. Ibid., 937–38.

86. Ibid., 938.

87. Ibid., 965–66.

88. Ibid., 966.

89. Ibid., 938.

90. Astell, *Job, Boethius, and Epic Truth*, 185.

91. Ibid., 184.

92. Lannois, "Job, sa femme et les musiciens"; Denis, "Saint Job"; Vötterle, "Hiob als Schutzpatron der Musiker"; Meyer, "Patron of Music."

93. The tradition goes back at least to biblical times, when David is reported to have used a lyre to bring relief to Saul (1 Sm 16:23; cf. 11QPs, which reports that David composed four psalms "for making music over the stricken"); J. A. Sanders, *Dead Sea Psalms Scroll*, 136–37). Plato (*Republic* 3.3) and Aristotle (*Politics* 8.7) acknowledge that different harmonies of music create different passions in people. In the late medieval period, the most celebrated encyclopedia, *De proprietatibus rerum* (thirteenth century) by Bartholomaeus Anglicus, identifies music as an agent in restoring the sick to health; see Long, *On the Properties of Soul and Body;* Seymour, *Bartholomaeus Anglicus.* For a

general overview of these matters, especially as they bear on the iconography of Job, see Cuttler, "Job-Music-Christ."

94. MacCracken, "Lydgatiana I," 368, lines 120–24.

95. For discussion of these aspects of the play, see Besserman, *Legend of Job*, 103–7; Meyer, "Patron of Music," 24.

96. Besserman, *Legend of Job*, 106.

97. Denis, "Saint Job," 272 and plate 9, 271.

98. *Job and the Musicians*, illumination, fourteenth century. Cantena sur Job 21:12 (LXX), Gr. 1231, fol. 285, Bibliothèque Nationale, Paris.

99. Jean Fouquet, *Job and His Three Comforters*, illumination, c.1459–60. *The Hours of Étienne Chevalier*, MS fr.71. fol. 26, Musée Condé, Chantilly, France. For discussion see Denis, "Saint Job," 274–75, plate 11; Meyer, "Patron of Music," 28–29.

100. *Job on the Dunghill and Three Musicians*, illumination, MS fr. 1226, fol. 40, Bibliothèque Nationale, Paris. For discussion see Cuttler, "Job-Music-Christ," 88; Meyer, "Patron of Music," 29, fig.10; Denis, "Saint Job," 272–73, plate 10. See also the *Job Altarpiece* attributed to the Master of Saint Barbara (discussed in the prologue), which depicts Job paying three minstrels for their music. For other artistic representations of Job paying the musicians, see the several examples discussed in Lannois, "Job, sa femme et les musiciens"; Denis, "Saint Job, patron des musiciens"; and Meyer, "Patron of Music," 29–30.

101. Minnen, "Culte de Saint Job." See also Minnen's essay "Den Heyligen Sant al in Brabant." I am grateful to be able to draw upon personal correspondence with Minnen over several years and to have been able to review an advance copy of this essay.

102. Réau, "Héros et Héroïnes," 312.

103. For example the Saint Job Hospital in Utrecht, Holland; Réau, "Héros et Héroïnes," 312.

104. For discussion of the history of the church and its patrons, see Arcangeli, "Sapienza nel silenzio."

105. For discussion of the details of the painting, see Hornik, "Venetian Images."

106. Ibid., 545.

107. Hartt, "Carpaccio's Meditation," 28.

108. Lauts, *Carpaccio*, 13.

109. C. Phillips, "Unrecognized Carpaccio," 145–46; Hartt, "Carpaccio's Meditation," 27.

110. Hartt, "Carpaccio's Meditation," 27. For the text see "Job dolens interpretatur. Typum Christi ferebat," in Migne, *Patrologiae latina* 23, col. 1475.

111. Dijon, *Bibliothèque communale*, MS 14, v. 3, fol. 13v.

112. Hartt, "Carpaccio's Meditation," 29–30.

113. Ibid., 28; cf. Terrien, *Iconography of Job*, 137; Hornik, "Venetian Images," 553–56.

114. Osten, "Job and Christ," 155.

115. Ibid., 156.

116. For a possible hermeneutical connection between this painting, the epilogue of Job 42:7–17, and Luke 24, see Balentine, *Job*, 718–21; and Balentine, "Who Will Be Job's Redeemer?" 277–83.

117. Hartt, "Carpaccio's Meditation," 32.

118. Lauts, *Carpaccio*, 13; cf. Hornik, "Venetian Images," 555.

119. Bolgar, "Hero or Anti-Hero?" 120.

120. For this summary of the "epic truth" about the nature of humankind that defines the heroic poetry of the ancients, see Astell, *Job, Boethius, and Epic Truth*, 6–20.

121. E.g., John Chrysostom, "Fragmenta in beatum Job," in Migne, *Patrologiae graeca*, 64, c511; Gregory, *Moralia*, 1.11.15.

Chapter 2: God and (the) Satan

1. Cf. P. Day, *Adversary in Heaven*, 76.

2. For discussion of the exegetical issues and their theological ramifications, see Balentine, "For No Reason"; Balentine, *Job*, 58–60; Balentine, "Traumatizing Job."

3. Various references to heavenly beings occur in the dialogues between Job and his friends (4:18, 5:1, 15:15, 16:19, 33:23–28). None are explicitly identified with the satan of chapters 1–2, and in no case is there a conversation between God and these heavenly beings.

4. M. Pope, *El in the Ugaritic Texts*; Handy, *Among the Host of Heaven*; Mullen, *Assembly of the Gods*; Mullen, "Divine Assembly" (1992); Mullen, "Divine Assembly" (2006–9); W. H. Schmidt, *Königtum Gottes*; M. S. Smith, *Origins of Biblical Monotheism*.

5. E.g., Ps 82:1 [MT 82:2], "council of El"; Ps 82:6, "sons of the Most High/Elyon"; Ps 89:7 [MT 89:8], "council of the holy ones." Perhaps the clearest pictures of the divine council are in 1 Kings 22:19–22, which describes God "sitting on a throne" with royal-like attendants to the right and left, and Daniel 7:9–14, which describes the "ancient of days" on a throne of judgment attended by thousands of couriers. See also Cross, "Council of Yahweh"; Robinson, "Council of Yahweh"; Whybray, *Heavenly Counsellor in Isaiah xl 13–14*.

6. For an overview of the use of the word *śāṭān* in Job and in the Hebrew Bible, see Balentine, *Job*, 53. For further reading see Kluger, *Satan in the Old Testament*; Forsyth, *Old Enemy*; P. Day, *Adversary in Heaven*; Martinek, *Wie die Schlange zum wurde*.

7. Newsom, *Book of Job*, 55–56.

8. Clines, *Job 1–42*, 1:25.

9. E.g., Carus, *History of the Devil*; Defoe, *Political History of the Devil*; Haag, *Teufelsglaube*; Kelly, *Satan*; Pagels, *Origin of Satan*; Roskoff, *Geschichte des Teufels*; Russell, *Devil*; Russell, *Satan*; Russell, *Lucifer*; Russell, *Mephistopheles*; Russell, *Prince of Darkness*. The ongoing work of J. H. Charlesworth, although not directly addressing the history of the satan, should also be noted: *Good and Evil Serpent* and the forthcoming *Serpent Iconography and the Archaeology of the Land from Dan to Bethsheba*.

10. Gammie, "Angelology and Demonology," 18–19.

11. The *Testament* omits not only God's conversation with the satan in the heavenly council, but also God's "whirlwind speech" in Job 38:1–42:6, replacing it with the words God speaks in the biblical epilogue (cf. T. *Job* 42:1–8).

12. Begg, "Comparing Characters," 436.

13. Quotations of the Greek text of the *Testament* are from Brock, ed., *Testamentum Iobi.*

14. On the structural importance of the opposition of "Job/revelation vs. Satan/deception," see Collins, "Structure and Meaning," 40.

15. *T. Job* uses *diabolos* (devil) in 3:3, but elsewhere the term is *Satanas* (Satan; e.g., *T. Job* 3:6, 4:2, and 6:4).

16. Kee, "Satan, Magic, and Salvation," 58.

17. The origin of the idea that Satan should appear in disguises is unclear. Some have suggested a Persian source (Philonenko, "Testament de Job," 28; Christiansen, *Premier homme,* 1:64–65; cf. Collins, "Structure and Meaning," 41n20), although this remains to be fully investigated. Others have noted parallels in both the testamentary literature (e.g., Testament of Reuben 5:6) as well as in the New Testament (e.g., 2 Cor 11:13–15; cf. 2 Cor 2:11; Spittler, "*Testament of Job*," 842, note c to 7:6; see also Schaller, "Testament Hiobs," 328n3d, for a list of comparable Jewish and Christian texts approximately contemporaneous with the *T. Job*). While the depiction of Satan in disguise has no clear antecedent either in the book of Job specifically or in the Hebrew Bible more generally, possible thematic connections have been suggested with Genesis 3, which depicts the serpent who deceives (Begg, "Comparing Characters," 439), and with Genesis 32, which recounts Jacob's wrestling with an angel or God disguised as a man (Collins, "Structure and Meaning," 47; Kee, "Satan, Magic, and Salvation," 58).

18. Collins, "Structure and Meaning," 40, 49–52.

19. For parallels to the *Testament*'s *agōn* motif in Hellenistic literature, see Jacobs, "Literary Motifs," 1–3.

20. Collins, "Structure and Meaning," 43.

21. The most extensive study of these Byzantine illuminated Job manuscripts is Papadaki-Oekland, *Byzantine Illuminated Manuscripts.* There is considerable debate on whether the archetype for the Byzantine miniatures is Jewish or Christian. Papadaki-Oekland assesses the evidence (303–22) and cautiously suggests that a Jewish archetype is "a reasonable conclusion" (322).

22. Papadaki-Oekland, *Byzantine Illuminated Manuscripts,* 76. See "Appendix II" of that work for the tabulation of correspondences between the book of Job and the illustrated folios of the fifteen Byzantine manuscripts Papadaki-Oekland surveys.

23. Some Byzantine manuscripts begin with a frontispage, pictorially unconnected to any specific text that follows, which depicts God, the "Ancient of Days," sitting on a throne surrounded by heavenly attendants, no one of which invites any connection with Satan; see Papadaki-Oekland, *Byzantine Illuminated Manuscripts,* 57, fig. 23 (Athos Vatapedi 590, fol. 144 [thirteenth century]).

24. Vaticanus Gr. 749, fol. 12v (ninth century); Papadaki-Oekland, *Byzantine Illuminated Manuscripts,* 83, fig. 53.

25. Vaticanus Gr. 749, fol. 13v; Papadaki-Oekland, *Byzantine Illuminated Manuscripts,* 83, fig. 54.

26. Sinaiticus Gr. 3, fol.13 (eleventh century); Papadaki-Oekland, *Byzantine Illuminated Manuscripts,* 87, fig. 64.

27. For discussion of these types, see Papadaki-Oekland, *Byzantine Illuminated Manuscripts,* 120–25.

28. Vaticanus Gr. 749, fol. 25 (ninth century); Papadaki-Oekland, *Byzantine Illuminated Manuscripts,* 122, fig. 113.

29. Bodleianus Baroccianus Gr. 201 (Oxford, twelfth century); Papadaki-Oekland, *Byzantine Illuminated Manuscripts,* 124, fig. 117.

30. Vaticanus Gr. 749. fol. 20 (ninth century); Papadaki-Oekland, *Byzantine Illuminated Manuscripts,* 110, fig. 92.

31. Vaticanus Gr. 1231, fols. 33v–34v (twelfth century); Papadaki-Oekland, *Byzantine Illuminated Manuscripts,* 78, figs. 47, 48.

32. Bodleianus Baroccianus Gr. 201 fol. 21 (Oxford, twelfth century); Papdaki-Oekland, *Byzantine Illuminated Manuscripts,* 114, fig. 99.

33. Vaticanus Gr. 751 fol. 1 (twelfth–thirteenth century); Papadaki-Oekland, *Byzantine Illuminated Manuscripts,* 114, fig. 100. The Vatican palimpsest of the *Testament,* Vaticanus Gr.1238 (dated 1195), presents the shepherds as messengers. A Paris manuscript of the *Testament,* Gr. 2658 (dated eleventh century), records that Job recognized Satan disguised as a messenger (Papadaki-Oekland, *Byzantine Illuminated Manuscripts,* 306n324). It is difficult to determine precisely whether Satan's representation/disguise as a messenger is based solely on the *Testament*'s version of Job's story. Legendary accounts likely also contribute to the general embellishment of the account. See, for example, post-Qur'anic interpreters who note that Satan was responsible for the calamities Job experienced and that he, disguised as a shepherd, delighted in announcing the details to Job (cf. Ginzberg, *Legends of the Jews,* 2: 225–42; Grünbaum, *Neue Beiträge,* 262–64).

34. Here I take my cue from a discerning observation by Terrien, *Iconography of Job,* 61.

35. *The Death of Job's Children,* twelfth century, La Daurade Priory; Terrien, *Iconography of Job,* 69, fig. 26.

36. *Job, His Wife, a Beggar, and Satan,* Église Saint-André-le-Bas, Vienne, France; Terrien, *Iconography of Job,* 73, fig. 30.

37. *Job, His Wife, His Friends, and the Devil,* thirteenth century, North Transept, Chartres Cathedral; Terrien, *Iconography of Job,* 74, fig. 31; see also Balentine, *Job,* 244.

38. For color reproduction of the frescoes, see Rackham, *San Gimignano,* 63. My discussion of the frescoes is informed by having studied them on site.

39. Opposite the Old Testament frescoes, the right wall of the basilica is frescoed with scenes from the New Testament. The arrangement mirrors the Old Testament frescoes: a row of lunettes at the top and two rows of rectangular frescoes underneath. These frescoes are usually attributed either to Barna of Siena or to his pupil, Giovanni of Asciano.

40. For additional discussion see Terrien, *Iconography of Job,* 96–99, fig. 49.

41. For additional discussion see ibid., 97–98, fig. 50.

42. Eisen, *Book of Job*, 4. In addition to his discussions of Saadiah and Maimonides, Eisen analyzes the works by Samuel ibn Tibbon (c. 1160–c. 1232), Zerahiah Hen (thirteenth century), Gersonides (1288–1344), and Simon ben Zemah Duran (1361–1444). For additional bibliographical listings, see Kimhi, *Commentary on the Book of Job*, xi–xii.

43. Here and throughout I follow the English translations of Saadiah's commentary in the critical edition by Goodman, *Book of Theodicy*.

44. For the English translation, see Saadiah Gaon, *Book of Beliefs and Opinions*. For English translations of portions of the work, see "Selections of *Beliefs and Opinions*."

45. For discussion of Jewish and Islamic antecedents for Saadiah's work, see Goodman, *Book of Theodicy*, 28–92.

46. *Book of Beliefs and Opinions*, 5:3; cf. Eisen, *Book of Job*, 18–20. In the same discussion (5.3), Saadiah observes that God does not give an explanation for Job's affliction, either in the prologue of the book or in the final chapters, because an explanation would spoil the purpose of a trial.

47. Goodman, *Book of Theodicy*, 123–25.

48. Ibid., 125.

49. Ibid., 128, 126.

50. Ibid., 127.

51. Ibid., 130.

52. Eisen notes that although antecedent Jewish and Christian (LXX) sources often connect Job to Abraham's genealogy, Saadiah goes beyond them by choosing Job, not Abraham, as the model for divine testing. This choice may also be indirectly indebted to rabbinic midrash, especially Bereshit Rabbah 57:4, in which Abraham pleads with God after the experience with Isaac on Mt. Moriah (Genesis 22) that he not be subjected to further trials. God grants Abraham's request by agreeing to transfer all his future trials to Job (*Book of Job*, 29–30, and 245n61).

53. Goodman, *Book of Theodicy*, 154. Goodman argues that Saadiah's identification of Satan as a human being, not a rebel angel, is "directly primarily against Midrashic, Christian, and Muslim readings of the Job prologue, . . . which in Saadiah's view, do violence to the tenets of monotheism" (167n28).

54. Ibid., 159.

55. Ibid., 411 (with reference to Job 42:13).

56. Eisen, *Book of Job*, 33.

57. E.g., Buber, *Prophetic Faith*, 188–97; Buber, "Dialogue between Heaven and Earth"; Kepnes, *Text as Thou*, 137–40; Susman, *Buch Hiob* (for a section of this work in English, see Glatzer, *Dimensions of Job*, 86–92); Oberhänsli-Widmer, *Hiob in jüdischer Antike und Moderne*.

58. Maimonides, *Guide of the Perplexed*, Introduction, 6.

59. Maimonides offers an analogy to explain the difference between the "vulgar" and the "elite." The former is like the person in a very dark night over whom lightning flashes sporadically; the latter is the person over whom "lightning flashes time and

time again so that he is, as it were, in unceasing light. Thus night appears to him as day" (*Guide of the Perplexed,* introduction, 7).

60. Maimonides, *Guide of the Perplexed,* 3.22.486. Subsequent citations are given parenthetically in the text.

61. This discussion of Maimonides's views on divine providence attempts little more than a cogent summary of his presentation, which is laced with difficulties and ambiguities that have generated enormous debate and discussion. I have drawn substantially on the following works: Reines, "Maimonides' Concepts"; Touati, "Deux theories"; Raffel, "Providence."

62. Eisen, *Book of Job,* 214.

63. Cf. ibid., 74.

64. Ibid., 206–17.

65. "Give the Devil his due" is a citation from Shakespeare's *Henry IV, Part 1,* 1.2.1597. The Faust story is based on the life of Dr. Johann Faustus, a sixteenth-century philosopher and theologian. Faust despairs that his vast knowledge has failed to provide him access to the mysteries of the cosmos. With the help of the devil, he turns to magic in an attempt to grasp knowledge through illusions, hallucinations, dreams, and other forms of so-called witchcraft. The first book devoted to Faust, published in 1587 by Johann Speiss, *Historia von Dr. Johann Faustus,* became known as the "Faust-book" and was the primary source for Christopher Marlowe's play *Tragical History of Doctor Faustus* (1588/1589; see Greg, *Doctor Faustus 1604–1616*). Goethe began working on his own adaptation of the Faust legend while still in his twenties and continued to work on it throughout his life. The completed work, *Faust: Eine Tragödie,* was originally published in two parts: part 1 in 1808 and part 2 in 1832. For the German edition, see Goethe, *Faust: Eine Tragödie.* For an English edition, see *Goethe's Faust.*

66. The commentary on Goethe's *Faust* is vast, and while Goethe's use of Job as a template, especially for the "Prologue in Heaven," is widely recognized, there is relatively little in-depth analysis of the Joban theme. For the latter I have consulted Carriere, "Satan, Mephisto, und die Wetten bei Hiob"; Gietmann, *Parzival, Faust, Job;* Zhitlowsky, "Job and Faust," including Matenko's introduction.

67. All parenthetical citations are to line numbers in *Goethe's Faust,* translated by Walter Kaufmann. Citations are from part 1 unless noted otherwise.

68. Goethe, *Goethe's Faust,* introduction, 24.

69. Sayers, "Faust-Legend," 7.

70. Cf. Goethe, *Goethe's Faust,* introduction, 17.

71. Ibid., 23.

72. E.g., Kafka, *Trial;* Wells, *Undying Fire;* Borchert, *Man Outside;* MacLeish, *J.B.;* and Wiesel, *Trial of God.*

73. All internal references are to this publication, Jung, *Answer to Job.* I reprise here my discussion of Jung in "Will You Condemn Me?" See also Schärf, "Gestalt des Satans."

74. Wells, *Undying Fire,* 85.

75. Frost, "Masque of Reason," 485.

76. Dietrich and Link, *Dunklen Seiten Gottes: Willkür und Gewalt;* Dietrich and Link, *Dunklen Seiten Gottes: Allmacht und Ohnmacht.*

77. Barton, "Dark Side of God," 134.

Chapter 3: There Was Once a Woman in the Land of Uz

1. Job's wife has received close inspection in recent studies. See, for example, Gitay, "Portrayal of Job's Wife"; van Wolde, *Mr. and Mrs. Job;* Penchansky, "Job's Wife"; McGinnis, "Playing the Devil's Advocate"; Greenstein, "Job's Wife"; Magdalene, "Job's Wife as Hero"; Seow, "Job's Wife"; Seow, "Reflections on the History," 573-74. The most comprehensive study to date of artistic representations of Job's wife is by Seow, "Job's Wife, with Due Respect."

2. Hartley, *Book of Job,* 84.

3. Cf. Linafelt, "Undecidability of *barak.*"

4. Mitchell, *Book of Job,* 73.

5. G. B. Gray, "Additions"; Gentry, *Asterisked Materials;* Witte, "Greek Book of Job."

6. Following here the translation by C. E. Cox, "Iob," 671.

7. Moore, *Tobit,* 189; Fitzmyer, *Tobit,* 197.

8. Van der Horst ("Images of Women," 95) notes that 107 of 388 verses in the *T. Job* deal with women, roughly thirty times more than the space allotted in the biblical book. For further discussion of women in the *T. Job,* see Collins, "Structure and Meaning"; Garrett, "Weaker Sex"; Kugler and Rohrbaugh, "On Women"; Legaspi, "Job's Wives."

9. All translations from Spittler, "*Testament of Job.*" Citations of the Greek text are from Brock, *Testamentum Iobi.*

10. Spittler adopts the conventional rendering of the name, Sistis (from *sitos,* "bread"), reasoning that it derives from Austis, the name of Job's country as given in LXX Job 1:1, 42:17b ("Testament of Job," 850). For the argument in support of Sitidos, see van der Horst, "Images of Women," 96-97.

11. On the shame associated with the cutting of a woman's hair, see Garrett, "Weaker Sex," 62-63.

12. Van der Horst, "Images of Women," 100; Collins, "Structure and Meaning," 40.

13. First suggested by Kohler, "*Testament of Job.*" The most influential study, with significant modifications to Kohler, is Philonenko, "Testament de Job et les Thérapeutes." Spittler offers a nuanced view of the proposal, suggesting that a text originating with the Therapeutae may have been reworked by Montanist Christians in the second century ("*Testament of Job,*" 833-34.). For a review and suggested refinements of the Therapeutae proposal, see Gruden, "Seeking a Context."

14. *De Vita Contemplativa* 68, cited by Garrett, "Weaker Sex," 58.

15. See van der Horst, "Images of Women," 100-101, and the literature cited there. For a reappraisal of Philo's *De Vita Contemplativa,* see Taylor, *Jewish Women Philosophers.*

16. Ginzberg, *Legends of the Jews,* 1:458.

17. Ibid., 1:460.

18. Terrien, *Iconography of Job*, 20, fig. 3.

19. E.g., Perraymond, *Figura di Giobbe*, 87, 90, 94, 97, 100, 101.

20. Ferrua, *Unknown Catacomb*, 120, fig. 110.

21. Wilpert, *I sarcophagi cristiana antichi*, 2:226, plate187(6); Perraymond, *Figura di Giobbe*, 90.

22. Terrien, *Iconography of Job*, 24–29, fig. 4 (*Job, His Wife, the Tempter, and Adam and Eve*). See also Malbon, *Iconography*; Verker, "Job and Sistis."

23. The scene of Job and his wife is now lost, but it has been preserved by Peirsec in a drawing; see Terrien, *Iconography of Job*, 28, fig. 5 (*Job and His Wife*); Le Blant, "D'une representation inédite," plate 17. My comments below on the scene showing the Samaritan woman and Jesus rely on Seow's description, "Job's Wife, with Due Respect," 358.

24. On the exposition of Job during the Middle Ages, see Besserman, *Legend of Job*; Schreiner, *Where Shall Wisdom Be Found?*; Eisen, *Book of Job*.

25. Duensing and de Santos Otero, "Apocalypse of Paul," 739–40.

26. For the Latin text, see *S. Gregorii Magni: Moralia in Job*. For English translations I follow Gregory the Great, *Morals of the Book of Job*.

27. Cf. Astell, who describes Gregory's reading of Job's wife as an example of medieval misogyny ("Job's Wife," 93–95).

28. Glatzer, *Dimensions of Job*, 32.

29. *Miroir de l'humane Salvation*, illumination, c.1358, MS 139/1363, fol. 26.22r, Musée Condé. Chantilly, France. See Terrien, *Iconography of Job*, 101, fig. 52.

30. Terrien notes that Job's wife is dressed in a full-length pastel robe and head-piece, which suggests innocence; her posture and gestures, on the other hand, "follow the medieval pattern of the harpy" (*Iconography of Job*, 100, 102).

31. Besserman, *Legend of Job*, 94.

32. The play survives in a single manuscript dated to 1475 but was performed, via successive editions, through the seventeenth century. Comments and line citations here follow Besserman's discussion (*Legend of Job*, 94–107), which relies on the edition prepared by Meiller, *Pacience de Job*.

33. School of Vlaamse (?), oil on canvas, c.1620. Chapel of the Beguines, Louvain. See Terrien, *Iconography of Job*, 189, fig. 100 (*Job, His Wife, and Demons*).

34. P. Lafond, *Hieronymus Bosch*, plates 32, 33; Schreiber, *Handbuch der Holz- und Metallschnitte*, nos. 1573, 1574, 1574a.

35. Altarpiece, 1360–66, Doberan Abby, Mecklenburg, Germany. See Schiller, *Iconography*, fig. 251.

36. The painting, now in the Wallraf-Richartz Museum in Cologne, is usually attributed to the "Master of the Saint Barbara Legend" (1485). See Friedländer, "Meister," 24–25, plate 8.

37. Astell, *Job, Boethius, and Epic Truth*, 85.

38. There are various sources for these legendary accounts of Job. In what follows I have relied on Muhammed ibn ʻAbd Allah al-Kisaʼi, *Qisas al-Anbiyaʼ*, English trans. by Thackston, *Tales of the Prophets;* Muhammed ibn Jarir al-Tabarī, *Tarikh al-rusul waʼlmuluk,* English trans. with annotation by Brinner, *History of al-Tabari,* 140–47, and Newby, *Making of the Last Prophet,* 87–98; Ahmad Ibn Muhammed al-Thaʼlabi, *Qisas al-Anbiyaʼ, al-musamma ʻAraʼis al-majalis,* English trans. by MacDonald, "Some External Evidence," and Johns, "Three Stories of a Prophet."

39. All citations of the Qurʼan are from Arberry, *Koran Interpreted.*

40. Cf. Johns, "Three Stories of a Prophet," 56.

41. From al-Thaʼlabi, as cited in MacDonald, "Some External Evidence," 156.

42. From al-Kisaʼi, as cited in Thackston, *Tales of the Prophets,* 201.

43. Ibid.

44. Ibid., 202.

45. From al-Thaʼlabi, as cited in MacDonald, "Some External Evidence," 159.

46. Seow, "Job's Wife, with Due Respect," 366n69.

47. Al-Nishapuri, illustration of *Qisas al-Anbiya (Legends of the Prophets),* 1580. Persian MS 46 fol.109, Spencer Collection, New York Public Library. See Vicchio and Edinberg, *Sweet Uses of Adversity,* 56. See also the images cited by Milstein, Rührdanz, and Schmitz, *Stories of the Prophets,* MS B, fol. 148b, MS L, fol. 91a, MS N, fol. 109a, MST-7, fol.126a.

48. Perry, "Patience and Pluck," 92.

49. The Morisco story of Job was recorded in Aljambia, a Romance language written in Arabic script. It was lost for some three hundred years, then recovered, translated, and published in the nineteenth century by Arabists in Spain. See Guillén Robles, *Leyendas moriscas sacadas,* 1:225–63; Vespertino Rodríguez, *Leyendas aljamiadas y moriscas,* 272–99.

50. Perry, "Patience and Pluck," 91, 96.

51. Ibid., 98.

52. Ibid., 99.

53. Ibid., 101.

54. Ibid., 100–101.

55. Line references are based on the *Riverside Chaucer* edition. In the interest of presenting Chaucer's words in contemporary language, all citations are from Chaucer, *Canterbury Tales,* translated by Coghill.

56. Astell, "Job's Wife," 95.

57. Ibid., 96.

58. Patterson, "For the Wyves," 678.

59. The earliest version of the Griselda story appears in Italian, in the last chapter of Boccaccio's *Decameron* (1352). It was translated into Latin by Petrarch (*Epistolae seniles*) in 1373, and in this version served as the source for Chaucer's introduction of Griselda to English readers in the late fourteenth century as "The Clerk's Tale." By the sixteenth century, translations and adaptations of the Griselda story appeared in

Italian, Spanish, Dutch, German, Polish, Portuguese, Hungarian, French, and English. See further, Griffith, *Origin.*

60. Cf. Bueler, *Tested Woman.*

61. Astell, "Job's Wife," 101; cf. Astell, *Job, Boethius, and Epic Truth,* 104; Astell, "Translating Job as Female," 59–69.

62. Besserman, *Legend of Job,* 112.

63. Note, for example, Astell: "The Clerk presents Griselda (via rhetorical copulatio) as a woman fit to be Job's wife, a Marylike New Eve at the side of a New Adam. Whereas Gregory compares Job to an unfallen Adam and Job's wife to a fallen Eve, Chaucer's Clerk represents Job's wife (in the person of Griselda) as Mary, turning 'Eva' into 'Ave'" ("Job's Wife," 101; Astell, *Job, Boethius, and Epic Truth,* 106–8).

64. Calvin, Sermons *from Job,* cited in Lamb, *Rhetoric of Suffering,* 3.

65. The left panel is now located in the Städelsches Kunstinstitut in Frankfurt. The right panel is in the Wallraf-Richartz Museum in Cologne.

66. For the argument that Job's wife threatens or castigates her husband, perhaps by pouring bilgewater on him as Socrates's wife did to her husband, see Pilger, "Sokrates in der Kunst der Neuzeit"; Anzelewsky, *Dürer,* 112–13; Gitay, "Portrayal of Job's Wife," 521. For the counterargument that both the water and the music are positive and therapeutic, see Wölfflin, *Art of Albrecht Dürer,* 137; Terrien, *Iconography of Job,* 140–42; Seow, "Job's Wife, with Due Respect," 366–69.

67. Terrien, *Iconography of Job,* 143–45. For the image see ibid., 144, fig. 78.

68. Cf. Seow, "Job's Wife, with Due Respect," 361, 368–69.

69. Caxton, *Book of the Knight,* 110 (sec. 80, lines 36–37).

70. The history of this painting, now located in the Musée departemental des Vosges in Épinal, France, is complex. Because both its attribution and its subject matter were originally unclear, the painting was first identified as *Saint Peter Delivered from Prison by an Angel* (Sterling, *Peintres de la réalité*). When the attribution to La Tour was confirmed and the scene was correctly identified as depicting Job and his wife, art historians gave the painting the title *Job Mocked by His Wife,* presumably relying on the regnant assumption that if the woman was Job's wife, then she could not be an angel (J. Lafond, "Tableau de Georges"; Weisbach, "L'histoire de Job").

71. Conisbee, *Georges de La Tour,* 128, plate 76; 122, cat. 27.

72. Ibid., 130, plate 78.

73. Seow, "Job's Wife, with Due Respect," 352.

74. The engravings are now located in various places, principally at the Pierpont Morgan Library in New York and at the Fogg Museum in Cambridge, Massachusetts. For discussion of the differences between the various versions of the engravings, see Cormack, *William Blake;* Rowland, *Blake and the Bible.*

75. Note the three wall panels behind Job and his daughters, which Blake uses to depict major episodes in Job's life. Viewed from left to right, the first panel depicts the slaughter of his sons, the second (middle) shows Job and his wife kneeling before the divine revelation, and the third shows the satan killing his plowman.

76. Raine, *Human Face of God,* 78; Gitay, "Portrayal of Job's Wife," 521–22.

77. Terrien, *Iconography of Job,* 228.

78. Cf. Wright, *Blake's Job,* xvi–xvii.

79. Beginning with the seminal work of Wickstead, *Blake's Vision,* it has been frequently noted that Blake's depictions of God and Job are usually almost identical.

80. Spark, *Only Problem,* 51.

81. J. Roth, *Job,* 3. Subsequent citations are given parenthetically in the text.

82. It is reported that Roth later acknowledged that he could not have written this happy ending if he had not been drunk at the time. See Aocella, "European Dreams," 84.

83. MacLeish, *J.B.,* 25. Subsequent citations are given parenthetically in the text.

84. Frost, *Masque of Reason,* 473–74. Subsequent citations are given parenthetically in the text.

85. E.g., Shaw, *Job's Wife;* van Wolde, *Mr. and Mrs. Job.*

86. Henriques, *Book of Mechtilde,* vii. Subsequent citations are given parenthetically in the text.

Chapter 4: Job's Words from the Ash Heap

1. A number of silences occur throughout the book: Job's initial silence in the company of his friends (2:13); his initial response to God's first speech (40:4–5); and his silence in the epilogue's narration of his life. These silences, as Newsom notes, gesture "to the unsayable that shadows speech" (*Book of Job,* 31).

2. Milosz, "Campo Dei Fiori," 35.

3. Neiman, *Evil,* 283 (emphasis added).

4. Sewall, *Vision of Tragedy,* 16.

5. Job 3:4–6: "darkness" (*ḥōšek*); "deep darkness" (*ṣalmāwet*); "settling clouds" (*ʿănānâ*); "blackness of the day" (*kimrîrê yôm*); and "thick darkness" (*ʾōpel*).

6. Fishbane, "Jeremiah IV 23–26," 153. Others have appropriated and expanded Fishbane's observations; see esp. Perdue, "Job's Assault on Creation"; Perdue, *Wisdom in Revolt,* 96–98; Perdue, *Wisdom and Creation,* 131–37.

7. I have adapted these parallels from my discussion in *Job,* 84, and have explored their subversion of the affirmations of the priestly creation account in "Job and the Priests."

8. I have adapted these parallels from my discussion in *Job,* 84, and have explored their subversion of the affirmations of the Priestly creation account in "Job and the Priests: 'He Leads Priests Away Stripped' (Job 12:19)," *Reading Job Intertextually,* eds., K. Dell, W. Keynes (New York: Bloomsbury, 2013), 42–53.

9. Cf. Job 7:7–21, 10:18–22, 14:7–17. See also Mathewson, *Death and Survival.*

10. The literature on ancient Near Eastern parallels to Job is extensive. For a comparative study of reproaches against the deity in Mesopotamia and Egypt, see Sitzler, *Vorwurf gegen Gott.*

11. Translations and line citations from Kramer, "Man and His God."

12. Translations and line citations from Lambert, "Poem of the Righteous Sufferer." See also the poem from Ugarit, translated by Nissinen as "The Just Sufferer," 184.

13. Lambert, "Poem of the Righteous Sufferer," 27.

14. Translations and line citations from Lambert, "Babylonian Theodicy."

15. Translations and line citations from Lambert, "Dialogue of Pessimism."

16. Müller, "Keilschriftliche Parallelen."

17. Zuckerman, *Job the Silent*, 102–3.

18. Translations, unless otherwise noted, follow Cox, "Iob."

19. Gard, "Concept of Job's Character," 186.

20. Some have argued that the translator sought to make intentional changes in the Hebrew text for theological reasons (Gard, *Exegetical Method;* Gard, "Concept of Job's Character"; cf. Gerleman, "Theological Approach," 231–40; Gerleman, *Studies in the Septuagint;* Urbach, *Sages,* 1:411, 2:866n66). Others argue that the translator was not motivated by any particular theological reasoning and attribute the divergences in the translation to a Hebrew original that differs from our present text or to difficulties in the Hebrew text the translator did not understand (Orlinsky, "Some Corruptions"; Orlinsky, "Studies in the Septuagint." For further reading on these and related matters, see Beer, *Text des Buches Hiob;* Heater, *Septuagint Translation Technique;* Fernández Marcos, "Septuagint Reading"; Gentry, *Asterisked Materials.*

21. On Job's patience see the prologue.

22. Translations from Spittler, "*Testament of Job.*" Quotations of the Greek text are from Brock, *Testamentum Iobi.*

23. See Papadaki-Oekland (*Byzantine Illuminated Manuscripts*), who notes the disproportionate number of illuminations devoted to the prologue and epilogue of Job.

24. Sewall, *Vision of Tragedy,* 24.

25. Ibid., 9.

26. Theodore's exposition of Job is extant only in four fragments; see Migne, *Patrologia graeca* 66:697–98. For commentary on Theodore's exegetical position, see Zaharopoulos, *Theodore of Mopsuestia.*

27. Kallen, *Job as a Greek Tragedy.* Kallen argues that the Greek influence on Job is "beyond question" (7). He hypothesizes that the Joban author visited Egypt, the Syrian coast, or other areas where Greeks lived under Persian influence. "Imagine him present, alone or with his guide, during one of the great festivals at a performance of Bacchae or Orestes or Bellerophontes or any other of the favorite dramas of the period. What would he see, and hear, and what, under such circumstances, would most stand out in his uncloyed mind?" (24).

28. Lamartine, *Cours familier de littérature,* cited in Glatzer, "Introduction," 43 (emphasis added).

29. On the connections between Job and Greek tragedy, see, for example, Montefiore, "Job as a Greek Tragedy"; Raphael, "Tragedy and Religion"; U. M. Kaufmann, "Expostulation with the Divine." On the connections between Job and Prometheus,

see, for example, Lindblom, *Job and Prometheus*; Irwin, "Job and Prometheus"; May, "Prometheus and Job"; Murray, "Prometheus and Job."

30. Murray, "Prometheus and Job," 58.

31. Hesiod, *Theogony*.

32. On the transmission of the Promethean myth through history, see Trousson, *Thème de Prométhée*; Blumenberg, *Work on Myth*.

33. Line numbers and translations from Aeschylus, *Prometheus Bound*. For a colloquial translation, see Roche, *Aeschylus: Prometheus Bound*.

34. Cf. lines 199–200, where Prometheus says, "Painful is it to me even to tell the tale, painful to keep silent—my case is hapless every way."

35. Yu, "New Gods and Old Order," 30.

36. Of the major characters in Aeschylus's drama, the only one who neither makes an appearance nor speaks is Zeus. While it is clear that Aeschylus departs from his previous portrayals of Zeus to portray a radically different god whose tyranny can only be corrected by Prometheus's intervention, there is considerable debate among classical scholars about how to understand "the twin masks of Zeus" (Yu, "New Gods and Old Order," 30–37; cf. Golden, "Zeus the Protector").

37. Yu, "New Gods and Old Order," 37.

38. Blumenberg, *Work on Myth*, 307.

39. Méautis, *Authenticité et la date*, 46–47.

40. For a review of different theories, see Podlecki, "*Prometheus Bound*" and "Appendix B." Aeschylus's discernments on the evils of tyranny clearly echo those of Plato and Aristotle (see, for example, *Politica* 5, parts 8–9). Podlecki's assessment is apt: "The play gives us the first formulation of any length of the new democracy's quarrel with the tyrant, who, as a law unto himself and beyond the check of legal redress, constituted an exact antithesis to the democratic process" ("*Prometheus Bound*," 115).

41. See for the example, the satire by Lucian of Samosata (second century C.E.), which sets the story in a brothel and portrays promiscuity as Prometheus's worst offense (*Selected Stories*, 125–35).

42. Cf. Bunker, *Bibliographical Study*, 197–200; Lathrop, *Translations from the Classics*, 142; Foster, *English Translations*, 2–7; L. S. Thompson, "German Translations," 348.

43. For discussion of Prometheus in eighteenth- and nineteenth-century literature, see especially Blumenberg, *Work on Myth*; for appropriations of the myth by musical composers in the Romantic period see, Bertagnolli, *Prometheus in Music*.

44. The move toward a more humanistic interpretation of Prometheus is anticipated in the fourteenth century by the Florentine Giovanni Boccaccio, who interpreted Prometheus as a benevolent teacher of human beings (see Trousson, *Thème de Prométhée*, 1:87–88), and by the Dutch scholar Erasmus (1466–1536), who viewed Prometheus as a hero who embodied and championed human potential (see Buck, "Über einige Deutungen," 90–92).

45. Blumenberg, *Work on Myth*, 465–522. On this connection see also Bloom, "Napoleon and Prometheus."

46. Wellbery, *Specular Moment*, 292.

47. Ibid.

48. Translations from W. Kaufmann, *Twenty German Poets*, 8–11.

49. Goethe entrusted his unpublished poem on Prometheus to Friedrich H. Jacobi, who assumed stewardship for approximately ten years. Jacobi shared the poem during this period with a number of readers, including G. E. Lessing, who is reported to have said that he agreed with Goethe's viewpoint. Jacobi published the poem in 1785. For discussion of this period before and after the publication of the poem, see Blumenberg, *Work on Myth*, 406–27.

50. Neiman, *Evil*, 58. Cf. Beiser, *Fate of Reason*; Neiman, *Unity of Reason*.

51. Blumenberg, *Work on Myth*, 556.

52. Nietzsche, *Birth of Tragedy*, 71.

53. Brandes, *Goethe*, cited in Bertagnolli, *Prometheus in Music*, 100.

54. Goethe, *Dichtung und Wahrheit*, cited in Blumenberg, *Work on Myth*, 413.

55. Byron, "Prometheus."

56. E.g., Samuel Taylor Coleridge, "On the *Prometheus* of Aeschylus" (1825); Elizabeth Barrett Browning, "Prometheus Bound" (1833); Henry Wadsworth Longfellow, "Prometheus, the Poet's Forethought" (1858).

57. Werblowsky, *Lucifer and Prometheus*, 47–66.

58. Modern renderings and line citations from Milton, *Paradise Lost*.

59. Citations and page references from Shelley, *Frankenstein*.

60. Shelley, "Prometheus Unbound." Internal citations are from this edition.

61. Bertagnolli, *Prometheus in Music*, 3.

62. Gide, *Marshlands and Prometheus Misbound*. Internal citations are from this edition.

63. Blumenberg, *Work on Myth*, 627.

64. Ibid., 627–33.

65. Ibid., 628, 633.

66. Ibid., 633–36.

67. Kafka, "Prometheus," 432.

68. Blumenberg, *Work on Myth*, 630.

69. Ibid., 636.

70. When biblical scholars have compared Job and Prometheus (see note 32), the usual approach has been to accent the differences between the two. The assessment of May is representative: "In contrast with the Promethean myth, the solution of the [Joban] drama is found not in a change of mind and heart on the part of the deity, but in the unquestioned submission of man to One with power and knowledge greater than his own" ("Prometheus and Job," 246).

71. Blumenberg, *Work on Myth*, 636.

72. Ibid., translaor's introduction, viii.

73. Ibid., 3.

Chapter 5: God on Trial

1. Shaffer, *Amadeus*. Internal citations are from this edition.

2. Sontag, "Aesthetics of Silence," 27.

3. On Job's use of the Psalms, see Kynes, *My Heart Has Turned into Weeping*.

4. Magdalene, *On the Scales of Righteousness*. The typical Neo-Babylonian pattern of litigation, Magdalene argues, is accusation; demand; investigation; summons; the defendant's oath; a possible second accusation/testimony by a corroborating witness; additional evidence; verdict; appeal; and execution of verdict (66). Magdalene distinguishes between the "inquisitorial system" common in the ancient Near East, which is characterized by a "higher degree of cooperation between the parties" and the adjudicating judge in finding the truth, and the "adversarial system," which is more familiar in modern judicial systems in the Unites States, Canada, and Great Britain (65).

5. For an examination of litigation terminology in the Hebrew Bible, see Bovati, *Re-establishing Justice*.

6. On the trial metaphor in the book of Job, see, for example, Roberts, "Job's Summons to Yahweh"; Dick, "Legal Metaphor"; Scholnick, "Meaning of *Mišpaṭ*"; Scholnick, "Oath of Innocence"; Scholnick, "Poetry in the Courtroom"; Chin, "Job and the Injustice of God"; Greenstein, "Forensic Understanding"; Schultz, "Cohesive Issue of *mišpāṭ*"; Sutherland, *Putting God on Trial*. Norman Habel's literary analysis of the trial metaphor in Job may be singled out as one of the more comprehensive arguments for its contribution to the book. Habel suggests that Job's quest for justice integrates the entire plot, which is constructed in a "ring composition" that moves from beginning to middle to end. The turning point in the development of the legal process, according to Habel's analysis, is Job 29–31, where Job declares an oath of innocence and formally challenges God to appear in court (*Book of Job*, 54). Habel's assessment was anticipated by Heinz Richter, who determined that 444 verses in Job were related to legal terminology, while only 346 verses were related to wisdom terminology (*Studien zu Hiob*, 131).

7. Magdalene, *On the Scales of Righteousness*, 145–76.

8. For Job's repeated insistence that he is innocent, see 6:28–30, 9:21, 10:7, 16:17, 19:6, and especially chapter 31 (cf. the prologue's comparable assessment: 1:1, 8, 22; 2:3, 10).

9. Job 13:15 is one of the many textually difficult verses in the book. The traditional rendering, "Though he [God] slay me, yet will I trust in him" (King James Version, New American Bible, New International Version), conveys the idea that Job will trust God come what may, a reading that sustains the piety informed by the "patience" of Job. An alternate reading, which follows a critical emendation based on manuscript and versional evidence, is represented by NRSV: "See, he [God] will kill me; I have no hope" (cf. NJPS). On this reading Job knows that there is no hope

winning a case against God, but he resolves, against all odds, to "defend my ways to his face." For discussion of the textual issues, see Balentine, *Job*, 210–13.

10. For a reproduction and discussion of the painting, see Balentine, *Job*, 361; Terrien, *Iconography of Job*, 250. Terrien reads the inscription differently: "Maintenant encore, my plainte est une *réussite*, et pourtant . . ." ("Even now my lament is a success, and yet . . ."). He suggests that the word *réussite* refers to winning at cards, and he interprets Gruber to be portraying Job as pondering that "life is a tragic game." When I viewed the painting in 1999, then on display at the Tate Modern Gallery, and discussed it with Chris Webber of the staff at the Tate, I was able to confirm that the word in the inscription is *revolte*, not *réussite*.

11. Soelle, *Suffering*, 32.

12. Sachs, "Landscape of Screams," 651.

13. Here I reprise my exegesis in *Job*, 164–76.

14. Stegner, "Impasse," 291.

15. Clines, *Job 1–42*, 1:323.

16. On the deity's silence in ancient Near Eastern and biblical texts, see Korpel and Moor, *Silent God*.

17. Frost, "Our Hold on the Planet," 349.

18. Schreiner, "'Why Do the Wicked Live?'" 141.

19. On the book of Job in the history of Jewish interpretation, see Susman, *Buch Hiob*; Oberhänsli-Widmer, *Hiob in jüdischer Antike und Moderne*.

20. Wiesel, *Trial of God*, 2. All internal citations are from this edition.

21. Ibid.

22. Susman, "Hiob-Problem," 49. See also, for example, Martin Buber, who regarded *The Trial* as the most important commentary on Job of his generation (Glatzer, "Introduction," 48); Frye, *Great Code*, 195; and the chapter on Job and *The Trial* in Wilk, *Jewish Presence*, 133–67. For a cautionary view of the trial metaphor in Kafka and Job, see Lasine, "Job and His Friends."

23. Kafka, *Trial*, 1. Subsequent citations are given parenthetically in the text.

24. Kafka's antecedents include not only biblical texts. His appropriation of the trial metaphor draws upon the emergence of legal fiction in the eighteenth and nineteenth centuries (especially the Russian fiction of Nikolai Gogol and Fyodor Dostoevsky). On eighteenth-century "fictions of the law," see Lamb, *Rhetoric of Suffering*, 128–50. Kafka also anticipates twentieth-century fictions that deal with the American system of justice run amok. See, for example, Gaddis, *Frolic of His Own*.

25. Cited in Steiner's introduction to *The Trial*, xviii.

26. Kafka's parable, variously called "Before the Law," "The Doorkeeper," or "The Man from the Country," was written separately from the novel and first published in 1915.

27. Steiner, introduction to Kafka, *Trial*, xx–xxi. See also Derrida ("Devant la Loi"), who cites the parable as an example of Kafka's insistence on the impossibility of interpretation.

28. These last sentences in the penultimate paragraph are typically elliptic. Why and to whom does K. spread out his fingers? Is he reaching out for the absent judge? Is he reaching out for the man in the house? Is he simply submitting silently to the execution? In the original version of the story, Kafka writes the scene differently: "Where was the Judge? Where the High Court of Justice? *I have something to say. I lift up my hands*" ("Passages Deleted by the Author," appendix 2 in *The Trial*, 263; emphasis added).

29. D. Cox, "Job as Bi-polar *Mašal*," 21.

30. Lamb, *Rhetoric of Suffering*, 29.

31. Ibid., 17. With respect to the appropriation of Job in eighteenth-century British law, Lamb notes that between 1749 and 1756, 306 persons were executed, more than in any other comparable span of time in the century. "Not for nothing," Lamb says, "was the Press-Yard of Newgate adorned with the Joban text, 'Man is born to Trouble as the Sparks fly upward [Job 5:7]'" (129).

32. Lowell, "Present Crisis." Lowell's poem was the inspiration for the magazine *Crisis*, which became the flagship publication of the National Association for the Advancement of Colored People, established in 1910 under the leadership of W. E. B. Du Bois.

33. Nussbaum, *Poetic Justice*, 73. For the concept of the "judicious spectator," Nussbaum draws upon the work of eighteenth-century British philosopher and economist Adam Smith, particularly his *Theory of Moral Sentiments* (1759).

34. Ibid., 91.

35. Ibid., 73.

36. Qtd. in ibid., 79.

37. Ibid., 82.

38. Whitman, "By Blue Ontario's Shore," 269–70.

39. Nussbaum, *Poetic Justice*, 81.

40. Whitman, "By Blue Ontario's Shore," 270–71.

41. Whitman, "Song of Myself," 48, 71, 75.

42. Ibid., 60.

43. Ibid., 48.

44. Whitman, "By Blue Ontario's Shore," 269.

45. Whitman, "Song of Myself," 78.

46. Dickinson, "#1551."

Chapter 6: Job's Comforters

1. The compositional history of the book invites questions (see the prologue). Newsom, for example, following Gordis, regards the report about the friends in Job 2:11–13 and 42:7–10 as an editorial hinge that has been added to the original prose tale to integrate the poetic dialogues. Newsom, *Book of Job*, 36; Gordis, *Book of Job*, 573–75.

2. For discussion of the alternatives, see Balentine, *Job*, 339–40, 381–83.

3. For the visuals see Wright, *Blake's Job*, plate 7, *Job's Comforters*, 22; plate 10, *Job Rebuked by His Friends*, 28.

4. The friends' gesture is likely modeled on Henry Fuseli's (1741–1825) depiction of the ghastly finger-pointing women in *The Three Witches*; Cormack, *William Blake*, 45.

5. Similar negative representations of the friends by artists and sculptors are extensive. A late fifteenth-century Lenten cloth by Konrad von Friesach, for example, depicts two parallel scenes. The Old Testament side of the cloth shows Job, his wife, the three friends, and the satan. The New Testament side portrays Christ as Job and his "friends" as mockers and torturers. One whistles at him, two others blow a wind instrument directly into his ear, and the fourth, a jester dressed as the satan, makes an obscene gesture with his hands; see Terrien, *Iconography of Job*, 114, fig. 59. The sixteenth-century artist Robert Falaise sculpted for the church of St. Martin in Champeaux-en-Brie the choir stalls, or "mercy seats," which included a number of scenes from the book of Job. In one of the Job scenes, Falaise depicts the three friends in a single, elongated dunce cap with donkey ears protruding from each side; see Terrien, *Iconography of Job*, 125, fig. 69; for further discussion see Balentine, *Job*, 202.

6. For a historical account of the event, see Kendrick, *Lisbon Earthquake*.

7. Voltaire, *Candide*, 12. Subsequent citations are given parenthetically in the text.

8. Leibniz, *Theodicy*, 150.

9. Leibniz, *Philosophical Essays*, 30.

10. Bayle, *Historical and Critical Dictionary*.

11. Leibniz, *Theodicy*, 132.

12. Ibid., 299–300.

13. Lamb, *Rhetoric of Suffering*, 92.

14. A. Pope, "Essay on Man," 1:9, 15–16. Subsequent citations are given parenthetically in the text.

15. Ibid.

16. Voltaire, *Oeuvres Complètes*. I follow here the English translation in Pendergast and Pendergast, *Reference Guide*, 1459–60. Subsequent parenthetical line citations are from this translation.

17. Lamb, *Rhetoric of Suffering*, 93.

18. Wood, *Book against God*, 188.

19. Kant, "On the Failure," 283.

20. Ibid., 290.

21. Ibid., 291.

22. Ibid., 292.

23. Ibid., 293.

24. Gelber, *Job Stands Up*, 3. Subsequent citations are given parenthetically in the text.

25. Levin, *Sorrows of Job*, 19. Subsequent citations are given parenthetically in the text.

26. Auden, "Quest," 286. Auden's lines are as follows: "Two friends who met here and embraced are gone, / Each to his own mistake."

27. Newsom, *Book of Job*, 201.

28. See Balentine, *Job*, 511–12.

29. Whedbee, *Bible and the Comic Vision*, 242–45. For further discussion see Balentine, *Job*, 511 (with accompanying commentary on the included CD: "The Great Reservoir of Comedy").

30. Newsom, *Book of Job*, 200.

31. E.g., Gordis, *Book of Job*, xxxi–xxxii, 546–62; Janzen, *Job*, 218; Habel, *Book of Job*, 36–37; Good, *In Turns of Tempest*, 7–9, 321; Balentine, *Job*, 511–13. Among recent commentators Clines argues that Elihu's speeches, even if secondary, which he doubts, have been misplaced in the history of the transmission of the book. Their original location, he contends, is after Job 27 and before Job 28 (also assigned to Elihu) (Clines, *Job 1–42*, 2:709).

32. Spittler, "*Testament of Job*," 862, note d. Spittler notes parallels between Eliphas's invective against Elihu and Jesus's execration against Judas Iscariot, as recorded in a Coptic gnostic apocryphon, *Book of the Resurrection of Jesus Christ by Bartholomew the Apostle*.

33. *Jerusalem Taphou* 5, fol.209v (c.1300; Papadoki-Oekland, Byzantine Illuminated Manuscripts, 241, Fig. 277. Cf. the almost identical miniature that accompanies the same Job text in Vaticanus Gr.231, fol. 371v (twelfth century; idem, 241, Fig. 278)

34. For Saadiah see Goodman, *Book of Theodicy*, 353–69; for Maimonides see *Guide of the Perplexed*, 491–97; for Gersonides see *Wars of the Lord*. For commentary see, for example, Carstensen, "Persistence of the Elihu Tradition"; Burrell, "Maimonides, Aquinas, and Gersonides"; Eisen, *Book of Job*, 17–41, 43–77, 143–73.

35. Maimonides, *Guide of the Perplexed*, 3.23.495.

36. Ibid.

37. For the image, *Job and His Friends*, see Terrien, *Iconography of Job*, 70, fig. 27.

38. For the image, *Job, His Wife, His Friends, the Devil, and the Angel*, see Terrien, *Iconography of Job*, 184, fig. 97.

39. Calvin writes that the "ignorance of providence is the ultimate of all miseries; the highest blessedness lies in the knowledge of it" (*Institutes* 1.17.11).

40. The sermons on Job are published in *Ioannis Calvini*, vols. 33–35. For an English version of selected sermons, see Calvin, *Sermons from Job*. Unless otherwise noted parenthetical references are to the Nixon translation.

41. Schreiner, *Where Shall Wisdom Be Found?* 132.

42. Cf. the movie *The Best Exotic Marigold Hotel* (2012), which features seven retirees who come to a not-so-exotic hotel in India to begin the next phase of their lives. When they are confronted with the dilapidated reality of the hotel and its promises, a young, invincibly optimistic hotel manager—a kindred spirit, perhaps, of Elihu (and Calvin)—assures them: "Everything will be all right in the end. . . . if it is not all right then it's not the end."

43. In this section I appropriate language from Clines, "Job's Fifth Friend," and on the "belated reader" from Newsom, *Book of Job*, 200–233.

44. Newsom, *Book of Job*, 202. The reference to Bloom is to his book *Agon: Towards a Theory of Revisionism* (1982), cited by Newsom on p. 204.

45. Ibid.
46. Ibid., 203.
47. Ibid., 204.
48. Clines, "Job's Fifth Friend," 233.
49. Ibid., 235.
50. Ibid., 247.

51. I concur with Newsom's apt summation of Elihu as a "dissatisfied reader." "The embodied, perspectival character of human understanding and the historicity of the moral imagination makes the act of interruption a necessity of every serious act of reading a disturbing text about a fundamental human dilemma. The signal contribution of the Elihu speeches may not finally be in their content but in the way they model this process. . . . The highest form of respect one can pay, of course, is to interrupt his own speech and to continue to quarrel with him as he quarreled with Job and his friends" (*Book of Job*, 233).

Chapter 7: "Then the Lord answered Job out of the Whirlwind . . ." (Job 38:1, 3)

1. Melville, *Pierre*, 290.
2. I take this apt metaphor from Wood, "All and the If," 30.
3. Melville, *Pierre*, 285.
4. Ibid., 290.
5. Ibid., 295, 297.
6. Ibid., 502.
7. See L. R. Thompson, *Melville's Quarrel with God*.
8. On the general theme, see Korpel and Moor, *Silent God*, esp. chaps. 3 and 5.
9. Newsom, *Book of Job*, 238.
10. In this section I reprise my overview of the divine speeches in *Job*, 625–40.

11. The primary Hebrew word for justice (*mišpāt*) does not occur either in the prologue or the epilogue. It occurs frequently within the poetic dialogues between Job and his friends, often with respect to God's justice, which is questioned by Job (e.g., 8:3; 9:19, 32; 14:3; 19:7; 27:2) and affirmed by the friends, especially Elihu (e.g., 22:4; 34:12, 17, 23; 36:6; 37:23).

12. Edwards, "Greatest of All People," 535.
13. Ozick, "Impious Impatience," 72.
14. Miles, *God*, 328.

15. See, for example, Perdue (*Wisdom in Revolt*, 197–98), who lists no less than eight major proposals.

16. E.g., Driver and Gray, *Critical and Exegetical Commentary*, lv; Fohrer, *Buch Hiob*, 534; Rowley, *Job*, 18–21.

17. See the oft-cited comments of Matitiahu Tsevat: "The God who speaks to man in the book of Job is neither just not unjust. He is God." Tsevat, "Meaning," 105.

18. Newsom, "Book of Job," 595–97; Newsom, *Book of Job*, 234–58.

19. Alonso-Schökel, "God's Answer to Job," 45.

20. The classic study by Jeremias (*Theophanie*) argues that the original setting for the theophany is a military context, in which God comes as a divine warrior to celebrate a victory against Israel's enemies (e.g., Ex 15:7–10; Dt 33:2–3, 26–29; Hb 3:3–15; Ps 68:8–9, 32–35).

21. Cf. Newsom, *Book of Job*, 248. Newsom and W. P. Brown (*Seven Pillars of Creation*, 115–40) interpret Behemoth and Leviathan through the hermeneutical lens of Edmund Burke's theory of the "tragic sublime," first propounded in his *Philosophical Enquiry* (1757), where the terror and beauty of these primordial creatures combine to produce in Job a sense of elation.

22. Glazov, "'Hand On the Mouth.'"

23. Tilley, "God and the Silencing of Job," 261; Tilley, *Evils of Theodicy*, 89–112. See, for example, Newsom ("Book of Job," 629), who cites five different translations as legitimate possibilities. For a review of the issues and possibilities, see Krüger, "Did Job Repent?"

24. Morrow provides the semantic survey, noting that of nearly seventy occurrences of *mā'as* in the *qal* stem, all but four are followed by direct objects (Job 7:16, 34:33, 36:5, 42:6). Morrow, "Consolation, Rejection, and Repentance," 214.

25. For discussion of the issues, see van Wolde, "Job 42:1–6."

26. E.g., Driver and Gray, *Critical and Exegetical Commentary*, 373; Tsevat, "Meaning," 91; Fohrer, *Buch Hiob*, 531; M. Pope, *Job*, 349. See also New American Bible, NJPS, Jerusalem Bible, Today's English Version.

27. E.g., Habel, *Book of Job*, 576, 582.

28. E.g., Patrick, "Translation of Job 42:6," 369–70; Morrow, "Consolation, Rejection, and Repentance," 212–15; Good, *In Turns of Tempest*, 376.

29. Curtis, "On Job's Response," 503.

30. E.g., Dhorme, *Commentary*, 646–47; Diewert, "Job XXXVI 5"; Krüger, "Did Job Repent?"; Clines, *Job 1–42*, 3:170, 172–73; W. P. Brown, *Seven Pillars of Creation*, 124.

31. E.g., Jo 7:6; 2 Sm 13:19; Is 58:5, 61:3; Jer 6:26; Ez 27:30; cf. Job 2:8, 12. See also Olyan, *Biblical Mourning*, 111–23.

32. Parunak, "A Semantic Survey of NHM." For the use of *nhm* with reference to God's change of mind, see Ex 13:17; 1 Sm 15:29; Jer 4:28, 20:16; Ez 24:14; Jon 3:9; Jl 2:14; Zec 8:14; Pss 106:45, 110:4. The only occurrence of the verb with reference to human action is Jer 31:19.

33. Job 2:11; 6:10; 7:13; 15:11; 16:2; 21:2, 34; 29:25; 42:11. For this verb with the same sense outside Job, see, for example, Gn 24:67, 38:12; 2 Sm 13:39; Ez 14:22. See also Willi-Plein, "Hiobs Widerruf?"; Boer, "Does Job Retract?" 192; Krüger, "Did Job Repent?"

34. A scribal correction (*Tiqqune Sopherim*) in Gn 18:22 suggests that "God remained standing before Abraham" (contrast NRSV: "Abraham remained standing before God"). On the parallels between Genesis 18 and Job, see Blenkinsopp, "Abraham and the Righteous," 126–27; Blenkinsopp, "Judge of All the Earth." Ben Zvi's commentary merits

attention: "The text [Gn 18:22–33] underscores the notion that when the ideal teacher defends the universal order and confronts God with the standards by which God ought to judge the world, *he is in fact fulfilling the role God has chosen him to fulfill*" ("Dialogue between Abraham and YHWH," 39; emphasis added). On the postexilic provenance of Genesis 18:22–33, see L. Schmidt, *"De Deo,"* 131–64.

35. Newsom, "Book of Job," 629.

36. Translations are from Gregory the Great, *Morals of the Book of Job.* Subsequent citations are given parenthetically in the text.

37. Schreiner, *Where Shall Wisdom Be Found?* 52.

38. See, for example, J. Day, *God's Conflict.* On the iconographic history, see Keel, *Jahwes Entgegnung an Ijob*; cf. Kubina, *Gottesreden im Buche Hiob.*

39. Cited in Beal, *Religion and Its Monsters*, 63.

40. For multiple versions of this image, see Papadaki-Oekland, *Byzantine Illuminated Manuscripts*, 192–93, figs. 211–13.

41. See Terrien, *Iconography of Job*, 46–48, figs. 9–11; Papadaki-Oekland, *Byzantine Illuminated Manuscripts*, 265–66, figs. 314–16.

42. Luther, *Luther's Works*, 13:31.

43. Milton, *Paradise Lost*, book 1, lines 192, 200–201.

44. I forgo here discussion of *Behemoth*, Hobbes's companion piece to *Leviathan*, which lays the blame for the Thirty Years' War on the ministers and members of the House of the Parliament for fomenting sedition.

45. See Mintz, *Hunting of Leviathan*, 39–62, and his appendix "Anti-Hobbes Literature [1650–1700]," 157–60. For the wider context of Hobbes in relation to the literature of the English Civil War, see N. Smith, *Literature and Revolution,* esp. 154–77.

46. Hobbes, *Life of Mr. Thomas Hobbes*, 2, as cited in Mintz, *Hunting of Leviathan*, 1.

47. K. Brown, "Artist of the *Leviathan* Title-Page."

48. Mintz, "Leviathan as Metaphor," 6.

49. For a survey see Schmitt, *Leviathan*, 16–36.

50. These and other etymologies have been collected by Steadman, "Leviathan and Renaissance Etymology." The citations are from page 576.

51. Beal, *Religion and Its Monsters*, 92.

52. For contrasting views on whether Hobbes's political covenant affirms or denies the possibility of a covenant between God and humans, see Curley, "Covenant with God"; Martinich, "Interpretation of Covenants"; Martinich, *Two Gods of "Leviathan,"* 136–82.

53. Hobbes distinguishes between sovereign power established by institution (*Leviathan*, 102–9), which he identifies with the threat of paternal punishment (110–11), and sovereign power established by acquisition, that is, by a conquering force, which exercises despotic force (*Leviathan*, 96, 111–12). But in all essential matters, as he says repeatedly, the rights and consequences of sovereign power are the same (e.g., *Leviathan*, 110, 112). For discussion of the comparable omnipotence of God and the monarch, see Freund, "Dieu Mortal."

54. For Hobbes's explication of the citation on the frontispiece, see *Leviathan*, 161–62.

55. See, for example, Greenlief, "Note on Hobbes," 28–31.

56. For the printing history of *Leviathan*, see MacDonald and Hargreaves, *Thomas Hobbes*, 27–30.

57. Cited in Mintz, *Hunting of Leviathan*, 62. For excerpts from Hobbes's contemporary critics, see Hobbes, *Leviathan*, 271–304.

58. Hobbes refuted his critics with published responses (for excerpts see *Leviathan*, 265–69). Despite his misgivings about his life and work, he concludes *Leviathan* on a hopeful note: "There is nothing in this whole discourse, nor in that I writ before the same Subject in Latine, as far as I can perceive, contrary either to the Word of God, or to good Manners or [tending] to the disturbance of the Publique Tranquility. Therefore I think it may be profitably printed, and more profitably taught in the Universities" (259).

59. Hobbes, *Leviathan*, 10.

60. For Hobbes's discussion of these three models for the commonwealth, see ibid., 102–9. In recognition of the 350th anniversary of the publication of *Leviathan,* see Sorell and Foisneau, eds., *"Leviathan" after 350 Years.*

61. On the "Enlightenment Bible" and the Joban revival, see Sheehan, *Enlightenment Bible*, 160–68, which includes discussion of Lowth's *Lectures on the Sacred Poetry of the Hebrews* (1753) and Herder's *On the Spirit of Hebrew Poetry* (1782).

62. Edmund Burke, *A Philosophical Enquiry into the Origin of Our Ideas of the Sublime and Beautiful* (1757); Thomas Carlyle, *On Heroes, Hero-Worship and the Heroic in History* (1840).

63. Blake, *Illustrations of the Book of Job* (1825); Goethe, *Faust* (1808, 1832).

64. Wood, "All and the If," 33. See also the section "Job and the Aesthetic Turn in Biblical Exegesis," especially with respect to Melville's work, in Pardes, *Melville's Bibles*, 20–25.

65. As cited in Parker, *Herman Melville*, 2:300; Delbanco, *Melville*, 252–53.

66. Thompson, *Melville's Quarrel with God*, 5–6.

67. Wood, "All and the If," 31–32.

68. See N. Wright, *Melville's Use of the Bible*. Wright identifies some 650 biblical allusions, two-thirds of which are to the Old Testament. Cf. Stout, "Melville's Use of the Book of Job"; Paffenroth, *In Praise of Wisdom*, 112–17; Kreitzer, "*Moby-Dick.*"

69. Holman, "Reconciliation of Ishmael," 477.

70. Cf. Thompson (*Melville's Quarrel with God*, 10–11, 153–54), who describes a triangulation between Melville's Job, Jonah, and Ahab.

71. E.g., VanZanten Gallagher, "Prophetic Narrator."

72. Melville scholars debate whether Father Mapple's sermon should be read as an affirmation or a parody of Calvinistic doctrine. See, for example, Thompson, *Melville's Quarrel with God*, 153–66; Vincent, *Trying-Out of Moby-Dick*, 70–75; Holstein, "Melville's Inversion of Jonah."

73. For a contemporary representation of God's presenting questions to Job and their impact on a family compelled to wrestle with their implications, see Terrence

Malick's 2011 film, *The Tree of Life*, which devotes almost twenty minutes to an extraordinary cinematic depiction of the beauty and terror of the creation of the world.

74. Wood, "All and the If," 34.

75. Thompson, *Melville's Quarrel with God*, 233.

76. As cited in Parker, *Herman Melville*, 2:312–13; Woods, "All and the If," 30; Kazin, *God and the American Writer*, 94.

77. As cited in Parker, *Herman Melville*, 2:316.

78. Wood, "All and the If," 39. In Wood's assessment *Moby-Dick* represents the "triumph of [the] atheism of metaphor" in Melville's work: "The Godhead is indeed broken into pieces. Truth is kaleidoscopically affronted. The whale is likened to everything under the sun, and everything under the moon, too—a portly burgher, an Ottoman, a book, a language, a script, a nation, the Sphinx, the pyramids. The whale is also Satan and God. The whale is 'inscrutable.' It is so full of meanings that it threatens to have no meanings at all" (37).

79. Cf. Holman, "Reconciliation of Ishmael," 487.

80. On *Moby-Dick* as a novel of testimony, a bearing witness by a survivor to trauma that requires articulation and compels hearers and readers to respond, see Peretz, *Literature, Disaster, and the Enigma of Power*.

Epilogue

1. Ngwa, *Hermeneutics of the "Happy" Ending*.

2. Clines, *Job 1–42*, 3:206.

3. Cf. van Wolde, "Job 42:1–6."

4. For the use of this term and its derivatives elsewhere in the Hebrew Bible and in Job, see Nam, *Talking about God*, 22–24.

5. Clines, *Job 1–42*, 3:197.

6. The collocation *'āśâ nĕbālâ* occurs frequently in the Old Testament, always with a strong negative connotation (e.g., Gn 34:7; Dt 22:21; Jo 7:15; Jgs 20:6; Jer 29:23). See also W. M. W. Roth, "NBL"; A. Phillips, "NEBALAH"; Saebo, "*nābāl*, fool." The comments of Driver (*Critical and Exegetical Commentary*, 26) are instructive: "The fault of the *nābhāl* was not weakness of reason, but moral and religious sensibility, an invincible lack of sense or perception, for the claims of either God or man."

7. Cf. M. Pope, *Job*, 347; Janzen, *Job*, 266; Good, *In Turns of Tempest*, 383. There is a suggestive echo here of Job's rebuke to his wife in 2:10 for talking like a "foolish woman" (*nĕbālôt*) by urging him to curse God. Just as Job dismisses his wife's counsel as foolishness, so now he appears to be unwilling to accept God's "foolish anger" toward the friends.

8. Balentine, "My Servant Job"; Balentine, *Job*, 712–13.

9. See, for example, the apocryphal Book of Tobit (second century B.C.E.), a story of a righteous Jew living in exile who, like Job, suffers the loss of his property, his standing in the community, and his health. His restoration includes a doubling of his life span (14:1–2).

10. F. I. Anderson, *Job*, 293; cf. Clines, *Job 1–42*, 3:202.

11. Clines, *Job 1–42*, 3:205.

12. Dostoevsky, *Brothers Karamazov*, 245.

13. On the theology of friendship in Job, see my discussion, "Let Love Clasp Grief"; Balentine, *Job*, 445–51.

14. The amount signified by the term *qĕśîṭâ* ("a piece of money") is uncertain. Jacob, for example, pays the sum of one hundred *qĕśîṭâ* to purchase a piece of land (Gn 33:19, Jo 24:32). LXX uses a word that means "lamb," which suggests an amount equivalent to the monetary value of such an animal.

15. Clines, *Job 1–42*, 3:208.

16. In a patriarchal world, which the book of Job assumes, daughters typically inherit only when there are no sons (Nm 26:33; cf. Nm 27:1–11, 36:1–12; and Ben-Barak, "Inheritance by Daughters"). It is not clear why the epilogue indicates Job does not follow this convention. Some commentators argue that the epilogue appropriates an old epic motif (Sarna, "Epic Substratum," 24; Coogan, "Job's Children," 146–47). Others debate whether the inheritance of the daughters subverts patriarchal convention or represents it (cf. Chittister, *Job's Daughters*; Pardes, *Countertraditions in the Bible*, 145–56; Morrow, "Toxic Religion"). On the embellishment of the daughters' role in the *T. Job*, see Machinist, "Job's Daughters."

17. Susman, *Buch Hiob*, 68.

18. Fackenheim, *God's Presence in History*; Fackenheim, *To Mend the World*. See also Berger, *Children of Job*.

19. Zuckerman, *Job the Silent*, 63.

20. Liptzin, *Flowering of Yiddish Literature*.

21. Wiesel, "Victims of God."

22. Zuckerman, *Job the Silent*, 34, 187. On commentators who have pursued Zuckerman's insights, see Balentine, *Job*, 709; Crenshaw, *Reading Job*, 34–35; Oberhänsli, "Job in Modern and Contemporary Literature," 278–79.

23. Zuckerman, *Job the Silent*, 34–45.

24. Perets, "Bontsye the Silent," 183. All subsequent parenthetical references are to Zuckerman's translation.

25. Ibid., 44.

26. Ibid. 64.

27. Ibid., 39.

28. Ibid., 67.

29. "What has happened to the [Yiddish] parodic tradition after the Holocaust is that no one is able to get the joke anymore. That is because everything Yiddish has automatically been shrouded in an aura of holiness. After the Great Destruction we can no longer view the Yiddish world as a paradise lost. All the archetypes are now protected by the Holocaust, so that parody of any kind becomes sacrilege" (Roskies, "People of the Lost Book," 23; as cited in Zuckerman, *Job the Silent*, 68).

30. Zuckerman, *Job the Silent*, 68.

31. Wiesel, "Use of Words," as cited in Zuckerman, *Job the Silent*, 66.

32. Wiesel, interview with H. Broun, in Abrahamson, "Introductory Essay," 1:56 (as cited in Zuckerman, *Job the Silent*, 65–66).

33. Wiesel, "Victims of God," as cited in Zuckerman, *Job the Silent*, 66.

34. Greenberg, "Y. L. Perets," stanzas 18, 19–20 (as cited in Zuckerman, *Job the Silent*, 69).

35. Ibid. (as cited in Zuckerman, *Job the Silent*, 69).

36. Leivick, "Jew—The Individual," 116.

37. Ibid., 118.

38. Leivick, *In the Days of Job*, 130. Subsequent references are given parenthetically in the text.

39. For commentary on Job's evocation of Genesis 4, see Balentine, *Job*, 257–60.

40. Wiesel, *Jew Today*, 207–08.

41. R. M. Brown, *Elie Wiesel*, 3.

42. Wiesel, "Job: Our Contemporary," 211. Subsequent citations are given parenthetically in the text.

43. I cite here the English titles, although all six books were first published in French: *Night* (1958); *Dawn* (1960); *The Accident* (1961); *The Town beyond the Wall* (1962); *The Gates of the Forest* (1964); and *A Beggar in Jerusalem* (1968). Subsequent parenthetical references are to the English editions cited in the bibliography.

44. Cargas, *Harry James Cargas*, 86, as cited in Brown, *Elie Wiesel*, 51.

45. Ibid., as cited in Brown, *Elie Wiesel*, 51.

46. See also Wiesel's comments on this passage in the first volume of his memoir *All Rivers Run to the Sea*, 321.

47. Cargas, *Harry James Cargas*, 86, as cited in Brown, *Elie Wiesel*, 51.

48. See especially the analysis in Brown, *Elie Wiesel*, who follows Wiesel's own characterization of these novels with a systematic discussion of the options he pursues. See also Wiesel's reflections in his memoirs *All Rivers Run to Sea* and *And the Sea Is Never Full*.

49. Wiesel, *All Rivers Run to the Sea*, 327.

50. Wiesel records the following in his diary about his first visit to Jerusalem in 1967 and the experiences that triggered the writing of *A Beggar in Jerusalem*:

> And here I am in Jerusalem. It took me a long time to get here, but here I am. I dream that I'm dreaming. I dream that my words become jumbled on my lips and that they burn my tongue.
>
> And yes, it is both a privilege and a duty to speak of Jerusalem.
>
> Of the heart that is full, so full that if it doesn't open it will burst. Of the alleyways of the Old City, which have made me want to sing like a madman, to sob like a child. To paraphrase Rabbi Nahman of Bratslav, I will have to make words of my tears. (*All Rivers Run to the Sea*, 390)

51. Wiesel, *Messengers of God*, 194–95 (emphasis added).

52. Wiesel, "Personal Response," 37.
53. Wiesel, *One Generation After*, 166.
54. Wiesel, "Jewish Values in the Post-Holocaust Future," 299.
55. Wiesel, *Souls on Fire*, 111.
56. Wiesel, *All Rivers Run to the Sea*, 326–27.
57. Wiesel, *One Generation After*, 189.
58. Wiesel, *All Rivers Run to the Sea*, 339.

BIBLIOGRAPHY

Abrahamson, I. "Introductory Essay." In vol. 1 of *Against Silence: The Voice and Vision of Elie Wiesel*, 9–83. 3 vols. New York: Holocaust Library, 1985.

Aeschylus. *Prometheus Bound.* In vol. 1 of *Aeschylus with an English Translation*, translated by H. W. Smyth, 211–315. 2 vols. Loeb Classical Library. London: Heinemann, 1922.

Agourides, S. "Apocalypse of Sedrach." In *The Old Testament Pseudepigrapha: Apocalyptic Literature and Testaments*, edited by J. H. Charlesworth, 605–13. Garden City, N.Y.: Doubleday, 1983.

Alonso-Schökel, L. "God's Answer to Job." In *Job and the Silence of God*, edited by C. Duquoc and C. Floristán, 45–51. Concilium. New York: Seabury, 1983.

Alter, R. *Canon and Creativity: Modern Writing and the Authority of Scripture.* New Haven: Yale University Press, 2000.

Anderson, F. I. *Job: An Introduction and Commentary.* Tyndale Old Testament Commentaries. Downers Grove, Ill.: Inter-Varsity, 1976.

Anderson, H. "4 Maccabees: A New Translation and Introduction." In *The Old Testament Pseudepigrapha: Expositions of the "Old Testament" and Legends, Wisdom and Philosophical Literature, Prayers, Psalms, and Odes, Fragments of Lost Judeo-Hellenistic Works*, edited by J. H. Charlesworth, 531–64. London: Darton, Longman & Todd, 1985.

Anzelewsky, F. *Dürer: His Art and Life.* Translated by H. Grieve. New York: Alpine, 1981.

Aocella, J. "European Dreams: Rediscovering Joseph Roth." *New Yorker*, January 19, 2004, 81–86.

Astell, A. W. *Job, Boethius, and Epic Truth.* Ithaca, N.Y.: Cornell University Press, 1994.

———. "Job's Wife, Walter's Wife, and the Wife of Bath." In *Old Testament Women in Western Literature*, edited by R.-J. Frontain and J. Wojcik, 92–107. Conway: University of Central Arkansas Press, 1991.

———. "Translating Job as Female." In *Translation Theory and Practice in the Middle Ages*, edited by J. Beer, 59–69. Kalamazoo, Mich.: Medieval Institute, 1997.

Arberry, A. J. *The Koran Interpreted.* 2 vols. New York: Macmillan, 1955.

Arcangeli, C. A. "La sappienza nel silenzio: Riconsiderando la pala di San Giobbe." *Saggi e Memorie di Storia dell'arte* 22 (1998): 9–54.

Auden, W. H. "The Quest." In *W. H. Auden: Collected Poems,* edited by E. Mendelson, 285–95. New York: Vintage International, 1991.

Balentine, S. E. "The Church of Saint Job." *Review and Expositor* 96, no. 4 (1999): 501–18.

——. "For No Reason." *Interpretation* 57, no. 4 (2003): 349–69.

——. *Job.* Smyth and Helwys Bible Commentary. Macon, Ga.: Smyth & Helwys, 2006.

——. "Job and the Priests: 'He Leads Priests Away Stripped' (Job 12:19)." In Dell and Kynes, *Reading Job Intertextually,* 42–53. Library of Hebrew Bible/Old Testament Studies, Book 574. New York: Bloomsbury, 2013.

——. "'Let Love Clasp Grief Lest Both Be Drowned.'" *Perspectives in Religious Studies* 30, no. 4 (2003): 381–97.

——. "My Servant Job Shall Pray for You." *Theology Today* 58, no. 4 (2002): 502–18.

——. "Traumatizing Job." *Review and Expositor* 105, no. 2 (2008): 213–28.

——. "Who Will Be Job's Redeemer?" *Perspectives in Religious Studies* 26, no. 3 (1999): 269–89.

——. "'Will You Condemn Me That You May Be Justified?'—The Character of God in Job." In *Community and Character Ethics in Ancient Near Eastern Wisdom Literature,* edited by K. M. Heim, forthcoming.

Barton, J. "The Dark Side of God in the Old Testament." In *Ethical and Unethical in the Old Testament: God and Humans in Dialogue,* edited by K. Dell, 122–34. New York: Clark, 2010.

Baskin, J. R. *Pharaoh's Counsellors: Job, Jethro, and Balaam in Rabbinic and Patristic Tradition.* Brown Judaic Studies 56. Chico, Cal.: Scholars, 1983.

Bayle, P. *An Historical and Critical Dictionary.* 4 vols. London: Harper, 1710.

Beal, T. K. *Religion and Its Monsters.* New York: Routledge, 2002.

Beecher, D. "Spenser's Redcrosse Knight: Despair and the Elizabethan Malady." In "Poetry and Religion 1545–1600." Special issue, *Renaissance and Reformation* n.s. 11 (1987): 103–20.

Beer, G. *Der Text des Buches Hiob.* Marburg: N. G. Elwertsche Verlagsbuchhandlung, 1897.

Begg, C. T. "Comparing Characters: The Book of Job and the *Testament of Job.*" In Beuken, *Book of Job,* 435–45.

Beiser, F. *The Fate of Reason: German Philosophy from Kant to Fichte.* Cambridge, Mass.: Harvard University Press, 1987.

Ben-Barak, Z. "Inheritance by Daughters in the Ancient Near East." *Journal of Semitic Studies* 25, no. 1 (1980): 22–33.

Ben Zvi, E. "The Dialogue between Abraham and YHWH in Gen 18:23–32: A Historical-Critical Analysis." *Journal for the Study of the Old Testament* 53 (1992): 27–46.

Berger, A. L. *Children of Job: American Second-Generation Witnesses to the Holocaust.* Albany: State University of New York Press, 1997.

Bernard of Clairvaux. "In Praise of the New Chivalry." In *The History of Feudalism,* edited by D. Herlihy, 288–98. London: Macmillan, 1970.

Bertagnolli, P. A. *Prometheus in Music: Representations of the Myth in the Romantic Era.* Aldershot, U.K.: Ashgate, 2007.

Besserman, L. *The Legend of Job in the Middle Ages.* Cambridge, Mass.: Harvard University Press, 1979.

Beuken, W. A. M., ed. *The Book of Job.* Bibliotheca ephemeridum theologicarum lovaniensium 114. Leuven: Leuven University Press, 1994.

Blake, W. *The Illustrations of the Book of Job.* New York: Pierpont Morgan Library, 1935.

Blenkinsopp, J. "Abraham and the Righteous of Sodom." *Journal of Semitic Studies* 33 (1982): 119–32.

———. "The Judge of All the Earth: Theodicy in the Midrash on Genesis 18:22–33." *Journal of Semitic Studies* 41 (1990): 1–12.

Bloom, H. "Napoleon and Prometheus: The Romantic Myth of Organic Energy." In *The Ringers in the Tower: Studies in the Romantic Tradition,* 81–84. Chicago: University of Chicago Press, 1971.

Blumenberg, H. *Work on Myth.* Translated by R. M. Wallace. Cambridge, Mass.: MIT Press, 1990.

Boer, P. A. H. de. "Does Job Retract? Job xlii 6." In *Selected Studies in Old Testament Exegesis,* edited by C. van Duin, 179–95. Old Testament Studies 27. Leiden: Brill, 1991.

Bolgar, R. R. "Hero or Anti-Hero? The Genesis and Development of the *Miles Christianus.*" In *Concepts of the Hero in the Middle Ages and Renaissance,* edited by N. T. Burns and C. J. Reagan, 120–46. Albany: State University of New York Press, 1975.

Borchert, W. *The Man Outside.* Translated by D. Porter. New York: New Directions, 1971.

Bovati, P. *Re-establishing Justice: Legal Terms, Concepts, and Procedures in the Hebrew Bible. Journal for the Study of the Old Testament:* Supplement Series 105. Sheffield: Sheffield Academic, 1994.

Brandes, G. *Goethe.* Berlin: Reiss, 1922.

Brock, S. P., ed. *Testamentum Iobi.* Pseudepigrapha Veteris Testamenti Graece 2. Leiden: Brill, 1967.

Brown, K. "The Artist of the *Leviathan* Title-Page." *British Library Journal* 4, no. 1 (1978): 24–36.

Brown, R. M. *Elie Wiesel: Messenger to All Humanity.* Notre Dame: University of Notre Dame Press, 1983.

Brown, W. P. *The Seven Pillars of Creation: The Bible, Science, and the Ecology of Wonder.* Oxford: Oxford University Press, 2010.

Buber, M. "The Dialogue between Heaven and Earth." In *On Judaism,* edited by N. Glatzer, 214–25. New York: Schocken Books, 1972.

———. *The Prophetic Faith.* Trans. C. Witton-Davies. New York: Macmillan, 1949.

Buchler, A. *Studies in Sin and Atonement in the Rabbinic Literature of the First Century.* Oxford: Oxford University Press, 1928.

Buck, A. "Über einige Deutungen des Prometheusmythos." In *Romanica, Festschrift für Gerhard Rohlfs,* edited by H. Lausberg and H. Weinrich, 86–96. Halle: Niemeyer, 1958.

Bueler, L. E. *The Tested Woman: Women's Choices, Men's Judgments, and the Shaping Stories.* Columbus: Ohio State University Press, 2001.

Bunker, R. A. *Bibliographical Study of the Greek Works in Translations Published in France during the Renaissance: The Decade 1540–1550.* New York: Kessinger, 1939.

Burrell, D. "Maimonides, Aquinas, and Gersonides on Providence and Evil." *Religious Studies* 20, no. 3 (1984): 335–51.

Burton, R. *The Anatomy of Melancholy.* Edited by F. Dell and P. Jordan Smith. New York: Tudor, 1927.

Byron, G. "Prometheus." In *The Poetical Works of Byron,* edited by R. F. Gleckner, 191. Boston: Houghton Mifflin, 1975.

Calvin, J. *Institutes of the Christian Religion.* Edited by J. T. McNeill. Translated by F. L. Battles. 2 vols. The Library of Christian Classics. Louisville: Westminster John Knox, 2006.

——. *Ioannis Calvini opera quae supersunt omnia.* Edited by W. Baum, E. Cunitz, and E. Reuss. 59 vols. Brunswick, N.J.: Schwetschke, 1863–1900.

——. *Sermons from Job by John Calvin.* Selected and translated by L. Nixon. Grand Rapids, Mich.: Eerdmans, 1952.

Cargas, H. J. *Harry James Cargas in Conversation with Elie Wiesel.* New York: Paulist, 1976.

Carriere, L. "Satan, Mephisto, und die Wetten bei Hiob." *Goethe* 20 (1958): 285–87.

Carstensen, R. "The Persistence of the Elihu Tradition in Later Jewish Writings." *Lexington Theological Quarterly* 2, no. 2 (1967): 37–46.

Carus, P. *The History of the Devil and the Idea of Evil from the Earliest Times to the Present Day.* New York: Open Court, 1900. Rpt., New York: Land's End, 1969.

Cassiodorus. *Exposito Psalmorum.* Edited by M. Adriaen. Corpus Christianorum Series Latina 97. Turnhout: Brepols, 1958.

Caxton, W., trans. *The Book of the Knight of the Tower.* London: Oxford University Press, 1971.

Charlesworth, J. H. *The Good and Evil Serpent: How a Universal Symbol Became Christianized.* Anchor Yale Bible Reference Library. New Haven: Yale University Press, 2010.

——. *Serpent Iconography and the Archaeology of the Land from Dan to Bethsheba* (forthcoming).

Chaucer, G. *The Canterbury Tales.* Translated into modern English by N. Coghill. Baltimore: Penguin Books, 1951.

——. *The Canterbury Tales.* In *The Riverside Chaucer,* edited by L. D. Benson, 3–328. 3rd ed. Boston: Houghton Mifflin, 2000.

Chin, C. "Job and the Injustice of God: Implicit Arguments in Job 13:17–14:12." *Journal for the Study of the Old Testament* 64 (1994): 91–101.

Chittister, J. *Job's Daughters: Women and Power.* New York: Paulist, 1990.

Christiansen, A. *Le premier homme et le premier roi dans l'histoire légendaire des Iraniens.* 2 vols. Stockholm: Norstedt, 1917–34.

Clines, D. J. A. *Job 1–42.* 3 vols. Word Biblical Commentary. Nashville: Nelson, 1989–2011.

———. "Job's Fifth Friend: An Ethical Critique of the Book of Job." *Biblical Interpretation* 12, no. 3 (2004): 233–50.

Collins, J. J. "Structure and Meaning in the *Testament of Job.*" In *Society of Biblical Literature: 1974 Seminar Papers,* vol. 1, edited by G. MacRae, 32–52. Cambridge, Mass.: Society of Biblical Literature, 1974.

Conisbee, P. *Georges de La Tour and His World.* Washington, D.C.: National Gallery Washington, 1996.

Coogan, M. D. "Job's Children." In *Lingering over Words: Studies in Ancient Near Eastern Literature in Honor of William L. Moran,* edited by T. Abusch, J. Huehnergaard, and P. Steinkeller, 135–47. Atlanta: Scholars, 1990.

Cook, D., trans. "Joseph and Aseneth." In *The Apocryphal Old Testament,* edited by H. F. D. Sparks, 473–503. Oxford: Oxford University Press, 1984.

Cormack, M. *William Blake: Illustrations of the Book of Job.* Richmond: Virginia Museum of Fine Arts, 1997.

Cox, C. E., trans. "Iob." In *A New English Translation of the Septuagint,* edited by A. Pietersma and B. G. Wright, 667–96. Oxford: Oxford University Press, 2007.

Cox, D. "The Book of Job as Bi-polar *Mašal:* Structure and Interpretation." *Antonianum* 62, no. 1 (1987): 12–25.

Crenshaw, J. L. *Reading Job: A Literary and Theological Commentary.* Macon, Ga.: Smyth & Helwys, 2011.

Cross, F. M. "The Council of Yahweh in Second Isaiah." *Journal of Near Eastern Studies* 12, no. 4 (1953): 274–77.

Curley, E. "The Covenant with God in Hobbes's *Leviathan.*" In *"Leviathan" after 350 Years,* edited by T. Sorrell and L. Foisneau, 199–216. Oxford: Clarendon, 2004.

Curtis, J. "On Job's Response to Yahweh." *Journal of Biblical Literature* 98, no. 4 (1979): 497–511.

Cuttler, C. D. "Job-Music-Christ: An Aspect of the Iconography of Job." *Bulletin de l'Institut Royal du Patrimoine Artistique/Koninklijk Instituut voor het Kunstpatrimonium* 15 (1975): 87–94.

Datz, G. *Die Gestalt Hiobs in der kirchlichen Exegese und der "Arme Heinrich" Hartmanns von Aue.* Göppingen: Kümmerle, 1973.

Day, J. *God's Conflict with the Dragon and the Sea.* Cambridge: Cambridge University Press, 2002.

Day, P. *An Adversary in Heaven: ŚĀṬĀN in the Hebrew Bible.* Atlanta: Scholars, 1988.

Defoe, D. *The Political History of the Devil.* Edited by I. N. Rothman and R. M. Bowerman. New York: AMS, 2003.

Delbanco, A. *Melville: His World and His Work.* New York: Knopf, 2005.

Dell, K., and W. Kynes, eds. *Reading Job Intertextually.* Library of Hebrew Bible/Old Testament Studies 574. New York: Bloomsbury, 2013.

Denis, V. "Saint Job, patron des musiciens." *Revue belge d'archéologie et d'histoire d'art* 21, no. 4 (1952): 253–95.

Derrida, J. "Devant la Loi." In *Kafka and the Contemporary Critical Performance,* edited by A. Udoff, translated by A. Ronell, 128–49. Bloomington: Indiana University Press, 1987.

Dhorme, E. *A Commentary on the Book of Job.* Nashville: Nelson, 1984.

Dick, M. B. "The Legal Metaphor in Job 31." *Catholic Biblical Quarterly* 41, no. 1 (1979): 37–50.

Dickinson, E. "#1551." In *The Complete Poems of Emily Dickinson,* edited by T. H. Johnson, 646. Boston: Little, Brown, 1961.

Dietrich, W., and C. Link. *Die dunklen Seiten Gottes: Willkür und Gewalt.* 5th ed. Neukirchen-Vluyn: Neukirchener, 2009.

———. *Die dunklen Seiten Gottes: Allmacht und Ohnmacht.* 3rd ed. Neukirchener-Vluyn: Neukirchener, 2009.

Diewert, D. A. "Job XXXVI 5 and the Root *m's* II." *Vetus Testamentum* 39, no. 1 (1989): 71–77.

Dostoevsky, F. *The Brothers Karamazov.* Translated and annotated by R. Pevear and L. Volokhonsky. New York: Vintage Books, 1990.

Driver, S. R., and G .B. Gray. *A Critical and Exegetical Commentary on the Book of Job.* Edinburgh: Clark, 1921.

Duensing, H., and A. de Santos Otero, "Apocalypse of Paul." In vol. 2 of *New Testament Apocrypha: Writings Related to the Apostles Apocalypses and Related Subjects,* edited by W. Schneemelcher. Rev. ed. of the collection initiated by E. Hennecke. Translated by R. M. Wilson, 712–48. Louisville: Westminster/John Knox, 1992.

Duhm, B. *Das Buch Hiob.* Kurzer Hand-Commentar zum Alten Testament 16. Freiburg: Mohr Siebeck, 1897.

Eccles, M., ed. *The Castle of Perseverance.* In *The Macro Plays: The Castle of Perseverance, Wisdom, Mankind.* Early English Text Society o.s. 262. London: Oxford University Press, 1969.

Edwards, C. "Greatest of All People in the East: Venturing East of Uz." *Review and Expositor* 99, no. 4 (2002): 529–40.

Eisen, R. *The Book of Job in Medieval Philosophy.* Oxford: Oxford University Press, 2004.

Fackenheim, E. *God's Presence in History: Jewish Affirmations and Philosophical Reflections.* New York: New York University Press, 1970.

———. *To Mend the World: Foundations of Future Jewish Thought.* New York: Schocken Books, 1982.

Fernández Marcos, N. "The Septuagint Reading of the Book of Job." In Beuken, *Book of Job,* 251–66.

Ferrua, A. *The Unknown Catacomb: A Unique Discovery of Early Christian Art.* Translated by I. Inglis. New Landmark, Scotland: Geddes & Grosset, 1991.

Fine, H. L. "The Tradition of a Patient Job." *Journal of Biblical Literature* 74, no. 1 (1955): 28–32.

Fishbane, M. "Jeremiah IV 23–26 and Job III 3–13: A Recovered Use of the Creation Pattern." *Vetus Testamentum* 21, no. 2 (1971): 151–67.

Fitzmyer, J. A. *Tobit.* Commentaries on Early Jewish Literature. Berlin: de Gruyter, 2003.

Fohrer, G. *Das Buch Hiob.* Kommentar zum Alten Testament. Gütersloh: Mohn, 1963.

Forsyth, N. *The Old Enemy: Satan and the Combat Myth.* Princeton: Princeton University Press, 1987.

Foster, F. M. K. *English Translations from the Greek: A Bibliographical Survey.* New York: Columbia University Press, 1918.

Freund, J. "Le Dieu Mortal." In *Hobbes-Forschungen,* edited by R. Koselleck and R. Schnur, 33–52. Berlin: Dunker & Humboldt, 1969.

Friedländer, M. J. "Der Meister der Barbara-Legende." *Jahrbuch für Kunstwissenschaft* 11 (1924): 20–25.

Frost, R. *A Masque of Reason.* In *The Poetry of Robert Frost: The Collected Poems, Complete and Unabridged,* edited by E. C. Lathem, 472–90. New York: Holt, 1979.

———. "Our Hold on the Planet." In *The Poetry of Robert Frost: The Collected Poems, Complete and Unabridged,* edited by E. C. Lathem, 349. New York: Holt, 1979.

Frye, N. *The Great Code: The Bible and Literature.* New York: Harcourt, 1983.

Gaddis, W. *A Frolic of His Own.* New York: Scribner, 1995.

Gammie, J. G. "Angelology and Demonology in the Septuagint of the Book of Job." *Hebrew Union College Annual* 56 (1985): 1–19.

Gard, D. H. "The Concept of Job's Character According to the Greek Translator of the Hebrew Text." *Journal of Biblical Literature* 72, no. 3 (1953): 182–86.

———. *The Exegetical Method of the Greek Translator of the Book of Job.* Society of Biblical Literature Monograph Series 8. Philadelphia: Society of Biblical Literature, 1952.

Garrett, S. R. "The Patience of Job and the Patience of Jesus." *Interpretation* 53, no. 3 (1999): 254–64.

———. "The 'Weaker Sex' in the *Testament of Job.*" *Journal of Biblical Literature* 112, no. 1 (1993): 55–70.

Gelber, S. M. *Job Stands Up: The Biblical Text of the Book of Job Arranged for the Theater.* New York: Union of Hebrew Congregations, 1975.

Gentry, P. *The Asterisked Materials in the Greek Job.* Society of Biblical Literature Septuagint and Cognate Studies 38. Atlanta: Scholars, 1995.

Gerleman, H. S. *Studies in the Septuagint I: The Book of Job.* Lund: Gleerup, 1946.

———. "The Theological Approach of the Greek Translator of Job 1–15." *Journal of Biblical Literature* 68, no. 3 (1949): 231–40.

Gersonides. *The Wars of the Lord.* Translated by S. Feldman. 3 vols. Philadelphia: Jewish Publication Society of America, 1984–89.

Gide, A. *Marshlands and Prometheus Misbound.* Translated by G. D. Painter. New York: McGraw-Hill, 1965.

Gietmann, G. *Parzival, Faust, Job und einige verwandte Dichtungen.* Freiburg: Herdersche Verlagshandlung, 1887.

Ginsberg, H. L. "Job the Patient and Job the Impatient." *Supplements to Vetus Testamentum* 17 (1969): 88–111.

Ginzberg, L. *Legends of the Jews.* Translated by H. Szold and P. Radin. 2nd ed. 2 vols. Philadelphia: Jewish Publication Society, 2003.

Gitay, Z. "The Portrayal of Job's Wife and Her Representation in the Visual Arts." In *Fortunate the Eyes That See: Essays in Honor of David Noel Freedman,* edited by A. Breck and A. Bartlett, 516–26. Grand Rapids, Mich.: Eerdmans, 1995.

Glatzer, N. "The Book of Job and Its Interpreters." In *Biblical Motifs: Origins and Transformations,* edited by A. Altman, 197–220. Cambridge, Mass.: Harvard University Press, 1966.

———, ed. *The Dimensions of Job: A Study and Selected Readings.* New York: Schocken Books, 1969.

———. "Introduction: A Study of Job." In Glatzer, *Dimensions of Job,* 1–48.

Glazov, G. Y. "The Significance of the 'Hand on the Mouth' Gesture in Job XL 4." *Vetus Testamentum* 52, no. 1 (2002): 30–41.

Goethe, J. W. von. *Faust: Eine Tragödie.* 2 vols. Basel: Schwabe, 1949.

———. *Goethe's Faust.* Translated and with an introduction by W. Kaufmann. New York: Doubleday, 1961.

Golden, L. "Zeus the Protector and Zeus the Destroyer." *Classical Philology* 57, no. 1 (1962): 20–26.

Good, E. M. *In Turns of Tempest: A Reading of Job with a Translation.* Stanford: Stanford University Press, 1990.

Goodman, L. E., trans. *The Book of Theodicy: Translation and Commentary on the Book of Job.* By Saadiah ben Joseph al-Fayyumi. New Haven: Yale University Press, 1988.

Gordis, R. *The Book of Job: Commentary, New Translation, and Special Studies.* New York: Jewish Theological Seminary, 1978.

Gordon, R. P. "KAI TO TELOS KYRIOU EIDETE (Jas. 5 v.11)." *Journal of Theological Studies* 26, no. 1 (1975): 91–95.

Gray, G. B. "The Additions in the Greek Version of Job." *Expositor* 19 (1920): 422–38.

Gray, P. "Points and Lines: Thematic Parallelism in the Letter of James and the *Testament of Job.*" *New Testament Studies* 50, no. 3 (2004): 406–24.

Greenlief, W. H. "A Note on Hobbes and the Book of Job." *Anales de la Catedra Francisco Suarez* 14 (1974): 11–34.

Greenstein, E. L. "A Forensic Understanding of the Speech from the Whirlwind." In *Texts, Temples, and Traditions: A Tribute to Menahem Haran,* edited by M. V. Fox, V. A. Hurowitz, A. Hurvitz, M. L. Klein, B. J. Schwartz, and N. Shupak, 241–58. Winona Lake, Ind.: Eisenbrauns, 1996.

———. "Job's Wife—Was She Right After All?" *Beth Mikra* 178 (2004): 19–31 [Hebrew].

Greg, W. *Doctor Faustus 1604–1616*. Oxford: Clarendon, 1950.

Gregory the Great. *Morals of the Book of Job*. Edited by C. Marriott. 3 vols. Oxford: John Henry Parker, 1844–45. Published in Latin as *S. Gregorii Magni: Moralia in Job*. Edited by M. Adriaen. Corpus Christianorum Series Latina, 143, 143a, 143b. Turnhout: Brepols, 1979–85.

Griffith, D. D. *The Origin of the Griselda Story*. Seattle: University of Washington Press, 1931.

Gruden, W. "Seeking a Context for the *Testament of Job*." *Journal for the Study of the Pseudepigrapha* 18, no. 3 (2009): 163–79.

Grünbaum, M. *Neue Beiträge zur semitischen Sagenkunde*. Leiden: Brill, 1893.

Guillén Robles, F. *Leyendas moriscas sacadas de varios manuscritos existentes en las Bibliotecas Nacional, Real, y de D. P. Gayangos*. 3 vols. Madrid: Tello, 1885.

Haag, H. *Teufelsglaube*. Tübingen: Katzmann, 1974.

Haak, R. "A Study and New Interpretation of qṣr npš." *Journal of Biblical Literature* 101, no. 2 (1982): 161–67.

Habel, N. *The Book of Job: A Commentary*. Old Testament Library. Philadelphia: Westminster, 1985.

Handy, L. K. *Among the Host of Heaven: The Syro-Palestinian Pantheon as Bureaucracy*. Winona Lake, Ind.: Eisenbrauns, 1994.

Hartt, F. "Carpaccio's Meditation on the Passion." *Art Bulletin* 23, no. 1 (1940): 25–35.

Hartley, J. *The Book of Job*. New International Commentary on the Old Testament. Grand Rapids, Mich.: Eerdmans, 1988.

Haas, C. "Job's Perseverance in the Testament of Job." In *Studies on the Testament of Job*, edited by M. A. Knibb and P. W. van der Host, 117–54. Society for New Testament Studies Monograph Series 66. Cambridge: Cambridge University Press, 1989.

Hauck, F. "*hypomenō, hypomonē*." In vol. 4 of *Theological Dictionary of the New Testament*, edited by G. Kittel, 581–88. Translated and edited by G. W. Bromiley. 10 vols. Grand Rapids, Mich.: Eerdmans, 1967.

Heater, H. *A Septuagint Translation Technique in the Book of Job*. Catholic Biblical Quarterly Monograph Series 11. Washington, D.C.: Catholic Biblical Association of America, 1982.

Henriques, A. R. *The Book of Mechtilde*. New York: Knopf, 1997.

Hesiod. *Theogony; Works and Days; Shield*. Translated by A. N. Athanassakis. Baltimore: Johns Hopkins University Press, 1983.

Hester, K. *Eschatology and Pain in St. Gregory the Great: The Christological Synthesis of Gregory's Morals on the Book of Job*. Eugene, Ore.: Wipf & Stock, 2008.

Hobbes, T. *Leviathan: Authoritative Text, Backgrounds, Interpretations*. Edited by R. E. Flathman and D. Johnston. New York: Norton, 1997.

Holman, C. "The Reconciliation of Ishmael: Moby Dick and the Book of Job." *South Atlantic Quarterly* 57 (1958): 477–90.

Holstein, J. A. "Melville's Inversion of Jonah in *Moby-Dick*." *Iliff Review* 42, no. 1 (1985): 13–20.

Hopkins, A. *The Sinful Knights: A Study of Middle English Penitential Romance.* Oxford: Clarendon, 1990.

Hornik, H. "The Venetian Images by Bellini and Carpaccio: Job as Intercessor or Prophet?" *Review and Expositor* 99, no. 4 (2002): 541–68.

Horst, P. W. van der. "Images of Women in the Testament of Job." In *Studies on the Testament of Job,* edited by M. A. Knibb and P. W. van der Host, 93–116. Society for New Testament Studies Monograph Series 66. Cambridge: Cambridge University Press, 1989.

Irwin, W. A. "Job and Prometheus." *Journal of Religion* 30, no. 1 (1950): 90–108.

Jacobs, I. "Literary Motifs in the Testament of Job." *Journal of Semitic Studies* 21 (1970): 1–10.

Janzen, J. G. *Job.* Interpretation. Atlanta: Knox, 1985.

Jeremias, J. *Theophanie: Die Geschichte einer alttestamentlichen Gattung.* Neukirchen-Vluyn: Neukirchener, 1965.

Johns, A. H. "Three Stories of a Prophet: Al-Ṭabirī's Treatment of Job in *Sūrah al-Anbiyāʾ* 83–4 (Part I)." *Journal of Qurʾanic Studies* 3, no. 2 (2001): 39–61.

Johnson, L. T. "The Letter of James." In vol. 12 of *The New Interpreter's Bible,* edited by L. Keck, 177–225. 12 vols. Nashville: Abingdon, 1994–98.

Johnson, T. J. *Now My Eyes See You: Unveiling an Apocalyptic Job.* Hebrew Bible Monographs 24. Sheffield: Sheffield Phoenix, 2009.

Joyce, P. M. "'Even if Noah, Daniel, and Job Were in It . . . ' (Ezekiel 14:14): The Case of Job and Ezekiel." In Dell and Kynes, *Reading Job Intertextually,* 118–28.

Jung, C. *Answer to Job.* Translated by R. F. C. Hull. London: Routledge & Kegan Paul, 1954.

Kafka, F. "Prometheus." In *Franz Kafka: The Complete Stories.* Edited by N. Glatzer, 432. New York: Schocken Books, 1971.

———. *The Trial.* Translated by W. Muir and E. Muir. Introduction by G. Steiner. New York: Schocken Books, 1992.

Kallen, H. M. *The Book of Job as a Greek Tragedy.* New York: Moffat, Yard, 1918.

Kant, I. "On the Failure of All Attempted Philosophical Theodicies." Translated by M. Despland in *Kant on History and Religion,* 283–97. Montreal: Queen's University Press, 1973.

Kaufmann, H. *Die Anwendung des Buches Hiob in der rabbinischen Agadah.* Frankfurt: Kauffmann, 1893.

Kaufmann, U. M. "Expostulation with the Divine: A Note on Contrasting Attitudes in Greek and Hebrew Piety." In P. S. Sanders, *Twentieth Century Interpretations,* 66–77.

Kaufmann, W. *Twenty German Poets: A Bilingual Collection.* New York: Random House, 1962.

Kazin, A. *God and the American Writer.* New York: Knopf, 1997.

Kee, H. C. "Satan, Magic, and Salvation in the Testament of Job." In *Society of Biblical Literature: 1974 Seminar Papers,* vol. 1, edited by G. MacRae, 53–76. Cambridge, Mass.: Society of Biblical Literature, 1974.

Keel, O. *Jahwes Entgegnung an Ijob.* Forschungen zur Religion und Literatur des Alten und Neuen Testaments 121. Göttingen: Vandenhoeck & Ruprecht, 1978.

Kelly, H. A. *Satan: A Biography.* Cambridge: Cambridge University Press, 2006.

Kendrick, T. D. *The Lisbon Earthquake.* Philadelphia: Lippincott, 1955.

Kennedy, B. *Knighthood in the Morte Darthur.* Cambridge, Mass.: Brewer, 1985.

Kepnes, S. *The Text as Thou: Martin Buber's Dialogical Hermeneutics and Narrative Theology.* Bloomington: Indiana University Press, 1992.

Kimhi, M. *Commentary on the Book of Job.* Edited by H. Basser and B. D. Walfish. Atlanta: Scholars, 1992.

Kisa'i, Muhammed ibn `Abd Allah al-. *Qisas al-Anbiya'.* In *Tales of the Prophets,* translated by W. M. Thackston, 192–204. Chicago: Great Books of the Islamic World, 1997.

Kluger, R. S. *Satan in the Old Testament.* Evanston, Ill.: Northwestern University Press, 1967.

Kohler, K. "*The Testament of Job:* An Essene Midrash on the Book of Job Reedited and Translated with Introductory Notes." In *Semitic Studies in Memory of Rev. Dr. Alexander Kohut,* edited by G. Kohut, 264–388. Berlin: Calvary, 1897.

Korpel, M., and J. de Moor. *The Silent God.* Leiden: Brill, 2011.

Kramer, S. N., trans. "Man and His God." In *Ancient Near Eastern Texts Relating to the Old Testament,* 3rd ed., edited by J. B. Pritchard, 589–91. Princeton: Princeton University Press, 1969.

Kreitzer, L. "*Moby-Dick:* Encountering the Leviathan of God." *Australian Religion Studies* 21 no. 3 (2008): 262–76.

Krüger, T. "Did Job Repent?" In Krüger et al,. *Buch Hiob,* 217–29.

Krüger, T., T. M. Oeming, K. Schmid, and C. Uehlinger, eds. *Das Buch Hiob und seine Interpretationen.* Abhandlungen zur Theologie des Alten und Neuen Testaments 88. Zurich: Theologischer Verlag Zürich, 2007.

Kubina, V. *Die Gottesreden im Buche Hiob.* Freiburger Theologischen Studien. Freiburg: Herder, 1979.

Kugler, R. A., and R. L. Rohrbaugh. "On Women and Honor in the *Testament of Job.*" *Journal for the Study of the Pseudepigrapha* 14, no. 1 (2001): 43–62.

Kynes, W. *My Heart Has Turned into Weeping: Job's Dialogue with the Psalms.* Beihefte zur Zeitschrift für die alttestamentliche Wissenschaft 473. Berlin: de Gruyter, 2012.

Lafond, J. "Tableau de Georges de la Tour au musée d'Épinal. 'Saint Pierre délivré' ou 'Job et sa femme?'" *Bulletin de la Société de l'histoire de l'art Francaise* (1935): 11–13.

Lafond, P. *Hieronymus Bosch.* Brussels: van Oest, 1914.

Lamartine, Alphonse de. *Cours familier de littérature.* Paris: Chez l'auteur, 1856.

Lamb, J. *The Rhetoric of Suffering: Reading the Book of Job in the Eighteenth Century.* Oxford: Clarendon, 1995.

Lambert, W. G. "The Babylonian Theodicy." In *Babylonian Wisdom Literature,* 63–91.

____, ed. and trans. *Babylonian Wisdom Literature.* Oxford: Clarendon, 1960.

——. "The Dialogue of Pessimism." In *Babylonian Wisdom Literature,* 139–49.

———. "The Poem of the Righteous Sufferer, *Ludlul Bēl Nēmeqi.*" In *Babylonian Wisdom Literature,* 21–62.

Lannois, M. "Job, sa femme et les musiciens." *Aesculape* 19 (1939): 194–207.

Lasine, S. "Job and His Friends in the Modern World: Kafka's *The Trial.*" In *The Voice from the Whirlwind: Interpreting the Book of Job,* edited by L. G. Perdue and W. C. Gilpin, 144–55. Nashville: Abingdon, 1992.

Lathrop, H. B. *Translations from the Classics into English from Caxton to Chapman, 1447–1620.* Madison, Wis.: Octagon, 1935.

Lauts, J. *Carpaccio: Paintings and Drawings.* Complete Edition. London: Phaidon, 1962.

Le Blant, E. "D'une representation inédite de Job sur un sarcophagi d'Arles." *Revue archéologique* n.s. 2 (1860): 36–44.

Legaspi, M. "Job's Wives in the Testament of Job: A Synthesis of Two Traditions." *Journal of Biblical Literature* 127, no. 1 (2008): 71–79.

Leibniz, G. W. *Philosophical Essays.* Edited and translated by R. Ariew and D. Garber. Indianapolis: Hackett, 1989.

———. *Theodicy.* Edited with an introduction by A. Farrar. Translated by H. M. Huggard. New York: Open Court, 1985.

Leivick, H. *In the Days of Job.* In *A Treasury of Yiddish Poetry,* ed. I. Howe and E. Greenberg, 126–45. New York: Schocken Books, 1969.

———. "The Jew—The Individual," as cited in *Three Great Jewish Plays,* translated by J. C. Landis, 115–18. New York: Applause Theatre, 1986.

Levenson, J. *The Book of Job in Its Time and in the Twentieth Century.* Cambridge, Mass.: Harvard University Press, 1972.

Levin, H. *The Sorrows of Job.* In *Modern Israeli Drama,* edited by M. Taub, 1–44. Portsmouth, N.H.: Heinemann, 1993.

Lewalski, B. *Milton's Brief Epic: The Genre, Meaning, and Art of "Paradise Regained."* Providence, R.I.: Brown University Press, 1966.

Linafelt, T. "The Undecidability of *barak* in the Prologue to Job and Beyond." *Biblical Interpretation* 4, no. 2 (1996): 154–72.

Lindblom, J. *Job and Prometheus: A Comparative Study.* Lund: Gleerup, 1939.

Liptzin, S. *The Flowering of Yiddish Literature.* New York: Yoseloff, 1963.

Long, J. R. *On the Properties of Soul and Body: De Proprietatibus Rerum Libri III et IV.* Toronto: Pontifical Institute of Mediaeval Studies, 1979.

Lowell, J. R. "The Present Crisis." In *The Complete Poetical Works of James Russell Lowell,* edited by H. E. Scudder, 67–68. Boston: Houghton Mifflin, 1897.

Lucian of Samosota. *Selected Stories of Lucian.* Translated by L. Casson. New York: Alden, 1962.

Lull, R. *The Book of the Ordre of Chyvalry.* Translated by W. Caxton. Edited by A. Byles. Early English Text Society o.s. 168. London: Oxford University Press, 1926.

Luther, M. *Luther's Works.* Edited by J. Pelikan and H. T. Lehman. 55 vols. St. Louis: Augsburg, 1955–86.

MacCracken, H. N. "Lydgatiana I: The Life of Holy Job." *Archiv für das Studium der neuern Sprachen* 126 (1911): 365–70.

MacDonald, H., and M. Hargreaves, *Thomas Hobbes: A Bibliography.* London: Bibliographical Society, 1952.

Machinist, P. "Job's Daughters and Their Inheritance in the Testament of Job and Its Biblical Congeners." In *The Echoes of Many Texts: Reflections on Jewish and Christian Traditions. Essays in Honor of Lou H. Silberman,* edited by W. G. Dever and J. E. Wright, 67–80. Atlanta: Scholars, 1997.

MacLeish, A. *J.B.: A Play in Verse.* Boston: Houghton Mifflin, 1956.

Magdalene, F. R. "Job's Wife as Hero: A Feminist-Forensic Reading of the Book of Job." *Biblical Interpretation* 14, no. 3 (2006): 209–58.

———. *On the Scales of Righteousness: Neo-Babylonian Trial Law and the Book of Job.* Brown Judaic Studies 348. Providence, R.I.: Brown University, 2007.

Maimonides. *The Guide of the Perplexed.* Translated with an introduction and notes by S. Pines. Chicago: University of Chicago Press, 1963.

Malbon, E. S. *The Iconography of the Sarcophagus of Junius Bassus.* Princeton: Princeton University Press, 1990.

Martinek, M. *Wie die Schlange zum wurde: Die Symbolik in der Paradiesgeschichte von der hebräischen Bibel bis zum Koran.* Studies in Oriental Religions 37. Wiesbaden: Harrassowitz, 1996.

Martinich, A. P. "The Interpretation of Covenants in Leviathan." In *"Leviathan" after 350 Years,* edited by T. Sorrell and L. Foisneau, 217–40. Oxford: Clarendon, 2004. 217–40.

———. *The Two Gods of "Leviathan": Thomas Hobbes on Religion and Politics.* Cambridge, Mass.: Cambridge University Press, 1992.

Mathewson, D. *Death and Survival in the Book of Job: Desymbolization and Traumatic Experience.* Library of Hebrew Bible/Old Testament Studies 450. New York: Clark, 2006.

May, H. G. "Prometheus and Job: The Problem of the God of Power and the Man of Worth." *Anglican Theological Review* 34, no. 4 (1952): 240–46.

McGinnis, C. N. "Playing the Devil's Advocate in Job: On Job's Wife." In *The Whirlwind: Essays on Job, Hermeneutics, and Theology in Memory of Jane Morse,* edited by S. L. Cook, C. L. Patton, and J. W. Watts, 121–41. *Journal for the Study of the Old Testament*: Supplement Series 336. London: Sheffield Academic, 2001.

Méautis, G. *L'Authenticité et la date du Prométhée.* Neuchatel: University of Neuchatel, 1960.

Meiller, A., ed. *La Pacience de Job: Mystére anonyme de XVe siécle (ms. fr. 1774).* Paris: Klincksieck, 1971.

Melville, H. *Moby-Dick.* Edited by H. Parker and H. Hayford. 2nd ed. New York: Norton, 2002.

———. *Pierre, or the Ambiguities.* New York: Grove, 1957.

Mende, T. *Durch Leiden zur Vollendung: Die Elihureden im Buch Ijob (Ijob 32–37).* Trierer Theologischen Studien 49. Trier: Paulinus, 1990.

Mies, F. "Le genre littéraire du livre de Job." *Revue biblique* 110, no. 3 (2003): 336–69.

Migne, J.-P., ed. *Patrologiae cursus completus: Series graeca.* 162 vols. Paris, 1857–86.

———, ed. *Patrologiae cursus completus: Series latina.* 217 vols. Paris, 1844–64.

Miles, J. *God: A Biography.* New York: Knopf, 1995.

Milstein, R., K. Rührdanz, and B. Schmitz. *Stories of the Prophets: Illustrated Manuscripts of Qisas al-Anbiya'.* Costa Mesa, Cal.: Mazda, 1999.

Milosz, C. "Campo Dei Fiori." In *New and Collected Poems, 1931–2001,* 33–35. New York: HarperCollins, 2001.

Milton, J. *Paradise Lost.* In *The Portable Milton,* edited with an introduction by D. Bush, 230–548. New York: Penguin, 1977.

Minnen, B. "Le Culte de Saint Job à Wezemaal aux XV and XVI Siècles." In *Congrès d'Ottignies-Louvin-La-Neuve: 26, 27 et août 2004. Actes des VII Congrès l'Association des cercles francophones d'histoire et d'archélogie de Belgique et LIV Congès de la fédération des cercles d'archéologie et d'histoire de Belgique,* 2:603–9. Brussels: Safran, 2007, 603–9.

———. "'Den Heyligen Sant al in Brabant.' The Church of Saint Martin in Wezemaal and the Devotion to St. Job 1000–2000. Retrospective: The Fluctuation of Devotion." In *Den Heyligen Sant al in Brabant.* Averbode: Uitgeverij Averbode, 2011.

Mintz, S. I. *The Hunting of Leviathan: Seventeenth Century Reactions to the Materialism and Moral Philosophy of Thomas Hobbes.* Cambridge: Cambridge University Press, 1969.

———. "Leviathan as Metaphor." *Hobbes Studies* 2, no. 1 (1989): 3–9.

Mitchell, S. *The Book of Job.* New York: Harper Collins, 1992.

Montefiore, H. G. "The Book of Job as a Greek Tragedy Restored." *Harvard Theological Review* 12, no. 2 (1919): 219–24.

Moore, C. A. *Tobit: A New Translation with Introduction and Commentary.* Anchor Bible 40a. New York: Doubleday, 1996.

Morrow, W. "Consolation, Rejection, and Repentance in Job 42:6." *Journal of Biblical Literature* 105, no. 2 (1986): 211–25.

———. "Toxic Religion and the Daughters of Job." *Studies in Religion* 27, no. 3 (1998): 263–76.

Müllner, I. "Literarische Diachronie in den Elihureden des Ijobbuches (Ijob 32–37)." In *Das Manna fällt auch Heute noch,* edited by F.-L. Hossfeld and L. Schwienhorst-Schönberger, 447–69. Freiburg: Herder, 2004.

Meyer, K. "St. Job as a Patron of Music." *Art Bulletin* 36, no. 1 (1954): 21–31.

Mullen, E. T. *The Assembly of the Gods.* Chico, Cal.: Scholars, 1980.

———. "Divine Assembly." In vol. 2 of *The Anchor Bible Dictionary,* edited by D. N. Freedman, 214–17. 6 vols. New York: Doubleday, 1992.

———. "Divine Assembly." In vol. 2 of *The New Interpreter's Dictionary of the Bible,* edited by K. D. Sakenfeld, 145–46. 5 vols. Nashville: Abingdon, 2006–9.

Müller, H.-P. "Keilschriftliche Parallelen zum biblischen Hiobbuch: Möglichkeit und Grenze des Vergleichs." In *Mythos-Kerygma-Wahrheit: Gesammelte Aufsätze zum*

Alten Testament in seiner Umwelt zur biblischen Theologie, 136–51. Beihefte zur Zeitschrift für die alttestamentliche Wissenschaft 200. Berlin: de Gruyter, 1991.

Murray, G. "Prometheus and Job." In P. S. Sanders, *Twentieth Century Interpretations*, 56–65.

Nam, D.-W. *Talking about God: Job 42:7–9 and the Nature of God in the Book of Job.* New York: Lang, 2003.

Neiman, S. *Evil in Modern Thought: An Alternative History of Philosophy.* Princeton: Princeton University Press, 2002.

———. *The Unity of Reason: Rereading Kant.* Oxford: Oxford University Press, 1994.

Nietzsche, F. *The Birth of Tragedy.* Translated by W. Kaufmann. New York: Vintage Books, 1967.

Newby, G. D. *The Making of the Last Prophet: A Reconstruction of the Earliest Biography of Muhammad.* Columbia: University of South Carolina Press, 1989.

Newsom, C. *The Book of Job: A Contest of Moral Imaginations.* Oxford: Oxford University Press, 2003.

———. "The Book of Job: Introduction, Commentary, and Reflections." In vol. 4 of *The New Interpreter's Bible,* edited by L. Keck, 319–637. 12 vols. Nashville: Abingdon, 1994–98.

Ngwa, K. N. *The Hermeneutics of the "Happy" Ending in Job 42:7–17.* Beihefte zur Zeitschrift für die alttestamentliche Wissenschaft 354. Berlin: de Gruyter, 2005.

Nissinen, M., trans. "The Just Sufferer." In *Prophets and Prophecy in the Ancient Near East,* edited by P. Machinist, translated by M. Nissinen, C. L. Seow, and R. Kitner, 184. Society of Biblical Literature Writings from the Ancient World 12. Atlanta: Society of Biblical Literature, 2003.

Nussbaum, M. *Poetic Justice: The Literary Imagination and Public Life.* Boston: Beacon, 1995.

Oberhänsli, G. "Job in Modern and Contemporary Literature on the Background of Tradition: Sidelights of a Jewish Reading." In Dell and Kynes, *Reading Job Intertextually,* 272–84.

Oberhänsli-Widmer, G. *Hiob in jüdischer Antike und Moderne: Die Wirkungsgeschichte Hiobs in der jüdischen Litertaur.* Neukirchen-Vluyn: Neukirchener, 2003.

Olyan, S. M. *Biblical Mourning: Ritual and Social Dimensions.* Oxford: Oxford University Press, 2004.

Orlinsky, H. "Some Corruptions in the Greek Text of Job." *Jewish Quarterly Review* 26, no. 2 (1935–36): 133–45.

———. "Studies in the Septuagint of the Book of Job." *Hebrew Union College Annual* 28 (1957): 53–74; 29 (1958): 229–71; 30 (1959): 153–67; 32 (1961): 239–68; 33 (1962): 119–51; 35 (1964): 57–78; 36 (1965): 34–57.

Osten, G. von der. "Job and Christ: The Development of a Devotional Image." *Journal of the Wartburg and Courtauld Institutes* 16, no. 1/2 (1953): 153–58.

Ozick, C. "The Impious Impatience of Job." In *Quarrel and Quandary,* 59–73. New York: Knopf, 2000.

Paffenroth, K. *In Praise of Wisdom: Literary and Theological Reflections on Faith and Reason.* New York: Continuum, 2004.

Pagels, E. *The Origin of Satan.* New York: Random House, 1995.

Papadaki-Oekland, S. *Byzantine Illuminated Manuscripts of the Book of Job: A Preliminary Study of the Miniature Illustrations, Its Origin and Development.* Athens: Brepols, 2009.

Pardes, I. *Countertraditions in the Bible: A Feminist Approach.* Cambridge, Mass.: Harvard University Press, 1994.

———. *Melville's Bibles.* Berkeley: University of California Press, 2008.

Parker, H. *Herman Melville: A Biography.* 2 vols. Baltimore: Johns Hopkins University Press, 1996–2002.

Parunak, H. Van Dyke. "A Semantic Survey of NḤM." *Biblica* 56 (1975): 512–32.

Patrick, D. "The Translation of Job 42:6." *Vetus Testamentum* 26, no. 3 (1976): 369–71.

Patterson, L. "For the Wyves Love of Bathe': Feminine Rhetoric and Poetic Resolution in the *Roman de la Rose* and the *Canterbury Tales.*" *Speculum* 58, no. 3 (1983): 656–95.

Pauphilet, A., ed., *La Queste de Saint Grail.* Paris: Champion, 1921. Translated by P. M. Matarasso as *The Quest of the Holy Grail.* Baltimore: Penguin Books, 1969.

Pearsall, D. "The Development of Middle English Romance." *Medieval Studies* 27 (1965): 91–116.

Penchansky, D. "Job's Wife: The Satan's Handmaid." In *Shall Not the Judge of All the Earth Do What Is Right? Studies on the Nature of God in Tribute to James L. Crenshaw,* edited by D. Penchansky and P. Redditt, 223–28. Winona Lake, Ind.: Eisenbrauns, 2000.

Pendergast, S., and T. Pendergast, eds. *Reference Guide to World Literature.* 2 vols. Detroit: St. James, 2003.

Perdue, L. G. "Job's Assault on Creation." *Hebrew Annual Review* 10 (1987): 295–315.

———. *Wisdom and Creation: The Theology of Wisdom Literature.* Nashville: Abingdon, 1994.

———. *Wisdom in Revolt: Metaphorical Theology in the Book of Job.* Journal for the Study of the Old Testament: Supplement Series 112. Sheffield: Almond, 1991.

Perets, Y. L. "Bontsye the Silent." In Zuckerman, *Job the Silent,* 181–95.

Peretz, E. *Literature, Disaster, and the Enigma of Power: A Reading of "Moby-Dick."* Stanford: Stanford University Press, 2003.

Perraymond, M. *La figura di Giobbe nella cultura paleocristiana tra esegesi patristica e manifestazioni iconografiche.* Studi di antichità cristiana 58. Vatican City: Pontifico Istituto di Archeologia Christiana, 2002.

Perry, M. E. "Patience and Pluck: Job's Wife, Conflict and Resistance in Morisco Manuscripts Hidden in the Sixteenth Century." In *Women, Texts and Authority in the Early Modern Spanish World,* edited by M. V. Vicente and L. R. Corteguera, 91–106. Hampshire: Ashgate, 2003.

Phillips, A. "NEBALAH—A Term for Serious Disorderly and Unruly Conduct." *Vetus Testamentum* 25, no. 2 (1975): 237–42.

Phillips, C. "An Unrecognized Carpaccio." *Burlington Magazine* 19, no. 99 (1911): 144–52.

Philonenko, M. "Le Testament de Job: Introduction, traduction, et notes." *Semitica* 18 (1968): 1–75.

———. "Le Testament de Job et les Thérapeutes." *Semitica* 8 (1958): 41–53.

Pilger, A. "Sokrates in der Kunst der Neuzeit." *Zeitschrift für Kunst und Kulture des klassischen Altertums* 14 (1938): 281–94.

Podlecki, A. J. "*Prometheus Bound.*" In *The Political Background of Aeschylean Tragedy,* 101–22. Ann Arbor: University of Michigan Press, 1966.

———. "Appendix B: The Date of *Prometheus Bound.*" In *The Political Background of Aeschylean Tragedy,* 142–47. Ann Arbor: University of Michigan Press, 1966.

Pope, A. "Essay on Man." In *Essays on Man and Other Poems,* 289–94. New York: Dover, 1994.

Pope, M. *El in the Ugaritic Texts.* Leiden: Brill, 1955.

———. *Job.* Anchor Bible 15. Garden City, N.Y.: Doubleday, 1979.

Prudentius. *Psychomachia.* In vol. 1 of *Prudentius.* Translated and edited by H. J. Thomson, 274–343. 2 vols. Loeb Classical Library. Cambridge, Mass.: Harvard University Press, 1969.

Rackham, P. *San Gimignano of the Beautiful Towers.* Sienna: Poggibonsi, 1998.

Raffel, C. M. "Providence as Consequent upon the Intellect: Maimonides' Theory of Providence." *Association for Jewish Studies Review* 12, no. 1 (1987): 27–52.

Rahlfs, A., ed. "Machabaeorum IV." In *Septuaginta,* 1157–84. Stuttgart: Württembergische Bibelanstalt, 1935.

Raine, K. *The Human Face of God: William Blake and the Book of Job.* New York: Thames & Hudson, 1982.

Raphael, D. D. "Tragedy and Religion." In P. S. Sanders, *Twentieth Century Interpretations,* 46–55.

Réau, L. "Héros et Héroïnes de la Bible." In *Iconographie de L'Art Chrétien. Vol.II: Iconographie de la Bible, I Ancien Testament,* 310–42. Paris: Presses Universitaires de France, 1956.

Reed, A. Y. "Job as Jobab: The Interpretation of Job in LXX Job 42:17 b–e." *Journal of Biblical Literature* 120, no. 1 (2001): 31–55.

Reines, A. "Maimonides' Concepts of Providence and Theodicy." *HUCA* 43 (1972): 169–205.

Richter, H. *Studien zu Hiob: Der Aufbau des Hiobbuches dargestellt an den Gattungen des Rechtsleben.* Theologische Arbeiten 11. Berlin: Evangelische Verlagsanstalt, 1959.

Roberts, J. J. M. "Job's Summons to Yahweh: The Exploitation of a Legal Metaphor." *Restoration Quarterly* 16, no. 3–4 (1973): 159–65.

Robinson, H. W. "The Council of Yahweh." *Journal of Theological Studies* o.s. 45 (1944): 151–57.

Roche, P. *Aeschylus, Prometheus Bound: A New Translation, Introduction, and Commentary.* Wauconda, Ill.: Bolchazy-Carducci, 1998.

Roskies, D. G. "The People of the Lost Book: A Cultural Manifesto." *Orim* 2, no. 1 (1986): 7–34.

Roskoff, G. *Geschichte des Teufels.* Leipzig: Brockhaus, 1869.

Roth, J. *Job: The Story of a Simple Man.* Translated by D. Thompson. Woodstock: Overlook, 2003.

Roth, W. M. W. "NBL." *Vetus Testamentum* 10, no. 4 (1960): 394–409.

Rowland, C. *Blake and the Bible.* New Haven: Yale University Press, 2011.

Rowley, H. H. *Job.* The Century Bible. Ontario: Nelson, 1970.

Russell, J. B. *The Devil: Perceptions of Evil from Antiquity to Primitive Christianity.* Ithaca, N.Y.: Cornell University Press, 1977.

———. *Satan: The Early Christian Tradition.* Ithaca, N.Y.: Cornell University Press, 1981.

———. *Lucifer: The Devil in the Middle Ages.* Ithaca, N.Y.: Cornell University Press, 1984.

———. *Mephistopheles: The Devil in the Modern World.* Ithaca, N.Y.: Cornell University Press, 1986.

———. *The Prince of Darkness: Radical Evil and the Power of Good in History.* Ithaca, N.Y.: Cornell University Press, 1988.

Saadiah Gaon. *The Book of Beliefs and Opinions.* Translated by S. Rosenblatt. New Haven: Yale University Press, 1948.

———. "Selections of *Beliefs and Opinions.*" Edited and translated by A. Altmann. In part 2 of *Three Jewish Philosophers,* edited by H. Lewy, A. Altmann, and I. Heinemann, 137–39. New York: Atheneum, 1969.

Sachs, N. "Landscape of Screams." In *Art from the Ashes: A Holocaust Anthology,* edited by L. Langer, 651–52. Oxford: Oxford University Press, 1995.

Saebo, M. "*nābāl,* fool." In vol. 2 of *Theological Lexicon of the Old Testament,* edited by E. Jenni and C. Westermann, 712. Translated by M. E. Biddle. 3 vols. Peabody, Mass.: Hendrikson, 1997.

Sanders, J. A. *The Dead Sea Psalms Scroll.* Ithaca, N.Y.: Cornell University Press, 1967.

Sanders, P. S., ed. *Twentieth Century Interpretations of the Book of Job.* Englewood Cliffs, N.J.: Prentice-Hall, 1968.

Sarna, N. M. "Epic Substratum in the Prose of Job." *Journal of Biblical Literature* 76, no. 1 (1957): 13–25.

Sawyer, J. F. A. "Job." In *The Oxford Handbook of the Reception History of the Bible,* edited by M. Lieb, E. Mason, and J. Roberts, 25–36. Oxford: Oxford University Press, 2011.

———. "The Role of Reception History, Reader-Response Criticism, and/or Impact History in the Study of the Bible: Definition and Evaluation." http://drchris.me/bbib comm/files/sawyer2004.pdf. Accessed July 19, 2013.

Sayers, D. "The Faust-Legend and the Idea of the Devil." *Publications of the English Goethe Society* n.s. 15 (1945): 1–20.

Schaller, B. "Das Testament Hiobs und die Septuaginta-Übersetzung des Buches Hiobs." *Biblica* 61 (1980): 377–406.

Schärf, R. R. "Die Gestalt des Satans im Alten Testament." In *Symbolik des Geistes: Studien über psychische Phänomenologie*, by C. J. Jung, 151–319. Psychologische Abhandlung 6. Zurich: Rascher, 1948.

Schiller, G. *Iconography of Christian Art.* Greenwich, Conn.: New York Graphic Society, 1972.

Scholnick, S. H. "The Meaning of *Mišpaṭ* (Justice) in the Book of Job." *Journal of Biblical Literature* 101, no. 4 (1982): 521–29.

———. "The Oath of Innocence and the Sage." *Zeitschrift für die alttestamentliche Wissenschaft* 95, no. 1 (1983): 31–53.

———. "Poetry in the Courtroom: Job 38–41." In *Directions in Hebrew Poetry*, edited by E. Follis, 185–204. *Journal for the Study of the Old Testament:* Supplement Series 40. Sheffield: Sheffield Academic, 1987.

Schmidt, L. *"De Deo": Studien zur Literarturkritik und Theologie des Buches Jona, des Gesprächs zwischen Abraham und Jahwe in Gen 18 22ff. und von Hi 1.* Beihefte zur Zeitschrift für die alttestamentliche Wissenschaft 142. Berlin: de Gruyter, 1976.

Schmidt, W. H. *Königtum Gottes in Ugarit und Israel.* 2nd ed. Beihefte zur Zeitschrift für die alttestamentliche Wissenschaft 80. Berlin: Töpelmann, 1966.

Schmitt, C. *Der Leviathan in der Staatslehre des Thomas Hobbes: Sinn und Fehlschlag eines politischen Symbols.* Hamburg: Hanseatische Verlagsanstalt, 1938.

Schreiber, W. L. *Handbuch der Holz- und Metallschnitte des 15. Jahrhunderts.* 8 vols. Leipzig: Hiersemann, 1926–30.

Schreiner, S. *Where Shall Wisdom Be Found? Calvin's Exegesis of Job from Medieval and Modern Perspectives.* Chicago: University of Chicago Press, 1994.

———. "'Why Do the Wicked Live?': Job and David in Calvin's Sermons on Job." In Perdue and Gilpin, *Voice from the Whirlwind*, 129–43.

Schrey, H.-H. "Geduld." In vol. 12 of *Theologische Realenzykopädie*, edited by G. Krause and G. Müller, 139–44. 36 vols. Berlin: de Gruyter, 1977–2004.

Schultz, C. "The Cohesive Issue of *mišpāṭ* in Job." In *"Go to the Land I Will Show You": Studies in Honor of Dwight W. Young*, edited by J. E. Colson and V. H. Matthews, 159–75. Winona Lake, Ind.: Eisenbrauns, 1996.

Seitz, C. R. "The Patience of Job in the Epistle of James." In *Konsequente Traditionsgeschichte: Festschrift für Klaus Baltzer zum 65. Geburtstag*, edited by R. Bartelmus, T. Krüger, and H. Utzschneider, 373–82. Orbis Biblicus et Orientalis 126. Freiburg: Universitätsverlag, 1993.

Seow, C. L. "Job's Wife." In *Engaging the Bible in a Gendered World: An Introduction to Feminist Biblical Interpretation in Honor of Katharine Doob Sakenfeld*, edited by L. Day and C. Pressler, 141–50. Louisville: Westminster John Knox, 2006.

———. "Job's Wife, with Due Respect." In Krüger et al., *Buch Hiob*, 351–73.

———. "Reflections on the History of Consequences: The Case of Job." In *Method Matters: Essays on the Interpretation of the Hebrew Bible in Honor of David L. Petersen*, edited J. LeMon and H. Richards, 561–86. Resources for Biblical Study 56. Atlanta: Society of Biblical Literature, 2009.

Sewall, R. *The Vision of Tragedy.* New Haven: Yale University Press, 1959.

Seymour, M. C. *Bartholomaeus Anglicus and His Encyclopedia.* Aldershot, U.K.: Ashgate, 1992.

Shaffer, P. *Amadeus.* New York: Signet, 1984.

Shaw, J. *Job's Wife: A Novel.* Brentwood, Tenn.: Wolgemuth & Hyatt, 1989.

Sheehan, J. *The Enlightenment Bible: Translation, Scholarship, Culture.* Princeton: Princeton University Press, 2005.

Shelley, M. *Frankenstein.* New York: Dover, 1994.

Shelley, P. "Prometheus Unbound." In *Shelley's Poetry and Prose: Authoritative Texts and Criticism,* edited by D. H. Reiman and S. B. Powers, 130–210. New York: Norton, 1977.

Sitzler, D. *Vorwurf gegen Gott: Ein religiöses Motiv im Alten Orient (Ägypten und Mesopotamien).* Studies in Oriental Religions 32. Wiesbaden: Harrassowitz, 1995.

Skeat, W. W., ed. *Aelfric's Lives of the Saints.* 2 vols. Early English Text Society 76, 82, 94, 114. London: Trübner, 1881–1900.

Smith, M. S. *The Origins of Biblical Monotheism: Israel's Polytheistic Background and the Ugaritic Texts.* Oxford: Oxford University Press, 2003.

Smith, N. *Literature and Revolution in England 1640–1660.* New Haven: Yale University Press, 1994.

Soelle, D. *Suffering.* Philadelphia: Fortress, 1975.

Sommerfeldt, J. R. "The Social Theory of Bernard of Clairvaux." In *Studies in Medieval Cistercian History,* edited by J. R. Sommerfeldt, 35–48. Cistercian Studies 13. Spencer, Mass.: Cistercian, 1971.

Sontag, S. "The Aesthetics of Silence." In *Styles of Radical Will,* 3–34. New York: Farrar, Straus & Giroux, 1969.

Spanneut, M. "Geduld." In vol. 9 of *Reallexikon für Antike und Christendum,* edited by T. Klauser et al., 243–94. 24 vols. Stuttgart: Hiersemann, 1950–2012.

Spark, M. *The Only Problem.* New York: Putnam, 1984.

Spenser, E. *The Faerie Queene, Book One.* In *The Works of Edmund Spenser: A Variorum Edition,* edited by F. M. Padelford. 1932; Baltimore: Johns Hopkins University Press, 1966.

Spiegel, S. "Noah, Danel, and Job: Touching on Canaanite Relics in the Legends of the Jews." In *Louis Ginzberg Jubilee Volume,* 305–55. New York: American Academy for Jewish Research, 1945.

Spittler, R. P., trans. *"Testament of Job* (First Century B.C.–First Century A.D. A New Translation and Introduction." In *The Old Testament Pseudepigrapha: Apocalyptic Literature and Testaments,* edited by J. H. Charlesworth, 829–68. Garden City, N.Y.: Doubleday, 1983.

Steadman, J. "Leviathan and Renaissance Etymology." *Journal of the History of Ideas* 28 (1967): 575–76.

Stegner, W. "Impasse." In *Collected Stories of Wallace Stegner,* 279–92. New York: Penguin, 1991.

Steiner, G. *Grammars of Creation.* New Haven: Yale University Press, 2001.

Sterling, C. *Les peintres de la réalité: L'Orangerie des Tuileries.* Paris: Éditions des Musées Nationaux, 1934.

Stout, J. "Melville's Use of the Book of Job." *Nineteenth Century Fiction* 25 (1970): 69–83.

Susman, M. *Das Buch Hiob und das Schicksal des jüdischen Volkes.* Freiburg: Herder-Bücherei, 1968.

———. "Das Hiob-Problem bei Franz Kafka." *Der Morgan* 5 (1929): 31–49.

Sutherland, R. *Putting God on Trial: The Biblical Book of Job.* Victoria, B.C.: Trafford, 2004.

Tabarī, Muhammed ibn Jarir al-. *Tarikh al-rusul wa'lmuluk,* 10 vols. Cairo: Dar al-Ma`arif, 1960–69. Translated by W. M. Brinner as *The History of al-Tabari.* Albany: State University of New York Press, 1991.

Taylor, J. *Jewish Women Philosophers of First-Century Alexandria.* Oxford: Oxford University Press, 2003.

Tennyson, A. "In Memoriam A. H. H." In *Tennyson's Poetry.* Edited by R. W. Hill Jr., 119–95. New York: Norton, 1971.

Terrien, S. *The Iconography of Job through the Centuries.* University Park: Pennsylvania State University Press, 1996.

Tertullian. *Of Patience.* In vol. 3 of *The Ante-Nicene Fathers.* Edited by A. Roberts and J. Donaldson, 1885–87. 10 vols. Rpt., Peabody, Mass.: Hendrickson, 1994.

Tha`labi, Ahmad Ibn Muhammed al-. *Qisas al-Anbiya', al-musamma `Ara'is al-majalis.* Cairo, 1954. Excerpt translated by D. B. MacDonald as "Some External Evidence of the Original Form of the Legend of Job." *American Journal of Semitic Languages and Literatures* 14, no. 3 (1898): 145–61.

Thomas, L. "To Err Is Human." In *The Oxford Book of Essays,* edited by J. Gross, 560–63. Oxford: Oxford University Press, 1991.

Thompson, L. R. *Melville's Quarrel with God.* Princeton: Princeton University Press, 1952.

Thompson, L. S. "German Translations of the Classics between 1450 and 1550." *Journal of English and Germanic Philology* 42, no. 3 (1943): 343–63.

Tillemont, M. L. de. *Mémoires pour servir à l'Histoire Ecclésiatique.* 2nd ed. 16 vols. Paris, 1693–1712.

Tilley, T. "God and the Silencing of Job." *Modern Theology* 5, no. 3 (1989): 257–70.

———. *The Evils of Theodicy.* Washington, D.C.: Georgetown University Press, 1991.

Touati, C. "Les deux theories de Maimonide sur la providence." In *Studies in Jewish Religious and Intellectual History,* edited by S. Stein and R. Lowe, 331–40. London: Institute of Jewish Studies, 1979.

Trousson, R. *La Thème de Prométhee dans la littérature européenne.* 2 vols. Geneva: Droz, 1964.

Tsevat, M. "The Meaning of the Book of Job." *HUCA* 37 (1966): 73–106.

Urbach, E. E. *The Sages: Their Concepts and Beliefs.* 2 vols. Jerusalem: Magnes, 1975.

VanZanten Gallagher, S. "The Prophetic Narrator of *Moby-Dick.*" *Christianity and Literature* 36, no. 3 (1987): 11–25.

Verker, D. "Job and Sistis: Curious Figures in Early Christian Funerary Art." *Mitteilungen zur christlichen Archäologie* 3 (1997): 20–29.

Vespertino Rodríguez, A. *Leyendas aljamiadas y moriscas sobre personajes bíblicos.* Madrid: Gredos, 1983.

Vicchio, S., and L. Edinberg. *The Sweet Uses of Adversity: Images of the Biblical Job.* Annapolis, Md.: IPP, 2002.

Vincent, H. P. *The Trying-Out of Moby-Dick.* Boston: Houghton, 1949.

Vötterle, K. "Hiob als Schutzpatron der Musiker." *Musik und Kirche* 23 (1953): 225–32.

Voltaire. *Candide.* In *Candide, Zadig, and Selected Stories,* translated by D. M. Frame, 1–96. New York: Signet, 2009.

——. *Oeuvres Complètes.* Paris: Société Littérarie-Typographique, 1785.

Wang, A. *Der 'Miles Christinus' im 16. und 17. Jahrhundert und seine mittelalterliche Tradition: Ein Beitrag zum Verhältnis von sprachlicher und graphischer Bildlichkeit.* Beiträge zur Literaturwissenschaft und Bedeutungsforschung 1. Bern: Lang, 1975.

Weisbach, W. "L'histoire de Job dans les arts: A propos du tableau de Georges de La Tour au musée d'Épinal." *Gazette des Beaux-Arts* 78, no. 2 (1936): 102–12.

Wellbery, D. E. *The Specular Moment: Goethe's Early Lyric and the Beginnings of Romanticism.* Stanford: Stanford University Press, 1996.

Wells, H. G. *The Undying Fire: A Contemporary Novel.* New York: Macmillan, 1919.

Werblowsky, R. J. Z. *Lucifer and Prometheus: A Study of Milton's Satan.* London: Routledge & Kegan Paul, 1952.

Wahl, H.-M. *Der gerechte Schöpfer: Eine redaktions- und theologiegeschichtliche Untersuchung der Elihureden- Hiob 32–37.* Berlin: de Gruyter, 1993.

Whedbee, J. *The Bible and the Comic Vision.* Cambridge: Cambridge University Press, 1998.

Whitman, W. "By Blue Ontario's Shore." In *Leaves of Grass,* edited with an introduction by J. Loving, 264–76. Oxford: Oxford University Press, 1990.

——. "Song of Myself." In Whitman, *Leaves of Grass,* 29–79.

Whybray, R. N. *The Heavenly Counsellor in Isaiah xl 13–14: A Study of the Sources of the Theology of Deutero-Isaiah.* Society for Old Testament Studies Monograph Series 1. Cambridge: Cambridge University Press, 1971.

Wickstead, J. *Blake's Vision of the Book of the Job.* London: Dent, 1910.

Wiernikowski, I. *Das Buch Hiob nach der Auffassung der rabbinischen Literatur in den ersten fünf Christlichen Jahrhunderten.* Breslau: Freishman, 1902.

Wiesel, E. *The Accident.* Translated by A. Borchardt. New York: Avon, 1970.

——. *All Rivers Run to the Sea: Memoirs.* Translated by J. Rothschild. New York: Knopf, 1995.

——. *And the Sea Is Never Full: Memoirs 1969–.* Translated by M. Wiesel. New York: Knopf, 1999.

——. *A Beggar in Jerusalem*. Translated by L. Edelman and E. Wiesel. New York: Avon, 1971.

——. *Dawn*. Translated by F. Frenaye. New York: Avon, 1970.

——. *The Gates of the Forest*. Translated by F. Frenaye. New York: Avon, 1969.

——. *A Jew Today*. Translated by M. Wiesel. New York: Random House, 1978.

——. "Jewish Values in the Post-Holocaust Future: A Symposium." *Judaism* 16 (1967): 266–99.

——. "Job: Our Contemporary." In *Messengers of God: Biblical Portraits and Legends*, 211–36. Translated by M. Wiesel. New York: Touchstone, 1976.

——. *Messengers of God: Biblical Portraits and Legends* New York: Touchstone, 1976.

——. *Night*. Translated by S. Rodway. New York: Avon, 1969.

——. *One Generation After*. Translated by L. Edelman. New York: Random House, 1970.

——. "A Personal Response." *Face to Face: An Interreligious Bulletin* 6 (1979): 35–37.

——. *Souls on Fire*. Translated by M. Wiesel. New York: Vintage Books, 1973.

——. *The Town beyond the Wall*. Translated by S. Becker. New York: Avon, 1969.

——. *The Trial of God (as It Was Held on February 25, 1649, in Shamgorod)*. Translated by M. Wiesel. New York: Schocken Books, 1979.

——. "The Use of Words and the Weight of Silence." Interview by L. Edelman. In vol. 2 of Abramson, *Against Silence*, 75–84.

——. "Victims of God." Review of *Selected Stories by I. L. Peretz*, edited by I. Howe and E. Greenberg. *New Republic*, September 21, 1974.

Wilk, M. *Jewish Presence in T. S. Eliot and Franz Kafka*. Atlanta: Scholars, 1986.

Willi-Plein, I. "Hiobs Widerruf?—Eine Untersuchung der Wurzel חםב und ihrer erzähltechnischen Funktion im Hiobbuch." In vol. 3 of *Essays on the Bible and the Ancient World: Isaac Leo Seeligmann Volume*, edited by A. Rofé and Y. Zakovitch, 273–89. Jerusalem: Rubenstein, 1983.

Wilpert, J. *I sarcophagi cristiana antichi*. 3 vols. Vatican City, 1929–36.

Witte, M. "The Greek Book of Job." In Krüger et al., *Buch Hiob*, 33–54.

——. "Die literarische Gattung des Buches Hiob: Robert Lowth und seine Erben." In *Sacred Conjectures: The Context and Legacy of Robert Lowth and Jean Astruc*, edited by J. Jarick, 93–123. New York: Clark, 2007.

Wolde, E. J. van. *Mr. and Mrs. Job*. New York: Trinity Press International, 1997.

——. "Job 42:1–6: The Reversal of Job." In Beuken, *Book of Job*, 223–50.

Wölfflin, H. *The Art of Albrecht Dürer*. Translated by A. and H. Grieve. London: Phaidon, 1971.

Wood, J. "The All and the If: God and Metaphor in Melville." In *The Broken Estate: Essays on Literature and Belief*, 26–40. New York: Random House, 1999.

——. *The Book against God*. New York: Farrar, Straus & Giroux, 2003.

Wright, A. *Blake's Job: A Commentary*. Oxford: Clarendon, 1972.

Wright, N. *Melville's Use of the Bible*. Durham, N.C.: Duke University Press, 1949.

Young, W. "The Patience of Job: Between Providence and Disaster." *Heythrop Journal* 48, no. 4 (2007): 593–613.

Yu, A. C. "New Gods and Old Order: Tragic Theology in the *Prometheus Bound*." *Journal of the American Academy of Religion* 39, no. 1 (1971): 19–42.

Zaharopoulos, D. Z. *Theodore of Mopsuestia on the Bible: A Study of His Old Testament Exegesis.* Mahweh, N.J.: Paulist, 1989.

Zhitlowsky, C. "Job and Faust." Translated with an introduction by P. Matenko. In *Two Studies in Yiddish Culture,* 75–162. Leiden: Brill, 1968.

Zuckerman, B. *Job the Silent: A Study in Historical Counterpoint.* Oxford: Oxford University Press, 1991.

Zupnick, I. L. "Saint Sebastian: The Vicissitudes of the Hero as Martyr." In *Concepts of the Hero in the Middle Ages and the Renaissance,* edited by N. T. Burns and C. J. Reagan, 239–67. Albany: State University of New York Press, 1975.

AUTHOR INDEX

Abrahamson, I, 210

Aeschylus. *See* subject index

Agourides, S., 24

Alonso-Schokel, Luis, 180

Alter, Robert, xx, 11

Anderson, Francis I., 5, 204

Anderson, H., 25

Anzelewsky F., 100

Aocella, J., 104

Astell, Ann. W., 33–41, 48, 59, 61, 65, 97–99

Arcangeli, C. A., 44

Auden, W. H., 171

Balentine, Samuel E., 33, 38, 46, 52, 53, 61,
     140, 158,160, 171, 204, 206, 207, 213

Barton, John, 76

Baskin, J. R., 17–19

Bayle, Pierre, 161, 164

Beal, T. K., 186, 189

Beecher, Donald, 39, 41

Beer, G, 120

Begg, C. T., 56

Beiser, F., 128

Ben-Barak, Z., 206

Ben Zvi, E., 183

Berger, A. L., 207

Bernard of Clairvaux, 37

Bertagnolli, P. A., 127, 129, 132

Besserman, Lawrence, xix, 34, 35, 40, 42,
     90, 92, 98

Blake, William, 101–3, 105, 159, 160, 193

Blenkinsopp, J., 183

Bloom, H., 175

Boer, P.A.H. de., 182

Bolgar, Raymond R., 37, 47

Borchert, W., 74

Bovati, P., 138

Brandes, Georgs, 129

Brock, S. P., 56, 84, 121

Brown, K., 188

Brown, R. M., 214

Brown, W. P., 181, 182

Buber, Martin, 65

Buchler, A., 18

Buck, A., 127

Bueler, L. E., 98

Bunker, R. A., 127

Burrell, D., 172

Burton, Robert, 41

Byron, G., 129–30

Calvin, J. 69, 99, 146, 152, 154–55 174, 187,
     196

Cargas, Harry James, 214–15

Carstensen, R, 172

Carus, P., 54

Cassiodorus, 33

Caxton, W., 100

Charlesworth, J. H., 54

Chaucer, G., 97

Chin, C., 138

Chittister, J, 206

Christiansen, A, 56

Clines, David J. A., 5, 53, 141, 171, 175–76,
     182, 202–4, 206

Collins, J. J., 56–57, 83, 86

SUBJECT INDEX